TOSCANINI IN BRITAIN

T O S C A N I N I
IN BRITAIN

Christopher Dyment

THE BOYDELL PRESS

First published 2012
The Boydell Press, Woodbridge

ISBN 978 1 84383 789 3

The Boydell Press is an imprint of Boydell & Brewer Ltd
PO Box 9, Woodbridge, Suffolk IP12 3DF, UK
and of Boydell & Brewer Inc.
668 Mount Hope Ave, Rochester, NY 14620-2731, USA
website: www.boydellandbrewer.com

A catalogue record for this book is available
from the British Library

The publisher has no responsibility for the continued existence or accuracy of URLs for
external or third-party internet websites referred to in this book, and does not guarantee
that any content on such websites is, or will remain, accurate or appropriate

Papers used by Boydell & Brewer Ltd are natural, recyclable products
made from wood grown in sustainable forests

Text pages designed and typeset by Tina Ranft, Woodbridge
Printed and bound in Great Britain by
CPI Group (UK) Ltd, Croydon, CR0 4YY

CONTENTS

ILLUSTRATIONS

FOREWORD

Harvey Sachs

A bunch of concerts and a handful of recordings in the 1930s and two more concerts in 1952: The End.

Some of us who know a thing or two about Arturo Toscanini have tended until now to think of his relationship with Great Britain in these overly drastic terms. It is true that the 1930s – when Toscanini was in his sixties and early seventies – probably constituted his peak decade as a symphonic conductor, and that the 1952 concerts gave London a chance to hear the eighty-five-year-old Maestro in a moment of musical grace, a year and a half before he brought his long career to an end. Still, there is no comparison, in either temporal or numerical terms, between Toscanini's British career and his careers in his native Italy (1886–1952, with a fifteen-year interruption for political reasons in the 1930s and '40s) and the United States (1908–15, 1920–21, 1926–54). Nor did Toscanini, renowned mainly as an opera conductor during the first half of his professional life (in South America and Paris, as well as Italy and the United States), ever conduct an opera in Britain.

And yet, as Christopher Dyment demonstrates in the pages that follow, the Toscanini-Great Britain relationship is well worth a thorough investigation. On the one hand, Dyment provides a panoramic view of the conditions of musical life in London during the first half of the twentieth century, and, on the other, a specific investigation of the efforts made by various musical organisations – the London Symphony Orchestra, Covent Garden, the Royal Philharmonic Society, the BBC Symphony Orchestra, HMV, EMI, the Philharmonia Orchestra and others – to secure the services of the most celebrated conductor of the day. Most of those attempts were unsuccessful, but the successful ones created an enduring impact. And in many ways the unsuccessful attempts are as telling as the successful ones: the organisational methods behind London's musical institutions from the Edwardian era to the post-Second World War period are laid bare, and major and minor personalities who in one way or another collaborated with those institutions appear as Dyment's story unrolls. The composers Giacomo Puccini, William Walton, Arthur Bliss and Benjamin Britten are all heard from, as are the conductors Adrian Boult, Thomas Beecham, George Henschel, Landon Ronald, Albert Coates, Malcolm Sargent and John Barbirolli; the recording pioneers Fred Gaisberg and

Walter Legge; many music critics, including Ernest Newman and Neville Cardus – and a former music critic named Bernard Shaw; a panoply of British orchestra musicians; various political and aristocratic figures, including a smattering of royals, and many other figures as well.

But Dyment does more than provide the background to and details of Toscanini's visits (and non-visits) to Britain. He analyses, authoritatively and in depth, the evolution of Toscanini's interpretative style, and – by way of example – he goes further than any other Toscanini-watcher has ever gone in establishing the origins of the Maestro's approach to Brahms and in comparing that approach with the styles of other Brahms conductors who were active during Toscanini's lifetime.

This book ought to be obligatory reading for anyone interested in Toscanini, in British musical life between 1900 and the early 1950s, and in the history of orchestral performance and recording.

Music historian Harvey Sachs's many books include *Toscanini* (a biography; 1978), *Reflections on Toscanini* (essays; 1991) and, as editor and translator, *The Letters of Arturo Toscanini* (2002). He is currently writing a completely new biography of Toscanini.

INTRODUCTION

Arturo Toscanini's supreme importance in the history of conducting is universally acknowledged. The standard of orchestral playing taken for granted in the twenty-first century owes more to him than to any other single figure; and the stylistic influence, today sometimes questioned, is still pervasive, if often unacknowledged or known only at second hand. That influence, however, is (for better or for worse) a product principally of his later years when he was in charge of the NBC Symphony Orchestra, a radio orchestra of unique stature whose recordings were disseminated worldwide.

Although Toscanini was recognised as supreme in his art far into the twentieth century, his career to some degree antedated that century's characteristic phenomenon, the peripatetic conductor. Such travellers were not unknown in his early years even amongst the finest conductors – Felix Weingartner in particular, together with Arthur Nikisch, Fritz Steinbach and other great names; but the careers of some of the very greatest were in that era fulfilled by the occupation of a relatively small number of posts that limited the number of appearances elsewhere. Just as for, say, Mahler, the progression from Hamburg and Vienna to his two New York posts was accompanied by a relative scattering of concerts across Europe, so with Toscanini the principal posts were similarly confined to two countries:[1] Turin and Milan in Italy; the Metropolitan Opera, the New York Philharmonic and NBC Symphony Orchestras in America. During the first half of his career concert engagements elsewhere were neither numerous nor geographically adventurous.

In the second half of his career Toscanini concentrated increasingly on the concert hall, beginning with extended tours by the reconstituted La Scala orchestra in 1920–21. Thereafter he spread his geographical wings: in addition to New York, major European capitals including Paris and Vienna heard him with their national

---

[1] Together with his many early operatic performances in South America and the Metropolitan Opera's visit to Paris in 1910 – see Chronicle p. xxii. Mahler's pan-European concert career began only after he resigned as conductor of the Vienna Philharmonic in April 1901. Until then, aside from his concerts as Kapellmeister at various posts, he had conducted only two dozen of his over three hundred concerts (including the five Paris concerts in June 1900 with 'his' Vienna Philharmonic): see Knut Martner *Mahler's Concerts* New York: Kaplan Foundation 2010 pp. 151, 165 and Appendix IV.

orchestras. In some the appearances were fleeting, in others there were annual series. Among these cities, from 1930 onwards London came to be the most favoured, visited most frequently and hearing him in the widest range of symphonic and other works. Even in concert life, no European city outside Italy could rival in sheer volume the forty-four symphonic concerts Toscanini conducted at Turin in 1898, the annual series he gave at the conclusion of each season at La Scala or the hundreds of concerts he led in New York between 1913 and 1954. But the thirty-one concerts he gave in London between 1930 and 1952 familiarised audiences and critics with his approach to a greater and more intimate degree than elsewhere, excepting only his principal centres of activity in Italy and the United States.[2]

Toscanini's Italian and American careers have been examined thoroughly on many occasions, most notably in Barblan's well documented book on the La Scala years, Harvey Sachs's authoritative biography and selection of letters, and Mortimer Frank's study of the NBC years. His style, musicianship and significance in musical history have also been the subject of many books, ranging from the insightful to the grotesquely misleading – more, indeed, than any other conductor. None, however, has documented systematically his activity in London, that third most favoured venue for his concert activities. The omission is not surprising, since only one of the many books about him is by a British writer – pianist and critic Denis Matthews's 1982 study, illuminated by his personal contact with Toscanini and presence at the London concerts. Slim as that volume is, its single chapter about London is virtually the only discrete source of information, supplemented by the histories of the BBC Symphony and Philharmonia Orchestras by, respectively, Nicholas Kenyon and Stephen Pettitt. But comprehensive though these works are (and I am indebted to them all), they remain general histories with many relevant details necessarily omitted.

The present volume presents the complete history of Toscanini's activities in London and assesses their significance in the context of his career as a whole. It has its origin in an essay for *Classic Record Collector* about Toscanini's HMV recording sessions in 1937–39. That in turn was stimulated by the realisation that, while those landmark sessions produced some of the most memorable symphonic recordings ever committed to disc, little had been written about the sessions themselves, and what little there was contained too many errors. For example, one CD transfer of the famous BBC Symphony Orchestra recording of Beethoven's *Pastoral* Symphony

[2]   The closest European rival was the combination of Vienna (nineteen concerts) and Salzburg (eleven), but their concerts involved more repetition of works/programmes than London's.

specified a scattering of recording dates on some of which Toscanini did not record, since he was not in the country. Another transfer of the same work produced in conjunction with EMI confined the recording dates to two days in October 1937; yet a glance at the matrix sequence of the recording shows that to have been impossible. Many other recording dates cited over the years have been erroneous. Since EMI themselves perpetuated some of those errors, still present in current issues, they were certainly excusable, but the need for further research was obvious. The absence of any complete and reliable information about Toscanini's concert programmes with the BBC Symphony Orchestra, which would demonstrate the variety of his repertoire and its interrelationship with the recording sessions, suggested the need to extend such basic data to a comprehensive concert listing. Annexes A and B therefore contain a detailed EMI discography and a listing of the London concerts setting out all the available information.

Originally designed as little more than a framework for the discography and concert listing, the main narrative expanded with the examination of substantial material never before fully researched into a broader examination of how Toscanini was captured for London. A subtitle for this book, later omitted, 'Conquest and Friendship', points to two significant themes which came to dominate this narrative. One, the friendship, is the central and hitherto unexplored role of the figure who became Toscanini's closest companion and friend in London, the BBC executive and later independent concert promoter, Owen Mase. His activities in attracting Toscanini back to London on several occasions are here fully documented for the first time. If on occasion Mase dominates the story, the focus on him is a measure of his unfailing devotion to the conductor and his interests in London and the assistance he willingly gave to the BBC and EMI/HMV. Without Mase both would probably have failed in their endeavours, as did Glyndebourne in its strenuous pre-war attempts to secure Toscanini's services. But with him, and through many a twist, turn and stratagem, they eventually succeeded in their efforts to induce the most famous living conductor to broadcast from London and, despite his aversion to the gramophone, to set down some recorded mementoes of his art. Recounted here in all surviving detail, the story could have no counterpart today; there is no-one of like dominance left to pursue.

Although much of the story concentrates on the years 1935–39, the exigencies of the ensuing worldwide armed conflict failed to dampen the BBC's ardour in attempting to lure Toscanini back to war-torn London in the years 1940–44. Moreover, EMI's efforts to capture his performances were not confined to concerts and recording sessions in London: they extended also to post-war concerts in

Europe with source material from them processed by EMI technicians in London in vain efforts to produce acceptable results. All this activity, unproductive though much of it was, finds its place here. The story is completed with the chequered history of Toscanini's appearance at London's Royal Festival Hall, including in particular the two Philharmonia concerts in 1952, with Mase once more to the fore throughout.

The second and still more significant theme, the conquest, describes Toscanini's extraordinary impact on London concert life. It is difficult today to recapture the sense of his unique vitalising force, right from the audience's first excited glimpse of him on 1 June 1930, when he led the first of the four concerts with which the New York Philharmonic-Symphony Orchestra closed its European tour. In the opinion of the great majority of witnesses, here was someone who was not just a great conductor among others, but a musician apart; not, certainly, immune from or above criticism – some of his limitations were noted from the start – but one gifted with such powers and penetration as to make comparisons with even the most talented of his colleagues a virtual irrelevance. Toscanini's dominance in critical opinion was thus substantially greater than anything achieved by his immediate predecessors – save possibly Nikisch – or his juniors in post-war years, such as Wilhelm Furtwängler, Erich Kleiber, Herbert von Karajan or even Otto Klemperer, for whom extravagant claims were made by some critics from the mid-1950s onwards.

Recapturing that impact requires contemporaries to speak for themselves. Here, then, are those who proclaimed Toscanini's supreme stature, led by Ernest Newman and aided and abetted by such other writers of distinction as W. J. Turner, Richard Capell and Ferruccio Bonavia, with the younger voices of Constant Lambert and Walter Legge adding their own paeans. But here, too, is the sometimes dissentient voice of Neville Cardus, tempering his appraisal of Toscanini's admittedly super-human qualities with caustic comment on what he heard as an increasing lack of the human touch. Ancient battles long ago, no doubt – but fought at a length and with a quality of writing that their modern counterparts might envy. Further, the summarised responses to Toscanini's concerts presented in the course of this narrative demonstrate the impression made by the conductor in his late prime upon a fraternity of distinguished writers who, observing the procession of the world's foremost conductors leading the BBC Symphony, London Philharmonic and London Symphony Orchestras as well as the finest visiting orchestras, were better placed than virtually anyone else worldwide to assess the Italian's true qualities and his status among contemporaries. In substance, then, the narrative's assessment of critical reaction to the concerts amounts to a study in reception which it would be impossible to replicate from sources elsewhere.

Another valuable aspect of this critical response is the clear evidence it presents of Toscanini's ongoing development as an artist. The reviews reflect a widespread critical perception – not limited to the intermittent grumbling from Cardus – of the conductor's changing approach to the symphonic repertoire over the relatively short period covered by his annual visits to London before war halted them: the sense of a style gradually on course to become less flexible and featuring tempos sometimes slightly faster than the norm which a later generation (often mistakenly) saw as typifying the standard approach taken by the conductor to the whole repertoire in his old age. In no other set of critiques is this change so closely and distinctly documented. The nature of the change and identification of the possible sources within Toscanini's personality and musicianship which gave rise to it are the subject of the final chapter, which also includes a study of the London recordings, official and unofficial, that seeks to answer other questions of contemporary interest: what makes the recordings special and why listen to them today? Annex C develops some of the themes briefly outlined in this chapter.

Throughout I have aimed to exclude most of the material more readily found in other sources such as the exemplary biographical studies cited above; but, given the limited time span of each of Toscanini's London visits, total exclusion of connecting tissue would have made for a misleading and discontinuous narrative. Hence the inclusion of the opening outline Chronicle and the brief descriptions throughout of the conductor's activities elsewhere, before and after his London visits.

The views of the author about Toscanini's attributes as a conductor are to the fore in the last chapter and also in the annotations accompanying the concert listing in Annex B. If I have not been wholly successful in eliminating hints of the hagiographic in the rest of the narrative, that failing in part reflects the range of (sometimes adulatory) critical opinion frequently quoted. But any such perceived bias also reflects my conclusion, based on more than half a century's listening and study, that in a wide range of masterpieces Toscanini possessed and projected to an ultimate degree a vision at once more comprehensive and more compelling than any other conductor known to recorded sound. That, after all, has been the real driving force in writing this book.

Christopher Dyment
June 2012

EMI Classics have advised their intention to issue a CD collection of Toscanini's recordings in their ICON series. It is to contain Toscanini's recordings with the BBC Symphony Orchestra and other recordings made by him for EMI. (September 2012)

ACKNOWLEDGEMENTS

I am indebted to several major sources of information without which this book could not have been undertaken. The BBC Written Archive made available to me its files concerning Toscanini (which commence in 1936) and I am indebted to its former Researcher Erin O'Neill for her assistance and for giving permission for use of quoted material. The archive of EMI Classics yielded copious information enabling the story of Toscanini's EMI recordings to be recounted in detail. Glyndebourne archives disclosed unexpected treasures and archivist Julia Aries, assisted by Jacqueline Noltingk, took immense trouble with my queries; I am grateful to Ms Aries for permission to quote from this material. The New York Public Library for the Performing Arts, housing the Toscanini Legacy collection of documents, scores and recordings, contained invaluable material and I am grateful to Bob Kosovsky, Curator Rare Books and Manuscripts, and Seth Winner, archivist of the library's Toscanini Legacy of sound recordings, for extensive assistance. Harvey Sachs provided many details supplementing his published work; his frequent advice and, in particular, his permission to use a substantial number of short quotations from his *Letters of Arturo Toscanini* (2002) are greatly appreciated.

I am grateful to the family of Owen Mase, his step-grandson Peter Agrell and Mr Agrell's daughter Sophie, guardian of the Mase archive, for permitting me to examine and copy all relevant surviving material – correspondence, memoranda, photographs – without which the account of Mase's activities would have been less complete. Further, I draw attention to Mase's two memoranda about Toscanini drafted in the course of his employment by the BBC and, later, the London County Council, preserved in his personal papers and reproduced substantially in Chapters 4 and 11; his only published essay about Toscanini's musicianship can also be found in Chapter 11. I am glad to acknowledge the permission to reproduce these pieces granted by the Mase estate, conveyed by Peter Agrell.

Other primary sources of information included the British Library and its Newspaper Library, the Westminster Music Library and the British Library Sound Archives containing the valuable, if fragmentary, recordings of the Leech Collection. I thank the Archive's staff for their assistance in identifying the relevant material and making it available for listening. I am grateful to Dr Jürgen Schaarwächter, of the Max Reger Institute Karlsruhe and the Busch Brothers Foundation, and to Irena Lucke-Kaminiarz, Weimar archivist and biographer of Hermann Abendroth, for further details enabling me to complete Annex C; Dr Schaarwächter also kindly provided some photographic material. I am immensely indebted to Michael H Gray for information about the technicalities of recording and all that relates to disco-graphical/cataloguing data.

I thank others for documentary, photographic and recorded material, suggestions, sources, facts, translations, perusal of early drafts and other forms of assistance, some of which is footnoted in the appropriate context: Peter Aistleitner (Hamburg), John Bird, Nicholas Chadwick, Clare Colvin (English National Opera archivist), Timothy Day (until mid-2006 Curator of the British Library Sound Archive), Donald Dean (whose generosity and constant encouragement were exceptional), Lewis Foreman, Mortimer H Frank, Rachel Hayes (Covent Garden Archives officer), Alexander Hermon, Martyn Jones (Philharmonia Orchestra archivist), Michael Kennedy, Nicholas Kenyon, Jerrold Northrop Moore, Clive Pearsall, Tully Potter, Libby Rice (London Symphony Orchestra archivist), the Royal Academy of Music's library, Alan Sanders, Jonathan Summers (Curator, British Library Sound Archive), Malcolm Walker and Stephen Wright.

David Hamilton's lecture on Toscanini in Britain at the New York Public Library for the Performing Arts on 4 December 2001 covered some of the same ground as this book. Courtesy Seth Winner, I heard it at a late stage in my own work but nonetheless benefited from its many stimulating comments.

The technical assistance provided by John Casey was invaluable and frequently saved my sanity, while his expert work on some aged sources made much of the pho-tographic material printable without flaws for the first time. Without his active help and guidance, I could not have submitted my text and photographs in good order. Submitted, that is, to Michael Middeke at Boydell, to whose tactful and sympathetic guidance I am greatly indebted. His colleagues were a constant source of ready assist-ance and information, for which I am grateful. David Harman contributed much to make this a better book – but its faults and shortcomings are my own.

In addition to the permissions noted above, I acknowledge the permissions given by *Gramophone* (Haymarket Publications) and © The Musical Times Publications Ltd. to quote material from those journals. I am grateful to the Toscanini family for permission to use several photographs and for Harvey Sachs's assistance in this regard. Further permission for photographic material was kindly given by Allan Steckler, manager and representative of the Toscanini estate. My thanks are due also to EMI Archives for permission to reproduce illustrations 8, 10 and 51; likewise to the Tulley Potter Collection for illustrations 13, 15, 16 and 23; to the BBC Written Archive for illustration 46; and to Donald Dean for illustration 48. Every effort has been made to locate the copyright holders, if any, of other photographic or quoted material. To any copyright holders not identified, acknowledgment is hereby made of their rights and apologies for any omissions on the part of the author in seeking their cooperation.

Christopher Dyment
June 2012

ARTURO TOSCANINI – CHRONICLE OF A LIFE, 1867–1957

1867 25 March: Born in Parma, eldest child and only son of Claudio and Paola Montani Toscanini.

1876 Enters Parma's Royal School of Music.

1885 Graduates with highest honours in cello and composition and maximum points in piano, first prize in graduating class.

1886 30 June: Conducting debut (Verdi's *Aida*) in Rio de Janeiro while principal cello and assistant chorusmaster of touring Italian opera company.
4 November: Italian conducting debut, Turin (Catalani's *Edmea*).

1887 5 February: Second cellist in world premiere of Verdi's *Otello*, La Scala, Milan.

1892 Conducts premiere of Leoncavallo's *Pagliacci*, Teatro Dal Verme, Milan.

1895 Principal conductor of Teatro Regio, Turin.
22 December: Opens season with first performance by an Italian company of Wagner's *Götterdämmerung*.

1896 1 February: Conducts premiere of Puccini's *La Bohème* at Turin.
20 March: Debut as symphonic conductor in Turin.
April: Debut at La Scala in four symphonic concerts.

1897 21 June: Marries Carla De Martini.

1898 1 May–31 October: Conducts forty-four symphony concerts at Turin for International Exposition, including Italian premiere of (three of) Verdi's *Four Sacred Pieces*.
26 December: Opens first season as La Scala's principal conductor with Wagner's *Die Meistersinger von Nürnberg*.

1899 26 December: Opens second season with first Italian production of Wagner's *Siegfried*.

1900   June: First visit to London to hear Felix Mottl conduct *Götterdämmerung* at Covent Garden.

1901   Conducts at Teatro de la Ópera, Buenos Aires, during Argentine winter season; again in 1903, 1904 and 1906.

1903   Leaves La Scala, freelances for three years.

1905   April: His first performance of Elgar's *Enigma* Variations in a Bologna concert.

1906   Resumes post at La Scala. December 21: conducts Italian premiere of *Salome* contemporaneously with Strauss at Turin.

1908   2 April: Conducts Italian premiere of Debussy's *Pelléas et Mélisande*. October: Having resigned from La Scala, arrives in New York to become principal conductor at the Metropolitan Opera, jointly with Mahler.

1910   19 May–25 June: Conducts Colonne Orchestra in eighteen performances of five Italian operas in Paris with Metropolitan forces.
10 December: Conducts premiere of Puccini's *La fanciulla del West* at Metropolitan.

1912   May–September: Conducts operas at Teatro Colón, Buenos Aires.

1913   19 March: Conducts American premiere of Mussorgsky's *Boris Godunov*.

1915   Leaves Metropolitan to conduct only benefit performances in Italy until 1918.

1920   Named plenipotentiary director of La Scala and reconstitutes orchestra.
23 October–29 November: La Scala Orchestra tours twenty-one Italian cities, giving thirty-three concerts.
15 December–2 April 1921: orchestra tours USA and Canada, giving sixty-eight concerts.
December 1920 (seven days) and March 1921 (eight days): first recordings with La Scala Orchestra in Camden, New Jersey.

1921   20 April–16 June: La Scala Orchestra's further Italian tour of thirty-six concerts in nineteen cities; Toscanini reorganises La Scala, which on 26 December reopens with Verdi's *Falstaff*.

1924   Conducts premiere of Boito's *Nerone* at La Scala.

1926   14 January: First appearance as guest conductor with New York Philharmonic Orchestra.
25 April: Premiere of Puccini's *Turandot* at La Scala.
October: First complete Beethoven symphony cycle with La Scala Orchestra
in Milan, repeated in Turin.

1927   Joint principal conductor of NYPO with Mengelberg.

1929   June: Conducts La Scala tour to Vienna and Berlin, after which leaves La
Scala.

1930   Principal conductor of combined (1928) New York Philharmonic-Symphony
Orchestra.
May–June: Conducts NYPSO European tour.
June–August: Conducts at Bayreuth, first non-Germanic conductor to do so.
November: First concerts with Philadelphia Orchestra.

1931   May: Assaulted by fascists in Bologna; determines not to conduct in Italy
for duration of fascist regime.
June–August: Conducts for second and final time at Bayreuth.

1932   17 June: Participates in Debussy memorial concert in Paris.

1933   Refuses to conduct at Bayreuth after Nazi accession to power.
October: Concerts in Paris, annually to 1936 (with visit to Brussels in 1934).
First concerts with Vienna Philharmonic, annually to 1937 (with visits to
Budapest and Prague).
December: Concerts in Stockholm and Copenhagen with Konsertförenin-
gens Orkester; again in Stockholm 1934 and 1937.

1934   August: First concerts in Salzburg with Vienna Philharmonic.

1935   June: First concerts with BBC Symphony Orchestra in London, thereafter
annually 1937–39.
29 July: Conducts first opera, *Falstaff*, at Salzburg, later Beethoven's *Fidelio*
with Lotte Lehmann. In 1936 adds *Die Meistersinger* and in 1937 Mozart's
Magic Flute.

1936 29 April: Final concert as principal conductor of NYPSO.
September: After Salzburg, extra performances of *Fidelio* at Vienna Staatsoper.
20 December: First concerts with Palestine Orchestra in Tel Aviv, Jerusalem and Haifa.

1937 March: Concerts in The Hague and Rotterdam with Hague Residentie orchestra, again in 1938.
25 March: Celebrates seventieth birthday in Milan, serenaded at dawn by the Busch Quartet.
17 October: Last concert with Vienna Philharmonic in Vienna.
25 December: First concert with NBC Symphony Orchestra, of which principal conductor until April 1954 (except 1941/42 season).

1938 16 February: withdraws from Salzburg Festival, foreseeing Nazi takeover of Austria.
April: Returns to conduct Palestine Orchestra; afterwards returns to Italy.
August: Conducts two concerts with specially formed orchestra in Lucerne as part of new Festival; after return to Italy, passport withdrawn until international campaign enables departure from Italy.

1939 June–September: After final BBC SO concerts, stays near Lucerne for seven Festival concerts in July–August.
22 September: Departs from Bordeaux for New York for duration of Second World War.

1940 13 June–10 July: Sixteen-concert NBC SO tour of South America.

1941 April: Guest conducts concert with Chicago Symphony Orchestra.
June–July: Conducts Colón Orchestra, Buenos Aires, in seven concerts.
November: Guest conducts Philadelphia Orchestra, again in January–February 1942.

1942 April–May: Guest conducts NYPSO in his last complete Beethoven cycle, six concerts in two weeks.
October–November: Further seven concerts with NYPSO, including his first complete Berlioz *Roméo et Juliette*.

1944 February: Last appearance with Philadelphia Orchestra (Beethoven concert).
19 April: Concert with Los Angeles Philharmonic Orchestra.

1946 23 April: Returns to Italy.
11 May: Conducts first of seven concerts reopening La Scala, followed by two concerts with La Scala Orchestra in Lucerne.

1948 10 June: Conducts Boito anniversary performance at La Scala, last occasion conducting fully staged opera performances.

1950 14 April–27 May: Conducts NBC SO's twenty-one concert transcontinental tour of USA.

1952 19 September: Conducts last, all-Wagner, concert with La Scala Orchestra.
29 September and 1 October: Final appearances in London, conducting Philharmonia Orchestra in Royal Festival Hall.

1954 4 April: Conducts final, all-Wagner, concert with NBC SO.
3 and 5 June: Conducts final recording sessions, correcting passages in *Un ballo in maschera* and *Aida*.

1955 28 February: Leaves Italy for the last time to live permanently in New York.

1957 16 January: Death at Riverdale, his home in New York.
18 February: Funeral in Milan, Victor de Sabata conducts the *Marcia funebre* from Beethoven's *Eroica* Symphony.

1 9 0 0 – 3 0 : T O W A R D S T H E
P H I L H A R M O N I C T O U R

Covent Garden – the performance of 9 June 1900

'Get the strongest possible cast and let them sing.' During his tenure as manager of the Metropolitan Opera House in the 1890s, Maurice Grau's recipe for presenting opera to the New York public was remarkably successful, especially in his vocally spectacular staging of Wagner's music dramas. The parade of talent was such that over half a century later the Met's historian judged that 'in no other period have so many of the greatest singers of the day been systematically presented to the New York public'.[1] A *Tristan* with Lillian Nordica and Jean de Reszke was but one highlight; other Wagnerian stars included Emma Eames, Milka Ternina, even Nellie Melba as Brünnhilde with, on the spear side, such famed exponents as Jean's brother Edouard, Ernest Van Dyck and Anton Van Rooy.

The excellence of Grau's reputation led the Grand Opera Syndicate at Covent Garden to engage him in 1896 to manage its long-established annual summer opera seasons at the Royal Opera House.[2] For four seasons the world's two major international opera houses ran in tandem under Grau's artistic direction; what London heard in the summer, New York often heard in the winter.[3] Grau's immediate imprint on his Covent Garden seasons was a sharp increase in the number of

---

[1] Kolodin p. 177; the opening quotation, ibid. Maurice Grau (1849–1907) was, with some intervals, manager at the Met 1891–1902.

[2] The Syndicate was formed in 1896 after the death of the impresario Augustus Harris and continued under the chairmanship of Henry V. Higgins until July 1914. With Higgins still *in situ* it resumed opera promotion from early 1919 until 1924; see Rosenthal pp. 277, 391 and 430.

[3] See Rosenthal p. 278 and, as to Grau's Covent Garden *Ring* cycles, ibid. pp. 286–7. The first London *Ring* cycles took place in 1882 but there were no further cycles until 1892. In 1899 Karl Muck conducted most of the Covent Garden Wagner performances but there was no *Ring* cycle.

Wagner performances: during his tenure they doubled from a previous average of one dozen to two, rising in 1898 to no fewer than thirty-two performances (out of a total of sixty-seven). That year saw the introduction of what until then had long been lacking – complete performances of the *Ring* cycle, repeated in Grau's final season in 1900.

In one vital respect Grau was persuaded to modify his New York practice, which paid little attention (and low fees) to conductors – 'no-one ever paid a nickel to see a man's back'.[4] The great Anton Seidl, for long New York's nonpareil among Wagner conductors, was imported into Covent Garden for the 1897 season. His early death in 1898 changed the course of musical history in the house and perhaps also the course of the present narrative. Grau's replacement for Seidl was Felix Mottl, already familiar to London audiences and critics from his frequent appearances at the Wagner concerts under the management of Alfred Schulz-Curtius, who until the outbreak of the Great War in 1914 ensured that the capital heard many of the most prestigious foreign maestros.[5] By the time of his Covent Garden engagement Mottl had attained almost legendary status within the German-speaking world for his Wagner performances at both Bayreuth and Karlsruhe.[6] With his arrival the management announced that, as at Bayreuth, the *Ring* cycle would henceforth be performed without cuts.

The *Ring* cycle of 1898, its cast assembled with the help of Schulz-Curtius, was perhaps Grau's finest achievement at Covent Garden; in particular *Götterdämmerung* on 2 July was hailed as a Wagner performance without peer. Brünnhilde was sung by Ternina, Siegfried by Jean de Reszke, and Hagen by his brother Edouard. For critics and public alike, the cast and conductor were incomparable.

The principal singers were reassembled for the 1900 *Ring* cycles, again with Mottl as conductor; but with the de Reszke brothers by then out of the picture, there were important cast changes. Could Grau and Schulz-Curtius once more find the 'strongest possible cast'? And would Grau's doubtless reluctant investment in a famed Wagnerian conductor continue to pay dividends? In the first performance of *Götterdämmerung* on 9 June 1900 Ternina once more took the part of

---

[4] Kolodin p. 178. As to Seidl, see further Annex C n. 105.

[5] The concerts were started by Schulz-Curtius in 1876 when he established his concert agency in London. During the First World War Schulz-Curtius, a German citizen, was interned as an enemy alien; Lionel Powell (1878–1931) then joined the agency and in the 1920s became the most active concert promoter of the era: see further p. 15 below and Scholes p. 203. Schulz-Curtius also oversaw the introduction of new stage machinery at Covent Garden similar to Bayreuth's; see Rosenthal p. 286.

[6] As to Mottl's career and his earlier London appearances, see further Annex C pp. 305–9.

Brünnhilde and the formidable Ernestine Schumann-Heink again sang Waltraute. Other parts, however, were now undertaken by artists known principally for their appearances at Bayreuth, for example, Ernst Kraus as Siegfried, the regular Eva and later exponent of the Bayreuth declamatory style Luise Reuss-Belce (Gutrune), as well as names of less renown today such as Robert Blass (Hagen) and Adolf Muhlmann (Gunther).[7]

The musical bush telegraph evidently alerted Wagnerians across Europe to the virtues of Grau's *Ring* presentations, for in the Covent Garden audience attending *Götterdämmerung* on the night of 9 June was the 33-year-old Arturo Toscanini, on vacation after the conclusion of his second season as conductor and artistic director at La Scala, Milan.[8] Recommended for that post by his long-time admirer Arrigo Boito, who years before had assured Verdi that here at last was a conductor whom he could trust, Toscanini was by the time of this London visit unquestionably his country's foremost conductor. The qualities which would lead to unexampled worldwide fame were already the subject of comment outside his native country. In October 1898 that voice of the British musical establishment, the *Musical Times*, had this to say: 'he grasps the general spirit and masters the detail of an art-work at a glance, unfolding it before his hearers with admirable clearness and plastic delineation ... An admirable stylist, conscientious in the handling of the minutest detail, there is nothing which escapes his solicitude and attention, with the result that his interpretations, both in the concert room and the theatre are, by common consent, absolutely masterly.'[9]

Other than Toscanini's presence at this performance of *Götterdämmerung* we

---

[7]   Milka Ternina (1863–1941) Austro-Croatian soprano, Munich 1890–99, Metropolitan 1899–1904. Ernestine Schumann-Heink (1861–1936) German contralto, Hamburg 1883–99, Bayreuth 1896–1914, Covent Garden 1897–1900, Metropolitan 1899–1932, creator of Klytemnestra (*Elektra*) Dresden 1909. Ernst Kraus (1863–1941) German tenor, Berlin Royal Opera 1898–1924, Bayreuth 1899–1909. Robert Blass (1867–1930) American/German bass, Bayreuth 1901, Covent Garden 1899–1900, Metropolitan 1900–10, 1920–22. Luise Reuss-Belce (1862–1945) Austrian soprano, Flower Maiden (*Parsifal*) 1882, Bayreuth (including Eva and Fricka) 1896–1912. Adolf Muhlmann (1865–?) German baritone, Covent Garden, San Francisco.

[8]   Toscanini's 1905 letter about his Covent Garden visit (ATL p. 72) refers to Mottl as conductor, but gives no date. Mottl conducted *Götterdämmerung* on 11 June and 2 and 5 July 1898, at which time Toscanini was engaged in his series of concerts at the Turin Exposition (from 8 May to 14 July, resuming from 28 August to 31 October: Nicotra p. 78, Taubman p. 83), and again on 9 and 29 June 1900. Toscanini concluded his 1899–1900 La Scala season with his usual four symphonic concerts, the last on 14 May 1900, and then took the orchestra on a tour of eight northern Italian towns; his next known engagements were rehearsals with a student orchestra for concerts on 21 and 28 June (Barblan p. 74, Sachs 1978 p. 73), therefore making the performance on 9 June 1900 the only one he could have attended.

[9]   Vol. 39, 1 October 1898 p. 662. It is possible that this quite lengthy article, published on the occasion of Toscanini's appointment to La Scala, was by Boito himself (translated).

FIG. 1 TURIN'S DEBONAIR WAGNERITE: TOSCANINI IN 1895

know nothing of this first London visit. Such interesting adjuncts as where and how long he stayed, who if anyone accompanied him and what other musical functions he may have attended, cannot now be traced. It is, however, easy to deduce why he was there. From his first encounter with *Lohengrin* in 1884 as a cellist in Parma, he had been a passionate Wagnerian, conducting his first Wagner opera, *Der fliegende Holländer*, at Palermo in February 1893. In December 1895 at Turin's Teatro Regio he conducted *Götterdämmerung*, the first performance in Italy by native forces; and at La Scala he opened his first and second seasons with Wagner – *Die Meistersinger von Nürnberg* in 1898 and *Siegfried* in 1899.

Between those two seasons Toscanini attended the fount of Wagner performances: on vacation with La Scala's administrative director Giulio Gatti-Casazza at Bayreuth in July 1899 he witnessed and admired Hans Richter's handling of the orchestra in *Die Meistersinger*. He also witnessed Franz Fischer conducting *Parsifal* and may also have attended the *Ring* cycle conducted by Siegfried Wagner. Of this we cannot be certain; it is, however, certain that he disliked much of what he witnessed. If Richter's conducting of the orchestra was an object lesson – Toscanini remembered years later how he had overlooked some of Wagner's expression marks until he heard Richter – the lack of ensemble he perceived between orchestra, chorus and singers was not. 'These Bayreuth performances are a real hoax for people like me who are hoping to hear perfection', he remarked in a letter from Bayreuth to his assistant at La Scala. That letter, virtually the sole documentation of Toscanini's several visits to Bayreuth around the turn of the century, measured the profound disappointment experienced on that occasion.[10]

Toscanini's Turin *Götterdämmerung* was cut by a quarter but in accordance with its new policy Covent Garden's was to be given complete. Moreover, the conductor was one of the foremost living Wagnerians and the Brünnhilde of extraordinary renown. After the disappointments of Bayreuth, what could be more tempting for

---

[10]   See ATL p. 66, Sachs 1978 p. 75. Taubman p. 92 is certain that Toscanini attended performances conducted by Siegfried Wagner in 1899 but, unless he was so informed by Toscanini himself, the letter quoted here is the sole source of information about this possibility. However, recent research by Harvey Sachs shows that Toscanini heard Fischer conduct *Parsifal* on the 1899 visit and that he also heard Hermann Levi and Felix Mottl conduct that work, respectively last led by them at Bayreuth in 1894 and 1897 (see Neupert p. 107); of these, he most admired Levi. Giulio Gatti-Casazza (1869–1940) Italian opera manager, director La Scala 1898–1908, Metropolitan jointly with Andreas Dippel 1908–10, sole manager 1910–35. Hans Richter (1843–1916) Austro-Hungarian conductor, Bayreuth 1876–1912, Vienna Hofoper 1875–98, Hallé Orchestra 1897–1911, Covent Garden appearances 1882–1910. Franz Fischer (1849–1918) German conductor, Mannheim, Munich 1879, Bayreuth (member of 'Nibelungen Kanzlei' 1876, conducted *Parsifal* 1882–84 and 1899); see further Annex C n. 15. Siegfried Wagner (1869–1930) son of Richard and Cosima, conductor, composer, in charge of the Bayreuth Festival 1909–30.

an ardent Wagnerian than a break from La Scala duties to attend this outstanding event? If, however, Toscanini was hoping for a model performance at Covent Garden, he was again disappointed. True, as the *Times* reported on 11 June in a review spanning the whole tetralogy, Schumann-Heink's 'beautiful voice told splendidly', while Ternina's Brünnhilde maintained the highest degree of excellence with 'a completeness and grasp of the whole creation' in marvellous measure. But, as Toscanini pointed out in a letter written five years later, the orchestra under Mottl was apparently sight-reading the opera's final scene. 'The audience noticed nothing and the press found the performance superb. Of course! An eminent maestro was conducting, and he was German to boot.'

Toscanini evidently did not see the *Times* review for, apart from the words of praise already quoted, not only was Kraus's Siegfried harshly dismissed – he was simply not up to the standard set by Jean de Reszke – but the orchestra and conductor came in for the heaviest criticism, the magic of Mottl's achievement only two years before seemingly dissipated. As the *Times* critic pointed out, the conductor was so well known in Germany for his 'funereal pace' in much of Wagner that 'a word formed from his name has enriched the German vocabulary of music ... The eminent conductor keeps his slowest rate of progress for the passages which have become familiar through Wagner concerts, allowing the band to get on quite at the ordinary measure in the intervals.'[11] And so 'the whole of the Waltraute scene and worst of all, the death march, were played in a way that robbed them of all impressiveness'. As for the orchestra, its quality was 'scarcely up to the level desirable for a proper performance': 'the first violins might have been supposed to be [sight] reading the solo passage at the scene of Brünnhilde's awakening' (in the third Act of *Siegfried*), while the horns were distinctly below average and much else in need of improvement. Every shortcoming noted by the *Times* matched Toscanini's own observations. This devastating review typified the London critics' cumulative impatience with the idiosyncracies observed in some of Mottl's Schulz-Curtius concerts and after this Covent Garden season he never again appeared in Britain. Grau then retreated to New York for his two final seasons at the Met.

Toscanini's negative experience at Covent Garden had two important consequences. In the first place, it surely confirmed his conviction that if he wished to secure performances of Wagner's music-dramas good enough to satisfy him, he could not look for models elsewhere, whether in Germany or Britain: it was up to

---

[11]   11 June 1900. See further Annex C p. 307 for Weingartner's attack on Mottl and the views of London critics. The playing at Covent Garden improved during the second cycle; see Philip 1992 p. 16.

him to set his standards which thereafter he did with characteristic determination. After his first two seasons at La Scala it was the turn of *Tristan* in 1901, in which the musical standards surprised the visiting Siegfried Wagner, whose positive report to Cosima drew forth her profuse thanks to the young Italian.[12] Probably in response to an invitation extended by Siegfried at the time, Toscanini visited Bayreuth again in 1902, when he doubtless established his first contacts with members of the Wagner family.[13] Almost certainly he attended Karl Muck's *Parsifal* and would have approved its breadth and meticulous attention to detail, although the other works performed that year, the *Ring* cycles of Richter and Siegfried Wagner and Mottl's *Fliegende Holländer*, can scarcely have held equal attraction. When, eventually, he conducted *Götterdämmerung* at La Scala during the 1907/08 season, his performances owed little or nothing to his Bayreuth and London experiences and almost everything to his own remarkable powers of analysis, empathy and projection. Those powers, exercised again in Toscanini's New York Metropolitan opera presentations and further La Scala productions during the 1920s, convinced the Wagner family that here was an interpreter of the music-dramas without peer; hence Siegfried Wagner's invitation to him to return to Bayreuth in 1930 as the first non-Germanic conductor to appear there.[14]

---

[12] Sachs 1978 p. 75.

[13] The 1902 visit is known only from a letter dated July 1902 addressed to Toscanini at Bayreuth from his wife, Carla, in ATC JPB 90-1 series L pt 1 folder L21A. He himself never wrote about it (or about his early visits during the 1890s) but, through Siegfried, he almost certainly became well known to various members of the Wagner family during the visit: he later addressed some of them such as Daniela and Blandine, Cosima's daughters by Hans von Bülow, as old friends (see Ch. 3 p. 55 and ATL pp. 116–17). There is, however, no evidence that he ever met Cosima Wagner. For Toscanini's relations with Bayreuth personalia from 1901 onwards, see Sachs 1991 Ch. 6. Karl Muck (1859–1940) German conductor, the long-term conductor of *Parsifal* at Bayreuth until 1930, conductor of the Boston Symphony Orchestra and in Hamburg 1920–33.

[14] Toscanini's Wagner performances at the Met: *Götterdämmerung* (1908), *Tristan und Isolde* (1909, 1911–15), *Die Meistersinger* (1910–12, 1914, 1915); at La Scala: *Die Meistersinger* (1922–25, 1928), *Tristan und Isolde* (1923), *Parsifal* (1928). Joseph Horowitz argues that New York critics did not rate Toscanini's Metropolitan Wagner performances as highly as those of other Wagner conductors of the time and in support cites one contemporary review in Millington & Spencer p. 181 and a few others in *Understanding Toscanini* New York: Knopf 1987 pp. 56–60. A more comprehensive cross-section of the reviews negates the thesis: see the author's review, 'Misunderstanding Toscanini', in ARSC Journal 1986, vol. 18, 1–3 pp. 144–171A, reprinted with corrections for Michael G. Thomas and members of the Toscanini Society in Britain. Horowitz's more general criticisms of Toscanini's musicianship and style in his book are not relevant to this narrative and are not further examined. For assessments of the approach and methodology employed in Horowitz's book, see Sachs 1991 pp. 137–47, 'Misunderstanding Toscanini', and Harris Goldsmith's review in *The Strad* May 1988 pp. 411–14. For a detailed examination of the book's techniques and use of evidence, see the author's article cited above. For a wider discussion of the issues raised by the critical approach exemplified by Horowitz, see Frank Ch. 4. See also Ch. 8 n. 5.

If at first you don't succeed ...

More significantly for this narrative, Toscanini's first encounter with London musical life was without doubt the principal reason for his declining the many and pressing invitations to conduct London orchestras over the next three decades. The very letter in which he described his Covent Garden experience, sent from Rome in March 1905 to a Mr Fano in contact with London agents, cited that performance in questioning the offer of an engagement for two concerts there with an unspecified orchestra, most probably the one assembled for the Schulz-Curtius concerts. His self-respect could not bear the thought of working in conditions so evidently lacking in rehearsal time, nor could he contemplate public and press enthusiasm for substandard performances; so, while he did not close the door on the invitation, he demanded details of the terms, of the number and length of rehearsals available, and of the criteria for programme content. Toscanini took the 'extremely kind' prospective engagement seriously and suggested guidelines for his fee (his Bologna engagements at the time paid him 1500 lire, about £60, now equivalent to over £5000), but nothing came of these negotiations. Nor did any of the invitations extended to him during the course of the next thirty years or so fare any better.

The first of these later invitations to be documented was in April 1907 when, just three years after its founding, the directors of London's only permanent orchestra, the London Symphony, considered requests for engagements by Mahler and Franz Schalk. As well as enjoying fame as the Vienna Court Opera's music director, Mahler was remembered for his skilful, if sometimes wilful, Wagner and Beethoven at Covent Garden in 1892,[15] while his Viennese first Kapellmeister Schalk had in 1906 appeared in London with the Vienna Philharmonic to critical acclaim ('Schalk is a great conductor', thought the sixteen-year-old Adrian Boult of his Queen's Hall concert).[16] Nevertheless, in a measure of Toscanini's growing reputation, the LSO's directors rejected the requests by these eminent conductors in favour of an invitation to the young Italian; as the minutes of their meeting on 28 April 1907 record, 'it was resolved to invite Signor Toscanini to conduct' in the 1907/08 season, along with Richter and Nikisch. Perhaps they remembered that *Musical Times* report from 1898 and were curious; certainly by the time of this invitation

---

[15] Rosenthal pp. 248–9.

[16] Kennedy 1987 p. 28, and see generally Dyment 'Franz Schalk'. For Sir Adrian Boult (1889–1983), see further pp. 34 and 317.

others were reporting to London that Toscanini 'was a man of genius, by far the best conductor in Italy, a man who can be ranked with Weingartner and Richter'.[17] Unfortunately nothing came of the LSO's invitation and the orchestra's directors were equally unsuccessful in their efforts to secure him during the Great War (1914–18), when hostilities prevented the appearance of such erstwhile Austro-German regulars as Nikisch, Weingartner and Fritz Steinbach.[18]

During the latter stages of the Great War there was a lull in attempts to lure the elusive Italian; when they resumed, they came from a source which had already proved ill-fated in his eyes and was to prove so again in the future. Covent Garden's Grand Opera Syndicate suspended its opera promotions during the Great War from July 1914 until the end of 1918. Soon after it reconvened, its preliminary prospectus in February 1919 not only promised the first European performance of Puccini's *Il trittico*, given its world premiere at the Metropolitan just two months earlier, but hinted that Toscanini would be engaged to conduct it and other proposed Italian operas including Verdi's *Simon Boccanegra*.[19] If ever there was any substance in the Syndicate's negotiations with Toscanini, they soon fell through, ostensibly because of the then ongoing quarrel between composer and conductor. As soon as Puccini had word of the Syndicate's intentions, he protested to his publisher Ricordi and also wrote in March 1919 to his English friend and one-time lover, Sybil Seligman,[20] asking her to intercede with chairman Henry Higgins because, 'I do not want that *pig* [in English] of a Toscanini. He has said all sorts of nasty things about my operas and has tried to inspire certain journalists to run them down.' It would have been entirely out of character for Toscanini deliberately to attempt to influence critics as Puccini maintained; but whatever truth lay in his allegations, it is unlikely that these negotiations would have succeeded in the best of circumstances. Toscanini would have had in mind his experience in 1900 and his consequent demands for rehearsals would have been of an order too stringent for the times. His low opinion of *Suor*

---

[17] EMI, letter from the Gramophone and Typewriter Company's Milan agent to London marketing manager Theodore Birnbaum, 26 June 1905. The Milan agent would have been able to compare Toscanini with the other named conductors at Turin in May 1904 when Toscanini and Richter (as well as such notables as Max Fiedler, Colonne and Chevillard) conducted concerts in the Teatro Regio; and in May 1905 when Toscanini and Weingartner both conducted concerts there; see Annex C p. 310 and Fig. 59. For the LSO invitation, see Foss & Goodwin p. 44; extract from the LSO minute book courtesy Libby Rice.

[18] Pearton p. 53.

[19] Rosenthal pp. 248–9.

[20] For Puccini's relationship and friendship with this cultured wife of a prosperous British banker, see Mary Jane Phillips-Matz *Puccini: a Biography* UPNE 2002 pp. 150–1. See also Lucas p. 149 and the authorities there cited, p. 348.

Angelica and *Il tabarro* would in any event have precluded his undertaking the premiere of all three works.[21] *Il trittico* had to await Covent Garden's 1920 season when Puccini himself supervised the performances conducted by the house's new Italian expert for the season, Gaetano Bavagnoli.[22]

1920: Toscanini returns to La Scala

In the same year Toscanini was nominated 'plenipotentiary director' of La Scala, an appointment that signalled the start of his third and most fulfilling period as musical head of the opera house, lasting until June 1929. Its orchestra had to be reconstituted after the disruptions of Italy's immediate post-war period and Toscanini commenced his tenure by honing it in a series of extended tours. These tours marked a mid-point in his career: he had spent thirty-four years on the podium and an equal period was to elapse before his retirement. The first tour began in October 1920 with thirty-three concerts in twenty-one Italian cities. There followed the vast trans-North America tour from December 1920 to April 1921 with sixty-eight concerts in over forty centres in the USA and Canada. After returning to Italy, the final tours took in a further thirty-six concerts in nineteen cities during April–June 1921.

Some of the critics attending the orchestra's New York concerts found fault with both players and conductor. For the *New York Times*, Richard Aldrich considered the La Scala forces, finely trained though they were, to be lacking in body and colour. Somewhat surprisingly, given Aldrich's elevated appraisal of Toscanini's Beethoven Ninth Symphony with Met forces in 1913, he also thought the Fifth Symphony in this opening concert of the tour too heavy, deliberate and free in tempo; a measure of the stylistic traversal that the conductor's approach to the Austro-German repertoire was to undergo in the second half of his career.[23] However, virtually all of Toscanini's contemporary colleagues disagreed with the critics. Fritz Kreisler, for example, preferred Toscanini's 'wrong' conception of the Beethoven Fifth to anyone else's 'correct' interpretation; and the Boston Symphony's Pierre Monteux appraised him shortly after the North American tour as 'the greatest of all'.[24]

---

[21] Cardus 1957 p. 16, and Mosco Carner *Puccini: A Critical Biography* 2nd. ed. 1974 p. 217.

[22] Lucas pp. 153–4. Bavagnoli lasted just one season, as he had at the Metropolitan, where on 28 January 1916 he conducted the world premiere of Granados's *Goyescas*.

[23] Aldrich p. 644, his critique of the 1913 Beethoven Ninth, pp. 396–7; see further Ch. 12 pp. 236–8.

[24] Sachs 1978 p. 146, which also quotes the contemporary views of other eminent musicians, e.g. Ernest Bloch, Paderewski and the Met's chief conductor Artur Bodanzky.

Toscanini was by now as experienced in the concert hall as in the opera house. To the forty-four concerts he gave at the Turin Exposition in 1898, necessarily covering an extensive repertoire, were added over twenty given with La Scala's orchestra before and during his earlier tenures at the house, an equivalent number with his Turin forces during those years, and more than fifty during and immediately after the Great War. When taken with the tours in 1920–21, Toscanini's tally of concerts to the mid-point of his career falls just short of three hundred. Of that total, however, over two hundred took place in Italy. Only with the North American tour did his stature as a symphonic conductor emerge for a wider, international audience.

Toscanini's access of fame stimulated renewed attempts to lure him to London. Shortly after the tours a London impresario tried to tempt him and his orchestra to the capital for a series of concerts,[25] embellishing this prospective attraction with many stories about the conductor's 'temperament' for the benefit of the newspaper gossip columns. This effort met with no success; nor in the end did that of the Royal Philharmonic Society for the following year. The fame of this venerable institution, with its intimate associations with Beethoven, Mendelssohn and Wagner among many others, meant that its claims could not lightly be brushed aside and the Society indeed secured a date for Toscanini to conduct its orchestra, 22 February 1923. It was not to be (a recurrent motif of this narrative). He was prevented by ill-health from travelling to London and in his place the young Eugene Goossens conducted a programme – including Dukas's *La Peri*, McEwen's *Solway Symphony* and Stravinsky's *Rite of Spring* – which clearly owed nothing to any plans that Toscanini may have had.[26] In any event, it seems that his ill-health was diplomatic in character: only three days after the agreed date he conducted his first post-war La Scala performance of Charpentier's *Louise* and the business of rehearsing his immense and illustrious cast (Fanny Heldy, Aureliano Pertile, Marcel Journet and Ezio Pinza among others) would certainly have occupied him for weeks beforehand.[27]

London doldrums

It was perhaps fortunate that Toscanini did not fulfil his engagement with the Royal Philharmonic Society. Its orchestra, the 'old' Royal Philharmonic Orchestra,[28] was

[25] Boult 1983 p. 86.
[26] Elkin pp. 110 and 151.
[27] Barblan p. 230.
[28] Not to be mistaken for the ensemble of that name founded by Beecham after the Second World War.

not a permanent body; instead, from the pool of London's finest orchestral players, which included many outstanding instrumentalists such as oboist Léon Goossens, some were regularly contracted to play for the limited number of concerts sponsored by the Society each season (six in the early 1920s, eight after 1927 when Beecham became more closely associated with the Society). Although the majority consistently performed for the orchestra, an ever-shifting penumbra of 'reserve' players was called upon to take the place of those unable to fulfil their Society engagements. If the orchestra was nonetheless capable of producing acceptable results on the customary minimal rehearsal, that achievement was a tribute to the sight-reading skills of the players and the technique of those conductors capable of energising them. The pinpoint delicacy of the scherzo from Mendelssohn's *Scottish Symphony* in Weingartner's 1929 recording of the work highlights what could be done; but where such authority was lacking, the results were appalling. A typical example, neither better nor worse than many another, is provided by Columbia's 1926 recording of Strauss's *Don Juan*, where even so eminent a maestro as Bruno Walter was unable to persuade the RPO to offer ensemble or standards of intonation remotely comparable with the great orchestras of the continent or the USA.[29] Such variable, improvisatory adaptability would not have met Toscanini's demands for precision, accuracy of intonation and tonal consistency.

Nor, it must be said, would any London orchestra of the time. After the depredations of the Great War, the one permanent London orchestra in the 1920s – still the LSO – attempted to recapture its glory days under Nikisch and other Austro-German luminaries by engaging Nikisch pupil Albert Coates to train and lead it, soon after his exit from Soviet Russia. After a couple of seasons of indifferent box-office returns, the orchestra dispensed with a permanent conductor in favour of a plethora of guests. The good and the great processed, each conductor engaged for a concert or two every season, among them Weingartner, Walter, Koussevitzky, Furtwängler and Beecham; with what degree of success may be judged by the verdict of the *Musical Times* in February 1925: 'We used to be proud of this Orchestra, and we shall be again – some day when it stops playing the fool with conductors from the ends of the earth (a different one for almost every concert) and settles down to a hard "grind" under a good man who will not spare its feelings in the effort to redeem its reputation.'[30]

The *Musical Times* was far from alone in its condemnation. Doyen of critics

---

[29] Weingartner's *Scottish* Symphony recorded on 27 March 1929, Columbia (UK) 9887–90, (USA) M 126 (67671–74D), CD Shinseido SGR 8534, Pristine Audio PASC 210. Bruno Walter's 1926 recording of Strauss's *Don Juan*, Columbia L 2067–68, CD Opus Kura OPK 2019.

[30] *Musical Times* vol. 66 February 1925 p. 165.

Ernest Newman took a year off to work in New York and on his return observed of a Weingartner concert in March 1925, 'the LSO, I suppose, ranks as our premier orchestra; and I am glad to be able to record that it compared not unfavourably with the orchestras in some of the New York picture houses' (which, it should be noted, contained such fine musicians as violinist and future conductor Eugene Ormandy).[31] He complained further of thin and scratchy strings, sour woodwind and blatant brass. Evidently Weingartner did not on this occasion exercise his sometimes magnetic powers. Toscanini was aware of the reputation of London orchestras and was as a result reluctant to accept any invitation from them during this period.[32]

Why did this state of affairs persist for so long? While a variety of conditions accounted for the stylistic characteristics of London orchestral playing in the 1920s,[33] particular factors, all germane to this narrative, undoubtedly contributed to stasis. First in importance was the long-standing deputy system still practised by the LSO, whereby any contracted player present at initial rehearsals was permitted to send a replacement to play in his stead at any subsequent rehearsal or at the concert itself, usually because of his having obtained a more remunerative engagement elsewhere. (This had been the catalyst directly responsible for the orchestra's foundation when, in 1904, Henry Wood had banned the practice in his Queen's Hall Orchestra.) Significantly, when circumstances made it impossible to operate the deputy system, the LSO's playing improved dramatically, as was demonstrated by Beecham's revelatory, light-footed *Messiah*, which reached London in December 1926 after the orchestra had toured for some weeks under his direction.[34] A similar change for the better occurred when the orchestra recorded with Beecham subject to the Columbia company's vetting of individual players. But so long as the deputy system lasted for the orchestra's London concerts, refinements of playing, let alone of interpretation, were virtually impossible to achieve.

Beyond some fretful members of the critical fraternity, widespread public acceptance of mediocre standards contributed to inertia. Specialist listeners who had access to the higher standards already audible in some recordings made abroad did not hesitate to make adverse comparisons; for example, in 1926 Compton Mackenzie, editor of the *Gramophone*, pointed to the fire and discipline of

---

[31] *Sunday Times* 29 March 1925, quoted in Kenyon p. 9 and Lucas p. 167. Ernest Newman (1868–1959) foremost British music critic of his generation, wrote for the *Sunday Times* from 1921 until 1958. See p. 31 for Newman's first notice of Toscanini in London.

[32] See the report of Toscanini's 1935 press conference, Ch. 2 p. 51.

[33] See the extended analysis in Philip 2004, Ch. 3.

[34] See Lucas p. 170; as to the vetting by the Columbia company, ibid. pp. 169–70.

Toscanini's 1920–21 La Scala Orchestra recordings by comparison with Weingartner's 1926 LSO Beethoven Ninth, where 'the ineluctable fact remains that life is
absent'.[35] But most concertgoers remained in ignorance of such delights. Indeed,
how could they question current standards when they were endorsed by a master
conductor such as Weingartner, whose praise for the LSO the Columbia company
made much of in his first post-war recordings for them in 1923? Only Hamilton
Harty's well-disciplined Hallé Orchestra on its forays to London provided any idea
of what could be, for the early 1920s saw virtually no visits from the great foreign
orchestras which were to become commonplace in future years. Just one arrived on
British shores in the immediate post-war years, the New York Symphony Orchestra
under Walter Damrosch in June 1920; but while the high standard of the playing
was noted (and, by a benighted critic or two, derided), its impact was vitiated by
Newman's vitriolic reviews of Damrosch's Beethoven and Elgar, so pointed that
Damrosch, an Elgar champion, dropped the composer from his repertoire.[36]

The first major wake-up call for London orchestras did not occur until December
1927, when the Berlin Philharmonic under Furtwängler visited the capital. If critics
appraised Furtwängler's technique and interpretative liberties somewhat coolly, press
and public alike were impressed by the orchestra's rich tone and – by comparison with
London orchestras – unanimity of ensemble. Still, even this demonstration of superiority failed to penetrate the complacency of the LSO management and the persistent
and increasingly vociferous calls for improvement in the London orchestral scene
continued to be undermined by the deputy system. Most savage of all, in the *New
Statesman* as late as 1929 W. J. Turner remarked that the LSO's lack of ensemble 'always
reminds me of what happens when you disturb an ant's nest with a stick'.[37] Of its
deputy system, he continued, 'as each member has the right to send a proxy should
he have another engagement, and as the proxies themselves send proxies, even to the
third and fourth degree, it is evident that the LSO is not a single homogeneous body
at all'. Although this attack merely echoed widespread critical views, the LSO man-

---

[35] *Gramophone* vol. 4 November 1926 pp. 210–11. Mackenzie's main point was that recordings
showed how demonically active conductors such as Toscanini and Albert Coates succeeded in
transferring their interpretations to disc while 'dignified' conductors such as Weingartner were
often unable to do so.

[36] See George Martin *The Damrosch Dynasty* Boston: Houghton Mifflin 1983 pp. 267–8.

[37] Quoted in Foss & Goodwin pp. 125–6. W. J. Turner (1889–1946) Australian poet and music
critic of the *New Statesman* 1916–39, was considered a writer of fierce integrity, although some
lack of musical training and his dislike of Wagner were held against him. As a friend of Schnabel,
he noted and often contested the latter's view that Toscanini was 'a flame but not a source'; see
further McKenna pp. 155–7 and Ch. 8 n. 15.

agement answered it by discontinuing all press handouts and soon after concert manager Lionel Powell, agent for (among others) the LSO and visiting orchestras, withdrew facilities for critics reviewing his contracted orchestras' concerts.[38]

The New York Philharmonic's European tour – the Maestro ascendant

This gloomy picture goes far to explain why, when Toscanini first conducted in London, he deemed it wise to bring his own orchestra with him – not by then an opera orchestra but one honed in symphonic music. In mid-1929, after a fêted tour to Vienna and Berlin with La Scala forces, Toscanini severed all connections with that opera house, exhausted by both musical and administrative work and the constant tussle with Mussolini's fascist régime outside its doors; he turned down all tempting offers to return. Shifting his focus to the concert hall, he became guest conductor with the New York Philharmonic Orchestra in January 1926, joint conductor with Mengelberg of the combined Philharmonic-Symphony Orchestra of New York from 1928 and by 1930 was the orchestra's principal conductor in all but name; that name became officially his in the following season.

As evidenced in the recordings made by Victor just a year before,[39] Toscanini had by now reached pre-eminence in his concert-hall career; but that pre-eminence was by no means unchallenged and even by the late 1920s only a relatively restricted audience could claim first-hand knowledge of his approach to the symphonic repertoire. North America had seen the Orchestra of La Scala on its tour in 1920–21, while New York had experienced his Beethoven Ninth Symphony as far back as 1913, a performance which for some critics overtopped all other contemporary efforts, including Mahler's just four years before.[40] Further, those critics had witnessed him in that work and much else in the four seasons with the Philharmonic since 1926. Europe, however, had little experience of this side of Toscanini's conducting. Two brief Swiss tours with his La Scala Orchestra in 1924 and 1925 awakened some to what was afoot but his other concerts in the 1920s were confined to La Scala.[41]

If European perceptions of Toscanini were soon to change, in-depth knowledge of what to expect was in the circumstances still lacking. A legion of stories circulated

---

[38] Scholes p. 402.

[39] See Ch. 12 p. 240.

[40] See the 'Musical Courier' 16 April 1913 and Aldrich n. 24; these contemporary reviews are collected in the author's article cited in n. 14.

[41] See Ch. 12 p. 245 and Annex C p. 319.

in the musical world about his fabulous memory, his explosive temper, the exhaustive rehearsals resulting in unprecedented precision in performance and so on – the more superficial, crowd-pulling adjuncts of the phenomenon, which fed the popular press. Attempts to analyse that phenomenon were less common and, in terms that would resonate with today's readership, largely confined once more to the New World.

Among early writers describing Toscanini's attributes, the critic Max Smith was one of the most enthusiastic, making much of the Toscanini personality and methods.[42] Crucially, however, he attempted as early as 1913 to convey in addition a detailed analysis of the musical process he observed. Significantly, he compared Toscanini's technique and approach with other conductors recently witnessed in New York:

> The movements of his right arm, though subtly varied and elastic, are at once broad, incisive, and sharply defined. Unlike certain other conductors – Nikisch, Strauss, Mahler and Mottl[43] – the Italian master is never satisfied with giving vague indications. While painting his colours he marks every important beat distinctly with his stick ... He has no sympathy with the trend of modern conducting, as exemplified by Nikisch, who ... shapes his reading to suit his individual taste ... His all-absorbing ambition is to reproduce music in a way absolutely true not only to the letter, but to the spirit of the creating mind.

Moving to Toscanini's interpretative approach, Smith expanded at length on his 'imaginative grasp of the movements best suited to express the emotional import of the score':

> His feeling for tempo, indeed, is one of Toscanini's most extraordinary gifts; for under his sway the metrical ebb and flow ... sweeping in waves now broad and placid, now light and fluent, now wildly propulsive and turbulent, creates the impression of something inevitable. His rhythm is always articulate ... Even the fluctuating and irregular pulsations of 'rubato' – and what a master of rubato Toscanini is! – rise and fall on a heaving

---

[42]   T. Max Smith (1874–1935), music critic for the *New York Press* (1903–16), *New York American* (1916–19 and 1923) and a foreign music correspondent for the *New York Herald Tribune*, latterly a friend and business associate of the Toscanini family. The extracts quoted are from Max Smith, 'Toscanini at the Baton', *The Century* vol. 85 (1913) pp. 691–701.

[43]   Arthur Nikisch (1855–1922) had appeared in New York as recently as April 1912 with the LSO (see Aldrich p. 362), Richard Strauss in 1904, Mahler at the Met in 1908–09, with the New York Symphony Orchestra in 1908 and the New York Philharmonic in 1909–11. Mottl guest conducted at the Met for five months in 1903–04; see further Annex C p. 312.

groundswell of rhythm. The unity and cohesion of Toscanini's musical per-
spectives, the perfect adjustment of one part to another, is striking ... the
most clashing contrasts are dovetailed into a seamless and homogeneous
whole. His crescendos are models of dynamic ascension, set at exactly the
right angle from the outset, no matter how distant the summit, and
beautifully graduated from start to finish; his accelerandos are as accurately
calculated as though they were impelled by the force of gravity. In the most
delicately interlaced network of tones ... no meshes hang loose. Every
filament is as closely related to those that are not yet disclosed as it is to
the threads that are not already spun. And as the impressions roll by, vitalized by a temperament that spans the whole gamut of human feelings, ...
one realizes that Toscanini has not been revealing merely a rapid succession
of pictures ... but a single gigantic canvas projected on the memory through
the wide-angled lens of his mind.

If somewhat technicoloured, the emerging portrait is a recognisable reflection of
the conductor, nonetheless emphasising elements such as the mastery of a frequently
used rubato which generations of those familiar with his work only through the late
recordings would be less willing to acknowledge.

As to Toscanini the symphonic conductor, the profound impression made by
his early seasons with the Philharmonic in the late 1920s is conveyed with great eloquence by the Russian-born composer-conductor Lazare Saminsky, whose estimate,
although in terms less specific than Smith, is nonetheless comprehensive in scope.[44]
For Saminsky, no executant artist's nature harmonised the 'Apollonian principle' –
thought plan and control – with the 'Dionysian element' – temperament and
intuition – as completely as did Toscanini's. Like Smith, Saminsky dealt summarily
with those who compared Toscanini to his disadvantage with 'romantic' conductors
such as Nikisch or Furtwängler:

> Toscanini's nature is priestly and Hellenic to the loftiest degree. He
> reaches out for nothing but the soul of the work ... He sacrifices every-
> thing – colour, brilliance, sonority, emotion too direct and crudely
> manifest – to the pure thought-substance, to the spiritual line of the
> music, he is bringing to life. Toscanini is the creator's trusted mouthpiece,
> devoted and honest to a martyr's degree. He is faithful to everything that

[44]　Lazare Saminsky (1882–1959), composer, conductor and author, specialising in Jewish music.
This estimate of Toscanini first appeared in his *Music in Our Day*, New York: Thomas Y Crowell,
1932 pp. 299–300. It was reprinted with revisions in Saminsky's *Essentials of Conducting*, London:
Dennis Dobson, 1958 pp. 57–60.

the music breathes, its inner dynamics, its rhythmic pulse, its spiritual essence. Not only his conscious self but the remotest recess of his instinct, loathes all that tastes of over-emphasis, the perfumery, the visible or veiled 'acting' that mark the inflated ego of today's deified conductor-emperor. His mastery of ensemble surpasses even Nikisch's in its delicacy, in its elfin agility and radiance of spirit. One marvels at the range of his interpretative grasp. It embraces the perfection of style in his reading of Mozart, the volcanic, flaming *credo* in his reading of the [Beethoven] Ninth Symphony, the lofty intensity of his Wagner readings ... Then one recalls the noble engraving in his recreation of Ravel's *Daphnis*, the torrential sound orgy evoked in Honegger's *Pacific 231*,[45] the light and radiant silhouette of 'his' *Till Eulenspiegel*. One is subjugated by this protean clairvoyance. In Toscanini's general predilections or in his technique, one may sense an affinity with the masters of the past, but in purely tonal taste he is entirely a musician of our day ... His very aversion for adorning music, for inflating it with meaning, with extra-musical content, for emotionalizing what is pure line and form, is the aversion of today's musician. He is bewitched by the very flesh of music, by its sonority and rhythmic flux; their plan and balance entrance him. In this he is a true neo-classic musician, both Hellenic and modern.

Concluding with remarks about Toscanini's technique, Saminsky again contrasted his 'leonine manner' with Nikisch's 'carefully restrained movements of the wrist':

At times, an incredible attention is demanded from the orchestra by Toscanini's gesture, in the execution, for example, of the orchestral *recitativo* that opens the finale of the Ninth Symphony. But we must bow before a superhuman will that achieves everything it desires, and with any means it may choose.

The passionate enthusiasm of Smith, the loftily synoptic view of Saminsky – both can now be seen as part and parcel of the New York reaction to Toscanini. If some New Yorkers during the late 1920s still championed the virtues of Mengelberg and, to a lesser degree, Furtwängler,[46] writers such as those quoted, as well as the

---

[45] Toscanini performed this work with the Philharmonic on several occasions in 1930 but never thereafter.

[46] E.g. B. H. Haggin (1900–87), who wrote for *The Nation* 1923–57 and was later known for his writings about Toscanini, still preferred the approaches of Muck and Mengelberg as late as October 1927; see his columns in *The Nation* vol. 123 no. 3197, 13 October 1926 pp. 382–3 and vol. 125

FIG. 2 THE NEW YORK PHILHARMONIC-SYMPHONY ORCHESTRA BOUND FOR
EUROPE ON SS *DE GRASSE*, 23 APRIL 1930, TOSCANINI, CENTRE, IN CAP AND
BOW TIE

daily press critics, notably Olin Downes in the *New York Times*, had by the close of
the decade played their part in establishing Toscanini as a unique force in New York
concert life.[47] Audience reaction, audience enthusiasm, did the rest.

After the close of the Philharmonic's 1929/30 season, in May and June 1930
Toscanini headed the orchestra on its epochal tour of Europe.[48] Among much else,
the tour would test whether the almost invariable acclaim for Toscanini's New York
concerts would be replicated in those centres of European musical culture which
had yet to experience his music-making. The 112 musicians drawn from thirty-four
nationalities (only about twenty native-born Americans) must have posed many
travel problems for customs and immigration officers across Europe; but so also
did Toscanini and his family, who were accompanied by twenty-six items of luggage,
a dog, two canaries and three bird cages. The line-up for the tour included many
musicians fabled in the annals of the orchestra, among them John Amans (flute),

---

no. 3249, 12 October 1927 pp. 405–6. Willem Mengelberg (1871–1951), conductor of the Concertgebouw Orchestra 1895–1945, made his debut with the Philharmonic in 1923, when Haggin
hailed him, with some reservations, as a 'genius' (*The Nation* vol. 116 no. 3009 p. 276).

[47]   Olin Downes (1886–1955) music critic of the *New York Times* 1924–55, an enthusiastic but
not uncritical writer about Toscanini.

[48]   For details of the tour, see Sachs 1978 pp. 198–202.

FIG. 3 ERICH KLEIBER GREETS TOSCANINI, BERLIN, MAY 1930

Bruno Labate (oboe), Simeon Bellison (clarinet), Bruno Jaenicke (horn), Harry Glantz (trumpet) and unsurpassed timpanist Saul Goodman. Remarkably, two prominent members, concertmaster Scipione Guidi and contrabassoonist William Conrad, were veterans of Henry Wood's old Queen's Hall Orchestra.[49]

Commencing with two concerts in Paris on 3 and 4 May 1930, the tour took in a total of twenty-three concerts in fifteen cities, in the course of which Toscanini conducted works by nine living composers and fifteen others. With but a single significant exception (dealt with in Chapter 12), the invariable reaction of critics, musicians and public everywhere was one of stupefaction at the perfection of the orchestral playing and transported amazement at the consistently exalted level of Toscanini's interpretative insight. Of the mass of appreciative appraisal emerging as a consequence of the tour's stopovers, it suffices to cite the verdicts of two outstanding musicians. One was a leading German conductor: for Otto Klemperer, Toscanini was at this time the 'king of conductors' whose interpretations of music from Haydn to Stravinsky were not merely beautiful but 'right'.[50] The other was the world's greatest living composer of Toscanini's generation: just a few years after the tour Richard Strauss expressed the view that 'the interpretation of Beethoven by most of our younger conductors suffers from the lack of any genuine tradition ... Toscanini alone ... makes a praiseworthy exception. Other conductors impose personal conceptions on their performances before – as von Bülow put it – they are able to read the score properly.'[51] Across Europe, then, the verdicts now echoed the transatlantic consensus.

The tour ended in London. The majority of cities heard just a single concert; Paris, Milan, Rome, Vienna and Berlin were honoured with two. If London had impatiently and for too long awaited its first sight of the 63-year-old conductor in action, this centre of Empire and the world's greatest city was now rewarded with no fewer than four concerts. The ground had been well prepared. The London concert scene so graphically condemned by Newman, Turner and many another had been leavened

---

[49] *Musical Opinion* vol. 53 July 1930 p. 890. The journal also claimed that Ernest Hall deputised throughout the London concerts for the orchestra's first trumpet who 'fell ill'; but see p. 26.

[50] *Der Dirigent Toscanini* in the *Berliner Zeitschrift* 'Das Tagebuch', 25 May 1931, reprinted in Klemperer pp. 49–50. Klemperer became more reserved about Toscanini only when the latter failed to support his claims to succeed him as the Philharmonic's principal conductor in 1936, favouring instead Furtwängler and Fritz Busch; see Heyworth vol. 2 pp. 57–60. See further Ch. 12 p. 240.

[51] *Recorded Sound* 24, October 1966 p. 110 (Strauss's introduction to his annotation of Beethoven's Symphonies, 1936, translated by Leo Wurmser). It is possible that Strauss attended Toscanini's Beethoven centenary concerts at La Scala in 1926 but more likely that he encountered Toscanini's Beethoven on the Philharmonic's tour in Vienna or Berlin (the *Eroica*) or Dresden (the Seventh).

by a series of visiting orchestras in the preceding months, including the Concertgebouw Orchestra under Mengelberg and both the Berlin Philharmonic and Vienna
Philharmonic under Furtwängler; in addition the Colonne Orchestra under Gabriel
Pierné was to appear on the day following Toscanini's final concert.[52] Despite Powell's
withdrawal of facilities, the European orchestras had drawn much critical appreciation
and further comment on London standards by comparison, but the public reaction
remained relatively muted with some less than full houses. Unused to tepid applause,
Furtwängler complained to Eugene Goossens about the cool reception given to his
programmes, especially to the then little-understood Bruckner, whose Fourth
Symphony he had conducted with the Vienna Philharmonic.[53]

Four London concerts: the critics enamoured

By contrast with the public reserve greeting other foreign visitors, the acclaim for
Toscanini and the Philharmonic was without precedent in its enthusiasm from the
moment of their first appearance. There were full houses both for the two concerts
in the 7000-capacity Royal Albert Hall and for the two in the smaller but acoustically
superior Queen's Hall. The first concert, on Sunday afternoon, 1 June, at the Albert
Hall, included Wagner's *Tannhäuser* Overture and Venusberg music, Brahms's
Second Symphony and Beethoven's Overture *Leonore No. 3*. The scene was set by
the *Daily Telegraph*'s veteran critic Robin H. Legge under banner headlines the
following morning:[54] 'On appearing through the tunnel which leads from the artists'
room to the conductor's desk (but Toscanini disdains any such desk), Toscanini
received an ovation the like of which is usually reserved for popular heroes ... Again
and again the great man bowed to the storm of applause, which ceased only when
the arrival of the King and Queen was signalled, when, of course, it burst out all
over again. Then there followed the two National Anthems ...' Royalty (not
renowned at the time for its musical enthusiasm) was indeed present, in record
numbers for a concert by a mere foreign conductor and orchestra; assorted princes,
dukes and duchesses of the blood royal accompanied King George V and Queen
Mary. Contrary to his usual custom, Toscanini was persuaded by Lionel Powell to

---

[52] Foss & Goodwin p. 127.

[53] Goossens p. 284. For *Musical Opinion*'s comparison between Toscanini and Furtwängler at this
time, see p. 31 – although this journal was one of the few to laud Furtwängler's Bruckner a few
weeks before this notice: vol. 53 June 1930 p. 776. These reviews were unsigned but may have been
the work of its associate editor, composer Havergal Brian (1876–1972).

[54] Robin H. Legge (1862–1933) music critic of the *Daily Telegraph* 1906–31. The complete programmes for all concerts conducted by Toscanini in Britain are set out in Annex B.

attend on this unprecedented constellation during the interval, when the King assured him of the uniquely high regard in which he was held.[55]

Other celebrities were also out in force. The venerable Sir George Henschel, friend of Brahms and first conductor of the Boston Symphony in 1881, rated Toscanini the greatest conductor in his experience.[56] Former music critic Bernard Shaw thought it a good concert but, while regaling orchestra and conductor with his views on Wagner at a post-concert reception given by Lord and Lady Howard de Walden, declined further detail with the observation that 'an article by me on Toscanini would be worth £5000'.[57] Again mixing social and critical comment, Robin Legge in the *Telegraph* was more forthcoming about the impact of orchestra and conductor: 'Those of us who were already familiar with the conductor as incomparably the greatest in the world enjoyed our pleasure at seeing our judgement confirmed by the huge audience in an ovation at the end of the concert such as has never been seen at an orchestral concert in the Albert Hall.' Newman, rarely given to unstinting praise – save from now on in writing about Toscanini – wrote to his wife, 'yesterday was a great day, the New York Philharmonic Orchestra is by far the best foreign orchestra we have had, and Toscanini is a marvellous fellow. He does no tricks with the music, but he makes it get right inside you.'[58]

---

[55]   According to 'Noblesse Oblige', memoir by Natalie (Mrs Lawrence) Townsend (*Opera News* vol. 21 no. 20, 25 March 1957, issued by the Metropolitan Opera Guild), Clarence H. Mackay, chairman of the orchestra's board of directors, asked her to secure attendance of the British royal family, a mission in which she was successful. The problem of persuading an adamantly negative Toscanini to conduct two national anthems was solved by Lionel Powell so demanding, on pain of his own ruination. At King George's behest, she continued, Toscanini was forced by Powell up to the tea room in the interval to receive the King's congratulation on his 'magnificent' conducting of the Brahms symphony; and in response to Toscanini's querying his knowledge of such matters, the King assured him that during a recent illness he had listened to all of Toscanini's records and hence grown to love them. While the truth of this detailed account cannot now be established, much of it lacks verisimilitude. Toscanini was punctilious in performing national anthems when needed, except when (as on the Italian leg of this tour) political considerations interfered. He would not in any event have conducted the anthems without notice or rehearsal. Guarded by his wife in his dressing-room, customarily he never saw royalty or anyone else during concert intervals, when he was drying himself and changing his shirt. However, the *New York Times* reported that he was presented to the King after the Brahms symphony in the first half of the concert and, given the importance of the occasion, the presentation may have taken place; but it is unlikely that Toscanini would have queried the King's familiarity with the work.

[56]   Henschel pp. 37, 81; Taubman p. 192. Sir George Henschel (1850–1934) conductor, composer and lieder singer, headed the Boston Symphony Orchestra 1881–84 and held various posts in Britain thereafter.

[57]   Taubman p. 192; *New York Times* report in ATC JPB 90-1 series L pt 2 folder L50D-1. Shaw made no written comment on Toscanini at the time. His only critique came in his final piece of music criticism at the end of his life in 1950, when in the context of observations about the (in his view) loss of traditions in the performance of Italian music, he maintained that Toscanini was better at German music than he was in Rossini; see *Shaw on Music* London: Bodley Head vol. 3 p. 768.

[58]   Vera Newman p. 91.

The voice of the critics in the following days was, however, somewhat muted principally because of Powell's 'churlish' behaviour in withdrawing facilities for them. Some journals, it seems, purchased tickets for their writers, but others were silent or, as in the case of the *Musical Times*, gave vent to hurt feelings in scornful depiction of an event which, professionally at least, they were prevented from witnessing – in this instance by means of an elaborate and exaggerated description of the scene culminating in the conductor leading the National Anthem. In any case, although Powell provided publicity material of the most lavish appearance, nobody knew in advance what the programme content was to be, another of the agent's devices again condemned in suitably thunderous tones on 2 June by the *Times*, whose critic (H. C. Colles) also felt that the hall's acoustics prevented full assessment of the orchestra's qualities.[59] Still, as this critic ventured, 'there could be no question about the clarity and finish of yesterday's performances, a clarity which even the Albert Hall could not obscure, at any rate for long at a time'. The *Times* continued by extolling the Wagner and Beethoven for their 'revelations' but, as was to be expected from the then unusual sight of an Italian conducting Brahms, it was the Second Symphony that caught its detailed attention. Despite the hall's aural fog, the symphony was 'the music thought of by Brahms relieved of all cloudiness ... and made eloquent without bombast', the slow movement in particular moving easily with every strand of melody 'perfectly poised', its relevance 'unmistakable'.

The second concert, including Haydn's *Clock* Symphony, Debussy's *La Mer* and Elgar's *Enigma* Variations, took place the following evening in the Queen's Hall. The next morning's critical superlatives were accompanied by relief at hearing the remarkable qualities of the orchestra in the acoustically sympathetic hall. For the *Times*, Toscanini's absolute control of his forces, their extraordinary virtuosity and his own vision transported the audience to a degree far surpassing other recent and brilliant visitors. The strings in the Haydn 'sounded like an enlarged quartet', with quiet passages having an 'infinite variety of nuance'. But with the *Enigma* Variations, the *Times* set hares racing which, as will be seen in Chapter 2, coursed through London concert notices over the next decade: the playing was 'wonderful' and *Troyte* had probably 'never been played with more electric energy, or *Nimrod* attained such

---

[59]   The writing of the anonymous *Times* critic, H. C. Colles (1879–1943), was, according to successive editions of *Grove's Dictionary* (which he edited for its 3rd edition), admired 'for its admirable qualities of comprehensive taste, sure and fair judgment' and for 'an unfailing tact and humanity that tempered even his severest strictures'. From 1925 he was assisted by Frank Howes (1891–1974), who was the *Times* critic from 1943 until 1960. For Powell's 'churlish' behaviour and the reaction of the *Musical Times*, see Scholes p. 402.

FIG. 4 LIONEL POWELL'S POSTER FOR THE PHILHARMONIC'S 1930 LONDON
CONCERTS, *SANS* PROGRAMMES

an overwhelming tonal climax', but Toscanini's ideas about the work were 'too
definite for a satisfying reading of Elgar'.

Turner (whose editor evidently bought him a ticket for this one concert) agreed
in essence – but started his lengthy *New Statesman* review with invidious, if
humorous, comparisons: 'How pleasant it is when a critic discovers that, owing to
his exactness of judgment and perhaps even more to his adjectival reticence, he has
a few epithets left for that rare, perhaps unique occasion when his enthusiasm is
left unbounded. I am now glad that I appreciated the merits of Furtwängler without
excitement, that, like Mengelberg, Bruno Walter and all the other famous conductors I have heard, he left one admiring with reservations.' He had never felt about a
conductor what he felt about Artur Schnabel as a pianist, 'until I heard Toscanini
this week at the Queen's Hall'. Nevertheless, in common with the majority of critics
– though not with the excited audience which in the interval (according to the

Times) could talk of nothing else – Turner was cool about the Elgar; it lacked the intimacy of expression present when it was given under the composer's admittedly 'somewhat feeble direction'. Again, in another letter to his wife, Newman remarked of this 'very fine' concert, that he did not much care for the Elgar: 'Toscanini evidently doesn't understand the English spirit. It was all very interesting but Italianized', views upon which he expanded in his review the following Sunday. By contrast, Richard Capell in the *Daily Mail* thought the performance 'incomparable', an event that, on his birthday, Elgar should have been present to hear.[60]

Decades later Capell's view was echoed in the memories of the orchestra's lead cellist (and the subsequent conductor) Alfred Wallenstein, who singled out this very performance of the *Enigma* Variations, together with the Berlin *Eroica* and *La Mer* the previous week, as among the most satisfying experiences of his life as a player: 'I've never heard it like that in my life ... it was the *most impeccable* playing and performance I've ever heard. It was fabulously beautiful; and the audience just went wild ... I've found a few players in the BBC and other English orchestras who were at that concert and still talk about how wonderful it was; but the majority of the people [now] tell you from hearsay that it was too fast, it wasn't English ... Hell, it was what Elgar wrote; and the sad thing was that Elgar, who was still living and should have been there, wasn't there.'[61] One of the appreciative players referred to was London's leading trumpeter, Ernest Hall, who in this concert helped out his transatlantic colleagues in *La Mer*, after (as he understood) too great an indulgence by one of the New Yorkers at their last stop in Brussels. He recollected the special rehearsal called by Toscanini to assure himself that Hall could play the third trumpet part, starting with the last movement to test his competence in the trumpet's repeated note figure and then returning to the earlier movements. 'And that was the complete rehearsal.'[62]

The following night's concert in the Albert Hall was devoted largely to colourful works, some of less than the first rank, including Strauss's *Tod und Verklärung* and the Mussorgsky/Ravel *Pictures at an Exhibition*, again enthusing the critics without qualification. The programme also included Eugene Goossens's *Sinfonietta*, a tribute to local talent. Goossens records that Toscanini had earlier given this work a superlative outing in New York (actually several performances in March 1930) and he now went backstage at the Albert Hall to thank him for a 'miraculously played'

---

[60]   Richard Capell (1885–1954), at this time the *Mail*'s critic, was chief music critic of the *Daily Telegraph* from 1933 until his death.

[61]   Haggin 1967 p. 183. Alfred Wallenstein (1898–1983) American cellist and conductor, principal cellist New York Philharmonic-Symphony Orchestra 1929–36, conductor Los Angeles Philharmonic Orchestra 1943–56.

[62]   Interview with the author, 1972.

performance.[63] He found 'the great man ... inconsolable and near to tears at what he considered fine performances ruined by the triple echo of the hall'. He refused to be comforted by any explanation, repeating '"non, non, non: orribile, brutto, spaventevole, acusticamente ridicolo", and further choice expletives'; the notorious acoustics were to remain largely untamed until the 1970s. However, 'at the Queen's Hall he was happier, but complained, "Molto risonante, ma troppo piccola per un gran' orchestra'".[64] As Goossens summed up the experience, 'Toscanini and the superb orchestra swept London like a fire', furnishing for years a yardstick of performance standards.

In particular, the *Eroica* Symphony in the final Queen's Hall concert on 4 June became a repeated reference point for critical comparisons in London for the rest of the decade, at least until Toscanini conducted it once more in the same hall in 1937. In this work Toscanini, said the *Times* on 5 June, did 'nothing' and 'everything', the rhythm 'at once steady and supple' with the *Marcia funebre* 'a superb example of vital rhythm kept even over a long stretch'. The concert also contained the Brahms *Haydn* Variations, 'each variation ... beautifully rounded and exactly adjusted to its neighbour', and Respighi's orchestration of Bach's Passacaglia and Fugue in G minor, commissioned by Toscanini as a showcase for the tour. If the *Times* was indulgent about the latter, Capell in that day's *Daily Mail* was vitriolic ('a vulgar din'), one of the few dissonant notes in the reception of the London concerts. This concert, and with it the whole tour, closed with the Prelude to Act 1 of *Die Meistersinger*; thereafter came the inevitable prolonged ovation from the capacity audience, led by Nellie Melba who stood close under the podium waving a white scarf shouting 'Bravo, maestro, bravo!'. Afterwards, said Wallenstein, she came round backstage – but Toscanini had already left for the post-concert reception.[65]

Throughout the tour Toscanini was for the most part in high good humour; his players reported that they had never seen him so happy. Such unprecedented contentment led him to give a speech to the guests at the Carlton Hotel reception on the evening of 4 June, aimed particularly at his orchestra. This gesture, which broke the habit of a lifetime, was premeditated: a draft of the speech, made earlier in the day at his Savoy Hotel, has been preserved.[66] He began by saluting his 'dearest

---

[63] Goossens p. 284.

[64] 'Horrible, nasty, dreadful, absurd acoustics'; 'plenty of resonance but a bit small for a big orchestra'.

[65] Haggin 1967 p. 183, Bonavia *Daily Telegraph* 5 June 1930.

[66] The text is in ATL p. 115, described as a letter to the players, but reports in two New York newspapers preserved in ATC make clear that Toscanini delivered it as a speech: JPB 90-1 series L pt 2 folders L50D-1 and 2.

friends', continuing, 'the thought that this evening we will give the last concert of a successful tour and that tomorrow we will have to separate after seven weeks spent in affectionate, familylike cordiality moves me profoundly'. He was very sure that 'all of us will always keep the sweet memory' that the tour had been 'a magnificent artistic success'. He had experienced great joy in becoming more aware every day of 'the enthusiasm and the faith that you've brought to making every concert turn out better than the previous one ... You have been really marvellous and I thank you ... not only am I proud of you but love you as faithful friends'. After the speech the concertmaster Scipione Guidi presented Toscanini with a bronze plaque as a gift from the orchestra in commemoration of the tour.[67]

The time had come for dispersal, with the players embarking for New York. For Toscanini there were personal memories as well as triumphs. One of his closest musical friends, Adolf Busch, whom Toscanini had already encountered at the Philharmonic's concert in Leipzig on 25 May, travelled with his wife Frieda and regular pianist partner Rudolf Serkin, to attend the London concerts.[68] Busch had first met Toscanini when he attended the *Falstaff* which reopened La Scala in late December 1921; thereafter they frequently attended each other's concerts. When they met again in London Toscanini asked Busch to perform with him in New York in 1931, an invitation later sealed with a September contract. As Toscanini reportedly put it, were a famous soloist to perform under his direction, it could only be Busch; for the violinist's fierce integrity of approach gave him the Maestro's ear on matters of musical interpretation, an access unique at the time.

There was also important correspondence for Toscanini to deal with before his departure. Perhaps the best documented was the exchange of greetings between George Henschel and the conductor. In his first letter to Toscanini, dated 4 June, Henschel asked that, 'the old conductor of the Boston Symphony Orchestra be permitted to express to you his profound admiration. Never in my life (and I am past 80) have I heard such marvellous orchestral playing as yours last night. It was simply perfect, and in spirit I grasp your hand and thank you for the supreme pleasure you have given me.' Toscanini's friendly reply and signed portrait stimulated Henschel's second letter of thanks the following day, which expressed the hope that they would meet in Boston at the concerts marking the half-century since his appointment as the orchestra's conductor.

---

[67]   Guidi ceased to be concertmaster at the end of the 1930/31 season, when he was succeeded by Mishel Piastro.

[68]   Lehmann & Faber p. 61; Potter pp. 309 (Busch's first meeting with Toscanini), 310 (Toscanini consults Busch on interpreting Mozart), 435 (their meeting in London in 1930) and 444 (the contract to play with Toscanini). For Adolf Busch, see further Annex C p. 318.

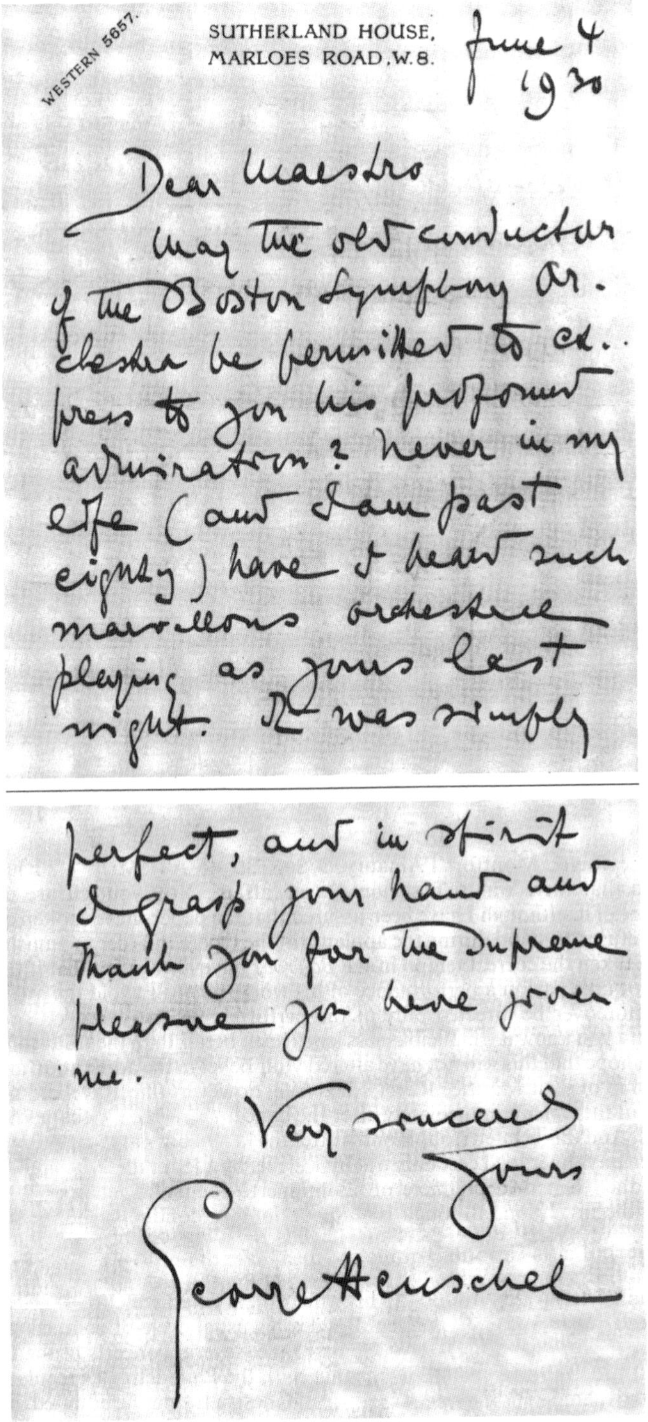

WESTERN 5657·

SUTHERLAND HOUSE,
MARLOES ROAD, W.8.

June 4
1930

Dear Maestro

May the old conductor of the Boston Symphony Orchestra be permitted to express to you his profound admiration? Never in my life (and I am past eighty) have I heard such marvellous orchestral playing as yours last night. It was simply perfect, and in spirit I grasp your hand and thank you for the supreme pleasure you have given me.

Very sincerely
yours

George Henschel

FIG. 5 SIR GEORGE HENSCHEL'S LETTER TO TOSCANINI
DATED 4 JUNE 1930

A younger musician addressed Toscanini in a letter dated 4 June in which he hoped that the conductor would 'forgive my writing to you to express my gratitude and admiration for your wonderful and inspired performances. Realising how fatigued you must be after your tour, it is with much diffidence and hesitation that I send to you three of my scores.' Perhaps William Walton was encouraged by the presence of the Goossens *Sinfonietta* in one of Toscanini's London programmes, for he judged 'from your programmes that you are always willing to see new works' and he hoped Toscanini would find time to go through his own. The selection of works enclosed with Walton's letter is now unknown but very probably his recent Viola Concerto was one of them. It appears that neither Henschel's hopes nor Walton's audacity was rewarded.[69] It was time for Toscanini to travel on to Italy for a brief vacation before heading for his first engagement at Bayreuth.

Post-Philharmonic fallout: the Newman effect

If visitors earlier in 1930 caused only temporary ripples across the stagnating surface of London concert life, the visitation of genius from New York contributed towards more permanent results. Moreover, Powell's attempt to undermine the critical fraternity by withdrawing facilities for them had the beneficial effect of enhancing the value of those notices that did appear. Two retrospectives on the Philharmonic's concert series provide an accurate measure of their impact. *Musical Opinion* was evidently so astonished by the Toscanini phenomenon that it reported on his concerts three times in a single issue.[70] Like Turner, the journal did not hesitate to make invidious comparisons with other conductors but, by naming names and giving its reasons for finding that Toscanini outdistanced even the most eminent of current and immediate past masters – Beecham, Furtwängler, Richter – the reviewer illuminated contemporary standards for today's readers. Toscanini, he wrote, did not indulge 'in the whipping up methods even a fine conductor like Beecham finds necessary', yet secured playing beautiful in detail, thrilling in ensemble and vitally musical. The Berlin Philharmonic's recent concerts were no less thoroughly and effectively rehearsed than Toscanini's orchestra, but their conductor Furtwängler 'seemed content to gather the fruits nurtured in rehearsal', while

---

[69] ATC JPB 90-1 series L pt 1 folders L49A and C. Henschel p. 37 confirms that the two conductors exchanged letters about Toscanini's performance of the *Eroica* symphony; that was, however, performed on 4 June, the date of Henschel's first letter wherein he refers to the previous night's concert. Since it is unlikely that Henschel wrote to Toscanini about the contents of the concert on 3 June, he probably wrote both letters preserved in ATC in the early hours and misdated them.

[70] Vol. 53 July 1930 pp. 877, 890 and 900.

for Toscanini 'the printed notes ... had to be kindled into meaningful sound on the spot' with a 'marvellous power of communicating the sense of song' to the players. And as long ago had been the case with Richter, there was the same negation of self but also 'a warmth and passion which Richter never knew'. Only one other conductor could be prayed in aid as a yardstick: Toscanini's intense concentration in recreating his composers' conceptions 'undoubtedly played a part in producing the most vital, and at the same time, technically perfect, orchestral playing heard since Nikisch was a wonder among the great conductors of history'.

Among individual works, *Musical Opinion* admired the *Enigma* Variations, which had 'a quality of beseeching tenderness', particularly in *Nimrod*; *La Mer* 'rose and fell like cascades of hot passion'; the *Tristan* Prelude, a 'vast irreproachable nocturne', again had a 'most unusual tenderness'; and the *Eroica* was without a coarse note in this 'passionate and triumphant' performance. By contrast with Capell's condemnation, the Bach/Respighi Passacaglia 'had a vastness which almost obliterated the Prelude to *Die Meistersinger*' in which, nonetheless, 'there was a welter of musical passion apparently produced by a minimum of effort'. And so 'Toscanini has become the hero of the hour'.

While these impressions vividly bring home Toscanini's impact for today's reader, it was Newman who, with his formidable resources of learning, experience and stylistic assurance, had the greatest contemporary effect. Newman prefaced his magisterial notice in the *Sunday Times* of 8 June, perhaps the longest concert review penned in Britain during the twentieth century, with the sweeping observation: 'That this has been the greatest week that the present generation of English music lovers can remember will be disputed by no-one' who had heard the four Toscanini concerts. For their technical perfection and flawless liaison between conductor and orchestra, he said, 'this week's performances stand supreme'.

Much of Newman's detailed account of what, for him, made Toscanini so outstanding may now seem to lack specificity or originality, but that would be to apply the wisdom of hindsight. Newman was attempting to convey qualities which were in some ways novel and, as he was often later to repeat, almost beyond analysis. For example, unlike the usual star conductors there was, he averred, nothing of the prima donna about Toscanini; Newman no doubt had in mind comparison with some familiar visitors such as Koussevitzky and Mengelberg. Again, in terms which may strike today's reader as uninformative, he emphasised the 'perfect musicality' of Toscanini's mind, by which he appeared to mean the conductor's complete freedom from any exaggeration in his approach. Every phrase was exquisitely modelled by the orchestra but the conductor's perfect taste ensured that he never thrusted himself forward at the expense of the work. 'On the rare occasions on which he indulges in a nuance that is not in the score we feel that even if it is not written over the music it is implied there.' Newman here cited the Andante of Haydn's *Clock* Symphony in which the oboe crescendo started earlier than the marked point, since the expression was already latent in it. He continued in his rather question-begging language, referring to Toscanini's 'magnificent common-sense' which, 'touched with genius', accounted for his 'superb feeling for form' that consistently avoided all exaggeration.

Newman's further observations were, however, more specific in content and to that extent more illuminating. For example, he said, if the music required a slight change of tempo, Toscanini would indulge in it, but 'where the whole effect can be got within the four containing lines of a frame he will hardly depart from these by so much as a hairs-breadth'. Newman here cited the *Tristan* Prelude and *Liebestod* which Toscanini 'built up to colossal proportions with hardly a moment's deviation from the tempo of the opening'. Even the 'comma' that Wagner marked in two places in the *Liebestod* involved – unlike the practice of other conductors – no breaking of the line: 'the quick breath-pause was enough to arrest the attention as Wagner intended it to do, but not enough to give the disturbed feeling of a sudden holding-up of the music and a beginning again'. Such architectural control over the longest spans was, he thought, extremely rare.

Newman disagreed with Toscanini only in his reading of one work – as with some other critics, the *Enigma* Variations. Some variations were of 'an incomparable beauty', *Nimrod* in particular, and 'the virtuosity of the playing in some of the more torrential passages was a marvel'; but he thought the interpretation, especially the finale, insufficiently English to be authentic. Surprisingly, he also thought some of the performances were those of an ageing man since 'the viewpoint was often that of an artist who has shed some of his youthful passion'. While the interpretation and playing of the Venusberg music were unbelievably beautiful, this was a 'Venus-berg spiritualised by the philosophy of advancing years'. Newman drew similar conclusions about *Tod und Verklärung* and the Brahms Second Symphony, even though the latter was (once more) 'incomparably' lovely. A few years later Newman was to change his views and even at the time others clearly disagreed: Adrian Boult, attending the first concert at a moment when he was finalising plans for the BBC's new orchestra, later recalled the Venusberg music in which Toscanini 'heaped climax on climax ... each height seeming to call up every ounce of the orchestra's power, only to be succeeded by one more thrilling and more intense'.[71]

---

[71]   Boult 1983 p. 88.

Taken as a whole, Newman's conclusions accorded with a widely-held consensus, although his analysis did not on this occasion advance significantly beyond what was discerned by his colleagues in the daily press; but such an extended and detailed exposition from the doyen of critics helped establish in Britain the view that Toscanini was without question the supreme exponent of the art of conducting, a view that was not seriously challenged for several decades to come. Newman's later writings deepened his analysis as well as his admiration even if he often felt that the secret of Toscanini's supremacy lay beyond the power of his language to describe.

Newman's review also continued his excoriation of orchestral conditions in London by comparison with New York. He described at length how economic conditions in the United States permitted both the hiring of the best musicians that money could buy and the ample rehearsal time resulting in the orchestra's miraculous ensemble, which in turn enabled Toscanini's genius to project 'ten thousand points' in the scores never before properly heard by his London audiences. None of this, said Newman, could be achieved with London orchestras, whatever the individual excellence of players. These comments did no more than reinforce what he and others had been repeating for years; but such was the impact of the Philharmonic's visit that renewed venom in the press directed at London orchestral life had one journal branding the LSO a 'national disgrace'.[72] In the face of this barrage the managements of London's orchestras realised that Powell's attempted critical lockout was counterproductive and that they could not revert to their accustomed defensive complacency.

The omens for change were by this time favourable. The LSO directors were already searching for a powerful agent of reform. To secure the services of a Toscanini would have been unrealistic; but, impressed by what Mengelberg had achieved with the Concertgebouw, the directors quickly engaged him to train and conduct the orchestra during the 1930/31 season. His one important condition was that the orchestra should abandon the deputy system, to which at last the management acceded, at least for the duration of Mengelberg's concerts; it was to be some years before the practice disappeared altogether.[73] Nevertheless, the beneficial results of Mengelberg's thorough training were immediately obvious in that season; coincidentally, shortly after it ended the orchestra lost its agent and promoter, Lionel Powell, who died suddenly at only fifty-three years of age.

---

[72] Foss & Goodwin p. 127.
[73] Morrison pp. 66, 70 and 86.

A new orchestra broadcasts

The BBC's concurrent activities were even more important for the future of London orchestral life. In the late 1920s negotiations between the BBC and Beecham with the aim of establishing an orchestra to serve both him and the BBC's musical plans foundered when it became clear that Beecham expected the orchestra to be subservient to his expanding aims in the concert hall.[74] Throughout these discussions the BBC made plain their emphasis on broadcasting which Beecham chose to ignore until their irreconcilable views became a matter for legal exchanges. From January 1930 onwards the BBC began to disentangle themselves from Beecham's ever-changing visions and concentrated instead on plans drawn up during the preceding months by two of their own executives, Edward Clark and Julian Herbage. Their scheme envisaged a large, permanent body of players capable of forming orchestras of varying sizes for different purposes, all of them exclusively devoted to the BBC's functions. Even as negotiations with Beecham were sailing unsteadily towards as yet unseen reefs, auditions began for a core of musicians. By the autumn of 1929 the BBC had succeeded in landing, among others, the prize of Arthur Catterall as putative leader of the first violins; Catterall was already pre-eminent in his chosen sphere as former leader of the Hallé Orchestra and first violin of his eponymous string quartet. Other future star players, attracted by the prospect of year-round salaried employment, were contracted before the year's end.

By the date of Adrian Boult's appointment on 15 May 1930 as the BBC's new Director of Music, disengagement from Beecham was virtually complete, although not without final protestations from his quarter.[75] Meanwhile Boult's campaign of recruitment was succeeding. At the time of Toscanini's concerts, he was coming to the end of his sustained attempts to sign up the finest players in the country for an orchestra destined to act as a showcase for both broadcasting and public concerts. By the end of July his plans were more or less complete; he and his assistants, who included a young pianist-composer turned BBC administrator named Owen Mase, had gathered a collection of players of the foremost talent. In addition to Catterall, principals included cellist Lauri Kennedy (grandfather of Nigel) who already had a burgeoning solo career; bass player Eugene Cruft, who had joined the LSO in 1910; first flute Robert Murchie, London's leading player of the instrument; first clarinet Frederick Thurston, who had been associated with music-making for the BBC since

---

[74] For the details, see Kenyon pp. 21–45. For Clark and Herbage, see Ch. 4 p. 69.
[75] Kenyon pp. 38–40; Kennedy 1987 pp. 139–41.

1923; illustrious horn player Aubrey Brain; Alec Whittaker, the Hallé's young but much prized first oboe; and, fresh from his appearance with the New York Philharmonic, Ernest Hall, formerly lead trumpet with the LSO.[76] Negotiations with players contracted to other orchestras were not always easy: because of his devotion to Hamilton Harty and the Hallé management's considerate treatment, Archie Camden was not recruited as principal bassoon until Harty left the Hallé in 1933; meanwhile the distinguished bassoonist Richard Newton filled that post. When Camden did reach London, he found, as he recounted at the end of his life, a very different atmosphere.[77]

During the summer season of 1930 members of the new orchestra played at the annual Henry Wood Promenade Concerts; the critics noticed the sudden improvement in the playing which until then sometimes suffered from Wood's extremely limited rehearsal time. The fully-fledged BBC Symphony Orchestra made its debut on 22 October 1930 at the Queen's Hall under Boult. The programme included two works which were specialities of Boult – also, as it happened, of Toscanini: the second suite from Ravel's *Daphnis et Chloé* and the Fourth Symphony of Brahms. Next day's press was unanimous in hailing Boult's achievement. The *Times* thought that 'the virtuosity of the Orchestra ... wiped out any reproach Englishmen may feel in the face of visiting Orchestras from abroad', while Newman in the *Sunday Times* of 26 October remarked simply, 'the new Orchestra is certainly the finest in the country'. The stage was set for visits by illustrious guests.

[76] Arthur Catterall (1893–1943) violinist, leader of the Hallé Orchestra 1912–25, leader BBC SO 1930–September 1936, first violin Catterall Quartet from 1910. Lauri Kennedy (1896–1985) Australian cellist, principal cellist BBC SO 1930–35, LPO 1935–36. Eugene Cruft (1887–1976) double bass, with the BBC from 1926, principal BBC SO 1930–49. Robert Murchie (1884–1949) principal flautist, BBC SO 1930–July 1938. Frederick Thurston (1901–53) clarinettist, with the BBC from 1923, principal BBC SO 1930–46. Richard Newton (1895–1977) bassoonist, with the BBC SO 1930–59. Archie Camden (1888–1979) bassoonist, principal Hallé Orchestra 1914–33, BBC SO 1933–46. Aubrey Brain (1893–1955) horn, with the BBC from 1928, principal BBC SO 1930–45 and January–August 1951. Alec Whittaker (1900–73) oboe, principal BBC SO 1930–37. Ernest Hall (1890–1983) trumpet, principal BBC SO 1930–53. Other BBC SO players referred to in later pages are Alex Nifosi (1905–75) cellist, BBC SO 1930–72; Bernard Shore (1896–1985) viola, principal BBC SO 1930–45; Paul Beard (1901–89) violinist, leader BBC SO October 1936–1962; Ambrose Gauntlett (1889–1978) cellist, with the BBC from 1925, principal BBC SO 1935–47, later a renowned gamba player; Sidonie Goossens (1899–2004) harpist, with the BBC from 1927, BBC SO 1930–80; Gerald Jackson (1900–?) flautist, principal BBC SO July 1938–46; Terence MacDonagh (1908–86) oboe, with the BBC SO 1930 as cor anglais player, principal oboe 1937–47, joint principal 1963–72.

[77] See Camden pp. 113 and 125–7, where he condemned the rigid management style of Christopher Pratt, orchestra manager 1930–46 (also quoted in Kennedy 1987 p. 165). Kenyon is silent on this contributory cause of the orchestra's variable standard in the 1930s, which, according to Camden, led to Alec Whittaker's erratic performance as principal oboe and probably contributed to his early departure in 1937; see Ch. 2 p. 42 and Ch. 4 p. 84.

1 9 3 1 – 3 5 : T H E L O N D O N M U S I C F E S T I V A L 1 9 3 5

Getting him back – at sixty-eight

The reform of London's concert life again stimulated invitations to the great foreign conductors who throughout the 1930s were the principal draw. Walter, Weingartner and Klemperer conducted the LSO in 1930–31; Weingartner and Klemperer returned during the following season. Given Turner's exalted estimate of Toscanini in 1930 and later in the decade, it is worth noting his views on Klemperer in February 1932, prescient in the light of this conductor's later prominence: he was 'the most satisfactory conductor I know of' – more satisfying than Furtwängler who had that very week again brought the Berlin Philharmonic to the Queen's Hall.[1] In 1933 the LSO extended an invitation to Toscanini to conduct during its 1933/34 season. The orchestra had recently undergone severe financial losses and its bank overdraft was colossal; not the best juncture, surely, at which to invite such an expensive guest. Toscanini's response was to offer one concert with a programme described by principal viola and orchestra director Anthony Collins as 'clam-bake' (details have not survived), for which he required nine rehearsals and a fee of £1000 (today equivalent to some £55,000). Such unheard-of demands seemed designed – probably were designed – to elicit refusal; the LSO duly declined them. Two years later, in December 1935, Albert Coates, once more the LSO's artistic adviser, wrote from Stockholm to invite Toscanini to conduct it but apparently he remained un-answered; and with that the LSO drops out of this narrative.[2]

In truth, if the ultimate but seemingly unattainable aim of inviting Toscanini

---

[1] *New Statesman* 13 February 1932 pp. 197–8; see also p. 53.
[2] Letter of 3 December 1935 to Toscanini, ATC JPB 90-1 series L pt 2 folder L66G.

back to conduct a London orchestra was to be achieved, only one body was capable of succeeding – the BBC alone had the necessary resources of money and matériel. The BBC Symphony Orchestra enjoyed a rapidly expanding reputation, in its first two seasons unassailably the finest in the country, with guests including Strauss, Weingartner and Walter. Throughout, its work was underpinned by the meticulous training of the Classically orientated Boult who was rewarded in May 1931 by his appointment as Chief Conductor. That year also saw the first mention of Toscanini among the conductors the BBC wished to invite (of the others listed, including Furtwängler, Stokowski and Koussevitzky, only the last-named was persuaded to conduct the orchestra before the Second World War).

The following year the BBC SO had to meet severe competition from Beecham's newly formed London Philharmonic Orchestra. The BBC took a number of initiatives in response, including the institution of the annual London Music Festivals, an end-of-season series of concerts by their orchestra showcasing particular artists and repertoire. The first Festival in May 1933 brought Koussevitzky together with Boult's already distinguished Brahms, the second Festival in 1934 Boult, Walter and, as ever eliciting particular press enthusiasm, Weingartner in Beethoven.

For the third concert of the second Festival, conducted by Boult on 9 May 1934, Toscanini's son-in-law Vladimir Horowitz travelled from Paris, where he was staying with the Toscanini family for the Maestro's Paris concerts, to join the BBC orchestra in Tchaikovsky's First Piano Concerto. The occasion was clearly to his great satisfaction, the *Times* reporting next day a 'splendid performance' which found 'unsuspected subtleties of phrase and expression'.[3] Obviously Boult gave a very different kind of support from the deliberately perverse effort Horowitz suffered with Beecham at his disastrous American concerto premiere in January 1928 – although later Beecham did make amends.[4] It was common knowledge at the time that Horowitz's experience with the BBC orchestra was a pivotal moment in the corporation's negotiations with Toscanini,[5] which, emboldened also by their success in securing Koussevitzky for the 1933 Festival, started in earnest soon after the pianist's visit.[6] Boult's assistant Owen Mase undertook the detailed work and his persuasive charms proved to be effective enough.

[3]   Plaskin p. 175 has Horowitz playing concertos with an orchestra conducted by Cortot in Paris that day but the *Times* review quoted here confirms that he played in the Queen's Hall that evening. Possibly the Paris concert was in the morning and the pianist flew to London later that day; but Boult would hardly have conducted the concerto without adequate rehearsal. See also Kenyon p. 98.

[4]   See Lucas pp. 178 and 210.

[5]   See the report of Toscanini's press conference, *Manchester Guardian* 14 June 1935.

[6]   Gaisberg p. 143 says: '... I was able to establish contact with Toscanini, and this led to his taking

By late 1934 terms were agreed for Toscanini to conduct four broadcast concerts during the third London Music Festival in June 1935. He was to have twenty rehearsals for four concerts in which a substantial number of items would be duplicated; in essence there were two programmes with variants within each pair. He would be paid £500 per concert (today over £27,000), a rate adhered to for all his concerts with the BBC orchestra until the close of the 1938 Festival. No other musical organisation in the country could have met such terms; but crucial in the equation was Horowitz's assurance to his father-in-law about the quality of the orchestra and the disciplined training it had received at the hands of its Chief Conductor.

Toscanini's arrival was timed for mid-Festival: the first four concerts of the 1935 Festival, one conducted by Boult, the others by Koussevitzky, had already taken place during May. The three under the latter already placed an exceptional strain on the orchestra, the difficulty of rehearsing such works as Stravinsky's *Rite of Spring* and Sibelius's Second Symphony heightened by Koussevitzky's choleric temper, severe demands and his threats of the still greater stress which the players would suffer under Toscanini. Tension was further fuelled by the BBC administration's anxiety at the prospect of the Maestro's expected displays of temperament and tantrums. His reputation for such behaviour elsewhere was without doubt well founded; but, as the course of this narrative demonstrates in relation to both the BBC orchestra and the Philharmonia, the last 'new' orchestra of his career, in some respects Toscanini's approach to an orchestra unfamiliar to him was not then well understood.

Whether or not these management anxieties were justified, the BBC could not have invited Toscanini back to London at a more appropriate time. In his public and professional life, he was at the age of sixty-eight incomparably successful, perhaps the most famous executant musician of the era and, so far as recorded evidence permits judgement, at the peak of his powers as a symphonic conductor. Nevertheless, although he was accepted throughout the musical world as the foremost

charge of the BBC London festivals'. This led Moore p. 211 to state, 'when the BBC wanted to secure Toscanini ... it was to Gaisberg that they turned for help'. Gaisberg (as to whom, see further Ch. 3 p. 58) may have advised the BBC who best to contact, either Carla Toscanini or Wanda Horowitz acting on Toscanini's behalf, since, as described in Ch. 3, he corresponded with Toscanini and Wanda about these concerts. However, given the history of relations between Toscanini and Gaisberg referred to in that chapter, and the well-established and active administrative structure in the BBC's music department further described in Ch. 4, it is unlikely that Gaisberg played any part in the negotiations. There is nothing predating 1936 concerning Toscanini in the BBC's Written Archive and nothing in EMI's archive before November 1934 indicating that HMV/EMI had any interest in the forthcoming BBC concerts. Gaisberg's claim, and the early history of BBC negotiations with Toscanini, cannot therefore be verified from these sources. In his 1943 *Gramophone* article, 'Toscanini', Gaisberg states that he helped Owen Mase in securing Toscanini for the 1937 Festival, but this is again doubtful; see further Ch. 4 n. 3.

conductor of his time (Nazi Germany excepted), engagements with orchestras outside his Philharmonic seasons were still relatively scarce. Two years before, he began what was to become a fruitful relationship with the Vienna Philharmonic, the first concerts in Vienna in late 1933 followed by more in Salzburg in 1934. His verdict on the orchestra – 'good, not excellent like mine in New York and above all not as disciplined'[7] – was a measure of the standards to which the BBC orchestra needed to aspire. How would this new orchestra, for all its excellent tutoring under Boult, compare with one of the world's most venerable and venerated institutions?

The year 1933 was also momentous in Toscanini's private life, for it marked the start of the most significant among his many extramarital liaisons. His passions in this all-consuming affair were ignited by Ada Mainardi, thirty years younger than him and wife, in a troubled marriage, of Italy's leading cellist, Enrico.[8] Toscanini first met her socially probably in 1917 and thereafter declared her to be the most attractive woman of her generation. Their intimacy began sixteen years later. Over the next seven years the affair stimulated – from a notoriously bad correspondent – an immense quantity of letters to Ada wholly uninhibited in character; even after the passage of four years, Toscanini admitted his 'sick, incurable mad love' in which 'I cling to you more than ever, held tightly in an erotic knot that nothing can loosen by so much as a thread'. The letters throw much light not only on the affair itself but on his approach to music, politics and his contemporaries, with many a revealing detail about the BBC seasons. But the affair was significant also for the extra and remarkable creative stimulus it inspired in Toscanini as a musician at a time when physical problems in his baton arm presaged the onset of old age – problems which, however, left no visible mark in an appearance that by common consent seemed, if anything, to improve over time.

The affair with Ada contrasts with (and was in part stimulated by) Toscanini's dissatisfaction with his own family situation. The family was used to the conductor's frequent extra-marital liaisons, although his wife Carla may well have known nothing of the affair with Ada. His attitude towards his marriage seems by the time of the BBC visits to have become a mixture of resignation and disappointment, bereft as it was after its first decade of any intimate physical contact.[9] Nevertheless, Toscanini held rigidly to a moral code permitting only one marriage – but any

---

[7] ATL p. 156 (letter to Ada Mainardi, hereafter AM, 22 October 1933).

[8] Ada Mainardi (1897–1979), wife of cellist Enrico (1897–1976). For more on her background and the start of her relationship with Toscanini, see ATL pp. 143–4; for the quoted letter, which also contains Toscanini's description of the impact made by Ada when he first met her some twenty years earlier, see ATL p. 265 (letter to AM, 3 July 1937).

[9] ATL p. 262 (letter to AM, 26 June 1937).

number of liaisons – which, when it went unobserved by others, precipitated the end of many a friendship. For all his frustrations, the marriage remained the focal point of Toscanini's personal life and Carla was in any event essential to him in guarding his business affairs, about which he was consistently vague, and his physical well-being, especially at the time of his concert engagements.

Toscanini's perpetual dissatisfaction also expressed itself in his attempts to prevent his daughters' marriages, always to suitors unacceptable in his eyes.[10] Vladimir Horowitz was, for him, as unacceptable as the rest of them. Although Toscanini admired the young pianist's unprecedented virtuosity, he felt he was not right for his younger daughter Wanda; family friends suspected he disapproved of Horowitz's close male friendships as a potential threat to a marriage – a not inaccurate forecast.[11] Wanda, however, possessed much of her father's iron will and was, furthermore, in love with Horowitz. Toscanini was eventually persuaded that the marriage should go ahead, subject to the couple's undertaking a trial voyage to Britain in November 1933 to test their compatibility. Chaperoned by Toscanini's elder daughter Wally, they successfully accomplished the voyage and were married the following month in Milan. For the time being, for better or for worse, Horowitz became part of the Toscanini household and, when his own commitments allowed, was often a member of the entourage surrounding Toscanini during his concert engagements in Europe.[12]

So it was that on 29 May 1935 Toscanini arrived from Italy for his first BBC engagements accompanied not only by Carla but also by Wanda and Horowitz. Assisted by Owen Mase, the two couples took up adjoining suites at Claridge's,[13] a short drive from the Queen's Hall. Boult's account of his and the orchestra's first encounter with Toscanini emphasised the nervousness of all concerned: his own in greeting Toscanini at his hotel when collecting him for the first rehearsal; the orchestra's in, at last, facing what all the players regarded as the ultimate challenge; and, not least, Toscanini's habitual nervousness in his first encounter with a new orchestra.[14] Boult's words of welcome to him in front of the orchestra were cut short

[10] See further Ch. 12 p. 239 and Sachs 1978 pp. 169–70.

[11] See Plaskin pp. 160, 163 and 259–60. As to Toscanini's admiration for Horowitz's pianism, see ibid. p. 218.

[12] Members of Toscanini's entourage at the time included: his wife Carla De Martini Toscanini (1877–1951) who acted as his business manager until his son Walter (1898–1971) took over; Wanda (1907–98) who married Vladimir Horowitz on 21 December 1933; Wally (1900–91) who married (Count) Emanuele di Castelbarco; and Vladimir Horowitz (1904–89), Russian-American pianist, pre-eminent keyboard virtuoso of his era.

[13] ATL p. 188.

[14] Boult 1973 p. 101.

FIG. 6 WALLY DI CASTELBARCO, WANDA AND VLADIMIR HOROWITZ, LONDON, 1933

the moment he described the guest as the 'greatest' conductor; Toscanini smilingly
controverted him: no, just an honest musician. Up on the podium in his alpaca
rehearsal jacket, standing head down for some seconds as if in a trance (a posture
with which the orchestra was to become very familiar)[15] and they were off.

The opening concert on 3 June was to include Brahms's Fourth Symphony and,
once more, the *Enigma* Variations. The first rehearsal began with the Brahms
and went smoothly and rapidly forward with few interruptions. Indeed, as Boult recollected, Toscanini played through the two middle movements without comment,
stopping only for brief words and repetition of a few bars, before moving to the
passacaglia finale, the whole full of slight but subtle differences from the orchestra's
way when playing under his own baton. The Brahms was followed by the Elgar,
where from the start, as recounted by Bernard Shore, Toscanini emphasised the lower
strings which he wished to hear in equal balance with the melodic line – 'only
'armony' but still 'lovely music and it must be alive. For me it is too dead';[16] and with

---

[15]   Broadcast talk by Alex Nifosi.
[16]   Shore 1938 p. 166.

that, a few bars on violas and cellos were repeated until they were as sensitive and coloured as the theme. That day Toscanini signalled his satisfaction; but as was clear from his subsequent public comments, he was at that stage testing the players' mettle: the detailed work was to come later.

Those rehearsals made an indelible imprint on the players. Shore, principal viola, has been quoted and will be again; but others, too, waxed eloquent about the experience. Perhaps the most considered, but also most enthusiastic, tribute came from Archie Camden. Although in 1935 Camden was a relatively recent recruit to the BBC orchestra, this premier exponent of the bassoon, like all his colleagues, considered himself a victim of the then heartless BBC orchestral management approach and the antics of some indifferent conductors, but the opportunity to play for the great maestros was consolation for such travails. In his mid-eighties he confessed to the author that his favourite among them was Bruno Walter, whose warmth and humanity came as a particular balm;[17] but as recounted in his subsequent memoirs written towards the end of his long life, the first encounter with Toscanini made the deepest impression: the 1935 concerts were 'a tremendous experience', Toscanini's impact again 'tremendous', the 'fine face, with sharply-cut features, dominated by those brilliant dark eyes ... caught one's instant attention. The spare figure ... gave the impression of suppressed dynamic energy even when still.' He seemed 'almost of another world' and 'when he swept us into the music, I felt something which has remained with me always: he was the High Priest of Music' – here echoing Walter's own appraisal of Toscanini.[18] As Camden remarked, there was none of the expected temperamental outbursts in rehearsals; had there been any, 'I'm sure we should have felt it was our fault'. Rehearsals progressed without incident, albeit, in Shore's summing up, with 'the most intense concentration'.

First concert: 'the world's master conductor' – and the Enigma dissected

After the first, long-sold-out concert on June 3, the following day's critics were unanimous in declaring Toscanini to be pre-eminent in his art. Indeed, one of them, Francis Toye in the *Morning Post*, was tempted to write 'simply "beyond criticism" and leave it at that'.[19] More typical, if more lyrical in terms than his sober colleagues,

---

[17]   Interview with the author, 1972.

[18]   Camden pp. 136–7; as to Walter's description, see Boult 1983 p. 87.

[19]   Francis Toye (1883–1964) also wrote for the *Daily Telegraph* after it took over the *Morning Post* in 1937 and was a noted Rossini and Verdi scholar. He once described Toscanini as the greatest of all musicians (BBC tribute, January 1957).

was the *Manchester Guardian*'s Neville Cardus in the first of his many Toscanini concert notices, which were to bring forth strongly coloured and sometimes conflicted responses.[20] For the moment, Cardus virtually deserted his critical faculties: he pronounced this occasion 'a musical experience of the rarest and finest kind – not, indeed, merely a concert but a revelation of the wonder and nobility of music and genius'; 'the world's master conductor', he concluded, whose interpretation of the Brahms was the 'fullest conceivable', 'eloquent yet direct, beautiful in its balanced line and energy, but always human and many-sided' and ending with a passacaglia which recalled Nikisch in its 'explosive and generating energy'. For the *Times* (doubtless the habitually more sober Colles), the Brahms was 'so nobly proportioned that one … stands amazed by the inevitability of its shape', a performance that 'said exactly what Brahms meant it to say with extraordinary clarity and certainty'. In the *Telegraph* the usually restrained Capell, perpetually dissatisfied and gloomy according to his fond colleague Ernest Newman, thought it 'a noble and memorable concert' by 'a great musician'. The Brahms was 'broad and full-blooded' with 'nobility and ease' in the second movement's rhythm and a 'boisterous and happy tempo' in the scherzo.

About the *Enigma* Variations views were less united. In the ordinary course the rigorous doyen, Newman, spoke with scarcely veiled disdain of the 'sensitised plate', his term for the colourful and impressionistic writings of reviewers such as Cardus. But on the subject of the *Enigma* Variations, there was a happy congruence between this incompatible duo, for, in addition to the lyrical praise of Cardus, Newman in the *Sunday Times* on 9 June at last fully approved, reconciled now to Toscanini's way, with 'each variation a model of clarity and beauty'; his reservations voiced in 1930 were banished. By contrast the *Times* remained unreconciled: while conceding that Toscanini's was a beautiful performance in which his 'insight into Elgar's imaginative outlook was penetrating', its critic still maintained that his 'standard of complete faithfulness sometimes resulted in too literal a reading' of the composer's markings, which were perhaps over-expressive in their nuances as an insurance against the haphazard orchestral responses of the 1890s.

These observations stimulated a famous correspondence in the columns of the *Times* from Sir Landon Ronald and Adrian Boult, both distinguished Elgarians.[21] On 6 June Ronald began his letter by setting out the then current understanding of Elgar's music: it was so English in character and feeling that it could be only really

---

[20] Sir Neville Cardus (1889–1975) was the *Manchester Guardian* music critic 1927–39 and again from 1951.

[21] Sir Landon Ronald (1873–1938) conductor of the New Symphony Orchestra from 1909 (renamed Royal Albert Hall Orchestra 1915–38); musical adviser to G&T/HMV from 1900.

understood and interpreted by his own countrymen, a view he himself had always strenuously denied. Toscanini's 'magnificent' performance of the *Enigma* Variations with the BBC orchestra had 'proved me to be correct. This great conductor rendered the work exactly as Elgar intended and the composer's idiom obviously had no secret for Toscanini. Some of the best performances I have ever heard were from the composer himself, but this one on Monday night last excelled because Toscanini has a genius for conducting and Elgar had not.' On 8 June Boult wrote in full agreement, adding that an artist of Toscanini's calibre 'seems to have the power of grasping the essence of the style of any music he touches, and it has been a great experience for us all to hear him unfolding the beauties of everything he has rehearsed with us, always in what seems to be inevitably the right musical language'.

These ripostes drew forth an extended *Times* piece on 8 June which subjected both Toscanini's interpretation and Ronald's views to minute examination. Too long to quote, it must nonetheless be summarised since it encapsulated particular and ongoing views held at the time about the performance of Elgar by Toscanini and other foreign conductors, which lost their validity and critical currency only when his music was taken up more widely in the international sphere. The *Times* critic (almost certainly Colles) admitted the value of Ronald's endorsement since he was himself widely recognised as a peculiarly sympathetic interpreter of Elgar's orchestral music; but Colles noted that the composer's intention comprehended two aspects, the letter and the spirit. There were many differences between Toscanini's performance and that of other conductors including the composer and Ronald himself, Colles citing two variations in particular, the first (CAE) and *Nimrod*.

At the start of the first variation, continued Colles, the woodwind had three or four strands of melody, with the first flute and first clarinet playing the main theme in octaves piano (*p*); meanwhile the second flute and second clarinet had a subsidiary idea in two-part harmony pianissimo (*ppp*) and the two oboes and bassoons interjected a triplet figure mezzoforte (*mf*). (Novello's score actually shows first flute and clarinet as pianissimo, oboes and bassoons as forte, but this error does not invalidate Colles's argument on its own terms.) In Toscanini's performance these gradations were more exact than they had ever been before, a result which raised the question whether Elgar meant them to be so exact and, if so, why his performances and those of his contemporaries had never observed them in the same way. 'To Toscanini's clear-thinking Latin mind exactitude is the key to the composer's intentions but it may be argued of this instance that inexactitude, a getting to the point without precise analysis of its nature, was a characteristic of Elgar's mentality which we recognise as English.' By referring in his first review to Toscanini being too literal, Colles raised the possibility that the expressed intention in notation might obscure the spiritual intention.

Nimrod presented an opposite case. Most people thought of it as the supreme example of Elgar's *nobilmente* quality. The BBC SO's playing of it was magnificent, but 'what we think of and cannot define as Elgar's nobilmente manner seemed to have vanished. Everything else was there in that crescendo ... the legato, legatissimo, largamente, sonore, all made their contributions up to the climax four bars from the end.' But the score, surprisingly, neither here nor elsewhere contained the *nobilmente* direction, which interpreters had read into this variation from later works. As Toscanini played it, the result called to mind that originally the music was not regarded as elegiac. 'The unbiased mind of Toscanini, taking the score at its face value, has cleared away a gloss for which possibly the composer's later feeling was in part responsible', thereby reinstating a view of the music when the 'idiom and tone of voice were new'. Colles suggested that there might be more national characteristics in Elgar's music than Ronald recognised, which could either escape or be especially attractive to the foreign conductor. These observations continued at length: the *Times* clearly wanted its critic to have the last and definitive word.

But was Colles justified in his comments about either Toscanini's performance or in his comparisons with what he took to be the composer's views? Recordings of Toscanini's BBC SO performance and of the composer himself now enable us to test his thesis. If it would be hazardous to examine relatively minor matters of orchestral balance in the first variation on the basis of these admittedly faded documents, the critique of *Nimrod* poses no such problem. Elgar's 1926 Queen's Hall recording of it, part of his complete *Enigma*, outpaces Toscanini's by some twenty-five seconds, a substantial difference in only three minutes-worth of music.[22] How accurately does it reflect the 'live' Elgar? His early hesitation about the initially brisk metronome mark, finally settling in 1903 on the slower but nonetheless forward-moving $\quarternote$ = 52, suggests that mark was his ultimate and considered preference. Further, internal evidence from the original discs makes it unlikely that time restrictions in recorded side-lengths had any influence on the composer's tempo; moreover, the recording was made in the hall rather than in the more artificial circumstances of a recording studio and Elgar seemed well enough content with the results at the time.[23] The recording remains the best evidence of the composer's view

[22] Elgar's recording with the Royal Albert Hall Orchestra made on 28 April 1926 (with retakes, not including *Nimrod*, on 30 August 1926), issued on HMV D 1154–57, various CD transfers including EMI 0956942. Toscanini's performance issued on CDH 7697842 (see the Discography, Annex A).

[23] See Philip 2004 p. 143 and, for an illuminating discussion of Elgar's recording, ibid. pp. 142–6, although the suggestion that the tempo might have been affected by recording in a 'dry studio' (p. 144) seems to be unsupported. For Elgar's reaction to the recording, see Jerrold Northrop Moore *Elgar on Record* OUP/EMI 1974 p. 61.

of the music, which overall is a world away from latterday funereal practice. In detail Elgar is, as always, remarkably elastic in tempo, starting at ♩ = 40, moving to the marked ♩ = 52 at the first forte, then to 56 before expanding for the final largamente and closing ritenuto. Save for a slight relaxation where the woodwind take over the melodic line at bars 20–4, Elgar's performance of *Nimrod* is virtually a long, fluctuating accelerando, riding through the first largamente in tempo and with no audible *nobilmente* until the final bars.

Toscanini starts below ♩ = 38, moving at the first crescendo in bar 4 to 42 and then back again. He steps up to 42 again at bar 9, maintaining this pace until the woodwind take over, where (unlike Elgar, although at a pace still slower than his) he increases the tempo to 46 which he maintains flexibly until a couple of bars before the final largamente where, unusually for him, he anticipates that marking. Toscanini's climax at this point is of overwhelming grandeur, his final ritenuto more pronounced than the composer's. Altogether Toscanini is as elastic in detail as the composer and, incidentally, in bar 6 tolerates an upward portamento in the violins more pronounced than any in Elgar's performance. As for *nobilmente*, it is difficult to conceive anything more so than his final peroration, but elsewhere, as in the composer's performance, this characteristic is conspicuously absent.

The *Times* critic's views doubtless appeared to be a persuasive analysis at the time but, faced with hard evidence, they do not survive close scrutiny. Toscanini's approach certainly differed in detail from Elgar's but no more than it differed from the composer's British champions at the time, while the elasticity in phrasing and tempo of composer and great conductor proclaimed a kinship which, two years later, was to be recognised by another and much younger composer-conductor, a perhaps unlikely witness to genius.[24]

Three more concerts, several diversions

Toscanini's Elgar was not the only issue to divide critical opinion after the opening concert: there was also some minor disappointment over the orchestra's contribution. It played 'magnificently' according to the *Times*, while Cecil Gray, deputising for its regular contributor Constant Lambert in the *Sunday Referee*, thought Toscanini 'made the orchestra play as it has never played since its foundation, with a subtlety and refinement of tone of which one could hardly have believed them capable, fine players though they showed themselves to be earlier in the Festival under Kousse-

[24] See Ch. 6 p. 121 and n. 25 below.

vitzky'.[25] But in letters to his future wife, oboist Evelyn Rothwell, Barbirolli thought the intonation in the first concert was 'bad' (his emphasis), although much improved in the second. For Newman the orchestra 'did not always rise to quite the expected heights' and at the second concert on 5 June, when the Brahms symphony and *Siegfried's Death and Funeral Music* from *Götterdämmerung* were repeated with the addition of Wagner's *Faust Overture* and excerpts from *Parsifal*, the *Times* on 6 June thought that, particularly in the *Parsifal* Prelude, a certain amount of ragged chording was to be laid at Toscanini's door. More perceptively, Ferruccio Bonavia in that day's *Telegraph* pointed correctly to the conductor's refusal here to subdivide his beat in order to uphold continuity of phrasing: 'Toscanini kept strictly to the directions of the score without altering the pace, giving four beats to the bar where some conductors give eight.'[26]

As for the interpretations, however, there was no division of opinion about the apocalyptic splendour of these Wagner excerpts and Barbirolli thought both the Brahms and Wagner 'unforgettable. Such nobility of music-making becomes a great inspiration'. The *Times*, probably for this second concert Colles's deputy Frank Howes, gave the Brahms symphony its ultimate imprimatur and, in claiming the performance to be a definitive and exhaustive statement of the music, propounded a view which later evoked some comment.[27] But at the time, such extravagant praise seemed the appropriate response; it was certainly not out of line with the general reception given to these first two concerts and to the series as a whole.

This enthusiasm extended beyond the critical fraternity to the musically educated public, among whom the most noteworthy comments came from that budding genius among British composers, the 21-year-old Benjamin Britten. In his youthful diary Britten summarily judged virtually all other conductors (save his

---

[25] *Sunday Referee* 9 and 16 June 1935. Cecil Gray (1895–1951) composer, writer and reluctant critic – his disagreements with and low opinion of Cardus led in the early 1930s to his resignation as a critic of the *Manchester Guardian*. Constant Lambert (1905–1951), composer, conductor and author, wrote for the *Sunday Referee* from 1931 but was conducting for the Vic Wells ballet company at the time of Toscanini's 1935 concerts. The paper ceased publication in 1939.

[26] Barbirolli quotation, Michael Kennedy *Barbirolli* London: McGibbon and Kee 1971 p. 96 quoted in Sachs 1978 p. 236. Ferruccio Bonavia (1877–1950) Capell's deputy in the *Daily Telegraph*, played for a decade as violinist in the Hallé Orchestra under Richter and later drew on his memories of Richter in his reviews of Toscanini concerts; see Ch. 4 p. 88 and Ch. 6 p. 120. He wrote for the *Telegraph* from 1931. NBC SO violinist Samuel Antek confirmed some years later that in the *Parsifal* Prelude Toscanini 'would give only the broadest indication of tempo and no more. He insisted that the men themselves make the subdivisions in eighths'. When this worked with a fully attuned orchestra, 'the spaciousness and nobility of the musical utterances were tremendously evocative' (Antek p. 52).

[27] See Ch. 12 p. 247.

teacher Frank Bridge) musically deficient, but found Toscanini's armour impene-
trable: if Bruno Walter was annoying, Furtwängler given to exaggeration, Beecham
careless and superficial and Boult perennially dull (frequently 'execrable'),
Toscanini's conducting of *Siegfried's Death and Funeral Music* was 'overwhelming'.
Toscanini, he thought, had a flair for the right tempos and the orchestra played
better for him than ever before, although it was still not first class. This verdict was
the first of many entries about Toscanini; even if Britten did not always agree with
him, his greatness was incontestable.[28]

Could Toscanini's health have been a factor in the less than fully polished finish
of some items in the first two concerts? He suffered from insistent bursitis pains in
his right arm and shoulder during earlier seasons with the Philharmonic, which
had caused him to cancel the second half of his 1931/32 season. Of the various
measures then taken to effect a cure, the one he favoured entailed a course of 'serum'
injections by a doctor of wide but questionable repute in Piazze, near Siena.
Toscanini underwent a further short cure there immediately before his arrival in
London, but wholly without benefit. Consequently he was at times in acute pain,
writing after the first two concerts to Ada that, 'my ailing arm leaves me a complete
wreck'.[29] His initial rehearsals for the next two concerts were, he said, a terrible effort
and between rehearsals the painful arm and shoulder were smeared with 'antiphlo-
gistine dressing' with a swathe of overnight bandages.

At all events, Toscanini's travails were to some extent eased by his pleasure in
the 'excellent, intelligent orchestra'.[30] That assurance enabled him to relax in the little
spare time available to him in a visit lasting just sixteen days. First port of call, on
the face of it somewhat surprising, was opera at Glyndebourne where at the time of
Toscanini's arrival in London the second season, under the aegis of its founder John
Christie and his soprano wife Audrey Mildmay, was already in progress. The draw
was Toscanini's friend Fritz Busch, a conductor whom he admired for his musicianship and for his open resistance to Nazi policies, which placed him among the most
eminent of German non-Jewish musicians to choose exile rather than rest complicit

---

[28] For Britten's views, see the diary entry for 3 June 1935 in Britten p. 265. The diary shows
(p. 221) that Britten apparently first heard Toscanini in a 'glorious' concert on the radio from
Salzburg, 23 August 1934; the programme, not mentioned by Britten, was Mozart's *Haffner*
Symphony, the Brahms *Haydn* Variations and Beethoven's Seventh Symphony. Britten attended
or heard on the radio thirteen Toscanini/BBC SO concerts, as noted throughout his diary, and
heard several more relayed from Salzburg. For Britten's views on Walter see ibid. pp. 198 and 209;
on Furtwängler pp. 98, 138 and 197; on Beecham pp. 260, 336 and 354; on Boult *passim*.

[29] ATL p. 188 (letter to AM, 8 June 1935).

[30] Ibid.

in government policies in his homeland.[31] Despite occasional and mutual reservations about their interpretative approaches, relations between Toscanini and Fritz
were, if less intimate than with brother Adolf, sufficiently close for Toscanini to
recommend him the following year (after Furtwängler's refusal) as his successor at
the Philharmonic; unfortunately Fritz declined.

It was, however, Adolf who, before Toscanini's arrival in London, enthused him
with the Glyndebourne dream. In 1933 he, with his devoted acolyte Frances
Dakyns,[32] was instrumental in securing Fritz for Glyndebourne; he was soloist in
Glyndebourne's inaugural concert in early June 1934; he, with his family and Rudolf
Serkin, attended the opening opera performance, events which were followed
immediately by their cross-channel attendance at Toscanini's Paris concert on 10
June that year. The socialising between the Busch and Toscanini families on such
occasions doubtless gave Adolf the opportunity to raise Glyndebourne among his
hottest topics of conversation. In addition, Toscanini's particular warmth towards
Fritz on account of his refusal, like Toscanini, to conduct at the Nazi-dominated
Bayreuth Festival in 1933,[33] made Glyndebourne during Toscanini's 1935 visit an
obvious and early priority on his agenda. So, only two days after arriving in London
he broke off rehearsals for his first BBC concert to journey down to the tiny Sussex
theatre for Fritz's *Magic Flute*. As Audrey Mildmay recorded in her diary for 31 May:
'Major and Lady Violet Astor ... in [the Christies' twelve-seater] box, rest of our party
in the theatre because Toscanini and his wife and daughter and her husband
Horowitz arrived and sat in our box and dined. Toscanini crept in at high speed into
the back row of the box. Didn't speak, but at dinner he expanded, but did not say
one word to me about the performance. He has enormous charm.' The reason for
Toscanini's silence about what he had just heard became apparent after a later visit
in 1937, detailed in Chapter 4. He was expected at *Così fan tutte* on 7 June but did
not go; no doubt pain and other diversions prevented his return.[34]

These diversions were less welcome. Toscanini received his assistant from the
Philharmonic, Hans Lange, who bore news of a proposed reduction in the strength
of that orchestra from 110 players to 95, in order to meet economic demands made

---

[31] John Christie (1882–1962) founded Glyndebourne Opera in 1934. Audrey Mildmay (1900–53)
English soprano, married John Christie in 1931. For the role of Adolf Busch in securing Fritz as
conductor, see Potter pp. 551 and 553.

[32] (1878–1960); for further details about Dakyns, see Hughes 1965 pp. 43–6 and Potter pp. 138–9.

[33] Fritz Busch p. 217.

[34] GA, manuscript entry for 31 May 1935. Mildmay's entry for 7 June 1935 noted 'Toscanini was
again expected but did not come'; the *Illustrated London News*, 15 June 1935, incorrectly reported
the (cancelled) visit to *Così*.

by the musicians union in New York; Toscanini made clear that, if the reduction came about, he would resign.[35] Less painful but hardly welcome was the full-scale lunch held by the BBC governors for him at Claridge's. He was sufficiently sociable to inform the domineering Director-General of the BBC, Sir John Reith, that there was no better orchestra in Europe than the BBC's[36] – an implicit judgement on the others, including the Vienna Philharmonic – but later made it known that he did not enjoy this kind of large-scale formal reception. More to his taste, friends from his circle of familiars appeared at rehearsals for the two later concerts, among them author Stefan Zweig, composer Vincenzo Tommasini and the newly-married Rudolf Serkin with his young wife, Adolf Busch's daughter Irene, who were welcomed before their onward journey to join the rest of their family at Glyndebourne.[37]

The two concerts on 12 and 14 June both featured *La Mer* and Beethoven's Seventh Symphony, with on 12 June works by Geminiani and Rossini and on 14 June Mozart's *Haffner* Symphony and the Nocturne and Scherzo from Mendelssohn's *A Midsummer Night's Dream*. The Debussy (for Britten, 'astounding') and the Mendelssohn Scherzo were heard under Toscanini in 1930, but his Beethoven Seventh was new to London. If all the critics commented on the fast tempo of the Trio and its proper, if revolutionary, observance of Beethoven's *assai meno presto*, only Newman in the *Sunday Times* of 16 June was moved to open dissent: he could not reconcile himself to 'the touch of flippancy' at this pace, 'especially the curt flicking away of the last two of the first three notes'. Britten, too, was unconvinced.[38]

Cecil Gray, however, again deputising for Constant Lambert in the *Sunday Referee* on 16 June, was more typical of the great majority of critical responses: 'the dynamic intensity of the pulse and rhythm was maintained throughout as one had never heard it done before and culminated in unimaginable splendour in the bacchanale of the last movement ... One felt that this was the first time one had heard

[35]   Hans Lange (1884–1960) assistant/associate conductor NYPO 1923–36, associate Chicago Symphony Orchestra 1939–46.

[36]   Reith p. 223. John C. W. (Sir, later Lord) Reith (1889–1971) general manager, later managing director, of the British Broadcasting Company 1922–27, Director-General of the Corporation 1927–38, subsequently Chairman of Imperial Airways and from 1940 a member of Churchill's wartime administration.

[37]   ATL p. 188 (letter to AM, 8 June 1935), Adolf Busch vol. 2 p. 327 (letter Rudolf and Irene (Busch-)Serkin to Adolf, 14 June 1935), Potter p. 613. Toscanini did not meet Adolf Busch in the course of his BBC engagements since none of their respective London visits coincided (information courtesy Tully Potter).

[38]   For Britten's comments on the concerts of 12 June (heard on the radio) and 14 June, see Britten pp. 266 and 267.

it performed as its creator had conceived it.' Similarly, Capell in the *Telegraph* on 13 June thought the Seventh's 'tale had been fully and nobly told', while for the *Times* on that same morning it became 'a work of almost terrifying energy'. In his first review of a Toscanini concert in the *Telegraph* on 15 June, J. A. (Jack) Westrup spoke of 'the triumphant god-like vitality of the Beethoven' and summed up Toscanini's unique qualities – he avoided the word genius but perhaps only just: here was 'a vivid presentation of the work as the composer, one felt, must himself have seen it in the act of creation ... Toscanini not only enables us to hear individual lines in the texture which too often are denied existence outside the score; he makes us hear them all simultaneously. The wood and the trees are one.'[39] Both Gray and Westrup, it may be noted, thought Toscanini penetrated the composer's mind as if at the moment of creation; this response may now seem extravagant, but it was a repeated refrain of widespread critical observation right through to the last of Toscanini's BBC concerts four years later.

At the end of the final concert, 'of course the crowd went mad', observed Britten in his diary, and 'of course they were right, he is a great man'. As Westrup recorded in the *Telegraph*, the applause lasted nearly ten minutes and when the leader gave the sign for the orchestra's departure, 'a crowd hurried to the artists' exit and cheered Toscanini as he drove away. So ended the visit of an artist who has given London so rare an opportunity of understanding and appreciating all that music can mean – its riches and its strength.'

A press conference and some retrospectives

On 13 June, between the second pair of concerts, Toscanini demonstrated in unprecedented fashion his pleasure at the fine quality of the orchestra and its state of preparedness: he held a joint press conference with Adrian Boult.[40] In the course of it he publicly praised the orchestra: 'it is one of the best orchestras I have ever conducted'. In explaining his refusal until then to conduct a London orchestra, he observed that English orchestras had the reputation among foreign conductors of promising marvellous things at a first rehearsal because of their remarkable powers of sight-reading; at subsequent rehearsals, however, they proved incapable of the process of polishing. By contrast he had found the BBC players so efficient that he had cut short several of the rehearsals and had, in fact, abandoned one because the

---

[39]   J. A. Westrup (1904–75) later Sir Jack and Professor of Music at Oxford University.
[40]   See reports in the *Daily Telegraph*, *Morning Post* and *Manchester Guardian* 14 June 1935; the event went unreported in the *Times*.

orchestra had reached such a stage of perfection. Moreover he was delighted to discover that the orchestra not only possessed a 'first rate Konzertmeister' (Catterall) but combined with efficiency and discipline the rarer qualities of humility, devotion and willingness. In answer to further questions, 'no, I do not mind women in my orchestras. In Italy there are nearly always five or more women playing under me [he had not conducted an Italian orchestra in Italy since 1929]. I do not mind either if part of the audience likes to sit on the platform behind the players.' As for broadcasting, 'if my concerts are heard by millions of listeners, then I am glad. It does not worry me to think of the microphones.' The same benevolence did not, however, extend to the gramophone: he would not make any more records because 'after I hear my own records once, I hate them'.

Then, as in later eras, trivia obtruded during the course of questioning: 'You tell me that Mr Walt Disney is coming to my concert tonight? [*sic* – there was no concert that night] I am so happy. Mickey Mouse is one of my favourite conductors' – this, be it noted, several years before Stokowski shook hands with that conductor in *Fantasia*. Among many more genuine tributes, he was most touched by a letter written by a lady in hospital, thanking him for the pleasure and benefit to her health from one of the broadcasts; despite her anonymity, she had been searched out and a signed photograph sent at Toscanini's express wish. He was asked 'Will you come back' and answered, yes, if you wish, turning to Boult, who asked if he would conduct choral works such as Beethoven's Ninth Symphony and the Verdi *Requiem*; and again, yes, he would be happy to meet an English choir. Only once was there a hint of anything other than complete urbanity, when a daring questioner, almost certainly the *Daily Express* critic Spike Hughes, submitted for consideration an alternative to Toscanini's rendering of certain appoggiaturas in the Allegretto of Beethoven's Seventh: 'the hypnotic eyes flashed and a quick hand swept past the maestro's ear'.[41] Such questions notwithstanding, he had enjoyed his stay in London enormously: 'London audiences are very enthusiastic indeed – quite as enthusiastic as Italian audiences.' And so to the end – 'I am not happy being questioned like this ... Still, good day, gentlemen.'

Toscanini's departure the day after his last concert did not end the debate accompanying his music-making. By contrast with the enforced silence after his concerts

---

[41] Patrick Cairns (Spike) Hughes (1908–87) jazz musician, critic and author; see Hughes 1951 p. 325: 'I asked him [on a later occasion] why he played the grace notes in the slow movement of Beethoven's Seventh Symphony the way he did: some editions show them to be before the bar-line, and Toscanini plays them after it. Toscanini listened while I sang the phrase I meant. [He merely answered] "Lika that? The way you sing it? Terrible! Terrible!"'

with the Philharmonic in 1930, on this occasion that voice of the musical establish-ment, the *Musical Times*, was able to make itself heard at length. Just three years before, this journal had distinguished itself after a visit by the Berlin Philharmonic with the observation that all the works given by that orchestra could be heard 'many times in a season played by English orchestras very little, if at all inferior to the visitors, under conductors certainly far superior to Furtwängler'.[42] Great care was, therefore, now required to guard against the appearance of too much enthusiasm for this Italian visitor. It is to the journal's credit that William McNaught's observa-tions got so close to the heart of Toscanini's approach, even if, as with Newman in later years, his analysis fell short of revealing the secret: 'What Toscanini does is at all times a personal intensifying of the music, but he does it without using the frame-work as the chief vehicle for expression. The text is enlivened from within by a com-plicated process for which the recipe "play according to the composer" is but a clearing for action. No formula, however subtly applied, will give a cue for the number of new lights and new angles that continually put revealing aspects upon the familiar music, and which nevertheless came within the principle of presenting the facts.' In illustrating these observations, there was full but cautious approval for the performance of all three symphonies and an *Enigma* Variations which was 'most revealing of all'.[43]

Caution was not a characteristic of W. J. Turner's approach and his extended ret-rospective in the *New Statesman* on 22 June was typically forthright and penetrating. Toscanini was, he thought, at his greatest in the finales of the Brahms and Beethoven symphonies, which were conducted with a 'purity and splendour' he had never encountered before, qualities which made him unique among conductors. 'Steadi-ness, accuracy, sensitivity and rightness of proportion are combined with a vitality that is unique as it is also so little manifested by outward physical exertion.' The two performances of Beethoven's Seventh Symphony were incomparably the finest that Turner had ever heard and watching him conduct it revealed precisely wherein lay the conductor's essential difference from all others: 'I was suddenly reminded of Berlioz's remark: "Do you think I make music for my pleasure?" I am certain that it is not a pleasure for Toscanini to conduct, but rather that he suffers. It is because of his extreme musical sensibility and intense concentration. Here lies the essence of his superiority. He suffers because he concentrates more than others. His self-

[42] March 1932, quoted in Fifield 2005 p. 218.

[43] Vol. 76 July pp. 647–8. William McNaught (1883–1953) was editor of the *Musical Times* from 1944 until his death.

forgetfulness is perfect and his awareness of the music is complete.' Uncannily, this verdict – the suffering, not the superiority – was echoed two years later by Toscanini himself in a letter to Ada: 'Bruno Walter, Furtwängler, enjoy their work; you see them smiling, almost fainting, while they conduct. I, on the contrary – you can see me suffer.'[44]

Physical suffering, in the shape of a painful conducting arm, certainly attended Toscanini's London concerts; that and all other troubles were relieved by his subsequent vacation at his home on the Isolino San Giovanni, close by Stresa on Lake Maggiore, to which he retreated with his entire family.[45] The Isolino was to become a familiar location for both BBC and HMV executives over the next four years.

[44] ATL p. 279 (letter to AM, 27 August 1937).

[45] Sachs 1978 p. 238. Toscanini rented the Isolino San Giovanni on Lake Maggiore from the princely Borromeo family from 1932 onwards; its monastery had been converted into a private residence: ATL p. 136. Bernard Shaw visited it in July 1927 when it had been let to one of Toscanini's predecessors; see Michael Holroyd *Bernard Shaw: The One Volume Definitive Edition* London: Chatto and Windus 1997 p. 553.

CHAPTER 3

RECORDING THE 1935 CONCERTS

The barricade

Toscanini's accommodating attitude on the occasion of his press conference was not in evidence during the parallel efforts to secure commercial recordings of his London concerts. He was aware from the outset that broadcasting the concerts was part and parcel of his bargain with the BBC, but his opposition to making records was adamant and of long standing. Since the series of recordings with the Philharmonic in 1929 (further described in Chapter 12) which, like all his released recordings up to that date, he heartily disliked, he had issued a consistent stream of negatives in response to requests for more. The attempts in the early 1930s to induce a change of attitude on his part are an integral element of the story of HMV's struggles before and after his arrival in London.

In the course of this story the authentic voice of Toscanini himself is heard only once, and then in addressing indirectly HMV's current rival, the Columbia company, whose recording manager, Arthur Brooks, was in Bayreuth for the 1930 Festival when Toscanini conducted *Tannhäuser* and *Tristan*. Brooks successfully recorded extensive and impressive extracts from Bayreuth Festival productions of *Parsifal* in 1927 and *Tristan* in 1928.[1] But he had no such good fortune with Toscanini, with whom he communicated through the conductor's friend Blandine von Bülow, Wagner's stepdaughter and widow of the Italian Count Gravina, who as a long-time resident of Florence spoke fluent Italian. The request from Brooks for extracts from *Tannhäuser* met with the conductor's response to the Countess dated 31 July 1930: 'In my actual condition of nervousness, which is spasmodical,

---

[1] *Parsifal* extracts conducted by Karl Muck and Siegfried Wagner, Columbia L 2007–14; *Tristan und Isolde* abridged, conducted by Karl Elmendorff, Columbia L 2187–206. Arthur H. Brooks (1875–1950) joined the Columbia Graphophone Company in 1910.

I feel it an absolute impossibility that I should undertake work so heavy and, above all, so very distasteful to me as would be that of performing discs. My aversion is so very deep-rooted that last winter I had to break off every commercial treaty with the New York Gramophone Society. So I beg that you, my dear and kind friend, will do your best to convince the honourable Mr Brooks that he must not insist on his wish, for it would only upset me further.'[2] The awkwardness of this translation from Toscanini's Italian does not disguise the implacable nature of his refusal. Brooks had to be content to record *Tannhäuser* (on thirty-six 78rpm sides)[3] with Karl Elmendorff conducting, accompanied, so it was reported, by amused but dismissive comments from the Maestro whenever he happened on the proceedings.

Next came the request from HMV's German arm, Electrola, which after the Festival performances of *Tannhäuser* and *Tristan* asked Hayes for recordings by Toscanini of the Overture and Prelude to Act 3 of the former and the Prelude to Act 1 of the latter. HMV referred the request to RCA in New York; the latter's eventual response on 20 July 1931 disclosed that, two seasons before, Toscanini had informed RCA of his refusal to record any more – this was no doubt the 'break' referred to in his letter to the Countess – and had insisted that, if they wanted further recordings, these should be made at concert performances without his knowledge, even though 'the very fact that he knew we were recording made him extremely nervous'. Fully aware of this hazard, RCA nonetheless went ahead with an attempt, the first of two, to capture Toscanini's Beethoven Fifth Symphony in live performances drawn from his Philharmonic concerts on 4 and 5 March 1931. The endeavour was a failure. After a small group of interested persons including Toscanini's concertmaster, Scipione Guidi, listened to the results, the company decided not to submit the records to him because, as RCA put it, they were not considered 'up to the standard of the orchestra'. Technical shortcomings including poor side-breaks contributed to the ultimate decision not to press ahead.

At that time HMV in Britain was on course to amalgamate with the Columbia company to form the giant EMI. Shortly before that event Rex Palmer was appointed Manager of the International Artistes' Department of the HMV company and, after amalgamation, of EMI. In the spring of 1933 Palmer learned that RCA had again attempted to record Toscanini, on this occasion by means of live recordings of Beethoven's Fifth and *Pastoral* symphonies drawn from the Philharmonic concert

---

[2] A shorter version of Toscanini's letter, which does not identify Brooks as recipient, is in ATL p. 117; the version quoted is preserved in EMI and ATC. By the 'New York Gramophone Society', Toscanini presumably meant RCA Victor.

[3] Columbia LX 81–98.

on 19 April 1933. In response to Palmer's enquiries, on 23 May Charles O'Connell, of RCA's Record and Recording Division and later in charge of RCA Victor's Red Seal records, first described the recording process: recordings were made on both film and disc over a 'high fidelity transmission line' from Carnegie Hall – to 411 Fifth Avenue, where the film recording was made, and to 153 East 24th Street, where the disc recording was made. RCA planned to make commercial records by transferring the film recording to disc, but O'Connell went on to explain that, although RCA considered their sound 'eminently successful' technically, Toscanini was dissatisfied with his own performances of the two symphonies.

Three weeks later O'Connell's letter of 15 June to Palmer promised him pressings of the Fifth Symphony, by now transferred from the film recording, but at great length betrayed his frustration at Toscanini's attitude. He admitted that there were minor technical deficiencies in the results as a consequence of transferring the film to discs, but maintained that, 'they are not very serious and did not disturb Toscanini, who found no fault with the recording whatever, but criticized only his own performance'. The conductor persisted in his disapproval even though 'people whom Toscanini himself asked to listen to the records for him were most enthusiastic'. Those people, as listed by O'Connell, read like a roll-call of familiars in any Toscanini history of the time, including Jascha Heifetz, Samuel Chotzinoff (then a music critic, later employed by NBC), Toscanini's intimate friends Max Smith and Bruno Zirato (assistant manager of the Philharmonic and Toscanini's conduit to its senior management), Hans Lange, together with Carla and Wanda. They made no impact: 'we have exhausted every argument we could think of', wrote O'Connell, and 'we positively will not make any more attempts to record him ... if we cannot get approval of these records', for, 'now that he himself admits there is no fault with the recording, it is certainly unfair for him to deny us the privilege of presenting the records to the public'.

In his final letter to Palmer on the subject, dated 5 June 1934, O'Connell remarked that he had exhausted every means of getting the records approved and he would not personally approach Toscanini again on the subject. He also mentioned that the film recording of the *Pastoral* Symphony was less successful and had not been transferred to disc; the recording did not survive. O'Connell's failure to secure a Fifth Symphony for commercial issue undoubtedly contributed to his later perspective when he wrote his sour and vindictive portrait of the conductor in *The Other Side of the Record*, his memoirs published in 1947 which presaged the lucubrations of some more recent writers. But fortunately for posterity, both the 1931 and the 1933 recordings of the Fifth Symphony survived to astonish later generations.[4]

---

[4]   Various issues, including Naxos CD 8.110844 (1931) and 8.110840 (1933).

Breaching the barricade

Such was the formidable wall of disapproval which, somehow, HMV had to breach if, as they first mooted in November 1934, they were to record the BBC SO concerts for commercial issue. The company was certainly well equipped to make the attempt. Negotiations for recordings of such significance had to be channelled through the American-born Fred Gaisberg, who in his capacity as impresario and recording manager exercised an influence both legendary and pervasive within EMI. Although in theory Gaisberg was answerable to various interlocking management committees within the company, his experience, brilliant judgement and the accumulated prestige of his decades of service since moving to London in 1898 ensured that his recommendations for recording the many world-ranking musicians with whom he was always in contact were invariably accepted. The 1930s witnessed the final flowering of Gaisberg's talents, with some remarkable recordings made later in the decade in difficult circumstances.[5]

Had the immediate circumstances of the upcoming BBC concerts been more propitious, recording Toscanini might have been the crowning achievement of Gaisberg's career. Unfortunately, Gaisberg understood neither of EMI's hottest conductorial properties in the 1930s, Beecham – and Toscanini.[6] Indeed he had quarrelled with Toscanini at La Scala years before, a dispute the source of which is now obscure. From his own viewpoint Toscanini had ample reason to distrust HMV and Gaisberg ever since Carlo Sabajno – his *maestro sostituto* in Turin days, later the company's Italian house conductor and Gaisberg's close associate – recorded rehearsals of the Maestro's 1926 La Scala Beethoven cycle with hidden microphones, much to Toscanini's anger on their discovery.[7]

Given this somewhat fraught scenario, it was as well for EMI's long-term interests that Gaisberg was surrounded by able administrators and assistants, some of whom he had himself nurtured. David Bicknell, for example, had in 1927 become

---

[5]   E.g. Mahler's Ninth Symphony with the Vienna Philharmonic and Bruno Walter in concert on 16 January 1938, a few weeks before the Nazi takeover in Austria: HMV DB 3613–22, various CD transfers including EMI CDH 7630292.

[6]   Moore pp. 210–11, quoting David Bicknell.

[7]   The recordings were made at La Scala over several days in September/October 1926 in co-operation with Toscanini's son Walter, with microphones set up in the Royal Box and recording machines hidden in a small room overlooking the booking office. The number of sides made was later estimated by Walter as at least two or three dozen. Of these, only a few survive in ATC: one side each of the scherzos of the Second and Fourth symphonies, two sides of the first movement of the *Pastoral* and two of its finale. Details in EMI, letters from Walter Toscanini to La Voce del Padrone, Milan, 5 June 1956 and to Saitz, RCA, 2 July 1959. See further Dyment *CRQ* Summer 2011.

Gaisberg's assistant at the age of twenty-one and on the latter's retirement was to take on his responsibilities within HMV. Musical supervision of many EMI sessions at the time was entrusted to Lawrance Collingwood, one-time conducting pupil of Maximilian Steinberg and assistant to Albert Coates in Petrograd. His dual role as musical adviser at company sessions and conductor both at Sadler's Wells and of many HMV recordings ensured that musical problems at recording sessions were anticipated or effectively solved. These personnel were, to varying degrees, answerable to the general manager of the International Artistes' Department headed until 1940 by Rex Palmer, an ex-BBC announcer and presenter.[8] This small department was responsible for a wide range of company business, such as international recording programmes, recording budgets, artists' contracts, royalties and record release dates. The greater part of the burden of transacting EMI's business with Toscanini was to fall on Palmer, although initially others were through force of exceptional circumstances obliged to share that task.

Whatever may have been his personal reservations about Toscanini, Gaisberg was well aware of his potential value to the company and early in 1935 he notified him of HMV's wish to record the concerts. His communication quickly elicited a counter-attack mounted at the conductor's behest for which Gaisberg had to summon all his tact. The attack was fronted by the formidable Wanda Horowitz, in London from late January 1935 for her husband's tour of Britain.[9] She wrote from the Grosvenor Hotel in Park Lane on 28 January 1935 to warn Gaisberg that she had received a letter from her father, referring to previous correspondence with HMV, which asked her to convey to the company his decision to forbid any recording of the concerts or rehearsals; only immediate and direct transmission of the concerts by the BBC would be permitted. Wanda's demands were categoric and unequivocal: 'no sound reproduction of any kind (not even temporary on records or films or platinofhone wire[10] or through telephone or any other system)'.

---

[8] F. W. (Fred) Gaisberg (1873–1951) HMV/EMI recording manager and impresario. David Bicknell (1906–88) manager EMI International Artists Division 1957–69. Lawrance Collingwood (1887–1982) conductor, adviser and record producer for HMV/EMI 1927–72. Rex Palmer (1896–1972) general manager of the International Artistes' Department, HMV/EMI, 1930–40. See further Martland pp. 164 and 166. Throughout the narrative of the pre- and immediate post-war period I refer to HMV rather than EMI because, notwithstanding the 1931 merger, at that time and until the 1950s HMV and Columbia maintained separate and competing artistic and administrative structures; see Southall et al. pp. 29–30.

[9] Horowitz's British tour: Plaskin p. 178.

[10] Probably a reference to the Blattnerphone recording machine then in use by the BBC. This early recorder using a thin steel tape was created in the late 1920s by Louis Blattner in England and manufactured in Germany for his British company, the Blattnerphone (Stille System) Co Ltd. The BBC used one for recording programmes in the early 1930s. See further the article by Professor Seán Street cited in Ch. 7 n. 51.

FIGS. 7–10 HMV QUARTET: FRED GAISBERG (top left), REX PALMER (top right), LAWRANCE COLLINGWOOD (L., WITH PROKOFIEV) (bottom left), DAVID BICKNELL (bottom right)

And she wanted both the company and the BBC, to which she copied her letter, to acknowledge and confirm in writing their agreement to Toscanini's conditions.

On behalf of the BBC, their Music Executive Owen Mase hastened to offer unequivocal assurances in his letter of 1 February: 'we unreservedly agree to Toscanini's prohibition of any recording of any part of his work with the BBC Orchestra. We shall not make any such recording of any kind without his written permission.' It is clear, however, that his response was closely coordinated with Gaisberg's (described hereafter) for, like Gaisberg, he raised the issue of unauthorised recordings made outside the country over which the BBC would have no control. To guard against this possibility he asked whether the best and most complete precaution would not be for Toscanini 'to arrange with the Gramophone Company a proper agreement, including such remuneration for himself, for the making and publication of authorised recordings. This would render unprofitable and therefore prevent the production in other countries of unauthentic recordings ... and would ensure the Maestro's financial position with regard to genuine authorised records.' And, like Gaisberg, he enclosed an Italian translation of his letter for Toscanini's perusal.

In his reply to Wanda on 31 January Gaisberg was rather more equivocal about recording Toscanini's concerts: he was, after all, intent on securing them for the company if he could.[11] Although he gave assurances that it was not HMV's intention to record his performances without his consent, he pointed to the copyright position in Britain which prevented copying without consent, at the same time warning of the ease with which her father's broadcast performances could be pirated outside Britain. But, he continued, 'if Maestro Toscanini authorised us, as agents for his recorded music, we could offer some protection against pirating' and he went on to offer generous financial terms provided they obtained 'say 10 successful records, including the Beethoven Symphony No. 7'. And since it was intended to carry out the recordings during the performance, 'Maestro Toscanini will be put to no fatigue whatever'.

Gaisberg's emphasis on the risk of pirated performances was to have adverse consequences in future years. Moreover, his reply evidently did not satisfy Wanda who summoned him to discuss further her father's wishes. After that meeting, on 7 February he again wrote at great length to her (now ensconced at Claridge's), recording his 'intense satisfaction' at having received her explanation of her father's

---

[11]   EMI, Gaisberg to Wanda Horowitz, 31 January and 7 February 1935. Mase's letter to Wanda in ATC JPB 90-1 series L pt 1 folder L66C, which also includes Gaisberg's of 31 January, both with their Italian translations.

viewpoint, particularly his frustration over the failed attempt to record Beethoven's Fifth Symphony in 1933. After expenditure of a great deal of money in paying the Philharmonic musicians for these records, they were, said Gaisberg, 'candidly a hopeless failure. I heard them myself and nobody would blame Maestro Toscanini for rejecting them. Under no conditions could he have accepted these hopeless records.' (Fortunately it is unlikely that O'Connell saw Gaisberg's comments.) He could, he said, understand Toscanini's prejudice against making another attempt at recording, but went on intrepidly to list the advantages of his doing so. First, no money would be hazarded or risked, since the musicians would only be paid if the records turned out successfully. Secondly, the technical advantages would be unprecedented and unlikely to recur: the perfect landline between the hall and recording studios round the corner, the repetition of programmes permitting two attempts to record the same work, and the two sets of machines running simultaneously in 'our home laboratory'. Gaisberg was here referring to recordings made by the mobile van recording unit and the simultaneous transmission of the recordings to the Abbey Road studios, technical matters further explained below and in the Discography, Annex A. Thirdly, continued Gaisberg, the Maestro would be put to no inconvenience and he guaranteed that the attempt would be made only with his consent; furthermore, the financial advantages set out in his previous letter would remain. Finally, Gaisberg guaranteed that the resultant records would be submitted to Toscanini for approval or rejection and, if they were rejected, would be 'destroyed immediately in his presence'. With elaborate and prolix courtesy, Gaisberg concluded, 'my dear Madame, I feel happy in having your support in making it possible to hand down to posterity something of Maestro Toscanini's life-time achievement. It is a grave responsibility which cannot be lightly cast aside ... Such a great opportunity may never occur again.'

For all the charm, indeed overkill, ladled out by Gaisberg, which sufficed to win some covert support from Carla and Wanda, these negotiations would undoubtedly have failed had he not hosted a Savoy lunch on 5 June 1935, the day of the second concert. The course of events was recorded in his diary.[12] Present were Toscanini, Carla, Wanda and her husband, Gaisberg, Rex Palmer, Carlo Clausetti (manager of Casa Ricordi in London) and John Barbirolli. The young conductor was fascinated by Toscanini's reminiscences of touring as a cellist with Barbirolli's violinist father,[13] with whom he had sat in the pit at the first performance of *Otello* in 1887; and he in turn amused the Maestro with the very idea of a woman oboist, Evelyn Rothwell,

---

[12]   Moore pp. 211–12, quoting Gaisberg's diaries.
[13]   Sachs 1978 p. 236.

his fiancée currently playing at Glyndebourne (Fritz Busch had engaged her and Natalie Caine for Glyndebourne since he disliked the tone of the LSO's oboe section).[14] After this mutual display of amiability, the conversation turned to the recording of the BBC concerts. Toscanini referred to his consistent refusal to record, which he loathed, and to his $20,000 retainer with the Philharmonic, with whom he felt he could not break faith. Again Gaisberg requested permission to make a test recording so that Toscanini could at least compare the results with the 1933 Beethoven Fifth Symphony. Toscanini grudgingly gave his consent – and Gaisberg thereupon, to sweeten the pill, offered to record a concerto with Horowitz and Toscanini, which the latter immediately agreed to put in his already mooted 1936 London Festival programmes for the purpose.

In fact, without Toscanini's consent HMV had already recorded the first concert on 3 June and went on to cover the remaining three. Under Bicknell's technical supervision, the recordings were efficiently transmitted by landline from the hall to the Machine Room at HMV's Abbey Road studios in north London; this room was a back-up studio supplementing Studios 1, 2 and 3, used for recording material from external locations.[15] Years later Gaisberg expressed his doubts about the results: 'every time the timpanist made a thunderous attack on his drums the controller would have a heart attack ... in some soft violoncello passage, Toscanini's voice singing the melody would drown the solo instrument. Pianissimos inaudible above the surface of the disc or fortissimos that sent stabs across the next groove.'[16] But at the time, like others in HMV, he was far more optimistic, judging the recordings, despite some awkward side-ends, to be among the finest they had ever produced.[17] Only the recording of the Geminiani Concerto Grosso disclosed defects irremovable by contemporary technology, caused by failure of the recording machine to record the start of the work at the correct speed.

A fatal delay

HMV were bound by their informal agreement with Toscanini to seek his permission to issue the concert recordings but, for the moment, did no more than tinker with the sound quality of the discs. Those parts of the recordings with faulty side-endings and other defects, limited to one side in the *Enigma* Variations and another

---

[14] See Morrison p. 186, Potter pp. 553–4.
[15] Details in the Discography, Annex A.
[16] Gaisberg 'Toscanini' *Gramophone* June 1943 pp. 6–7; Moore p. 212.
[17] EMI, Palmer's letter to O'Connell, 31 December 1935.

in the *Parsifal* excerpts, were redubbed in July to produce better continuity and other improvements. Crucially – as it turned out – before he left London Toscanini expressed interest in hearing the recordings and asked for some to be delivered to his island home on Lake Maggiore where he had the latest gramophone equipment.[18] However, HMV apparently felt that Toscanini would not give his approval unless he were to hear the discs in the optimum conditions; and such conditions, they thought, would only be present when he returned for his planned BBC SO concerts in 1936. They therefore did nothing.

The delay undermined HMV's chances. Not until 31 December 1935 did Palmer write to O'Connell with a list of the HMV concert recordings, pointing to Toscanini's refusal to permit any of them to be released until he had taken the matter up with the New York Philharmonic Society, to which he felt morally, if not actually bound. Palmer requested O'Connell's good offices in reminding Toscanini of the position. 'Once the position is clear, we do not anticipate any great difficulty in getting Toscanini's approval of the records … when he visits London in May.' Gaisberg supplemented this letter with his own two weeks later to Toscanini himself (not preserved), referring to the recordings.

In his reply of 29 January addressed to Gaisberg, O'Connell disclosed that Toscanini was not happy over the fact that the records had been made and would not consent even to listen to them. 'I have exhausted every resource, and so have Mr Judson [who headed the Philharmonic's management] and Mr Zirato, with the idea of interesting Mr Toscanini to the point where he will at least consider these records, but I have been completely unsuccessful.' O'Connell cited as reasons Toscanini's intense dislike for recording and for anything mechanical applied to music, his reluctance to record with any orchestra other than the Philharmonic as well as his sense of obligation to it. But, with barely disguised *Schadenfreude*, O'Connell was glad to inform Gaisberg that he had completed arrangements for recording Toscanini with the Philharmonic on 8 February – a move that further diminished HMV's chances.

Enter Newman

HMV were not openly downcast by the news of Toscanini's attitude or his forthcoming Philharmonic recordings because, as Palmer informed O'Connell on 6 February, they had learned that Toscanini had specifically asked Ernest Newman

[18]   EMI, Bicknell's note to Palmer, 19 June 1935.

to hear the Queen's Hall records and let him have his opinion of them. 'We are in close touch with Mr Newman and hope that his report, which we believe will be highly favourable, may induce Toscanini at least to give the records a hearing when he again comes to England this spring.' Palmer hoped that, since the new recordings with the Philharmonic would then be an accomplished fact, Toscanini would thereby be encouraged to hear the BBC orchestra recordings and permit their release.

Newman's role as *deus ex machina* needs some explaining. His name was in itself enough to open all doors for his wife Vera to attend the BBC orchestra's rehearsals in June 1935, since Toscanini's omnivorous reading included all of Newman's books, in particular his *Wagner as Man and Artist*, which he greatly admired. Horowitz introduced Vera to the Maestro who wanted to meet her husband; but Newman determinedly kept his distance, as he did with most artists he reviewed. It was the critic's fondness for gambling and winter sunshine that undermined his resolution. Monaco was a yearly draw for him and there, on 1 January 1936, it happened that Toscanini was to conduct a programme of Beethoven, Debussy, Wagner and Verdi with the Monte Carlo orchestra. Strolling in the gardens towards the Casino on 29 December, the Newmans met the Maestro, who spotted them before Newman saw him; he could not avoid the encounter. Back at Toscanini's hotel the two men conversed for an hour, after which Newman remarked: 'What a brain! What a fascinating man! I wish I had known him years ago. *There* is someone I can listen to and talk to with pleasure.'[19]

Returning to his Surrey home Newman duly listened to the BBC orchestra test discs and his verdict was on the whole favourable. He singled out *La Mer* and the Brahms Fourth Symphony as being particularly good and the discs containing these works, which remained in his collection, were much played by him into old age.[20] Taped copies of his pressings of the symphony, 'blasting' at climactic moments, were the basis for its first and unofficial release in the USA on Toscanini Society long-players in the late 1960s. Newman must have been well aware of the obvious defects, among them the conductor's prominent vocalising superimposed on the music and the distortion unavoidable on contemporary equipment, but his verdict was duly conveyed to Toscanini, including in particular his commendation of *La Mer*.

---

[19] Vera Newman pp. 146–7 and 150.

[20] Vera's letter to Walter Toscanini, 31 December 1958, ATC JPB 90-1 Appendix series L pt 1 folder L205C.

Losing him ...

By then, however, time was running out for Toscanini to audition any of the recordings in London as HMV had hoped; bungling bureaucracy elsewhere soon ensured
the extinction of any such possibility. After the 1935 London Music Festival
Toscanini said he wished to return for the next Festival in May 1936 and negotiations went ahead during the winter of 1935–36 for him to conduct a series of
concerts in the spring of 1936.[21] According to Boult's autobiography, the series was
originally to consist of eight concerts with a total fee agreed by the conductor, but
later the number of concerts was reduced to seven. Another account suggests the
perhaps more likely number of six concerts with a repetition of one of them; for
such repetitions the BBC customarily paid a lower fee. Whether the total was eight
minus one or six plus a repetition, BBC accountants duly revised the fee down-
wards – but that, as Boult remarked, was not how Toscanini's mind worked or
could have been expected to work. Correspondence abruptly ceased and by the
time the reason for this became evident it was too late to resume negotiations. On
5 February 1936 a curt telegram from Bruno Zirato to Boult announced the conductor's decision not to come at all because he was very annoyed about the 'too
many misunderstandings' concerning the 1936 concerts: 'sorry, regards'.

Desultory negotiations continued despite the seeming finality of Zirato's
telegram, enthusiastic on the part of Boult but with polite and non-committal
responses from Zirato and (through him) Toscanini. Boult's letter of 19 February
to Zirato enclosed his handwritten letter of that date to Toscanini, sent, as he
remarked to Zirato, in the hope that the Maestro would reconsider his decision.
To Toscanini Boult stressed 'keen and sincere regrets' about the misunderstandings
and also the longing of the public, the broadcast audience and the orchestra for
fulfilment of the 'provisional promise' to repeat the 'wonderful experience' of the
June 1935 concerts. He still hoped that Toscanini would consider coming to
conduct for the BBC again immediately on his return to Europe, to celebrate the
fiftieth anniversary of his conducting career. This letter, Zirato assured Boult in
his reply of 2 March, was read by Toscanini 'with immense interest' but he pleaded
his heavy load of engagements in deciding to leave matters in abeyance. Further
correspondence went little beyond exchanges of courtesies, although Zirato did
disclose in a letter of 30 March that Felix Greene, the BBC's first North America
correspondent, spoke personally to Toscanini on behalf of Boult. The exchanges

---

[21] See Boult 1973 pp. 103–4, Kenyon p. 127.

terminated with an acknowledgement dated 21 April of Zirato's considerable help from Boult's assistant, Owen Mase.[22]

By the date of this last letter, however, the 1936 London Music Festival had already been cancelled, since Koussevitzky, considering himself overshadowed by the attention given to Toscanini in 1935, declined to step in. Rumours in the London press alleging that Toscanini stayed away for political reasons were rebutted by Zirato, who stressed his fatigue; and indeed Toscanini himself said that the London concerts would have allowed him insufficient time to rest before his Salzburg engagements in July/August.[23]

If cancellation of the Festival extinguished HMV's chances of direct communication with Toscanini, they still thought Newman's recommendations would carry some weight with him and continued to hope that he might hear the records when he returned from America to Europe.[24] They also turned for assistance to those close to him. Rudolf Serkin, recently soloist with the Philharmonic under Toscanini, asked to hear some of the discs on his London visit in March 1936 and Gaisberg played him the recordings of the Brahms Fourth Symphony, *La Mer* and parts of the Beethoven Seventh Symphony.[25] Shortly afterwards Gaisberg also played them to Wanda and Horowitz. These listeners were all duly impressed and Toscanini himself had as yet made no final decision. After his last Philharmonic concert on 29 April 1936, he boarded ship on 2 May, heading for Paris for an extended stay. Wanda and Horowitz joined him there after the latter's concert in Trieste on 2 May, his last appearance before his first retirement from the concert platform.[26] Gaisberg lost no time in pleading his cause further in the most fervent, in retrospect almost desperate, terms: in a letter dated 4 May to Toscanini in Paris (*chez* Horowitz) he recounted the auditions by Serkin, Wanda and Horowitz, remarking, 'I do not know if you realise what magnificent results were obtained ... especially of the Brahms Fourth. If you could hear this, I think you would be very much impressed. We were all unanimous in saying that we have never heard anything like it and that it is a

[22]   Zirato's telegram in ATC JPB 90-1 series L pt 1 folder L69A. For more about Zirato, see ATL p. 120. The further correspondence here summarised, courtesy Harvey Sachs and the Toscanini family. Felix Greene was a cousin of Graham Greene; see further Ch. 7 n. 3.

[23]   ATL p. 198 (letter to AM, 11 April 1936).

[24]   EMI, Palmer to O'Connell, 6 March 1936.

[25]   This audition most probably occurred around the time of Serkin's Wigmore Hall recital on 11 March 1936, shortly after his second concert appearance in the USA (three concerts with Toscanini and the Philharmonic during February); see Potter p. 627.

[26]   See Plaskin p. 182.

major achievement.'[27] In a final plea, 'I wish you could make it convenient to let me play these for you in Paris. I think you would then agree that they ought to be made available for the public.'

Such unsubtle pleading was unlikely to be persuasive and, indeed, served only to stoke the conductor's mistrust for the future. Toscanini did, however, trust Newman's judgement and, in response to Gaisberg, indicated through Wanda his desire to hear the recording of *La Mer*. HMV duly sent the discs but, somewhat oddly, their courier (it seems at Wanda's prompting) was Sybil, Marchioness of Cholmondeley, one of a number of eminent London society hostesses in love with the evidently magnetic 69-year-old conductor, whose attendance on the object of her devotion was as constant as his travels permitted; she figures with some frequency hereafter. Gaisberg's letter to Wanda of 19 May recording despatch of the precious discs to the Marchioness remarked that he 'quite expected that of all the records made you would only ask for *La Mer*, notwithstanding a magnificent Brahms No. 4. Mr Ernest Newman told me after he heard the records that he thought *La Mer* stood out as being particularly good.'[28] He concluded once more with a plea for the Maestro's permission to issue it on 'liberal terms'. Again, however, Gaisberg prayed in vain: despite Newman's commendation, nothing more was heard. Fortunately Gaisberg did not carry out his earlier promise to destroy the (presumptively) rejected recordings. Toscanini had not heard most of them and HMV could therefore rightly maintain that they knew nothing of his views whether of approval or otherwise; consequently the masters were left undisturbed in storage until given fresh life on expiry of Britain's fifty-year copyright period in 1985.[29]

---

[27]   ATC JPB 90-1 series L pt 1 folder L69F.

[28]   EMI, Gaisberg to Wanda Horowitz in Paris, 19 May 1936, thanking her for her letter of 17 May 1936 (not preserved). See Ch. 4 n. 57 and ATL pp. 258, 267 and 273 for further details of the London society hostesses.

[29]   See issue details on LP and CD in the Discography, Annex A.

CHAPTER 4

1936-37: THE LONDON MUSIC FESTIVAL 1937

... getting him back again

Without massive persuasion it was unlikely that Toscanini would return to the BBC Symphony Orchestra. Who best could apply the requisite pressure? Boult himself could not be expected to chase the Maestro across Europe; indeed, he could not have maintained his remarkable dual role as Director of Music and Chief Conductor at all without substantial delegation and highly competent assistants. Crucial in the direction and organisation of programmes were Edward Clark, an inspirational and innovative musician with extensive European contacts, and Julian Herbage, whose organisational talent dealt with detailed scheduling and practical aspects of broad-casting requirements. Clark's departure from the BBC in March 1936 left a void almost impossible to fill but it is not surprising that the BBC dispensed with his services. Hardly a conventional organisation man, many of his activities raised hackles among his colleagues and others whom he managed to offend. All too typical of Clark's way of operating was the tale of his mission to establish contact with Toscanini in Monte Carlo in January 1936 in the course of one of his European trips, in order to discuss the conductor's programmes for the 1936 Festival. He became so distracted by musical matters more to his immediate interest that he lost sight of this important mission altogether,[1] with a consequent further diminution in Toscanini's esteem for the BBC.

After Clark's departure there was only one person who stood any real chance of recapturing Toscanini. Owen Mase has already been noted in this narrative

---

[1] Kenyon pp. 118–19. Edward Clark (1888–1962) BBC programme planner *extraordinaire* 1927–36, later married composer Elisabeth Lutyens. Julian Herbage (1905–76) BBC programme planner 1927–46, later BBC contributor and presenter.

recruiting members of the BBC orchestra during 1929–30 and assisting Boult in securing Toscanini for London in 1935. In the 1920s he attained some distinction as an accompanist and composer but put these talents to one side soon after he joined the BBC Music Department in 1927. In 1930 he was appointed Music Executive, having direct contact with artists and rehearsal arrangements. He became Assistant Music Director in May 1931 but reverted to his old title in 1933, a change that, if it resulted in minor loss of a more prestigious title, also relieved him of some routine business.[2] In his capacity as Music Executive he had immediate charge of Toscanini on his arrival at Claridge's in May 1935 and established a personal connection with the conductor and his family. Because of this already well-developed link, he was deputed by Boult in the spring of 1936 to bring Toscanini back to the BBC fold.

That objective was achieved – but only after three journeys: to Paris and Italy in June, to Salzburg in August and finally back to Italy in September/October to get Toscanini's signature on a contract. Were such elaborate efforts really necessary? Boult at least thought so: Mase, in his view, expressed repeatedly then and later, had succeeded where no-one else could; and without the persistence, guile, tact and persuasive powers displayed by Mase in the whole enterprise, in retrospect few could doubt that London would never have seen Toscanini again and HMV would have had little to hand down to posterity. Mase's own writings show how he set about this task. In January 1937 he wrote up his experiences in a memorandum entitled 'Getting Toscanini' with a covering minute to Boult containing some more general comments on his adventures.[3] Boult remarked to Reith that the memorandum was amusing and deserved circulation, but it was too long for submission to the BBC governors as Mase intended. Reith, however, was so impressed that he not only singled out Mase for his achievement – 'we are very grateful to him and congratulate him on this service' – but ensured that the memorandum was indeed circulated to everyone concerned. Doubtless lost in the rounds, it did not survive

---

[2]   For published details about Owen Mase (1892–1973) see Lewis pp. 69–74, Kenyon p. 65. When Mase reverted to the title of Music Executive in 1933, Boult wrote regretting the change but hoped it would be more satisfactory to him in the loss of routine work: letter 6 June 1933 in MA.

[3]   With covering minute of 25 January 1937, both in MA. Reith congratulations: BBCA, manuscript endorsement of Boult minute, 26 January 1937. Although Mase did not mention other consultations, Gaisberg claimed credit for enabling Toscanini's visits to the BBC orchestra, in his memoirs for the 1935 visit, in his article 'Toscanini' (*Gramophone* June 1943 pp. 6–7), for the 1937 visit. For reasons already given (see Ch. 2 n. 6) it is unlikely that he assisted in the initial negotiations for the 1935 visit, but his mention in the *Gramophone* of assisting Owen Mase in securing Toscanini's return for the 1937 visit makes it possible that Mase consulted Gaisberg before departing in pursuit of Toscanini in June 1936: they were clearly co-operating in 1935 – see Ch. 3 p. 61.

in the BBC's archives; but Mase, well aware of its historic significance and proud of his achievement, kept a copy in his personal papers, probably unexamined again for some decades to come.

As Mase said in his covering minute, his endeavours were preceded by 'exhaustive steps', including contacts with the BBC's representative in New York, Felix Greene, and Toscanini's agents there,[4] his continental agents, letters, telegrams and transatlantic telephone conversations by Boult himself; some of the exchanges with Toscanini's friend Bruno Zirato are outlined in the preceding chapter. Mase might have mentioned, but tactfully omitted, the vain efforts of a BBC representative sent down to Plymouth in May where Toscanini's ship docked when he was en route to Paris. In any event, as Mase put it, all attempts 'were completely abortive and the matter was given up'. But 'higher authority', presumably Reith himself, wanted to know if anything further could be done and Mase, 'having personally secured Toscanini in 1935' (a pardonable exaggeration), was willing to try again if he were given a free hand with programmes and, within agreed financial limits, administration. 'I was given the authority and carried on', concluded Mase's covering minute; and, although his memorandum gave only the bare bones of his many conversations, these were indeed prolonged, for it was 'necessary to walk warily and generally go "to Paradise by way of Kensal Green".[5] Nevertheless, insisted Mase, his memorandum was 'exactly true'. The following transcript of it is virtually complete and as Mase wrote it:

> Through old personal contacts in the impresario and concert world I learned that Toscanini had said he would not broadcast again. He had been very badly treated in Paris where, at one of his concerts, microphones were hidden in the ferns and records made and sold (even in Italy) without his knowledge or consent (which he would never have given), and of course without any fees. The natural result was that he determined 'no more microphones anywhere, ever'. To a man of his temperament broadcasting is broadcasting, no matter under whose auspices, and he damned the lot. There were political fears too because of Sanctions [presumably against Mussolini over Abyssinia] and I sensed later that there was some friction left over from a previous contact between

---

[4]   Carla Toscanini was in sole charge of Toscanini's business affairs at the time but Mase was presumably referring to others who had her ear and perhaps also to Zirato; see also n. 6 below.

[5]   'For there is good news yet to hear and fine things to be seen,/Before we go to Paradise by way of Kensal Green': quotation from G. K. Chesterton's *The Rolling English Road*.

Toscanini and [Edward] Clark. I don't know exactly what and it was not wise to probe it, but by the way his name was brought in on one occasion I suspect personal incompatibility of some kind.

Early last summer Toscanini was back in Paris and I got in touch with Horwitz, whom I know and who looks after Toscanini on the continent, and arranged with him that I would run over to Paris at once and try with his friendly help to have a word with the great man at the least stormy moment that could be found. Just before I left [in early June], Horwitz 'phoned me that it was no use, as Toscanini had refused to conduct his last concert in Paris and gone off in a rage to his home in Italy.[6]

This was rather damping. But I went to Paris all the same and saw Horwitz in order to sense the general atmosphere for myself. It certainly was stormy. Toscanini was not prepared to see anyone at all. But having told Horwitz to say nothing to anybody I determined to go on to Italy and try to renew acquaintance with Madam Toscanini, to whom I had been able to show some little courtesies when she was in London in 1935 ... .

It was useless trying to make an appointment ahead, since correspondence had proved entirely unproductive even of a refusal except on one occasion [presumably a reference to Zirato's telegram, page 66]. I was also unable to get exact information as to which island in Lake Maggiore was Toscanini's home – his agents deal always with his Milan address. I went therefore into the blue to Stresa on the shores of the lake. The first day there was spent in getting the actual island located. I made friends with the woman who runs Cook's agency in Stresa and she told me it was the little island of San Giovanni. I tried to get the telephone number but it was not in the directory and she did not know it, neither did anyone else in Stresa or else, which I suspect, those who do (possible tradesmen etc.) are under promise to keep it secret. Eventually, while we drank cocktails, the Cook's lady remembered a girl friend in the main telephone exchange and spoke on the 'phone to her and persuaded her to give the

---

[6]   F. Horwitz was a Paris agent, also Emanuel Feuermann's agent at this time (Morreau p. 182), probably one of those of whom Toscanini later became suspicious; see Ch. 5 p. 107. If any unofficial recordings were made at Toscanini's Paris concerts, they seem not to have survived. Toscanini was due to conduct only one concert in Paris at this time, on 22 May 1936, to raise money for a monument to Saint-Saëns, and this took place; there is no mention elsewhere of a cancelled concert. It is more likely that his early departure from Paris was occasioned by his agitation over (unspecified) events at Salzburg; see Sachs 1978 pp. 245–6. The omission from the memorandum referred to Mase's Paris consultations with Darius Milhaud, whom he persuaded to be satisfied with a BBC studio performance of *Christophe Colomb* in place of a Queen's Hall public production previously agreed with him.

FIG. 11 THE ISOLINO SAN GIOVANNI, LAKE MAGGIORE

number. It was against regulations but we got it. She then rang the number and got reply from the Italian head-servant that 'the Maestro is not here, Madam is not here, no-one is here, and no-one knows when they are going to be here'. I took the phone and tried to get better results with no effect. While 'phoning I heard an American voice saying something to the servant at the other end.

I went for a walk along the shore of the lake for an hour before dinner to sort out the situation and could not see much of a loophole, since the island is a very small one, (only big enough for house and garden) and landing is strictly forbidden.

During the walk I got into conversation with some boatmen and found that one of them had been Toscanini's private boatman a year before. I at once engaged him and his motor boat for next day and he agreed, for a consideration, to take me over the next morning at 10, land me on the island, and cruise in sight until I was ready to come off.

I landed and by way of the gardener got the head-servant to come and talk. We spoke French and he only repeated what he had said on the 'phone, like a parrot. Eventually I steered the conversation on to Italy, England, politics etc., and, on the plea of finding it difficult to understand all he said, I asked him if the American lady, whose voice I had heard the night before, would be willing to come and help. He went to ask and she came out, a very charming American girl of about 22, who, with her mother, was staying with the Toscaninis.[7] I was careful to thank the head-servant in material form (since I might want him again at some time) and then spent over an hour in conversation with Miss Whitman (the American). I learned from her that Toscanini was there but would see no-one; that Madam was not there but was expected back from Milan in a day or two, possibly the next evening. Miss Whitman promised to do her best to get Madam to see me and asked me to ring her up next evening and she would let me know progress.

Next afternoon at about 5 I was sitting at an outside table at a café in Stresa when Toscanini himself with Miss Whitman and her mother came and sat a few tables away. I resisted a strong temptation to go over and speak to him, as I realised he was on holiday and had given definite orders he was not available to anyone, and contented myself with bowing from a distance. Presently Toscanini went off to a paper shop and Miss Whitman came over to me, took me to meet her mother, and told me they had heard Madam Toscanini was returning that evening. They asked me to go over to the island next morning. Mrs. Whitman told me Toscanini had recognised me and had said it was very nice of me not to have gone over to break in on them at their table. So I had done the right thing (or refrained from doing the wrong).

Next morning I went over at 10 and Miss Whitman met me and said that she was very sorry that Madam Toscanini had not arrived but had 'phoned to say she could not get back till that evening. There was nothing to do but wait at Stresa till next morning.

Next morning I went over again to the island and Miss Whitman brought Madam Toscanini to see me. Madam was frigidly polite; said she was pleased to renew acquaintance but that my visit was hopeless as far as the main object was concerned because the Maestro was adamant. However, I said at least my journey was rewarded by seeing her again and her lovely home. After much conversation we got to arguing about

---

[7]   Mrs Lucilla de Vescovi Whitman (with her daughter), a close family friend, was an Italian who married an American (ATL p. 136). 'Mr. Goldsmith', also mentioned by Mase, is unidentified.

what I told her was the Maestro's complete mistake in classing the BBC, a fine independent organisation enjoying a monopoly, with commercial broadcasting organisations in other countries. We could arrange that all should be governed by his artistic wishes, no unauthorised recordings etc. etc. Eventually she said I must leave it with her and she would take some suitable opportunity of opening the matter again with the Maestro and would try to let me know by letter if she had any success at all, but she could hold out no hope. I caught the night train back to England.

By the end of July I had heard nothing so, knowing Toscanini was in Salzburg to conduct at the Festival, I went there in August. Here again no-one seemed to know where he was staying – it was not in Salzburg and his address was only known to the Festival authorities. I thought it out and went to the Festival Office and talked to the woman in charge on the subject of help to find less noisy accommodation than I had secured and said 'surely Toscanini does not stay in this terrible noise'. She said 'Oh no, he stays at ...' (naming a village some way out).[8] I asked no more as I did not want to get a refusal, or to get the girl into trouble for having said as much as she did.

I got a car next day and went out to the village and a villager pointed out a large villa with grounds where 'a conductor from the festival' was staying. I called and found the same head-servant from Italy. He was very friendly now and said Madam was out but would be there at lunch and would I come back. I left a little note for her and called again at 2.30 and was shown into a room with closed double doors separating it from the dining room. The maid said Madam wanted me to wait and in a quarter of an hour she came in. Her first remarks were – 'How did you find us again? You do get about!' She said she was really sorry but she had been unable to move the Maestro at all. (Sounds of revelry came from the dining room and evidently a big family luncheon party was still un-finished.) I expressed my sorrow and the great regret all over England the news that he would not come would cause, especially in such a celebration year as our Coronation. I'm not sure I did not imply that our whole coronation would be spoiled. I said also that I had personally looked forward to her own coming as well, because we wanted her to be our guest on this occasion.

Count Castelbarco (son-in-law) came into the room then. He bemoaned that he wanted to give an exhibition of his pictures (he is a painter) in London at Coronation time and all his society friends had

---

[8] Mase omitted the name; Toscanini rented a villa at Liefering in 1935–36 (ATL p. 211).

failed to get him a gallery because there was no gallery disengaged. I promised to do what I could and am glad to say that with Mr Goldsmith's invaluable help, a gallery has been found and the exhibition arranged.

Toscanini's daughters (Madam Horowitz and Countess Castelbarco) then joined us from the dining room. I had met the former before and we talked of many things art, music, etc. Presently Madam Toscanini said 'He seems happy now. I will go and tell him you are here again.' She was gone a long while and when she came back said 'I believe he will come' – I said 'Do you mean come to see me?' – she said 'No – come to make your concerts.' Then the Maestro 'appeared' (there is no other word for it) and shook hands with me and said 'I will come' and went straight back into the dining room. I discussed dates with Madam and she took my suggestions through to him and brought them back agreed.

While we had coffee Madam asked me how long I was to be in Salzburg and I told her that as no tickets had been obtainable for weeks for the Maestro's performances I was going home next day. She went through to the Maestro again and came back with a message that he wanted me to stay to hear his Meistersinger next evening and that she would arrange for an extra seat in their family party and I was to join them. This was a great honour and pleasure, not detracted from by the looks of hatred I received from three impresarios (an English, American and Continental, all of whom I know) when they saw me there in that company.[9] They had all three been in Salzburg for a long time, mainly to get hold of Toscanini, and he had received none of them.

It was impossible to tackle the question of programmes then in the middle of heavy rehearsals so I promised to go to Italy in early October and discuss them.

I felt strongly that, in view of the present and of the possible future, the social side of my contact with the Maestro and family should be strengthened. So in October I took my wife with me to Italy. She proved invaluable in making friends with them and we are to meet them in England. I had wired to the Maestro that I was coming as I felt certain this would not now bring a refusal to receive me as it would have done before.

On arrival in Italy I found a wire from him saying he was detained in

---

[9]   Although Mase does not disclose the identity of the 'impresarios', Gaisberg 'hovered around' (his own description) the Salzburg Festivals in 1935, 1936 and 1937 in the unfulfilled hope of recording operas or extracts conducted by, among others, Toscanini: Moore p. 213.

Vienna but would be back in two or three days and would I wait.[10] I waited and a few days later I went over to the island with my wife. We were received by the Maestro himself and spent two hours discussing programmes in detail. At this meeting I went through the score of Elgar's *Falstaff* with him and asked him if he would do it (he did not know it). He shrank from the hard study required for this difficult work and I suggested he keep it and think about it. Eventually he said 'All right – you have asked me to play it – I will play it for you.'

After we had finished programme discussion he insisted on showing us over his lovely island and asked us to go to see them again the next day when Madam Toscanini would be there. We went and had a very pleasant meeting. The Maestro signed a firm contract with me and I gave him a copy to retain. They came out to wave good-bye as our boat left.

Fairly early in the affair Madam Toscanini had insisted that they would only communicate with and receive communications from me personally. She said they had been so badly let down many times by people in many parts of the world that they wanted to deal only with someone they had got to know and trust. It was very silly, since they would be quite safe in dealing with the Corporation, but as that is their temperament I readily agreed and promised to do my best to see they were looked after in every way possible.

The whole business was rather arduous and a little anxious. A mistaken action, or wrong remark in any of the many conversations (carried out in mixed Italian French and English), would, I know, be quite sufficient to make them 'shy off' again. But I think a firm and friendly acquaintanceship at least has been established, and the Maestro does not now include us in his general damnation of broadcasting and its personnel. I had to promise that we would not give permission to any other broadcasting organisations to relay his performances as he mistrusts them all.

Each journey brought Mase nearer to his goal. On his first, his initial conversations with Carla took place in Toscanini's island home on the Isolino. Mase reported back to London in a note dated 6 June that, if the BBC were to have any hope of capturing Toscanini, they would have to assure him that none of his broadcasts

[10] Toscanini conducted several performances at the Staatsoper in September as a gesture to his friend Bruno Walter at the start of his tenure as music director: Sachs 1978 pp. 247–8; ATL pp. 218 and 220. Toscanini's letters show that he was back on the Isolino by 28 September (ATL p. 222, letter of that date to AM), sufficient evidence that Mase's third journey took place at the end of September rather than in October, as his memorandum states.

would be transmitted on shortwave frequencies (from Droitwich) to avoid the risk of unauthorised recordings abroad. Evidently Toscanini had been alerted to this possible transgression by Gaisberg's letter to Wanda of 31 January 1935, referred to in Chapter 3, which had been specially translated for him, as well as by his experience in Paris. For the BBC this demand presented no real problem. All Toscanini concerts were broadcast nationally, the majority on the BBC's National programme reserved for the most significant cultural and other events, the rest on its regional network.[11] Shortwave transmissions were important for maintaining contact with the Empire but their use for information and propaganda was still in its infancy. The BBC therefore agreed to Toscanini's demand without hesitation, even though at that stage it was no more than an outcome of Mase's discussions with Carla. Nevertheless, Gaisberg's earlier insistence on the benefits of authorised recording of the broadcasts to forestall pirate recordings abroad now had the perverse effect, for posterity, of threatening to prevent recordings in any form of future London Music Festival performances.

Mase's second journey, to Salzburg in August, established personal contact with Toscanini once more, secured his commitment to return to London, without, however, the vital signature on a binding contract. But Mase's personal invitation to Carla on this occasion was essential to the whole operation.[12]

Mase's third journey, to the Isolino once more in September/October, at last secured the missing contractual signature. The agreement, dated 22 September – it must have been ready prepared and dated by the BBC – was for six concerts to take place in May 1937. To accord with Toscanini's demands for restrictions on broadcasting and possible illegal recordings, the contract duly contained a clause limiting broadcast of Toscanini's concerts to the wavelengths designed for reception in the British Isles with 'every possible safeguard' to be taken to prevent any recording. While in itself the latter undertaking may well have been unenforceable by the BBC, the clause had its practical effect in the total absence of surviving recordings from the Festival other than a few private off-air attempts within Britain. For the same reason, a few months later the BBC flatly rejected the request by NBC's London

---

[11]   The National programme was transmitted throughout the United Kingdom, the Regional programme transmitted from London was simultaneously broadcast through regional transmitters with, however, some local contributions; but 'three-star' programmes of national importance, such as Toscanini concerts, were always broadcast on all Regional programmes: Asa Briggs *The History of Broadcasting in the United Kingdom (2) The Golden Age of Wireless 1927–1939* Oxford: OUP 1995 pp. 28–31 and 36–7. Thus all Toscanini's BBC SO concerts, whether broadcast on the National or Regional programmes, were received nationwide.

[12]   BBCA, Mase's minute, 13 October 1936.

agent for shortwave transmission of the 1937 Festival concerts to the United States. Still, Mase's discussion of programmes also bore fruit: although Toscanini did not take up the proffered Elgar *Falstaff*, he did programme instead the *Introduction and Allegro*, a work he first performed in Turin in 1906 but, unlike the *Enigma*, relatively rarely thereafter.

Overall, Mase had ample reason to be triumphant. But in a note to Boult after his return from his second visit to Italy he was careful to emphasise once more how important had been his personal invitation for Carla to accompany her husband, an extra attraction authorised by Boult earlier in June as one of the 'concessions' Mase was empowered to offer.[13] Carla was so used to being merely a 'background' but now it was 'her friendship firmly gained in the first place' that led to her supporting Mase in the discussions with Toscanini, resulting in the conductor's 'recantation'.

Another vital consequence of Mase's efforts was the personal bond between him and Toscanini cemented by their contact during their meetings; the importance of that bond for the BBC, for future concerts in London, and also in due course for HMV, cannot be over-estimated. For the time being the BBC were content to accept the position without demur since, as Mase said in his covering minute in January 1937, really important artists such as Toscanini 'do not deal readily with an impersonal Corporation'. Thenceforward Mase was at all times centre stage in matters relating to the Maestro's London visits. Toscanini's contracts with the BBC were agreed and concluded with him, even after he left BBC employment in late 1937; in effect he acted as the conductor's agent in London right through to his last, post-war concerts. Mase was assisted by his wife Georgina, a published poet with a special love of nature and woodland whose verse was set to music by her husband and by other composers including Cecil Armstrong Gibbs.[14] Together they willingly undertook the duty of guiding and entertaining the Maestro and Carla throughout many weeks spent in London bereft of their usual intimate circle, a function evidently carried out to their lasting satisfaction.

---

[13]   BBCA, Boult's memorandum, 18 June 1936.

[14]   Margery Georgina Mase (1890–1967) was first married to Swedish/British businessman Harald Olof Agrell, when she was known as Margery Agrell. After her marriage to Owen Mase, she was always known as Georgina Mase (details courtesy Peter Agrell). Recently some sources have mistakenly stated that the name Margery Agrell was the pseudonym for English soprano and songwriter Ursula Greville: see e.g. Hyperion CDA 67337 containing settings by Cecil Armstrong Gibbs of, among others, Georgina under both her names. Greville, sometime editor of *The Sackbut* and married to music publisher Kenneth Curwen, also, like Owen Mase, set verse by Georgina; and Curwen published both Greville's and Mase's songs. The confusion was no doubt caused by these multiple connections and the mystifying disappearance of the name Margery Agrell after Georgina's marriage to Owen.

Back at last – to a 'better orchestra'

Fortunately the arrangements made for Toscanini's visit in May/June 1937 went without hitch. In early May he was in Paris to discuss performances of Debussy's *Pelléas et Mélisande* in the autumn[15] and travelled by air to London on 11 May, leaving Carla and other family members to follow on later the same day by train and boat. Boult (Sir Adrian since February) sent a letter of welcome referring to the visit two years before as the orchestra's 'summit of achievement', while on 12 May Mase took Toscanini, Carla and Sonia, the three-year-old daughter of Wanda and Horowitz, to a favoured spot outside Westminster Abbey to view the coronation procession of King George VI.

The first concert was not due for a full two weeks, a period which allowed ample time for the press and publicity excitement to generate in its now expected fashion. Spike Hughes's half-page in the *Daily Express* was typical: headlined 'They Pay Him £500 for Conducting One Concert – And his wife cuts his hair for him', the article[16] was so detailed in its disclosure of domestic life that Carla was moved to ask where he could have learned so much about her husband – 'we don't know anybody called Spike Hughes, I think'. This kind of treatment caused headaches for those in charge of box-office arrangements: the enormous public interest required special measures, since the hall management and the BBC agreed that first come, first served, favouring those who could queue all night, would be unfair. Following the announcement that only written ticket applications would be accepted for a ballot, the Queen's Hall box office received over 17,000 letters. All were numbered and tickets drawn from a drum, with applications being dealt with in the order in which the numbers were drawn. As the hall manager put it, 'there was no other way for anybody to get into a Toscanini concert'.[17] All tickets were sold on the day booking opened.

Rehearsals for the first concert began on 19 May. Toscanini found the orchestra 'excellent – better than two years ago',[18] yet its personnel had remained remarkably stable during that period. What, then, accounted for the change? In 1935, as mentioned in Chapter 2, not all critics thought the orchestra's playing immaculate during its opening concert and, indeed, some less than impeccable string articulation and

---

[15] ATL p. 255 (letter to AM, 9 May 1937).

[16] Kenyon p. 137, Hughes 1951 p. 320, who there explains that he drew on his gossiping with opera singer Margaret Sheridan, a friend of the Toscanini family.

[17] Berta Geissmar *The Baton and the Jackboot* London: Hamish Hamilton 1944 p. 301.

[18] ATL p. 256 (letter to AM, 24 May 1937).

FIG. 12 TOSCANINI AND CARLA STEP OUT IN LONDON, c.1937

occasional faulty intonation in wind and brass are audible in the recordings of the concerts released by EMI in the 1980s, notably in the Brahms Fourth Symphony. If that is a reflection of the standards expected at the time, along with the pronounced string portamenti in *Nimrod* and elsewhere that Toscanini clearly tolerated, overall the orchestra excelled themselves for him. A comparison with, say, the fitfully ragged ensemble in Koussevitzky's live (and thrilling) recording of Sibelius's Seventh Symphony from the 1933 Festival or the sometimes wayward intonation permitted by Bruno Walter in his 1934 BBC SO recording of Brahms's Fourth Symphony, makes clear the benefits of Toscanini's intensive rehearsals in 1935 and also provides an accurate measurement of mid-1930s London orchestral standards and technique.[19]

Several factors made for improvements in the intervening two years, of which the most obvious was the change of leadership. Although as a leader Arthur Catterall was a prestigious figure who had been a major influence in the orchestra's early success, he was not a full-time player: in his absence on solo or quartet performances, deputy leaders took his place, as they did at the annual Promenade concerts. After Catterall's resignation in July 1936 in order to pursue his increasing outside interests,[20] Boult secured the replacement he wanted from Beecham's London Philharmonic Orchestra in the person of Paul Beard, who joined the BBC SO in October 1936; he knew Boult of old from their years with the City of Birmingham Orchestra. With ambitions from his earliest years to be an orchestral leader, Beard applied himself exclusively to his new post. His distinction and vigour undoubtedly led both to a sharp reduction in the pronounced string portamenti evident in earlier years and, taken overall, to a cleaner focus and tighter discipline resulting in a recognisably modern sound.[21] As the *New Grove Dictionary* put it, 'although his leadership tended to be autocratic, his influence on raising orchestral standards was quite exceptional'. In addition, although the long-serving Ambrose Gauntlett succeeded Lauri Kennedy as principal cellist in October 1935, for the 1937 Festival Kennedy was recalled at Toscanini's request to lead and strengthen the cello section; in the programmes his name appeared before Gauntlett's.

As important as these few but significant changes in personnel was the extra drilling the orchestra received at the hands of Mengelberg in a concert at the beginning of the 1936/37 season.[22] For all his hours of talking at rehearsals, this supreme orchestral trainer's insistence on absolute precision and faultless intonation paid off at the concert, particularly in *Ein Heldenleben* with Paul Beard as soloist, with brilliant results of astonishing clarity. This lesson had, it seems, an indelible effect

---

[19] Bruno Walter's Brahms Fourth Symphony: see p. 327; Koussevitzky's Sibelius Seventh Symphony recorded in concert on 15 May 1933, issued on HMV DB 1984–86, CD Naxos 8.110168.

[20] Kenyon, p. 128.

[21] For the reduction in string portamenti in the LPO and BBC SO under Beard's leadership, see Philip 1992 pp. 186 and 188. For an examination of the standards of London orchestral playing in the 1930s, see Philip 2004, Ch. 3, and of the styles of orchestral woodwind Philip 1992 Ch. 5.

[22] See Shore 1938 pp. 113–14, Kenyon p. 132.

FIGS. 13–16 A QUARTET OF BBC SO PLAYERS: PAUL BEARD (top left), FREDERICK THURSTON (top right), ARCHIE CAMDEN (bottom left), ERNEST HALL (bottom right foreground)

for, on the basis of such recorded evidence of the 1937 London Music Festival concerts as survives, the discipline of the strings and just intonation of the woodwind displayed all the best characteristics of British pre-war instrumental playing; and they continued to do so throughout Toscanini's subsequent visits. The artistry of principal clarinet Frederick Thurston who, like his New York Philharmonic counterpart, Simeon Bellison, played with little or no vibrato, was particularly admired by Toscanini; but no less distinguished were the virtuosity of Aubrey Brain's horn and the exceptional technique and artistry of Archie Camden's bassoon. Toscanini's perception of overall improvements in the orchestra, shared by all the critics reviewing the forthcoming concerts, was doubtless an important factor in persuading him to embark on his series of HMV studio recordings with them, as described in the next chapter.

Toscanini also showed his pleasure in the orchestra's extra responsiveness by his remarkable patience in some – but not all – rehearsals for the 1937 Festival. He had, for example, difficulty in conveying to harpist Sidonie Goossens the correct phrasing in her solo at the start of the second suite from Ravel's *Daphnis et Chloé*, demonstrating afterwards the desired imitative effect with the clarinet on an old upright piano in the artists' room; all was crystal clear, and he dismissed her with a pat on both cheeks and 'bene, bene ...'[23] Even the great Heddle Nash's explanation for his tardiness in attending rehearsal for his off-stage vocalising in Busoni's *Rondò Arlecchinesco*, proffered in what seemed to Toscanini to be operatic Italian, was met with no more than the mild reprimand to 'speak in English, per Dio santo!'[24] His patience did, however, sometimes wear thin. The orchestra was still not of uniform excellence and its weaknesses, such as the sometimes erratic principal oboist Alec Whittaker who failed to flourish under the orchestra's rigid management style, were an occasional irritant. His solos in the second movement of Brahms's First Symphony were met in rehearsal with constant comments: 'It is so cold ... you play correct, yes, you play too correct ...' and so on.[25] Later in the year Terence MacDonagh was promoted and held the principal's chair for extended periods until his retirement in 1972; Whittaker found fulfilment elsewhere.

---

[23] Broadcast talk. This incident was not his only mark of appreciation for her: after Beethoven's *Prometheus* Adagio and Allegretto in the concert on 24 May 1939, he tapped her hair with his baton while leaving the platform, saying 'molto intelligente' which, as she remarked, she would have liked in writing.

[24] Broadcast talk by Alex Nifosi. Heddle Nash (1896–1961) foremost English tenor.

[25] Shore 1938 pp. 177–8. See Ch. 1 p. 42 and nn. 76 and 77. Whittaker was the first principal oboist of the Philharmonia Orchestra in 1946 and later freelanced.

The first concert – greatness revealed and analysed

Daily Mail critic Edwin Evans set the scene for the opening concert on 26 May: 'There were extraordinary scenes at Queen's Hall last night ... When Toscanini stepped on the platform and the orchestra rose as usual, the majority of the audience followed its example ... Every work in the programme was followed by rapturous applause ... an extraordinary spirit prevailed.'[26] And the press was unanimous as to the results Toscanini elicited from the BBC SO: they had never experienced the like from a British orchestra. Constant Lambert delivered a breathless, interim report after the first concert on 30 May: 'I have never heard such astounding performances in all my life.' Writing in the *Sunday Referee* on 6 June, he singled out the opening concert's Ravel as 'the most remarkable orchestral performance I have ever heard ... in spite of having an extraordinary dynamic force and sonority, it had all the clarity of a string quartet ... even in the most complex passages one could look at any individual instrument ... and hear what it was playing.' But Lambert cautioned against those who praised Toscanini for simply playing 'as written': such views showed extreme ignorance of the conductor's art. Toscanini neither imposed himself on the music, as did 'virtuoso' conductors, nor played just what was written, as did a mere craftsman; rather, he 're-creates what is in the composer's mind and it hardly seems just to describe him merely as an executive artist'. As will be seen, this verdict aligned Lambert's views with one of the principal thrusts of Newman's appraisal of Toscanini and, in its reference to Toscanini's power of recreating the composer's very thoughts, sustained a critical refrain evident already in 1935, which continued over the next three years.

Lambert's colleague on the *Times* was only a shade more sober on 27 May. For this critic, the incendiary *Coriolan* Overture and Brahms First Symphony were 'personal readings of the kind which defy imitation', notable for subtle rubatos in the overture and a symphony which he judged 'a triumph of concentrated musical thought' with an overwhelming finale which closed with 'torrential energy'. Britten, confiding his enthusiasm to his diary, was once more profoundly impressed: the Ravel was 'a revelation; it can never have sounded like that before – all the colours melted into each other', yet 'never was the colour all important'. *Coriolan* was 'great' and even the symphony, by a composer for whom he already nurtured what was to be a lifelong detestation, was 'as good as it could be'.

It fell to Cardus in the *Manchester Guardian* on 27 May to sound the first

---

[26] Quoted in Kenyon p. 137.

substantial note of a pained dissent which was to recur in many of his assessments of Toscanini's BBC concerts. He heard no rubato in *Coriolan*, which was 'entirely lacking in humanity ... superbly mechanical, with great chords chopped as though by an axe'. The first movement of the Brahms symphony suffered from 'compressed' rhythms, which rendered it 'matter-of-fact' – although 'the man's genius was asserted in the remaining movements' and the orchestral playing throughout was 'the best I have heard in this country'. Cardus was always to concede Toscanini's pre-eminence in his pre-war performances but his roller-coaster attitude towards the conductor's interpretations – sometimes, as here, dyspeptic, at others ecstatic – led to some extreme and even contradictory verdicts. His observations on this and subsequent occasions did, however, have the virtue of pinpointing the start of those changes in Toscanini's interpretative approach which led in his post-BBC years to an austerity and sometimes to an increased velocity that some have viewed as characteristic of his later music-making.

As if in answer to Cardus, the extraordinary impression left by the first concert was reinforced on 29 May by the *Times* critic's acute analysis of Toscanini's operation in the Brahms symphony. Toscanini was, said the *Times* critic (probably Colles), supreme in his capacity to keep the whole in mind while working over the detail. Throughout the symphony the critic was constantly hearing things which generally escaped attention, 'particularly those little overlappings of the ends of phrases, notably in the second theme of the first movement, which often fade away into one another. It would be easy to make such things too prominent, but they never were; they were just present.' By contrast with the virtuoso conductor bent on dynamic effect, this characteristic demonstrated the way in which Toscanini 'always finishes a phrase through'. Although the entry of instruments was the primary care of a conductor, their exit was too frequently left to look after itself while he attended other entries – but that was not Toscanini's way: his 'power of carrying through ... often gives the impression that he is not only playing on the orchestra ... but that he is really playing each instrument. And just as the single phrase is carried through, so is the group of phrases, the period, the movement, so that ultimately the whole symphony is modelled to completeness.' Certain instrumental tones insisted on might be striking in themselves, for example, the roundness of the horn in the last movement's introduction or the penetrating oboe throughout, but 'such characteristics are all made relative to what he conceives to be Brahms's symphonic scheme'.

The *Times* critic went on to compare Toscanini's tempos with those of other conductors, particularly Hans Richter, pointing out that tempos were not absolute – the right tempos were those in which everything needful could be said without haste on the one hand or ponderousness on the other. If a German conductor would probably require a little longer than Toscanini for his complete expression of the Andante sostenuto second movement, that would no doubt be right in its context: anyone insisting on exactly a particular tempo because it was Toscanini's would be wrong. 'The players said of Hans Richter that there was always room in his beat for all the notes which had to be put into it. The same might be said of Toscanini's beat'; and, although there was a considerable difference between their tempos for Brahms, 'both were proved right in their results'.

As with some of Bonavia's reviews, the value of this analysis was enhanced by the writer's personal memories of the hallowed leader of a previous generation. Bonavia cited Richter because (as he saw it) of his similarities with Toscanini; the citation by the *Times* critic emphasised their differences in choice of tempo, both being (again as he saw it) equally valid. Timings for Richter's performances of Brahms's First Symphony have not survived, but those for his 1877 premiere of the Second Symphony in Vienna suggest that he was faster than any recorded Toscanini performance of that work save in the second movement;[27] but some twenty years later, when Richter was performing the First in Manchester and London, he may in any event have broadened his tempos. Furthermore, venerated as Richter was by many in England early in the twentieth century, Brahms was not always content with his work and, as is discussed further in Chapter 12 and Annex C, Toscanini had the benefit of absorbing the interpretative approach of the composer's favourite conductor, Fritz Steinbach; Toscanini's way with Brahms in pre-war days is analysed in more detail in that context.

Three more concerts: the Maestro is happy

The second concert on 28 May precipitated its expected shower of encomiums, most lyrical and high-flown of all being the *Manchester Guardian*'s often contrary Walter Legge, standing in for Cardus, who on 29 May thought Toscanini 'cosmic in his understanding, clairvoyant in his sympathies. There seems to be no weakness or chink in the man's artistic armour'. If Elgar's *Introduction and Allegro* seemed at first insufficiently expansive, 'two minutes later we were lifted out of our seats by the noble surge of Elgar's melody made real as we have never heard it before'. Throughout the concert there was 'playing the like of which we have never heard before from an English orchestra or any orchestra except under Toscanini's direction'. The Berlioz *Queen Mab Scherzo* was 'more lovely, more transparent, more

---

[27] See Musgrave & Sherman, pp. 115–17; as to Brahms's views on Richter, see Annex C p. 297.

entrancing than any we have ever imagined'. Legge was in 1937 already an experienced recording producer for EMI and, in the light of his subsequent notorious perfectionism, such uninhibited enthusiasm is not only significant as an assessment of Toscanini's achievement at the time, but goes far to explain the extraordinary lengths, as described in Chapter 11, to which Legge went in his attempts to lure Toscanini back to London fifteen years later.

If other critics were less colourful in language, they were unequivocally appreciative of Toscanini's interpretative powers and the playing he secured. Newman, covering the first two concerts in the *Sunday Times* on 30 May, thought the Ravel 'indescribably beautiful' and the orchestral playing 'superb', even if the conductor's typical virtue of rhythmic counterplay 'defies analysis' (one of Newman's recurrent phrases in reaction to the Toscanini experience). For the *Times* on 29 May, the Cherubini Symphony in D 'glowed in the incandescence which is Signor Toscanini's gift ... he does not throw light on music from without but makes it glow from within'. Bonavia in that day's *Telegraph* commented on the 'ravishing finesse' of the Berlioz and the 'incredible brilliancy' of the closing *Meistersinger* Prelude. Later, in reviewing the same concert for the *New York Times* on 20 June, he drew on his memories of Hans Richter, under whom he played as a Hallé violinist at the turn of the century: 'it is Richter that Toscanini recalls in this [ability to draw more than others from his players] as in the considered tempos and in the climaxes which retain the right balance between different families of instruments at their loudest.'

Although there was a large measure of agreement about the supreme quality of the performances, the first two concerts also marked the start of complaints about the miscellany of items played, a refrain continued during the next season to the effect that, however masterful Toscanini the interpreter might be, that mastery did not always extend to his programme-building. The Elgar *Introduction and Allegro* was, for most critics, wonderful, the *Queen Mab Scherzo* magical, the *Meistersinger* Prelude for all listeners virtually indescribable in its majesty – except for the *Times* critic for whom Toscanini's 'too brilliant, too aristocratic, too dry-eyed' way de-Wagnerised it. These two items in the second concert were also the highlights for Britten who thought them a 'fantastic show'.[28] But, on the debit side, Cherubini? 'Nice but spotty' thought Britten, and the critics (Newman excepted) voted his symphony dull in content, saved only by Toscanini's transformational conjuring. And Tommasini's *Carnival of Venice*? Not even Toscanini could save this work from critical downsizing, typified by Turner's sarcastic observation that its inclusion demonstrated only that the conductor 'possesses a great capacity for friendship'.

[28] Britten p. 434. For Turner, see *New Statesman* 5 June 1937.

FIG. 17 TOSCANINI AND TOMMASINI RELAX BY LAKE MAGGIORE

True enough in this instance; and in rehearsal, after complimenting the orchestra on its sight-reading virtuosity ('I do not understand – how can you have seen this music before?'),[29] he spent hours rehearsing his friend's composition 'like a boy with a toy as the orchestra exerted itself to read appalling passages at sight and to make the work sound like a masterpiece'.[30] The composer arrived from Italy in time to attend the morning dress rehearsal and received a warm ovation in the hall when he stood in response to Toscanini's gesture to him in the audience.[31] This occasion was not the last on which the conductor would demonstrate publicly his esteem for him in the Queen's Hall.

Whatever the critical reservations about the programmes, some perceptive writers sensed Toscanini's genuine joy at working with the BBC players. Of the first concert, Capell in the *Telegraph* on 27 May remarked that the orchestra 'had for a week been rehearsing ... under a conductor who unites passionate intellectual power with the gift of instantaneous physical expression of his mental intention'. In the result, even the most captious listener could not fail to have been conquered by the 'supreme effect of the union of thought and energy' in the music-making, with

[29] Matthews 1966 p. 69.
[30] Shore 1938 p. 169.
[31] ATL p. 256 (letter to AM, 31 May 1937).

Toscanini in 'unbuttoned' mood, his 'extraordinarily exuberant and sweeping' gestures giving the impression that he was 'in his intense way, enjoying himself', an impression reinforced when Toscanini 'himself applauded the players the moment the [Brahms] symphony ended'. Toscanini was indeed for once content: as he wrote to Ada after the second concert, 'if only you knew how happy I am with this orchestra! It's a real joy to be working!'[32]

Toscanini's euphoric mood continued through the third and fourth concerts on 2 and 4 June, containing respectively the *Pastoral* and *Eroica* symphonies as their weightiest pieces. Rehearsing them after a near-sleepless night 'swept me away, and everything disappeared in the divine enchantment' of the works; his friends Tommasini and pianist 'Miecio' Horszowski, present at the rehearsal, 'expressed their wonderment at how the orchestra understands me and responds to my every sign'. His patience was again exceptional; almost half the total time spent in rehearsing the *Pastoral* Symphony was devoted to the exposition of the first movement, modifying ever so slightly certain dynamic markings, for example, to enhance the sense of awakening wonder. By contrast, in rehearsing the *Eroica* only the *Marcia funebre* and finale were dealt with in detail; the other movements were played straight through without pause, the concentrated fire of Toscanini's conducting conveying to the orchestra almost all that was needed.[33] A few weeks later he wrote again, 'the orchestra is truly admirable for its discipline and ability ... I think I have never conducted [the *Eroica*] better. The orchestra was possessed, like me, and like the audience afterwards'.[34] Such joy was for him rare and on this occasion apparently unaccompanied by his usual obliterating doubts, probably because the letter's recipient, Ada Mainardi, was considered by the conductor at this time to be the fount of his inspirational drive.

By and large the critics shared Toscanini's enthusiasm. For the *Times* on 3 June the *Pastoral* Symphony had a sense of 'easy, almost lazy, relaxation' in the first two movements and finale, giving them an 'unusual spaciousness' in which, however, the rhythmic tension seemed 'like a steady undercurrent carrying the music ever onward beneath any surface variations of the tempo'. On 5 June the *Times* thought the *Eroica* was 'as perfect an example as could be desired of the conductor's aims and methods', the whole 'given in its highest concentration and greatest purity'. Newman, covering the third and fourth concerts in the *Sunday Times* of 6 June, inveighed in terms that were to become characteristic against those who laboured under the 'illusion' that Toscanini was an 'objectivist': his art was far more subtle

---

[32] ATL p. 257 (letter to AM, 31 May 1937).
[33] See Shore 1938 pp. 173 and 179; and see further Ch. 12 p. 253.
[34] ATL p. 259 (letter to AM, 18 June 1937).

and comprehensive than any such simplistic label and this series of performances was of unsurpassable 'clarity and luminosity'. Britten's diary comments were less sophisticated: hearing the *Pastoral* on the radio, he thought it a 'really good show', with Toscanini's rhythm 'glorious'. Attending the *Eroica* concert, he found it a 'fine, simple and direct' performance – everything in the work was there.[35]

Of other works featured in the third and fourth concerts, critical attention centred on the conductor's remarkable velocity in the fifth *Haydn* variation – 'reckless' according to Westrup in the *Telegraph* on 5 June; but as will be noted in Chapter 11, Toscanini was here drawing on his memories of Fritz Steinbach. More to critical tastes was the conductor's extraordinary handling of *Tod und Verklärung* which ended the third concert. Typical comment again came from Westrup, who remarked that the work rose 'to a climax that seemed temporarily to remove the roof and expose the firmament'. This achievement was a fruit of the most intensive rehearsing of the whole piece, especially the opening bars and the middle 'fever' section where the orchestra for the first time faced an outburst of score-mauling and baton-hurling.[36] Even so, for principal trumpet Ernest Hall performing this work was a highlight remembered indelibly three and a half decades later: 'I have never, never heard such a crescendo ... He brought the orchestra right up and then came down in such a fashion that I think the Queen's Hall must have rocked. Everything went black in front of me for that moment and I thought "My God!" – and I had to pull myself together because a few bars later the trumpets had to come in together in a triad.'[37] The crescendo in question was preserved by Kenneth Leech in one of his many off-air recordings and may be heard in the British Library's Sound Archive; neither Westrup nor Hall exaggerated its effect.

A special interest attaches to the reaction to Toscanini's reading of two works in the fourth concert, the *Eroica* Symphony and the still unfamiliar Shostakovich First Symphony which preceded the *Eroica*. The *Times* critic's response to the Beethoven is summarised above, but two comments of detail in the course of this review have a particular significance for later generations. Its critic noted the peculiar quality of sound which Toscanini drew from the orchestra in this work: 'the tone, even of an abrupt *fortissimo* chord, [is] full saturated and quite free from noise'. This description of Toscanini's tonal preferences, which were the subject of repeated comment in reviews of later concerts, suggests the degree to which so many of his later NBC

---

[35] Britten p. 435
[36] See Shore 1938 p. 181.
[37] Interview with the author, 1972. For Leech, see Ch. 12 n. 36 and, as to this recording, see Annex B p. 282.

recordings falsified the very sound of his orchestra – particularly in the notoriously poor recorded sound of his performance of this work two years later (further described in Chapter 12).

The *Times* critic also noted that the *Marcia funebre* was 'unsurvivingly rigid from beginning to end at a stately pace', resulting in a heightened intensity in the fugal passage. Recorded evidence shows that Toscanini did, in fact, vary the pace in all his performances of this movement, particularly during the fragmentation of the first theme towards the end; but the *Times* comment suggests that distinct variations of pace between first and second subjects and the fugue were quite usual at the time. Such variations were certainly characteristic of Weingartner's approach, with which the critics were familiar both from his 1936 recording with the Vienna Philharmonic and from two recent Queen's Hall performances, in May 1935 with the Vienna Philharmonic and March 1937 with the LPO in a Royal Philharmonic Society concert; a 'live' recording of Weingartner conducting this work at the Salzburg Festival in July 1935 suggests that his concert hall approach to this movement was yet more extreme in its variations of pace than his Columbia recording. If that inference is correct, it is the less surprising that the *Times* critic was moved to comment on Toscanini's contrasting approach, which has since become virtually the norm.

The Shostakovich First Symphony was the only modern work of substance in the Festival programmes and the composer had yet to gain the praise showered on him by critics after the Second World War. Toscanini had long championed the work, giving it his first reading in April 1931, just three months after the first British performance with Harty and the Hallé Orchestra. Subsequently Nicolai Malko conducted the work at a BBC studio concert in February 1932; but it had to wait until 1935 for its concert premiere in London, on that occasion played by the LSO under Malko, followed by a Henry Wood Promenade Concert. According to the *Times* review of Toscanini's concert, these earlier British performances, as well as Stokowski's Philadelphia recording, suggested the work's affinities with Tchaikovsky, whereas Toscanini's lucid and logical reading emphasised the composer's individuality: 'its colour scheme is bright enough, but colour was not allowed to obtrude on the lucid exposition of the thought, and its brilliant passages fell into place as means whereby the concise argument was clinched'.[38] Newman, too, who had little good to say of Shostakovich at the time, was impressed by the eloquence of the per-

---

[38] For the reception of this work at its first British performances and of Shostakovich's work in general before the Second World War, see Fairclough pp. 266–70. Stokowski's 1933 Philadelphia recording was issued in Britain on HMV DB 3847–51S (CD Pearl GEMM CDS 9044). Harty's

formance, while Capell in the *Telegraph* on 5 June remarked that the 'devotion and intensity' which Toscanini brought to the work would be remembered to his honour.

To Oxford

The gaps in Toscanini's London engagements during his five-week stay, in particular the ten days between the first four concerts and the last two, once more allowed him time for diversions and expeditions outside the routine of hotel and rehearsals. His most important out-of-town engagement was the visit on 8 June to Oxford with members of the BBC orchestra. This was to be Toscanini's only British concert outside London. The event had its origin in a multi-pronged offensive aimed at getting him to the university town, the brainchild of the principal instigator, Sir Hugh Allen, Professor of Music at Oxford, Director of the Royal College of Music and a major influence in British musical life between the two world wars. Allen's views about the BBC were virulent, even after his appointment as chairman of their Music Advisory Committee in 1926, although, after its enlargement and reconstitution under his chairmanship in 1936, he became more amenable – which did not stop the BBC's Music Department viewing the Committee as a millstone round its neck. Explosive and imperious by temperament, Allen habitually got what he wanted; and what he wanted was Toscanini at Oxford in order to confer on him an honorary doctorate, together with the BBC's orchestra for a concert under the conductor's direction.[39]

Allen had no hesitation in using his position to further his purpose and as early as February 1937 he proposed to the BBC that the orchestra be 'borrowed' to play under Toscanini in Oxford; the proposal was duly approved. Early in March Mase contacted Carla in The Hague, where Toscanini was preparing a concert with the Residentie orchestra, and later reported to Allen that the idea of a concert in Oxford had been planted in Toscanini's mind; but Carla was doubtful because things had gone so badly with the Hague orchestra.[40] Toscanini described it as crude and

---

premiere was on 21 January 1931, Malko's studio concert on 5 February 1932, his London concert premiere on 31 March 1935 and the Henry Wood Promenade Concert performance on 19 September 1935; see further Britten pp. 255, 278 and 435. Toscanini's first performance of this work with the New York Philharmonic took place on 8 April 1931 and he had at the time of the London performance recently conducted it with the Vienna Philharmonic (22 November 1936).

[39]   Sir Hugh Allen (1869–1946), conductor of the Oxford and London Bach Choirs, Director Royal College of Music 1918–37, Professor of Music Oxford University 1918–46. For Allen's views on and relationship with the BBC, see Bailey pp. 95–6 and Kenyon pp. 11, 111–12 and 130. The negotiations described in the next paragraph are in BBCA, memoranda from Allen (23 February 1937 with endorsement by the Music Department Executive) and Mase to Allen (8 and 18 March 1937).

[40]   ATL p. 238 (undated letter to AM, early March 1937).

FIG. 18 SIR HUGH ALLEN IN 1938

lacking in discipline and threatened to cancel his appearance. The threat and the
consequent infusion of fresh personnel transformed the orchestra, which he then
expressed himself as glad to conduct. However, the extreme stress caused by these
events led Carla to decline the invitation to Oxford on his behalf. Mase duly
reported the bad news to Allen with the emollient comment that Toscanini was

aware of Oxford's great tradition and knew the honour was the greatest that its university could bestow; but with such troubles, 'he becomes ten years older and his mind refuses to encompass anything except the immediate tragedy affecting him', transforming himself into 'a young man with terrific energy' only when the problem was solved.

A month later back in Milan, Toscanini came upon earlier correspondence from the University sent to Italy's London embassy notifying him of the University's intention to confer on him the honorary degree of Doctor of Music at a date con-venient to him.[41] Since, for well-known reasons, the conductor was not in good odour with the Italian government, the correspondence had not been forwarded at the time through ordinary channels. Again Toscanini did nothing to further the matter. After he arrived in London Mase asked him repeatedly if he would be willing to conduct in Oxford but he remained consistently non-committal until Carla intimated that the proposed degree conferment was the obstacle: as Toscanini himself explained to Mase, he had a horror of the pomp and ceremony and of wearing 'a funny hat'.[42] If all this were dropped, he would be happy 'to come and conduct a concert for you anywhere for nothing'. A telephone call to Allen was sufficient for the degree proposal to be dropped and Toscanini immediately consented to the concert as an appropriate gesture by which, as he later put it, 'to avoid being honoured with investitures and Latin orations'.[43]

As its programme announced, the concert was to be 'given by Maestro Toscanini as a gesture of goodwill to the University of Oxford' with proceeds devoted to the Oxford University Appeal Fund.[44] It took place on the afternoon of 8 June in Oxford's New Theatre with seventy-five players;[45] compared with the Queen's Hall complement, a little less than the full strength for the two main items, the *Pastoral* and Brahms First symphonies, but more than enough for the opening Rossini Overture *L'italiana in Algeri*. Some accounts, which appear to have originated with an error in the performance list in Robert Charles Marsh's 1956 monograph on the conductor, suggest that Toscanini also prepared Haydn's *Oxford* Symphony specially for the occasion; but this item appeared neither in the programme nor in press reviews (including the local *Oxford Mail* which would certainly have mentioned

---

[41] ATL p. 248 (letter to AM, 10 April 1937).

[42] Mase *Memories*.

[43] ATL p. 257 (letter to AM, 10 June 1937).

[44] A copy of the programme is in ATC JPB 90-1 series L pt 3 folder L75A-1.

[45] Based on a string complement of 14-14-10-9-8 (the number of first and second violins, violas, cellos and double basses) compared with the strength listed in the 1937 Queen's Hall programmes of 20-16-14-13-12.

this compliment to the city).[46] Nor did Fritz Busch, present in the audience, refer to it in a letter to Adolf, in which his admiration for Toscanini showed its limits: '[the concert] was very lovely, of course, but by no means as exciting as many of the things in his Wagner concert [the following week] ... The Pastorale was to my mind the least bit too fast all the way through, the "Awakening of cheerful impressions along the Arno" and the Brahms I still have in my memory even more warmly and convincingly as a whole by Steinbach'[47] – this last a significant assessment in the context of Fritz's own approach described further in Annex C.

Press reviews, by contrast, were without dissent. The *Times* on 9 June commented only on the 'justness' of the performances, which closely reflected those already heard by its critic in London. Westrup in that day's *Telegraph* commented on the playing's 'spirit of uncompromising vitality, precision that transcends exactness, and truthfulness that stirs up heart and mind'. He thought the dry acoustic of the theatre would have shown up any weaknesses in Toscanini's musicality or in the playing – but there was none in either, a fact which made the listener 'appreciate even more vividly the stature of the orchestra and the mastery of the hand that guided it'. A few days later Allen echoed this verdict in a letter to a friend: 'He [Toscanini] was delightful and never was such an audience in Oxford yet seen, nor more beautiful playing heard.'

Toscanini was happy with the event and motored back from Oxford via the 'wonderful' Windsor Great Park. Later he noted with satisfaction that by giving his services free for the occasion, the Appeal Fund earned more than £1000 (some £50,000 in today's terms).[48] On 11 June Allen wrote to Mase expressing his thanks for the 'marvellous musical experience' which created a whole new host of friends for Toscanini among undergraduates who would then and there have elected him President of the Oxford Union if they could.[49] All this, said Allen, was thanks to Mase's exercise of supreme diplomacy; and the following year he saw to it that, in place of Toscanini, Mase was awarded an honorary degree for these services to music and the University.

---

[46] See Marsh p. 227, Matthews p. 63, ATL p. 258. Shore 1938 p. 168 and Shore 1949 p. 5 refer to Toscanini conducting Haydn; no work by Haydn otherwise featured in the BBC SO programmes. Toscanini may therefore have prepared the work but dropped it for the concert, a possibility made the more likely by his taking up the work for one performance with the NBC SO (concert of 19 March 1944). See also the *Oxford Mail* 9 June 1937.

[47] Adolf Busch vol. 2 p. 370 (letter dated 27 July 1937).

[48] ATL p. 258 (letter to AM, 10 June 1937). Allen's letter to his friend quoted in the preceding paragraph gave a figure of £800; see Bailey p. 127.

[49] Letter 11 June 1937 from Allen at the RCM in MA. Degree of MA Oxon, listed in CV in MA, prepared by Mase in the 1940s, probably when applying for the post of Concerts Adviser to the London County Council in 1950.

Distractions and expeditions

The day following the Oxford expedition was, if devoted wholly to relaxation, exceptionally busy. In the morning Toscanini and Carla motored down to Tadworth to visit
Ernest Newman at his Surrey home, causing Vera Newman perturbation over her
limitations as a cook. She knew that Toscanini's favourite dish was scrambled eggs
with asparagus tips and this was duly prepared with care by her housekeeper; but she
need not have worried since Toscanini wanted little more than to talk with Newman.
This they did continuously for several hours, sparing little time for the table. The conductor's memory was demonstrated when, in discussing a particular phrase in *Tristan*,
he correctly identified the page, line and bar while Newman hunted for the score.[50]

Continuing down to Glyndebourne, Toscanini and Carla arrived in time for *The
Magic Flute*, their second Glyndebourne experience of the work under Fritz Busch
and the last performance of the season; afterwards, with Sybil Cholmondeley, they
dined with the Christies. Audrey Mildmay's diary for 9 June duly recorded 'Toscaninis
and Lady Cholmondeley to opera and dine'. By most accounts the Busch-Ebert *Magic
Flute* was a fine collective achievement, controversial only in Fritz's piano accompaniment for the recitatives and in his treatment of appoggiaturas. Toscanini picked up
on the latter, amongst much else, when he later admitted to Ada his boredom with
Fritz's approach – the tempos were slow where they should have been moderate or
andante, even slower in the Larghetti, and 'enough to asphyxiate you in the Adagios',
with all the embellishments (in his view) wrongly interpreted. As he put it, the opera
was 'full to the brim' of instances where 'the interpretation is right when it embellishes
the melody that is decorated by it'.[51] Having been equally unhappy with a performance
at the Vienna Staatsoper two months earlier, Toscanini was able to put his own ideas
into practice in Salzburg later that year.

Toscanini's private thoughts about what he heard were, as on the occasion of his
first visit in 1935, shielded from the rest of the company. Towards Fritz, for example,
his behaviour was impeccable: in the lengthy letter to brother Adolf already quoted,
Fritz remarked that Toscanini 'was very kind as always', although preoccupied with

---

[50] Vera Newman p. 164. Vera does not specify the date but, since Tadworth lay in the direction
of Glyndebourne, it seems likely to have been on the same day as the visit to the latter, 9 June 1937.
As against that, Sybil Cholmondeley was in the party at Glyndebourne but she did not figure in
the photograph of Newman with his visitors, nor did Vera mention her; but she probably travelled
from London by the Glyndebourne train.

[51] ATL p. 260 (letter to AM, 24 June 1937). As to the Vienna *Magic Flute*, see ATL pp. 251–2:
Toscanini attended the Staatsoper performance on 18 April 1937 conducted by Josef Krips, which
he heartily disliked, although its principals, Jarmila Novotná, Helge Roswaenge and Alexander
Kipnis, sang in his Salzburg *Magic Flute* in August that year.

FIG. 19 TOSCANINI, CARLA AND ERNEST NEWMAN AT TADWORTH, JUNE 1937

problems at Salzburg.[52] Fritz went on to compare the attitudes of Toscanini, who was anxious to pay for his party's tickets (in fact they were seated in John Christie's private box in the tiny theatre), and Furtwängler, in London for Covent Garden *Ring* cycles, who on his subsequent visit behaved like royalty but was received with reluctance. Fritz avoided all contact with his ex-colleague and freely blamed what he perceived as Furtwängler's weakness in serving only his own interests. By contrast, Toscanini's visit signalled the start of prolonged efforts to engage him as conductor at Glyndebourne.

Toscanini's other diversions were less strenuous, if equally pleasurable. He was busy, as he was almost throughout the year, with correspondence relating to the formation of the NBC Symphony Orchestra. He appealed internationally by private correspondence for funds for the impoverished widow of Ferruccio Busoni, 'one of the greatest musicians of our time'.[53] He ministered to the teenaged, rebellious – but as yet by no means wholly anti-Nazi – daughter of Siegfried and Winifred Wagner, Friedelind, up from a school in Arundel, Sussex. He was to see her again during his visits later that year and in 1938, by which time her hatred for Hitler and his régime had crystallised; the Nazis' treatment of Frida Leider and her husband that year was the tipping point. Thereafter Friedelind

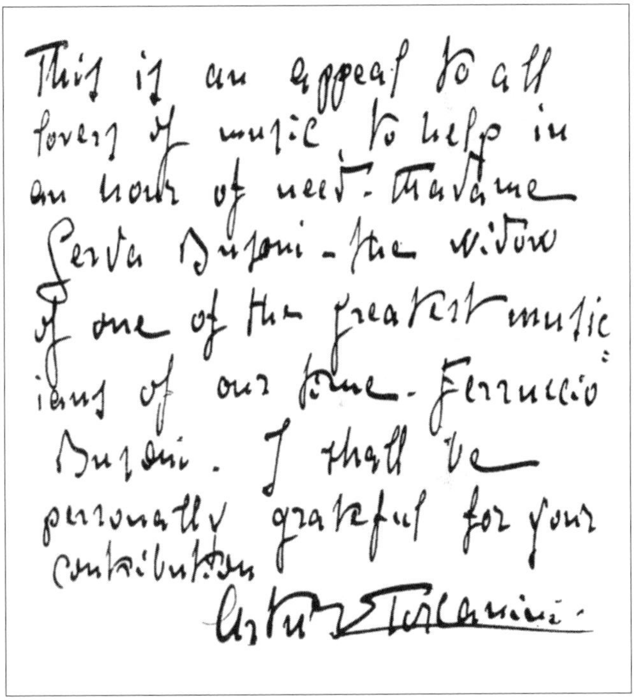
This is an appeal to all lovers of music to help in an hour of need. Madame Gerda Busoni – the widow of one of the greatest musicians of our time – Ferruccio Busoni. I shall be personally grateful for your contribution.
Arturo Toscanini.

FIG. 20 TOSCANINI'S APPEAL ON BEHALF OF BUSONI'S WIDOW, PROBABLY WRITTEN IN LONDON, JUNE 1937, AND DISTRIBUTED INTERNATIONALLY

[52] Adolf Busch vol. 2 pp. 370–2; for these 'problems', see Ch. 6 and n. 3.

[53] ATL p. 264.

FIG. 21 TOSCANINI, BRUNO WALTER AND STEFAN ZWEIG, SALZBURG, 1934

left Germany for Switzerland and in 1940 managed to reach London where, because of security service doubts about her, she was sent to Holloway gaol as a preliminary to her internment as an enemy alien. Toscanini exerted all his influence to secure her release.[54]

---

[54] ATL pp. 261 (letter to AM, 24 June 1937), 376 (letter to AM, 14 August 1940) and 378 (telegram to Friedelind Wagner, 12 March 1941); Friedelind Wagner pp. 163, 165 and 175; see further Ch. 9

Other musical entertainment was frequent and varied. Toscanini attended two operas at Covent Garden: *Pelléas* under Albert Wolff and *Tosca* under Barbirolli.[55] Accompanied by Tommasini, he spent a whole day with exiled author Stefan Zweig in the latter's Hallam Street flat near the Queen's Hall, examining his autograph manuscripts of 'truly exceptional importance: Mozart, Beethoven, Wagner, Bach, Goethe etc'. Zweig's collection was, indeed, of world-ranking importance and in 1986 went to the British Library. He attributed his latterday concentration on musical interests to Toscanini after he became closely acquainted with the conductor at the author's pre-exile home in Salzburg. In 1935 Zweig there penned the most eloquent of all essays by a non-musician about Toscanini's art; and, just two months before this London meeting, he wrote an extravagant greeting to Toscanini in Milan on the occasion of his seventieth birthday, ending with 'one more wish *for us* – that you always remain the same – the highest example of artistic perfection in our poor times, and a hero of moral independence in the midst of universal weariness ...'[56] As a member of Toscanini's intimate circle, Zweig often attended the London rehearsals.

In love with the Maestro

Less consistently welcome were the attentions of various over-zealous society hostesses who professed their love for the Maestro,[57] among them the 73-year-old Margot Asquith, who later that year he found tiresome to the point of impertinence.

---

p. 184. Friedelind Wagner (1918–91); for a full account of her changing attitude towards the Nazis, her escape to London in 1940, the views of the British security services and British efforts to secure her release from internment, see Carr pp. 206–9 and 211–20. Frida Leider's Austrian Jewish husband, Rudolf Deman, concertmaster of the Berlin Staatsoper orchestra, lost his Austrian citizenship after the Nazis invaded Austria and was forced to flee to Switzerland for the duration of the war. Leider lived in Germany in reduced circumstances: Carr pp. 211–12.

[55] Sachs 1978 p. 260.

[56] See ATL p. 258 (letter to AM, 14 June 1937). Stefan Zweig (1881–1942), a renowned writer, lived in London 1934–40 before leaving for New York and later Brazil, where he and his second wife committed suicide. His collection of literary and music manuscripts was gifted by his heirs to the British Library in May 1986; see further Arthur Searle *Stefan Zweig Collection: Catalogue of the Music Manuscripts* British Library 1999 pp. xxix-xxx. Zweig's essay on Toscanini constitutes the Foreword to Stefan; Toscanini was eager to know what Zweig had written – ATL p. 194 (letter to AM, 9 September(?) 1935). Zweig's birthday greeting is in ATC, reproduced in Sachs 1987 (exhibition catalogue). As to Toscanini's awakening Zweig's greater interest in music, see Zweig *The World of Yesterday* (trans. Anthea Bell) London: Pushkin Press 2009 p. 372.

[57] ATL p. 258 (letter to AM, 14 June 1937) and, as to Margot Asquith, p. 310 (letter to AM, 3 November 1937). Emma Alice Margaret 'Margot', Countess of Oxford and Asquith, née Tennant (1864–1945), married Herbert Asquith (Prime Minister 1908–16). Sybil, Marchioness of Cholmondeley, née Sassoon (1894–1989), as to whom see further Stansky pp. 211–12; Yvonne Rothschild, née Cahen-d'Anvers (1899–1977), married Anthony de Rothschild, a leading light in the banking family.

After importuning him for a photograph with a dedication 'with love' (declined), 'is it possible', he asked Ada, 'that a woman should still have *subversive* notions' at her age. In extreme contrast with this pertinacious elder was the 'very dear and very correct ... *reserved* and *restrained*' Yvonne Rothschild, a friend of his daughters Wally and Wanda, in whose company he felt relatively safe and unembarrassed, even though in 1937 she followed him devotedly to Salzburg and New York in quest of his company.

More troublesome for Toscanini were the attentions of prolific correspondent Sybil, Marchioness of Cholmondeley, whom we have already met as Paris courier of BBC SO test discs from HMV in May 1936. Scion of two pre-eminent Jewish families, the Sassoons and, on her mother's side, the Rothschilds, at the age of nineteen she married into the most senior ranks of English aristocracy, partly to escape the embrace of the latter family, and eventually became an Anglican convert. Her husband's accession to the title of fifth Marquis of Cholmondeley in 1923, and with it the hereditary post of Lord Great Chamberlain, confirmed her position at a pinnacle of pre-war British society, reflected in the multiple portraits by the family's friend, John Singer Sargent. Over a seventy-year period at the Norfolk family seat, Houghton, and at their magnificent London home at 12 Kensington Palace Gardens, she pursued her intensive cultural interests, particularly in music. Although Sybil was not a society hostess in the conventional sense, her intimate dinner parties for musicians were nonetheless appreciated, particularly by Arthur Rubinstein and Toscanini.

After first meeting Toscanini in 1935, Sybil conceived a long-term but never consummated passion for him; thereafter she was a constant attendant at his concerts, including the Oxford excursion, and accompanied him on his Glynde-bourne visits. Toscanini first complained to Ada of her attentions (and on this occasion Yvonne's) while still in London in June 1937, repeating his complaints and his embarrassment about Sybil more explicitly a few weeks later in a letter to Ada from the Isolino.[58]

Matters came to a temporary head after Sybil wrote from Paris on 30 June to Toscanini at the Isolino, professing her love for him in the most sincere and touching terms: being 'just a "cosy friend"' was hard to bear; 'my life is ... dedicated to that love, it is the only good and perfect thing in it. It has blossomed for you & by you & I always want to be worthy.' She could not bear to cause him worry but 'I can

---

[58] ATL pp. 258 (letter to AM from London, 14 June 1937), 266 (letter to AM from the Isolino, 5 July 1937) and 272 (letter to AM from Salzburg, 28 July 1937); see also Stansky pp. 211–12.

endure anything except not seeing you sometimes'. She was coming to Salzburg to
see him conduct: she 'hardly dared think of that but it makes my whole life golden'.
She accepted that he would be surrounded by others, but 'I shall be near you sometimes & I shall be happy & content just to be with you'. After Sybil arrived in
Salzburg, as Toscanini told Ada, he 'tried to give her paternal advice, but it's all been
futile. I find myself in an embarrassing and slightly ridiculous situation.' He showed
her letters to Ada with the comment, combining compassion and good humour,
that they 'will give you an idea of my comical status with respect to this kind, dear
lady, with whom I have always had a most cordial friendship'.

The friendship, as we shall see, continued for several years. But, profoundly sympathetic though Toscanini was to the plight of German Jewry and to Jewish aspira-
tions generally, some disobliging remarks in the cited letters about the Jewish
ancestry of these women showed that, by their constant attentions, he sometimes
felt he was their 'victim' on his London visits. In any event, much as he was partial
to the attention of younger women, he was too engrossed in his relationship with
Ada Mainardi to take advantage of anything other than the lavish entertainments
proffered by these would-be inamorata; and always to Ada he addressed his frequent
but resigned complaints about their unlooked-for pressures.

The two final concerts

Refreshed by his varied entertainments and expeditions, Toscanini returned on 10
June to rehearsals for the last two concerts. The fifth concert on 14 June once again
offered a miscellany of works of wildly varying gravity that nonetheless drew critical
hosannas. At one stage Toscanini intended to programme Haydn's Symphony No.
98, which had joined his repertoire in a recent Vienna Philharmonic concert, but
he decided eventually to adhere to his first preference for the BBC concert, Mozart's
great G minor Symphony.[59] Perhaps surprisingly his performance was widely
approved, Capell in the *Telegraph* on 15 June, for example, regarding it as the most
memorable item of all. That day's *Times* called it 'robust': 'delicate nuances are not
allowed to divert attention from the broad sweep of the rhythm, though they are
always present at need to add the final touch'. Britten thought the performance
simply 'quite a lovely show'.[60] By contrast, in his detailed study of Toscanini

---

[59] ATL p. 247 (letter to AM, 8 April 1937); Toscanini first conducted Haydn's Symphony No. 98
in Vienna on 25 April 1937.
[60] Britten p. 437.

performances Spike Hughes expressed his disappointment at length (the London performance was 'a very dismal experience indeed') and Toscanini's interpretation, strongly influenced by descriptions of Bülow's passionately driven approach, has remained controversial.[61]

Most fully acclaimed were Sibelius's *En Saga* and Debussy's *Iberia*, the latter for the *Times* of 'scintillating brilliance'; for Capell of a 'dark and sensuous beauty' which 'can never have been more ardently believed in or realised'; and for Britten in his diary a 'splendid' performance of a 'great, adorable' piece. Many years later Toscanini remembered how well the orchestra executed *En Saga*, especially the long and difficult arpeggio passages;[62] but moments in *Iberia* caused difficulty in rehearsal, especially the viola/oboe solo in the first movement where only constant repetition and experiments (such as adjacent seating for the two soloists), during which Toscanini was patient to a fault, produced ensemble and intonation sufficiently exact to satisfy him.[63] Still, after the performance he was heard to mutter that he would never conduct it again: getting the balance he wanted was just too difficult.[64] In fact, he conducted many further performances and it became a favoured touring vehicle with the NBC orchestra.

The last concert two nights later, consisting of Wagner excerpts, repeated some of the items heard two years before with even finer results, at least in the estimation of those, such as Bonavia in the *Telegraph* on 17 June, who heard both. 'Even the last run of the violins [in the *Faust Overture*], a notorious snag, was soft, unanimous and crystal clear. The [*Siegfried*] *Idyll*, superbly played by the reduced strings, set also in relief the qualities of the woodwind, which seemed purged of original sin.' Likewise for that day's *Times*, 'all had a beauty unmatched in one's experience', with a *Siegfried's Rhine Journey* that had 'besides tenderness, a towering heroic stature'.

Fritz Busch, again taking time off from Glyndebourne, was more doubtful about Toscanini's *Rhine Journey*. In describing the concert in his July letter to Adolf,[65] he also responded to his brother who had expressed incredulity at Fritz's forgoing the opportunity of hearing Toscanini ('*such* a man') conduct *Falstaff*,

---

[61]   Hughes 1959 p. 170. Toscanini never saw Bülow conduct but Puccini's description of witnessing Bülow's Mozart G minor Symphony in the 1890s, with 'bite in the strings' and a 'strongly pas- sionate' first theme, provided Toscanini with the key to a work he had until then found puzzling: Taubman p. 301. Toscanini continued to regard Bülow as an 'incomparable artist' (ATL p. 342, letter to Bülow's daughter Daniela Thode, 19 August 1938); see further Annex C pp. 297–8.

[62]   Matthews 1966 p. 126, Matthews 1982 p. 72.

[63]   Shore 1938 p. 171.

[64]   Broadcast talk by Alex Nifosi.

[65]   Adolf Busch vol. 2 p. 370, 27 July 1937.

Meistersinger and *Fidelio* in Salzburg that August. For Fritz, this Wagner concert gave pleasure – up to a point: it 'had incredible things in it, and I learned a lot', he said; but 'the programme was hideous, and I heard a number of notes … that I had never heard in Wagner heretofore, as he didn't write them' – he referred here to the 'highly unusual' arrangement of the *Rhine Journey* with Toscanini's own concert ending. And in answering Adolf's enthusiastic devotion to the Maestro, the more hard-headed and less idealistic Fritz observed that 'one ought not to stop being objective, especially when one is in love'; so he preferred to work and rest amid the idyllic surroundings of Glyndebourne rather than undergo the 'abhorrent' commotion of Salzburg.

Critics, however, were undoubtedly 'in love': some, such as Bonavia, Lambert and Walter Legge, without restraint, others in tones more measured. Those with the space at their disposal – and far more was dispensed then than now – analysed the Toscanini operation at length. In particular, although Newman was brief in his coverage of individual concerts, he spent successive Sunday articles on the subject, summarising his conclusions by quoting a player who 'said the other day when asked why it was that the orchestra thought so highly of Toscanini, "Because we feel we are being brought face to face with the truth."'[66] As for those paying for their seats, Toscanini himself remarked to Ada that, 'I can't begin to describe the audience's frenzy'.[67] The phenomenon had reached a peak about which, as his correspondence with Ada showed, the conductor was anxious to tell her as evidence of his continuing youthful vitality.

Just one voice later communicated a retrospective reserve – as ever, that of the more insular element of the establishment in the *Musical Times*. Recovering from its subdued enthusiasm in 1935, the journal, with a conspectus of the whole series again penned by William McNaught, summed up its view of Toscanini as a symphonic conductor:[68] the performances in which Toscanini 'most actively expresses himself' could not include the Mozart or the Brahms symphonies, since 'few would give classical symphonies a high place among Toscanini's power' – a viewpoint at odds with the rest of the critical fraternity which, as the preceding pages have demonstrated, valued the conductor most fully in precisely that repertoire. Still, Toscanini was 'a supremely gifted observer' who saw 'everything that is visible and implied in the score' and composed an interpretation to express those elements in

---

[66] *Sunday Times* 27 June 1937.
[67] ATL p. 259 (letter to AM, 18 June 1937).
[68] Vol. 78 July 1937 p. 644.

full. This approach produced arresting results in the 'hackneyed' Wagner concert and in the Shostakovich symphony, given 'a new air of balanced thought and sweet reason' where earlier performances pictured it merely 'as a field of wild oats'. Elsewhere the Toscanini dazzle was clearly too blinding for this observer whose circumlocutory efforts to diagnose his reservations toppled into verbal paradox – 'he seems to need the whip in order to show the power of his curb' – before conceding at the close that from beginning to end the orchestral playing was 'electric and luminous. The players knew, better than the listeners, that to go through half a dozen Toscanini concerts was an experience of a lifetime.'

CHAPTER 5

THE FIRST HMV RECORDING SESSION

Persuasion

In the ordinary course Toscanini would have left the country on 17 June, the day after the final concert of the 1937 Festival, but two important pieces of business detained him an extra day. Such had been the level of enthusiasm for the Festival and so content was Toscanini with the orchestra that, not only did he agree in principle to a further Festival in 1938, but on the morning of 17 June he was happy to sign an agreement with Mase for two autumn concerts in the orchestra's forthcoming standard series, to take place in October/November.[1] As he recognised, this agreement made it impossible for him to fulfil the Paris plans for *Pelléas* on or around the same dates.[2] He had in any case been in some doubt about the motives of impresarios involved and the vocal estate of the proposed Mélisande: fourteen years had elapsed since Fanny Heldy (now forty-nine) had sung that *Louise* which occasioned his 'indisposition' for a Royal Philharmonic Society engagement and eleven since she had sung her renowned Mélisande under his baton at La Scala. Moreover, further weighting the scales in favour of the BBC, the two autumn concerts would enable Toscanini to redeem the promise made at his press conference in 1935 to conduct a British choir, since the two principal works in the planned programmes were to be Brahms's *German Requiem* and Beethoven's Ninth Symphony. The Verdi *Requiem*, also mentioned in 1935, would have to await the next Festival.

The second piece of business on 17 June was a recording session with HMV engineers. In advance of the 1937 Festival visit Toscanini forbade any recordings of

---

[1]   BBCA, BBC memorandum, 17 June 1937.
[2]   ATL p. 259 (letter to AM, 19 June 1937). As to Heldy, see ATL p. 244 (letter to AM, 2 April 1937).

FIG. 22 TOSCANINI AT HIS HOME IN RIVERDALE, NEW YORK, IN THE 1950s WITH
(l. to r.) MRS CHOTZINOFF, LADY AND SIR LOUIS STERLING, DAUGHTER-IN-LAW
CIA (FORNAROLI) AND SAMUEL CHOTZINOFF

the kind made by HMV in 1935. Furthermore, in February 1937 both Boult and
Mase rebuffed advances by Rex Palmer urging that proper recordings be made to
avoid the risk of record piracy abroad.[3] Mase pointed out that, since Toscanini had
forbidden any shortwave broadcasts, there would be no such risk, while Boult
remarked that, far from wanting to make new recordings, Toscanini would prefer
to withdraw those he had already made. How, then, was Toscanini's volte-face
accomplished? Within HMV Gaisberg was, from Toscanini's viewpoint, tainted by
his part in the ill-fated 1935 concert recordings. Sir Louis Sterling, Managing
Director of EMI, was aware of the ill feeling between Toscanini and Gaisberg and
gave instructions to Palmer to sideline Gaisberg as tactfully as possible in any
matters relating to the Maestro during 1937.[4] Sterling was fully mindful of the
sensitivities involved: he intimated that, rather than wound Gaisberg, he was
prepared to sacrifice Toscanini. That such sacrifice proved unnecessary was in itself
a tribute to this businessman of warm and hospitable character who at No. 7 Avenue
Road, near Regent's Park, kept open house for artists appearing in London. For
many, including Toscanini, the house became a second home, particularly in the
closed gloom of pre-war British Sundays; and it was doubtless there that Sterling

[3]   BBCA, letters Palmer to Boult, 9 February 1937; Boult to Palmer, 15 February 1937; Mase to
Palmer, 18 February 1937.
[4]   See Moore p. 211.

exercised his persuasive powers upon the conductor. Years later Gaisberg was to refer in his memoirs to 'Toscanini's friend Louis Sterling', fortunately wholly without rancour.[5] The friendship was to last many years.

But if it was Sterling who captured Toscanini for HMV, negotiations as to terms were conducted, not via the conventional channel of EMI's International Artistes' Department, but through the BBC's Owen Mase – no doubt at Toscanini's behest.[6] As well as according with the Maestro's very particular wishes, this unusual arrangement helped maintain conditions of utmost confidentiality; the curtains were drawn tight to ensure that nothing was publicly known that might cause the conductor to reconsider his agreement to record. By late summer the negotiations were successfully concluded and in the meantime Toscanini agreed to make some test recordings in the Queen's Hall on his last day in London.

17 June 1937

For this important event, which would decide the future of Toscanini's London recordings, Palmer was in administrative charge and Lawrance Collingwood[7] was in attendance, as he was to be at all future Toscanini/HMV sessions. The names of the technicians have not survived but the senior balance engineer and manager of the Abbey Road studios, Edward Fowler, must have been present. As with the financial negotiations, confidentiality was the watchword: no official session material survives about precisely what was recorded or when and, had not Toscanini himself written to Ada about the occasion, some of those details would have been lost. Moreover, the precautions taken to secure optimum working conditions attractive to the Maestro and to get the very best results were virtually unprecedented. Studio test recordings on the standard 12-inch HMV matrix series used at the Abbey Road studios (at the time the 2EA series) were commonplace and would have posed no exceptional problem; but it seems that Palmer and Collingwood guessed rightly that any attempt to entice Toscanini to record at Abbey Road would have been hazardous. Indeed, when they tried to do so the following year, their endeavours ended disastrously. But they also knew that recordings made at Abbey Road by

---

[5]   See Gaisberg pp. 202–3 and MacKenzie. Sir Louis Sterling (1879–1958), American-born businessman, with G&T from 1903, Managing Director Columbia 1918, Managing Director EMI (from merger) 1931, knighted 1937, left EMI in 1940 following a history of boardroom differences with EMI's Chairman, Alfred Clark: Martland pp. 104 and 147–8.

[6]   EMI, HMV to Edward Wallerstein, RCA, 5 August 1937, referring to 'negotiations … conducted through the medium of the BBC', meaning Mase.

[7]   See Ch. 3 and n. 8.

means of direct landline transmissions from the Queen's Hall, the course adopted for Toscanini's 1935 concerts, were not yet acceptable to him.

To circumvent all the problems, on 17 June the engineers recorded Toscanini and the BBC orchestra in the Queen's Hall direct on to test recordings, which, because side-breaks overlapped, required no break in continuity: the music could be performed from start to finish without interruption. These TT (Technical Test) matrices were used primarily for live events when start or finish or recording levels and the like could not be determined in advance.[8] They were now pressed into service to record Toscanini and the orchestra performing the first and second movements of the *Pastoral* Symphony, an obvious choice given that conductor and orchestra had already performed the work in concert twice that month, on 2 and 8 June. As Toscanini later wrote to Ada from the Isolino on 29 June, 'the last day [in London] I recorded the first two movements of the *Pastoral* to see whether they [HMV] make records well'.[9] During the session the engineers avoided the use of buzzers or lights; each movement was recorded complete, with a single signal to begin the performance of the movement, conditions which, as Palmer later remarked, 'were therefore practically that of an actual performance'.

Test discs were not intended for commercial issue and needed dubbing to other matrices to ensure satisfactory side-breaks. On various dates in June and July Toscanini's test recordings were therefore transferred in the Transfer Room at the Abbey Road studios on to matrices in the standard (2EA) series. The elaborate preparations for securing his approval of the dubbed transfers set a pattern for the future. Since he had retreated to the Isolino after his London concerts, tactically it seemed wise for HMV to take the test pressings there, despite its unreliable electricity supplies. But who was to be entrusted with the precious discs? Once again HMV turned to Mase for assistance, which he willingly gave. From the Isolino Toscanini wrote in the above-quoted letter that a 'BBC big-wig' (Mase) was coming that day, 29 June, 'to show me that they make *records* better than in New York' (the italicised word in English). On 5 July Palmer was able to inform Sterling of the success of Mase's island mission and of Toscanini's approval of the recording conditions in the Queen's Hall.[10] Moreover the conductor was very pleased with five out of the six dubbed test pressings and he promised Mase that he would complete

---

[8]   These technicalities are further explained in the Introduction to the Discography, Annex A p. 260.

[9]   'L'ultimo giorno feci due tempi primi della pastorale per provare se fanno bene i records'. New translation courtesy Harvey Sachs; cf. ATL p. 263.

[10]   EMI, Palmer's memorandum to Sterling, 5 July 1937.

his recording of the *Pastoral* when next in London. Palmer expected that Toscanini would also record two works by Brahms, the First Symphony and *Tragic Overture*, as well as Rossini's *William Tell* Overture; of these items, only the second was actually made.

Friends or rivals?

HMV's optimism was clouded only by complications with RCA, who were alerted by NBC's local agents to rumours of Toscanini's contacts with HMV. RCA cabled the agents to say that they did not wish to enter into competitive bidding with HMV, which would thereby raise costs for all concerned. They also asked HMV for details of their activities, complaining that they appeared to be in competition with RCA for Toscanini's services, a situation which they regarded as 'very foolish'. In Palmer's absence on holiday, Bicknell acted quickly and effectively to urge RCA to prevent NBC agents competing and to maintain confidentiality about HMV's own negotiations. On 5 August he warned RCA of the BBC's stipulation (doubtless direct from Mase) to observe 'the utmost secrecy' if they were 'to bring the negotiations to a successful conclusion'. As he explained, 'we have made great efforts to prevent the knowledge of our recording reaching the press or general public. Owing to the artiste's uncertain temper, premature disclosure might still jeopardise the success of our plans'. He attempted to mollify RCA with his concluding assurances that HMV never intended their negotiations to interfere with RCA's proposed recordings with the NBC Symphony and 'we see no reason why they should do so'.[11]

Bicknell's response proved so persuasive that RCA promptly furnished their wish list of prospective BBC SO recordings by Toscanini, including Beethoven's Fifth and Ninth symphonies, as well as the Brahms Fourth and various Haydn symphonies. Palmer countered in mid-August with HMV's own desired Toscanini repertoire list including, for the BBC orchestra, Beethoven's *Eroica* and Fifth, Sibelius's Fourth and Mozart's *Jupiter* symphonies, listing also a work that Toscanini never performed complete, Berlioz's *Symphonie fantastique*. For the Palestine Orchestra, somewhat tentatively Palmer further proposed overtures by Mendelssohn, in recognition of Toscanini's interest in the welfare of that orchestra with which he 'might be persuaded to make some records when next visiting Haifa'.[12] Such (from our present perspective) dream lists were unfulfilled; at that stage only completion of the *Pastoral* Symphony was in prospect.

[11]   EMI, HMV to Wetherald, RCA, 5 August 1937.
[12]   EMI, Wetherald, RCA, to HMV, 6 August 1937; Palmer to Wetherald, 16 August 1937.

CHAPTER 6

AUTUMN 1937: TWO CHORAL CONCERTS AND MORE RECORDS

Preparations and return

On 18 June Toscanini left London with relief for the Isolino where, as we have seen, he received Mase on 29 June. That visit was only one of Mase's activities at the time in furtherance of the Maestro's interests in London. He was in contact with the family (principally Carla) to conclude negotiations on behalf of HMV. In his capacity as a member of the Royal Philharmonic Society's Management Committee, he also sounded her out about the possibility of Toscanini accepting the Society's Gold Medal 'without ceremony or fuss' during his October visit.[1] And he persuaded Toscanini to relax his ban on the broadcasting of his two forthcoming autumn concerts abroad on shortwave frequencies,[2] a change of mind that led to NBC's agents in London concluding an agreement with the BBC for their transatlantic transmission. To Mase's persuasive powers, then, we owe the preservation, albeit in primitive sound, of Isobel Baillie's beautifully sung solo in the Brahms *Requiem* in the first of the two autumn concerts on 30 October.

For Toscanini himself, this was a period of rest and contemplation; the remarks on the beauty of nature in his letters to Ada from the Isolino are lyrical in the extreme. He was also making preparations for his engagements that summer at what was to prove his last Salzburg Festival. Events affecting these preparations caused him unwelcome stress in consequence of, as he saw it (with ample justification in contemporary circumstances), the unlooked-for presence of Furtwängler at the forthcoming Festival.[3] The international situation was no doubt one reason for his

---

[1]   BBCA, Mase's letter to Carla Toscanini, 9 July 1937.
[2]   BBCA, Mase's memorandum, 27 August 1937.
[3]   For Toscanini's remarks on nature, see ATL p. 262 (letter to AM, 25 June 1937). The Vienna authorities' invitation to Furtwängler to conduct at the 1937 Salzburg Festival angered Toscanini

reluctance to discuss his plans for the future with the many agents pressing round him throughout that August in Salzburg.

There was, however, one welcome arrival for whom Toscanini made, then as in the future, an exception: Owen Mase. One of only two outsiders allowed into Toscanini's Salzburg rehearsals, Mase discussed arrangements for the 1938 London Festival concerts with the conductor in the intervals of his work during the latter days of August, while other agents milled around in the vicinity in vain efforts to gain the Maestro's attention. Their talks centred on Toscanini's requirements for Verdi's *Requiem*, which the BBC were keen to mount. The omens were favourable. Toscanini regarded Mase's appearance at this juncture as almost heaven-sent: after his success with the Salzburg performance of the *Requiem* on 14 August, he had already expressed to Carla his wish to conduct it in London. Because of the sheer amount of labour and rehearsal involved, he wanted to perform it twice ('as I had anticipated', remarked Mase). He was, however, exacting about the choice of soloists: he wanted his Salzburg quartet – Zinka Kunz, Kerstin Thorborg, Helge Roswaenge and Alexander Kipnis – a stellar and expensive cast by comparison with the British-based soloists in prospect for the London Ninth Symphony. In any case, Kipnis was not available for 1938; of the alternatives discussed, Toscanini preferred Josef von Manowarda and for the moment got his way. Characteristically, Mase was exuberant about the success of his negotiations, particularly in persuading some of the distinguished soloists to agree to reduce their fees for the two performances of the *Requiem*.[4] After concluding his Salzburg engagements at the end of August, Toscanini took the cure at Bad Gastein for two weeks, welcoming Ada Mainardi in his isolation there before returning to the Isolino.

Typically, the conductor's preparation at the Isolino for the two BBC autumn concerts called for an intensive restudy of Beethoven's Ninth Symphony, even though it was wholly committed to memory and had featured in his final season with the Philharmonic in February 1936. His ecstatic correspondence with Ada after their time together illuminated his approach to a work he held in supreme reverence and, as to the first movement, dread. His restudy sparked a vision of the Adagio recorded in a late September letter: 'Elysian Fields, Paradise – I feel what is inexpressible. It lifts me off the earth, removes me from the field of gravity, makes

because, while that invitation appeared to him to be an act to please the German Nazi régime, the régime had refused to release the German singers needed for Toscanini's Salzburg operas. Eventually all the artists were released to participate in the 1937 Festival but Toscanini failed to stop Furtwängler's appearance there (ATL p. 270).

[4] Mase's negotiations with Toscanini were recorded in a memorandum for the BBC, 31 August 1937, BBCA.

me weightless.' Where the music modulated to E flat (bar 83), he always, he said, conducted with eyes closed, so intense was his vision of 'bright lights far, far away', of moving, disembodied shadows penetrated by rays, whence the music seemed to be descending – a 'mysterious spell that wraps around me during those sixteen bars'. And so this remarkable paean to the ineffable continued, diverted by his chance alighting a few days later on a BBC broadcast of the work under Sir Henry Wood with, as he remarked to Ada, 'the same [forces] I'll have next month'. Unfortunately Wood, as Toscanini put it, transformed the first movement into a funeral march, went 'completely off the rails' in the scherzo taken at ♩.= 138 instead of the 'just right' 116, made the Adagio adagissimo and boring, and the finale so choppy as to anger his distinguished listener before he found refuge in sleep – 'And besides calling himself a maestro, he is also a *Sir*. Incredible!'[5] By the time Toscanini reached London he was 'full of dread at the thought of confronting that *colossal, marvellous first movement*' which he always felt he was doing for the first time and never understood well enough. Over bar 512, where the louring passage in the coda commences, he inscribed his score with Dante's words marking the Gate to Hell which resounded in his brain every time he conducted the passage: 'it's enough to make you quake!'[6]

More recordings

After further engagements with the Vienna Philharmonic in Salzburg, Vienna and Budapest, Toscanini arrived in London by air from Vienna on Monday 18 October. His first task was to audition Isobel Baillie as soprano soloist for the Brahms *Requiem*, which he did without fuss at the Queen's Hall.[7] 'She sings right in the middle of the note', he is reported to have remarked; and, later on, 'Che bella voce'. But he was doubtless also taken by her musical intelligence, the quality he always sought in his singers, the absence of which in one eminent vocalist during the 1938 Festival was to lead to his agonised frustration.

Soon after this audition he plunged into two days of rehearsals of the Brahms with the BBC Chorus and Choral Society; he found them well prepared and ever afterwards spoke warmly of the chorusmaster Leslie Woodgate. The concerts, as he proudly remarked to Ada, were already sold out, with a ballot again necessary to

---

[5] ATL pp. 298, 301 and 307 (letters to AM, 29 September, 3 and 24 October 1937).

[6] In Sachs's translation, the lines Toscanini inscribed on the score read: 'Through me one goes into the sorrowing city,/Through me one goes into eternal sorrow,/Through me one goes among the lost people' (see ATL p. 308).

[7] Baillie p. 56, Donald Brook *Singers of Today* London: Rockliff 1949 p. 31.

cope with the 14,000 applications for tickets: 'so the old maestro is still of interest'.[8] On this and future occasions he stayed at the Langham Hotel close by the Queen's Hall, which he found he preferred to Claridge's.

For the following three working days, Thursday 21, Friday 22 and Monday 25 October, he was in the Queen's Hall for more HMV sessions, during which he recorded Beethoven's *Pastoral* and First symphonies and Brahms's *Tragic Overture*. Palmer and, as always, Collingwood, attended, together with (according to surviving documentation for the *Pastoral* alone) three engineers, Edward Fowler, Arthur Clarke and Douglas Larter. Unlike the session on 17 June, these recordings were not made continuously throughout each movement; instead Toscanini was persuaded to pause for about five seconds between sides, with a manual signal given by Palmer to recommence. Two machines recorded each take, one relayed by landline from the hall to Abbey Road, the other to HMV's mobile recording van outside the hall. 'In this way', remarked Palmer in a letter to O'Connell some months later, 'the tension was maintained and the orchestra did not relax until the end of the movement.'[9] Although later events suggest that even these short pauses taxed his patience, Toscanini's ever-present desire for continuity of musical line and thought was to some degree met by the decision to record the whole of the *Pastoral* Symphony on 21–22 October, even though he had approved the dubbed June recording of the Andante during Mase's island visit at the end of July. The June version of the Andante was, indeed, used in the issued records and the recording of that movement made in the October sessions was scrapped.

Toscanini's letters to Ada document the growth of his hostility to the microphone.[10] On 24 October he simply noted that he was recording the three works; but on the evening of 25 October he described two sessions that day totalling almost six hours which 'knocked me out', in the morning rehearsing the first movement of Beethoven's Ninth, in the afternoon recording (according to available documentation with Edward Fowler as the sole engineer) Beethoven's First Symphony and the Brahms *Tragic Overture*: 'these recording sessions are killers for me! I even finish up with a headache – an illness virtually unknown to me.'

Nevertheless, he was well enough pleased with the sound that HMV captured;[11]

---

[8] ATL p. 304 (undated letter to AM, October 1937). In preparing his chorus, Woodgate was assisted at the piano by the 22-year-old Charles Groves (see Robert Ponsonby *Musical Heroes* London: dlm 2009 p. 37).

[9] EMI, Palmer to O'Connell, 25 March 1938.

[10] See ATL p. 307.

[11] ATL p. 313 (letter to AM, 17 November 1937).

according to HMV's optimistic assessment to RCA in early November, 'Signor Toscanini has expressed himself as being delighted with the result'. Indeed, HMV could hardly suppress their jubilation: by the end of October they secured Toscanini's approval of the complete *Pastoral* Symphony, which, despite his earlier approval of all but one of the June dubbings of the opening Allegro, included the new recording of that movement. The symphony was promptly issued the following month. Toscanini also approved the *Tragic Overture* and all but the first part of the Beethoven First Symphony's finale, which awaited re-recording on his next visit. This last disappointment was mitigated by HMV's decision to issue the *Tragic Overture* with the First's scherzo as a fourth-side filler; when completed, the First Symphony on seven sides would have a single-sided scherzo, thereby enabling purchasers of both recordings to avoid duplication. Purchasers of US RCA Victor pressings, however, had to await completion of the First Symphony's recording in 1938, when it was issued paired, rather incongruously, with the *Tragic Overture* in a single album.

Meanwhile, HMV had the satisfaction of planning with RCA their further recordings with Toscanini for sessions in the spring of 1938 to take place during the next London Music Festival. HMV were eager to take up Toscanini's suggestions of Beethoven's *Coriolan* and Rossini's *La scala di seta* overtures, but 'unfortunately' he also suggested *Pictures at an Exhibition*, which RCA had just recorded with Ormandy and the Philadelphia Orchestra (HMV were apparently unaware that, while Toscanini performed only Ravel's orchestration, Ormandy had used the version by Lucien Cailliet); HMV countered Toscanini's suggestion by proposing the *Eroica* Symphony to him.[12] Regrettably, only the Maestro's preferred Rossini was to bear fruit.

Two concerts, several diversions

In the midst of the recording sessions Toscanini received Chaim Weizmann, leader of the World Zionist Organisation, who advised him against his impending second visit to Palestine contrary to urgent promptings from Tel Aviv; disturbances between Jewish settlers and Palestinian Arabs would present unacceptable risks for the conductor.[13] Toscanini accepted Weizmann's advice and postponed his trip until the following April. The attempted manipulations from Tel Aviv scarcely improved the

[12]   EMI, Palmer to Wetherald, RCA, 3 November 1937; Palmer to Wallerstein, RCA, 4 November 1937.
[13]   Chaim Weizmann (1874–1952) first President of Israel in 1948; see ATL p. 307 (letter to AM, 24 October 1937).

ill temper aroused by the recording sessions and it was with relief that he turned to further rehearsals for the two concerts.[14] On 27 October he reported to Ada, 'it's very easy to rehearse with this orchestra. For me, it's superior to all others, at least for its magnificent discipline.' In some sessions he was in obvious good humour. When baritone Harold Williams's opening recitative in the Ninth Symphony's finale was sung too strictly in tempo, the conductor corrected him in his own fashion: 'Why you sing so correct? It must be rubato, rubato, rubato. Sing it freely. Who told you to sing it so correct?' On hearing that it was Koussevitzky, Toscanini, ever the cellist, exclaimed 'Oh, der bass player!'[15] And he assured soprano Isobel Baillie that, if his *poco adagio* tempo for the quartet's last passage in that movement made it 'very, very difficult, I will take it a little faster – it will not harm the music'.[16]

There were also pleasures outside the hall. One diversion which indulged Toscanini's love of Shakespeare was a 'magnificent performance' of *Richard II* at the Queen's Theatre on Shaftesbury Avenue, with the 'marvellous' John Gielgud directing and leading the cast, the staging in 'exquisite taste and thoroughly worked out'.[17] Another fruitful visit was to the British Museum to view the score of the Ninth Symphony sent by Beethoven to the Philharmonic Society which Toscanini was eager to see in order to find out what light it might throw on certain textual problems in the work.[18] He spent a considerable time examining Beethoven's annotations and admiring other scores in the collection.

As for the Society itself, in response to Mase's query earlier in the year Toscanini felt gratified by its wish to present him with the Gold Medal but could not undergo a public presentation; so Mase arranged a small private lunch party attended by fellow musicians when the medal was given without ceremony 'except the expression of our affectionate regard for him',[19] after which it remained one of his prized possessions. Another distinguished Beethovenian, Felix Weingartner, had already received the medal at the usual public presentation in a concert interval in March that year. The

---

[14]   ATL p. 308.

[15]   Shore 1938 p. 7. Baillie recounts the same incident but in her version of events it was Williams's singing of the final word of his recitative in a single breath ('freudenvollere' according to her, although the performance was sung in English) which sparked Toscanini's comments (see Baillie p. 57).

[16]   Parry Jones's untitled memoir in *Opera* vol. 8 no. 3 March 1957 p. 141.

[17]   ATL pp. 308–9 (letter to AM, 28/29 October 1937). Sir John Gielgud (1904–2000) British actor and finest exponent of Shakespeare's verse. This *Richard II* was one of his triumphs, 'one of the rarest blazes of theatrical light this century' (Harold Hobson in the *Sunday Times*; see Robert Morley *John G – The Authorised Biography of John Gielgud* London: Hodder 2001 pp. 152–4).

[18]   Boult 1983 p. 90.

[19]   Mase *Memories*.

presentation of a second medal within about six months, an exception to the Society's usual practice, demonstrated its wish to honour Toscanini at the first opportunity.[20]

The good humour engendered by such diversions could not last. Wood's September broadcast of the Ninth Symphony with BBC forces upon which Toscanini chanced gave forewarning of trouble to come. On 28 October Toscanini cut short a rehearsal after less than an hour when, in the first movement of the Ninth, he felt the orchestra was not giving its utmost. As Mase reported to his colleagues, 'the incident was really very trivial. Toscanini thought it would be better to abandon the rehearsal ... so he stopped it and walked out ... he told me he still thinks it is one of the finest orchestras there is.'[21] He left behind an invited and distinguished handful of spectators, including the Queen of Spain, Vaughan Williams and Alfred Cortot; the last-named, Toscanini later remarked, was in tears afterwards – so it seemed that 'something a little out of the ordinary emerged'. He restored his equanimity with the theatre visit already referred to; but his walkout inevitably fed the press with precisely the sensation for which, given his reputation, it had long been waiting. The incident was duly reported, but with such a degree of fabrication by the *Telegraph* that it had to withdraw the report, which dilated on a passage allegedly in the *third* movement inaccurately played by the oboe – a slight on the remarkable if eccentric Terence MacDonagh, lately graduating to the principal's chair. Once started, however, the press was fed by another incident, when Toscanini allegedly struck out at a flashbulb-wielding photographer outside the Langham Hotel on his way to rehearsal and accidentally hit Carla, who was intervening between them; later Toscanini termed this incident 'pure fabrication' by reporters.[22]

Despite, perhaps in part because of, this sensationalist publicity, the two concerts on 30 October and 3 November were triumphs with the public and, on the whole, with the critics. The latter received the Brahms *Requiem* with respect rather than huge enthusiasm, although any reservations were principally on account of the nature of the work itself: despite its popularity with the major choral societies, its reputation had perhaps not fully recovered from Bernard Shaw's contemptuous dismissal a generation or more before – 'patiently borne only by the corpse'. Britten naturally loathed the work, but thought that Toscanini's efficiency and inspiration obviously discerned 'what was at the back of [Brahms's] mind, and what he hadn't the skill to put on

[20] The list of Society Gold Medallists in Elkin pp. 134–5 shows an irregular pattern of frequency after the initial batch in 1871 but between the two World Wars there were other instances of two presentations in one year on only three occasions, 1925, 1930 and 1934.

[21] Kenyon pp. 139–40.

[22] ATL p. 315 for this and the other 'fabrication' outlined below.

paper'.[23] More conventionally, the *Times* on 1 November pointed to the superb balance and sense of line achieved with a modest choir of only one hundred voices. The conductor gave the impression of 'intense concentration on each moment as it passes', yet 'the size and shape' of each movement was his primary concern, with slow tempos that were 'inexorable'. If there was some critical reserve, principally from Cardus who on the same day categorised Toscanini's tempos in this 'woeful and pious' work as 'rigid and austere', everyone agreed about Isobel Baillie's 'angelic' contribution (Capell's term), while Turner in the *New Statesman* on 6 November praised the preceding *Tragic Overture* for providing the finest orchestral playing London had recently experienced. With typical idiosyncracy, he also criticised aspects of the choral singing in the *Requiem* about which others were unanimous in their praise – but these failings were no fault of the conductor: 'that would be quite impossible, for every musician worth his salt must recognise that Toscanini is a real master, a conductor such as we shall probably not hear for another hundred years'.

Toscanini's wish that the concert should close in silence and without applause was insufficient to damp an initial outburst of enthusiasm. Allegedly he declined to take a bow, duly reported again as a minor sensation in the popular press; but once more Toscanini later described such reports as a fabrication.

Nor did matters proceed entirely smoothly at the second concert, Beethoven's First and Ninth symphonies. Anticipation about this, Toscanini's first London Ninth, was immense; but it started six minutes late to allow royalty (the Duke and Duchess of Kent) and Prime Minister Neville Chamberlain, delayed by typical London fog, to take their seats, drawing many a sigh from the impatiently pacing conductor backstage: 'what a life!' he finally shrugged to the attendant soloists. The delay was such that, awaiting the shortwave transmission in New York, NBC felt obliged to fill in time with an unscheduled anonymous string orchestra contribution; but the wait also gave Helen Henschel, daughter of the late Sir George and present at rehearsals, opportunity to lean over and whisper to budding pianist Denis Matthews, 'you have never heard anything like the first movement'.[24]

Indeed, no-one had. For the first time the press was less than unanimous in its overall verdict, with reviews spanning the whole gamut. Augmenting his relatively restrained animadversions earlier in the year, Cardus, in the *Manchester Guardian* on 4 November – now without restraint – thought the first movement revealed 'a complete indifference to the music's usual emotional significance': with tempos

---

[23]   Britten p. 460; for Shaw's remark see Shaw vol. 1 p. 19.

[24]   Baillie p. 60, Matthews 1982 p. 71. Helen Henschel (1882–1973) singer and broadcaster. Denis Matthews (1919–88) British pianist, author and broadcaster.

'hammered out inexorably ... the symphony thundered over intimacy of expression like a juggernaut. The rigid precision cast a fierce light on everything.' Yet even for him there were many wonderful moments and in the finale 'Toscanini seemed to comprehend all things ... it was in its finish and extent a cosmic scheme which had no use for the nuance of merely mortal pathos'. On the same day both the *Times* and Bonavia approved but kept their heads. In contrast to Cardus, the former heard the first movement as 'boldly carved, but the time was anything but rigid', while the last movement, with a choir over twice as large as that for the *German Requiem*, kept its 'dithyrambic character ... without any sacrifice of the purely musical detail'.

Bonavia expanded his *Telegraph* notice for a detailed report on Toscanini's achievement in the *New York Times* on 21 November, one of the most acute pieces of observation ever penned about Toscanini's approach to the Ninth. Not for the first time apropos Toscanini, Bonavia invoked the shade of another hallowed master, pointing out that, although the pace of the second movement's Trio sounded rapid, it was not more so than Richter's. Moreover, the first movement, although quick in tempo, 'slackened very slightly in one or two places for the sake of clarity and in order to give a rapid passage time to make its full effect felt'. In the scherzo 'titans hurled defiance at one another' but without excess; and if the timpani solos sounded loud, 'the effect was obtained by the careful grading of dynamic force elsewhere, not by brute effort'. The Adagio rose to an 'irresistible eloquence' in the D major episode and somehow the conductor persuaded his second violins 'to play with the quality of tone seldom heard in first violins', with the 'exquisite embroidery subservient to the main theme' but made to tell 'by the perfect equilibrium of each contributory part'.

At the opposite pole from Cardus, and with an acuity of observation virtually Bonavia's equal, Constant Lambert in the *Sunday Referee* on 7 November, delivering his last piece about Toscanini, indulged in a rhetorical opening gambit under the headline 'The Genius of Toscanini'. How, he asked, could he possibly convey to someone not present at the concert that Toscanini's performance of the Ninth's first movement was 'the best performance ever given of the greatest symphonic movement ever written? One can analyse talent but one can't analyse genius.' Lambert did his best to supply an answer to his outsize question. Toscanini, he said, 'never obscures the main design of the work by spotlighting details. He conducts in one unbroken line' – which did not mean Lambert took the 'idiotic view' according to which Toscanini always followed the score and never varied his tempo. 'Passages that require a slight easing up are given it but the main curve of the rhythm remains unbroken.' Lambert thought him the greatest living Beethoven conductor because, 'with some miraculous telepathy, [he] seems able to live through and suffer the actual creative process of the composer'; so, for him, it was as if Beethoven himself were 'endowed with a conducting technique'. Remarkably, Toscanini's general approach during these concerts reminded Lambert of only one other conductor – Elgar: both had 'the same impetuous onrush, the same steady line, the same unobtrusive flexibility'.

Given that Lambert was a noted creative talent and, in the view of many, a first-rate conductor, his witness stood in significant contrast to the experienced but essentially amateur ear of Cardus; furthermore, his review as a whole penetrated the stylistic character of Toscanini's performances in the pre-war era as few others managed. The validity of the comparison with Elgar, examined in more detail in Chapter 2, is not here germane: what is relevant is that an outstanding musician with a composer's ear thought to draw it. Still, another and even finer composer, but at the time a lesser critic, took a rather different view: for Britten, although the concert was a 'magnificent example of disciplined playing' and the First Symphony 'grand', the Ninth's first movement 'raced along and all majesty was lost', although the scherzo was 'terrific' and the end 'glorious'.[25] That first movement, in a series of Toscanini renditions stretching from 1936 to his 1952 RCA recording, continued to divide opinion. However, as younger, mainline orchestral conductors in the next century, such as Riccardo Chailly and Gianandrea Noseda, outpaced Toscanini in the movement, his performances took their place in musical history, prescient of things to come but with an instinctive flexibility others lacked.

Toscanini departed for Milan on 4 November; not, however, before sending on to Ada a brace of letters from attendant London society hostesses (Margot Asquith and Yvonne Rothschild) still professing their perpetual devotion, to his amusement and irritation. He disappointed Sybil Cholmondeley by his failure to contact her on arrival but there is little doubt that she met him once more, if only at the rehearsals that she asked permission to attend. On the day of his departure her telegram to him in Milan, referring to the previous evening's weather that delayed the start of the Ninth Symphony, mourned that 'the only fog now is the unhappiness of your going away which is more lasting and harder to endure'.[26]

A week before, on the very day of his truncated rehearsal of the Ninth Symphony, Toscanini indicated his continuing satisfaction with London by signing an agreement with Mase for six concerts in the following year – the 1938 London Music Festival.

[25] Britten p. 461.
[26] See ATL pp. 305, 310 (letters to AM, 22 October and 3 November 1937) and Stansky p. 212.

||: CHAPTER 7

1938: THE LONDON MUSIC FESTIVAL 1938

Changes and exchanges

Soon after Mase contracted Toscanini for the 1938 Festival, he decided that his various interests, including the personal connection forged with the conductor, would justify his pursuing a career as concert promoter and administrator outside the BBC structure. After leaving the corporation late in 1937 he began a prolonged process of co-opting a committee which would plan and direct the following year's London Music Festival; once in place, the committee duly appointed him Director of the Festival.[1] According to Sir Henry Wood's memoirs, Mase's 'release' from the corporation had 'the full blessing of the BBC';[2] but while relations between them necessarily remained close, the BBC cannot have been entirely happy for their erstwhile employee to assume a position as the (in substance) self-styled Director of the Festival, an event featuring their own orchestra and starring the most eminent of all conductors who was until then contracted (through Mase) with the corporation.

Tensions soon grew, stemming from Toscanini's complaint in February 1938 to NBC, quickly relayed to the BBC, that he had not received promised copies of the as yet unissued *Tragic Overture* recorded three months before. In fact Mase had arranged for copies to be sent by the quickest means possible from HMV to RCA in New York but RCA had failed to deliver them to Toscanini's home. As soon as he heard about the complaint, Mase sent an explanatory and propitiatory letter to Toscanini but at the same time, in a letter addressed to the BBC's North America correspondent Felix Greene, adjured him in the strongest terms not to allow NBC

[1]   Mase's speech prepared in 1939 for the launch of that year's Festival, in MA, explained the gestation of that and the previous year's Festivals, their management structure and aims; see further Ch. 8 p. 152.
[2]   Wood p. 335.

or anyone else to intervene in his negotiations with Toscanini on behalf of the BBC: 'I know my man better than anyone in the world, except his wife!'[3] Fortunately the Controller of Programmes and Deputy Director-General, Cecil Graves, to whom Mase copied his warning, agreed: Mase was, he pointed out, the sole channel for communication between the BBC and Toscanini in England and his dealings had been extremely successful where everybody else had failed.[4] 'Mase *does* understand Toscanini ... I think we must just agree to adopt whatever procedure Mase considers necessary. We have done this for two or three years and Mase has always been proved right.' The carte blanche Mase wanted was secure for the time being although it was to be challenged again. For the present he was to attend on Toscanini throughout his 1938 visit; for the future he was to conclude the agreements with him for BBC concerts, assigning them to the corporation for their execution. Whatever the BBC's reservations, there is no doubt that Mase's dealings with Toscanini, conducted, it is true, with a degree of possessiveness but also with complete integrity, were to the enormous benefit of London's musical life. The Toscanini connection was in any event only one string in Mase's bow: he was also appointed Director of Opera at Sadler's Wells theatre in 1937, where he was to entertain Toscanini during the two remaining Festivals, and until 1942 was a member of the Royal Philharmonic Society's management committee.[5]

As for the object of all this solicitude, Toscanini stayed in Milan for several weeks after his return from London in November 1937, preparing for his first season with the newly formed NBC Symphony Orchestra. His first concert with them took place in Studio 8H, New York City, on Christmas night 1937 and he stayed in New York until completion of his first RCA sessions with the orchestra in 8H on 7 and 8 March 1938. Over the two days he recorded Haydn's 88th and Mozart's G minor symphonies together with his frequently favoured string orchestra versions of the two inner movements from Beethoven's Op. 135 quartet. There followed what were to be Toscanini's final engagements with both the Residentie orchestra in The Hague and Rotterdam, for which Mase joined him, and the Palestine Orchestra. From Palestine he returned to Italy on 29 April for a brief stay before travelling on to

---

[3] BBCA, Mase to Felix Greene, copied to Graves, 11 February 1938. The whole incident is curious since Toscanini had already received at least one (? test) copy of the *Tragic Overture* recording, upon which he commented favourably in a letter to AM dated 17 November 1937 (ATL p. 313; see Ch. 6 n. 11). Probably he wanted copies of the already issued HMV pressings; as noted at p. 116, RCA delayed its issue until later in 1938.

[4] (Sir) Cecil Graves (1892–1957) later joint Director-General of the BBC 1942–44; see p. 178. Memorandum from Graves, 14 February 1938.

[5] In Mase's CV in MA.

London. Toscanini arrived there on 15 May for the six concerts of the 1938 Festival, the outstanding events of which were to be the two performances of Verdi's *Requiem* (preceded by the *Te Deum*) on 27 and 30 May. The day before his arrival, in an exchange of courtesies, Boult conducted the first of two concerts with the NBC Symphony; the second took place a week later and Boult returned to London in time for the last of Toscanini's series on 10 June.

Rehearsals for Toscanini's first concert started on 16 May. Two days later he made use of the top-of-the-range radiogram installed by HMV in his suite at the Langham Hotel, a facility also provided for his visit the following year. RCA had sent over to HMV test pressings of the NBC recordings, including the two symphonies;[6] and, with Palmer on hand to supervise the demonstration, Toscanini approved the Haydn and all but the Andante of the Mozart, which he thought lacked 'lightness and refinement'.[7] Although on this occasion he also disapproved the two movements from Op. 135, RCA later persuaded him to allow their publication.

HMV were for their own purposes deeply interested in RCA's methods and programme of recording. At the end of March Palmer asked O'Connell whether RCA had adopted HMV's method, used in the *Pastoral* Symphony, of dual machines stopping for five seconds at suitable moments or whether Toscanini had been willing to 'make each side separately, according to normal practice'; he needed to know in order to prepare for HMV's upcoming sessions with the Maestro. And what about RCA's recording of Toscanini conducting Beethoven's Ninth Symphony, of which HMV were aware but lacked all detail?[8] In his reply of 26 April, O'Connell disclosed that for the Haydn and Mozart symphonies RCA had used four turntables 'not interrupting the performance except at the end of a movement' and finding 'fairly satisfying interruption points' from which the occasional hangover reverberation could be eliminated. As for the Ninth Symphony, recorded in concert on 6 February, O'Connell had little hope of rescuing it since, not only had two bars been lost at the start of the finale – due to Toscanini commencing the movement without break from the Adagio – but 'the performance itself was not a distinguished one, and I am sure that if Mr Toscanini did hear the records he would reject them'. The latter explanation, while typical of O'Connell's attitude of distaste towards RCA's hottest conductorial property, was at the very least disingenuous, given New York's hyper-

---

[6]   EMI, Palmer to O'Connell, 19 May 1938.
[7]   ATL p. 336 (letter to AM, 19 June 1938).
[8]   EMI, Palmer to O'Connell, 25 March 1938; O'Connell to Palmer, 26 April 1938.

bolic press reaction to this Ninth and Toscanini's own euphoric post-concert report to Ada ('I was a devil. I conducted, I believe, as never before in my very long career ... The orchestra did wonders').[9] In any event, for the moment HMV ignored RCA's forewarning about uninterrupted recording methods; on 19 May Palmer was content to inform O'Connell of HMV's recording plans and to relay Toscanini's approval of most of RCA's efforts.

Two concerts and a soloist – Cardus and Newman agree

After experiencing a dozen BBC concerts with Toscanini in the Queen's Hall, there could have been no surprises for London audiences about either the miscellaneous character of some of his forthcoming programmes or the expected superlative level of the orchestra's accomplishment. The first concert on 19 May duly met these expectations: Mozart's *Magic Flute* Overture, Beethoven's Fourth Symphony, Vaughan Williams's *Tallis* Fantasia (the sole representative of British music in the series and Toscanini's first performance of a work by this composer), the Weber/Berlioz *Invitation to the Dance* and Smetana's *Vltava*. Such, however, was the level of musicianship of all concerned that any complaints about a programme featuring popular classics as a Festival item were stilled. For the *Times* on 20 May, in each item 'Toscanini captured the mood of the composer unerringly'. The first movement of the Beethoven was 'magnificently broad and measured', the Adagio had 'never sounded more lyrical' and the playing in the *Tallis* Fantasia 'made one feel that it had never been heard before in its full beauty'. Capell, in that day's *Telegraph*, agreed, the Beethoven 'memorable', the 'rare spirit' of the Vaughan Williams 'at once serene and passionate'; overall, the impression remained of the conductor's 'fierce and apostolic earnestness' and 'the sacredness of his trust'.

Cardus in the *Manchester Guardian* on 20 May, as was by now to be expected, disagreed with his colleagues, so much so that he might have been attending a different concert. Alone he judged the Beethoven 'as flawless as a machine and ... as impersonal': the chording in every fortissimo passage 'had the explosive exactitude of a railway train leaving a station ... in the end I for one longed for the freedom of humour'. But even he thought the *Tallis* Fantasia 'gorgeous' and, of the concert as a whole, 'there was no question, of course, that the greatest of all conductors was in action, exercising his power with a noble simplicity'.

With but one day's rest, rehearsals for the second concert on 23 May began on

---

[9]   ATL p. 324 (letter to AM, 9 February 1938).

the morning of 21 May. For the first time in a London Toscanini concert there was to be a major instrumental soloist, Emanuel Feuermann in Strauss's *Don Quixote*. Toscanini's earlier performances of the work with the Philharmonic featured his lead cellist, Alfred Wallenstein, a practice that certainly aided his ever-present desire for unity of conception and purpose in any work he conducted with solo performers. By mid-1938 Feuermann was by contrast accepted in the United States as the foremost cellist in the country, according to his own assessment – he was not shy of such self-appraisals, given that Casals had not toured the USA since 1928. But he had not yet achieved equivalent status in Britain and apparently was not the conductor's first choice: despite Enrico Mainardi's craven attitude towards the fascist regime,[10] it seems that Toscanini had initially suggested Ada's husband, perhaps on the strength of his 1933 recording of the work conducted by the composer.[11] As early as 25 November 1937 Mase wrote to Toscanini in Milan that the BBC did not consider Mainardi to be satisfactory: he had attended a recital given by the cellist in London and found that, although his intonation was 'generally good', his tone was not quite full enough for a concerto with orchestra.[12] Moreover, his readings 'suffered too much from being in separate compartments and one did not feel the work as a completely related whole'. Mase preferred Lauri Kennedy, another cellist admired by Toscanini, who had been leader of the cello section in both the BBC orchestra and Beecham's LPO; at Toscanini's request, he had returned to reinforce the BBC cello section in the 1937 Festival concerts. By March 1938, however, it became clear that Kennedy, now pursuing his own freelance career, would be on tour in Australia at the time of the forthcoming concert; and in mid-March Toscanini, then in The Hague, recommended Feuermann to the BBC.

Feuermann had already played the solo part in *Don Quixote* with the BBC orchestra during the second London Music Festival in 1934, on that occasion with Bruno Walter, meeting with modest critical approval – although Britten thought him (but not Walter) 'first rate'.[13] If Feuermann, despite his friendship with Walter, had reservations about his musical approach, Toscanini was a different matter: he 'was flat on his stomach in admiration of Toscanini. He loved his way of

[10] Sachs 1987 p. 157.

[11] By the Berlin Staatskapelle conducted by Richard Strauss, various Polydor 78 issues, Decca Polydor LY 6087–91, CD Dutton CDBP 9746.

[12] BBCA, Mase's letter to Toscanini in Italy, 25 November 1937. Toscanini recommended Feuermann, according to Mase's memorandum, BBCA, 18 March 1938, in which Mase also said that Lauri Kennedy was unavailable. Emanuel Feuermann (1902–42) Austro-American cellist.

[13] 11 May 1934; see Britten p. 211.

conducting.'[14] But what would Toscanini think of him, given the conductor's memory of his 'rotten' playing in Zürich a decade earlier, about which Feuermann unburdened himself when they first met in New York in February 1938?[15] Since Zürich, Toscanini had heard more of his work through radio broadcasts and he may also have heard some of the monumental series of four concerts with the National Orchestral Association under Leon Barzin in New York during February and March 1938 when the cellist played thirteen concertos, a series that confirmed him as supreme in critical opinion.[16] By the time Feuermann reached *Don Quixote* in that series, however, Toscanini was in Milan preparing for Palestine and the cellist approached the forthcoming BBC SO engagement in a state of nerves. He need not have worried: the Queen's Hall rehearsals went without incident and, as was usual with a soloist whom he respected and was musically in accord, Toscanini 'didn't say one word'.[17]

For both Toscanini and his soloists, including principal viola Bernard Shore as Sancho Panza, this central item of the concert on 23 May was an unreserved triumph. Gerald Moore later recalled that Feuermann 'created such a sensation that the Queen's Hall audience – Toscanini leading the applause – went wild with enthusiasm';[18] and the critics were likewise unanimous. Toscanini himself thought Feuermann 'played very well'.[19] The most extravagant encomiums were, however, reserved for the conductor's guiding hand in recreating a *Quixote* combining unprecedented structural clarity and vividness of characterisation. For the *Times* on 24 May, this was a 'magnificent' performance, with 'refinement and rhythmic point in every detail'. The music created 'a total impression of aristocracy without toning down the freakish and vulgar elements' – 'no small achievement'.

If the praise of this critic was unequivocal enough, the most significant pointer to Toscanini's achievement was the united critical hosannas from those polar opposites among musical commentators, Newman and Cardus. Their critiques provided

---

[14] Morreau p. 184 quoting his wife, Eva, in 1994. For Feuermann's differences with Walter, see Seymour W. Itzkoff *Emanuel Feuermann, virtuoso* Schweinfurt: Internationale Kammermusik-Akademie 1995 2nd ed. pp. 92 and 152.

[15] Morreau p. 177; ibid. for Toscanini's comment on Feuermann's 'rotten' playing.

[16] Morreau pp. 177 et seq. Morreau p. 183 suggests that Feuermann's *Don Quixote* on 27 March may have influenced Toscanini's choice, but the conductor had by then left the USA. Morreau pp. 180–1 quotes Feuermann's view of his own status in the USA, which reflected critical opinion at the time.

[17] Morreau p. 184, quoting Feuermann.

[18] Morreau p. 183, quoting the text of a BBC broadcast appreciation in 1942.

[19] ATL p. 333 (letter to AM, 24 May 1938).

on this occasion textbook examples of their profoundly different approaches, but for once reached unanimous conclusions. Cardus, in the *Manchester Guardian* on 25 May, used typically colourful, sometimes almost ecstatic language to describe his soul-baring reaction, intermixed, as was his habit, with meditations upon the nature of the music. In summary, he thought this performance was one of the conductor's finest, in which:

> Toscanini achieved a perfect fusion of parts, and the playing ... was constantly eloquent – now audacious, now vivid, now warm and wise, and always accurate, balanced, natural ... he seemed to create *Don Quixote* whole while we sat enchanted there ... The shape of the composition, its originality of technique in evolution of pattern and the weaving of a satisfying orchestral tissue – to these musical qualities were added splendour of dramatic and poetic vision. The music sang and spoke wit and poetry at one and the same time ... Nowhere did Toscanini miscalculate the style ... Toscanini caused the passage of the bleating sheep to sound – as seldom before has it sounded – a masterpiece of humorous onomatopoeia ... Again in the assault on the army of the Emperor Alifanfaron, the gorgeous comedy of Sancho's panic-stricken warnings was brought out as never before ... In none of the mainly realistic episodes was a point missed. The reflective or lyrical moments were dignified always. ... The death scene brought moisture to the eyes; Strauss was made to sound wise and not just sentimental ... And the gentleness of the coda: Toscanini translated it simply as 'once upon a time – long ago'. ... The closing emulations of appoggiatura were treated with a rare and heart-swelling beauty of curve. At the end of the work one conductor of fame in the audience was almost beside himself with admiration. 'To conduct such a performance, to make it all so real and beautiful!'

Newman, in the *Sunday Times* on 29 May, was typically more cautious, analytical, ever the rationalist – yet here exposed more explicitly than ever before his ongoing admission that the Toscanini operation lay in some respects beyond the scope of even his ample lexicon to pin down. Perhaps because of this admission, there was also a strong element of paradox in his analysis, which strove to convey the subtleties both of the performance and of his critical reaction to it. Although, Newman said, Strauss's textures were here 'crystal clear, with the smallest nuance indicated in the score made evident without being insisted on in the slightest degree', the performance's 'overwhelming effect' came about 'from something far subtler':

FIGS. 23–24 *DON QUIXOTE* SOLOISTS EMANUEL FEUERMANN AND BERNARD SHORE

Toscanini's peculiar virtue is not that he makes us hear a score sound as it is written ... The strange and paradoxical thing is that with all this fidelity to what is in the score ... Toscanini effaces his own personality in the act of asserting it. The total result is unmistakeably Toscanini and no-one else; but at the same time it is still more the work and the composer ... Instead of imposing his own imagination upon us, he liberates ours; we stand face to face with the work itself. ... We seemed to be looking at each incident in turn not through our own or the conductor's eyes but through Quixote's; even the sheep took their proper place in the scheme ... and became a real vision, one-third serious, one-third grotesque, one-third pathetic. Emanuel Feuermann and Bernard Shore played their parts worthily in a performance of the most extraordinary beauty and nobility.

Agreement between Newman and Cardus on the virtues of a Toscanini performance was rare and, until Cardus wrote once more about Toscanini's final London concert fourteen years later, this performance marked virtually their last coincidence of view.

The performance was preserved in recordings from the shortwave transmission, albeit in primitive sound with some discontinuities; an unfortunate consequence of the 1938 concerts being available for transmission to various European countries including Finland and Czechoslovakia, but not to the USA, where techniques for recording such relays were more sophisticated. Even so, what survives suggests an account of greater spontaneity and delight than the (still superlative) NBC broadcast with Feuermann in October 1938. Four years after the BBC concert, virtually to the day, Toscanini was a pallbearer at Feuermann's funeral in New York.[20]

For the opening Bach Second Brandenburg Concerto there was less enthusiasm ('thin and scratchy' strings, said Newman), despite the extreme care Toscanini lavished on its preparation. As shown by his correspondence, he had studied critically Adolf Busch's chamber orchestra performances; in September 1934 he attended the Busch Chamber Players' Brandenburg cycle in Basle[21] and he had a high regard for their 1935 recordings. But to Ada he wrote after the present concert[22] of his discovery 'after several years' of how to interpret a trill at the end of the Andante: 'I trill in the violin part, right in the last bar, which everyone including Busch omits ... I made the discovery very early yesterday morning [the day of the concert], while I was sitting at the piano (but not playing), and you can imagine my joy ...' His (roughly) Busch-sized small string orchestra, based on a complement of four first and second violins, four violas, three cellos and two basses, also used a harpsichord continuo, stylistically more appropriate than Serkin's piano. These precautions did not prevent controversy, centred on Toscanini's last-minute decision to substitute clarinet for high trumpet, which the press understood to be 'for the sake of balance'; but Ernest Hall, great lead trumpet though he was, did not play the piccolo trumpet and probably none of sufficient agility was available for the brisk pacing of the outer movements, uncontroversial though these now sound in the light of tempos since adopted by historically informed specialists.[23]

As was to be expected, the press gave a more positive reception to the Beethoven Fifth Symphony which concluded the programme, Toscanini's first performance of the work since 1934: 'once again a thrilling adventure pursued untiringly' to the end, said the *Times* but, for Newman, once again beyond the grasp of his (consid-

---

[20] Morreau p. 262.

[21] ATL p. 195 (letter to AM, 18 September 1935), Lehmann & Faber p. 74, Potter p. 615.

[22] ATL p. 333 (letter to AM, 24 May 1938).

[23] Toscanini's string forces in ATL p. 333 (letter to AM, 21 May 1938); for Adolf Busch's forces, see Potter pp. 610 and 633. Toscanini substituted clarinet for trumpet in his New York Philharmonic-Symphony Orchestra performance on 3 February 1935 explicitly because of the difficulty of the trumpet part, according to the broadcast announcement, even though his tempos on that occasion were slower than the BBC SO performance. He retained the trumpet (Bernard Baker) for the speedy NBC SO performance on 29 October 1938 (on Guild GHCD 2364). Ernest Hall participated in the recording of the Brandenburg Concertos conducted by Anthony Bernard for Brunswick, 30137–38, but his solo part in No. 2 (probably recorded in October 1928) was there transposed down an octave. (The set was abruptly withdrawn immediately prior to its March 1929 release date and few copies survive.)

erable) powers of rational analysis. If the symphony was played 'just as it is', there was in addition, he maintained, 'some inner impulse, indefinable and unseizable in itself' with an extraordinary power to impress the composer's, rather than the conductor's, vision on the listener's consciousness.

Travails and two requiems

After another day's rest rehearsals began for the first of the two performances of the Verdi *Requiem*.[24] They tired the conductor to the extremity of his endurance, which was tested all the more by renewed pains afflicting his right arm and shoulder leading to sleepless nights. And there was trouble with one of the soloists. Not, certainly, with Nicola Moscona, a substitute for Manowarda who, as Mase told Toscanini in April, was unavailable.[25] In his place Mase secured this Greek bass, who had performed the work with Toscanini and the NBC Symphony in March that year and was to do so again on later occasions. Nor were his chosen mezzo and tenor, Thorborg and Roswaenge, at fault. It was, rather, the soprano Kunz, now transformed by marriage into Milanov, who tested Toscanini's patience past breaking point – somewhat curiously, given that she, too, had participated in the March performance.[26] The accounts of their exchanges at rehearsal have many variants; perhaps the most true to life was that recounted by Boult: a player sitting close by overheard Toscanini say under his breath 'De voice it is so 'igh, there is no room for any brain in de 'ead.'[27] Whichever version is preferred, it is clear that Toscanini admired her voice more than her intellect; but notwithstanding baton and score hurled in frustration at her musical shortcomings,[28] she remained imperturbable and virtually unaware of the despair she engendered ('Is Maestro referring to me?' she queried, after various imprecations from the rostrum).

Despite the many frustrations, despite the pain and 'a *horrible*' final rehearsal, Toscanini was buoyed by his love for the work ('I adore it more and more') and his belief that he could do it justice as the composer conceived it; and, at last, as he reported to Ada, the first performance on 27 May '*went along* as it should have'.

---

[24] See ATL pp. 333–4 (letters to AM, 25, 26 and 28 May 1938).

[25] BBCA, Mase's cable to Toscanini, 19 April 1938.

[26] The singer used her maiden name (sometimes Kunç) until her marriage in 1937 to actor Peter Milanov.

[27] Boult 1973 p. 103.

[28] Broadcast talk by Alex Nifosi. Despite his frustrations, Toscanini worked with Milanov again in later years, including the BBC SO *Missa Solemnis* in 1939 and the NBC SO Verdi *Requiem* in 1940.

The critical response was naturally more enthusiastic than the conductor's modest assessment in his correspondence with Ada. The *Times* on 28 May was struck by Toscanini's deliberateness, the absence of excitability – as distinct from excitement: he displayed 'the majestic lines of melody and the tremendous breadth of the structure through an amazing energy of rhythm which included all incidental *rubato* in its sweep'. It was a performance 'supreme in conception and magnificent in execution, one by which standards can be corrected and others may be judged'. The same qualities informed the preceding *Te Deum*, where the soprano solo, originally billed as Milanov, was actually taken by Sybilla Marshall, a member of the tireless BBC Singers.

Cardus, in the *Manchester Guardian* on 29 May, was uncharacteristically brief, struck virtually dumb by what he had heard: 'It is impossible to go on and on praising Toscanini; yet there is little else to do.' As his earlier reviews demonstrated, Cardus found the alternative easy enough; but in sharp contrast, here was an occasion 'blasphemed by the term performance. It was a moving experience for the spirit ... Toscanini controlled everything and everybody.' Milanov had clearly learnt her lesson, for Cardus had 'never heard finer soprano singing'. For once he found himself in precisely the same dilemma as Newman – how to analyse what seemed beyond and above analysis; it was, for him, difficult to explain how the conductor 'asserts his mastery and individual point of view and yet seldom, if ever, stands between the listener and the music'. He concluded that it was simply Toscanini's understanding of music and his 'power of personal presence'.

Three days later the same forces repeated the programme, when Britten was present: 'Heaven itself. A grand show', was his diary verdict.[29] In both performances the overpowering effect of Toscanini's deliberate but inexorable tempo for the *Dies irae* was enhanced by use of a gigantic bass drum borrowed from the Royal Academy of Music, where it had resided since Stanford had it specially made for one of the work's earliest London performances.[30]

Whether it was at the 'horrible' dress rehearsal of the *Requiem* or at one for a later concert cannot now be determined, but at about this time occurred the one incident of the Festival – indeed, of all Toscanini's pre-war visits – with markedly unpleasant consequences. After a morning rehearsal in the Queen's Hall, some of the players, as was their wont, retired for lunch to the nearby 'Gluepot' (actually the George public house, nicknamed by Sir Henry Wood for its retentive effects on afternoon punctuality). Emboldened by the liquid lunch, during the afternoon

---

[29] Britten p. 473.

[30] Hughes 1965 pp. 144–5 fn.

rehearsal the famed principal flautist Robert Murchie answered Toscanini back after being in receipt of his critical attention. The considerable audience at the rehearsal witnessed his explosive, score-throwing response and departure for the dressing-room, where Carla tried to calm the weeping conductor.[31] After half an hour the rehearsal resumed but the incident marked the virtual end of Murchie's tenure at the BBC; as a result of the exchange, Gerald Jackson took his seat at the end of July.

Entertaining Maestro Toscanini

Fortunately the contretemps with Murchie was an isolated incident, no doubt exacerbated by Toscanini's problem with his painful conducting arm. The pain did not, however, prevent his leading a considerable social life, as he had on previous visits. Mase took Carla and her husband to relax at his cottage near Great Missenden in Buckinghamshire where Carla made a particular friend of Georgina's pet donkey, Haiyu. More lavishly, Toscanini attended post-concert functions with his devoted admirers:[32] after the first concert at Sybil Cholmondeley's, where he dined with the future Prime Minister Anthony Eden, who had recently resigned as Foreign Secretary in disagreement with the government's appeasement policy (doubtless on that account 'molto simpatico', as Toscanini put it); after the first *Requiem* at Yvonne Rothschild's, where he admired the sumptuous and refined surroundings; and after the second *Requiem* at the Cornwall Terrace home of the passionate music devotee (and one-time lover of Arthur Rubinstein) Irene Curzon, who had inherited the barony of Ravensdale on the death of her father Lord Curzon.[33]

This last entertainment had a substantial history. In April Reith remarked that an American visitor, NBC programme manager (later NBC vice-president) John Royal, was amazed that the Director-General's only contact with the Maestro had until then been a handshake at rehearsal, 'speedily removing myself thereafter'. Royal was also surprised at the absence of any parties for the conductor by comparison with the constant stream of such events in New York. Boult pointed out that Toscanini was there surrounded by long-term friends and acquaintances, of whom

---

[31] Jackson p. 75 (where Murchie's name is not disclosed) and the author's interview with Ernest Hall, 1972.

[32] ATL pp. 333–4 (letters to AM, 26 and (?)30 May 1938).

[33] Irene Curzon, 2nd Baroness Ravensdale (1896–1966), was created a life peer with the same title in the first batch of life peers in 1958. Her liaison with Rubinstein ceased only on his wedding night in 1932, after his wedding feast at Sybil Cholmondeley's London home – see Stansky p. 181, Anne de Courcy *The Viceroy's Daughters* 2000 p. 186 and, as to Irene Curzon's attendance at the *Requiem*, p. 304; also Harvey Sachs *Arthur Rubinstein* London: Weidenfeld 1995 pp. 246–7.

FIGS. 25–27 ENTERTAINING THE
MAESTRO: SYBIL CHOLMONDELEY
(SARGENT'S CHARCOAL DRAWING,
1912), IRENE CURZON IN 1923,
PAGANI'S (see p. 161)

there were relatively few in London; he himself had enjoyed just one meal with
Toscanini and only Mase had exceeded that quota. Mase also responded, extolling
the virtues of the post-concert intimate supper parties at which Toscanini was
accustomed to unwind into the small hours and warning against repetition of the
formal lunch given in 1935: mention of it 'produces the "bleak" look I know so well'.
The eventual upshot was Reith's invitation to the post-*Requiem* function at Lady
Ravensdale's home, attended by Toscanini and his entourage, his soloists, a few

senior BBC people, lead players from the orchestra, the conductor's English friends (corralled by Mase) and, of course, Lady Ravensdale herself, an eager listener at that evening's concert. Lady Ravensdale, if not among the very richest of London socialites, was nonetheless accustomed to the best that money could buy and the party was evidently a convivial occasion. Her secretary billed the BBC for the costs (£46 16s 7d – £46.83, equivalent now to £2400), which her Ladyship hoped would be considered reasonable, given the large quantity of champagne consumed – of a quality, the BBC were assured, far superior to any available in London's hotels.[34]

Musical entertainment for the Maestro was of high quality. Not long after his arrival in London, Mase took Toscanini to Sadler's Wells for a performance of *Boris Godunov*, which he himself had introduced to New York a quarter of a century before; on this occasion Ronald Stear sang Boris and the producer at Toscanini's HMV sessions, Lawrance Collingwood, conducted. Toscanini was surprised and delighted; the performance far exceeded his expectations and he sent his thanks and congratulations to the company.[35]

Glyndebourne plots

The principal musical entertainment in 1938, as it was in the preceding year, lay at Glyndebourne; but Toscanini's visit came only after substantial plotting among the opera house's principal actors designed to bring him to Glyndebourne that year as conductor rather than as a mere honoured guest. His visits in 1935 and 1937 showed how much he appreciated Glyndebourne's standards and way of working, even if Fritz Busch's *Magic Flute* was not to his taste. The retention of that goodwill was a factor in John Christie's thinking from 1936 onwards. In August of that year, discussing the possibility of a Glyndebourne *Falstaff* with Fritz, he feared Toscanini might view its attractions as 'unfriendly' competition with his own presentations at Salzburg and be offended with Fritz; in December 1936, rather contrarily, he wanted Fritz to have the best possible cast for the 1937 *Magic Flute* to ensure that Glyndebourne would be 'quite certain of beating' Toscanini's upcoming Salzburg performances.[36]

---

[34] BBCA, Reith's memorandum, 11 April 1938; Boult's reply, 13 April 1938; Mase's response, 2 May 1938; Lady Ravensdale's bill with secretary's letter, 6 June 1938, and further letter, 23 June 1938.

[35] This visit was noted in the *Times*, 24 May 1938, which dates it as just before the Feuermann concert on 23 May; but ENO archives show there was only one performance of *Boris* at Sadler's Wells during May while Toscanini was in London, on 17 May (information courtesy Clare Colvin).

[36] GA, Christie's letters to Fritz Busch, 19 August and 22 December 1936.

'If impossible to beat, let him join us' appeared to be the thinking early in 1938; that, and the news that Toscanini had abandoned Salzburg, anticipating the Nazi takeover in Austria. Fritz himself, working in Copenhagen, was the prime mover: from there his daughter Margareta ('Eta') wrote on 21 February to Glyndebourne manager Rudolf Bing[37] with her father's proposal for additional performances of *The Magic Flute* and perhaps *Falstaff* at the end of the 1938 season, both under Toscanini's baton.[38] Fritz's brother Adolf, for long an intimate friend of Toscanini, was also among the fervent supporters of this invitation. The incentive for Fritz lay primarily in the propaganda coup for Glyndebourne; but while Christie eventually agreed that the approach be made,[39] Bing's stream of concerned letters to Fritz and Eta conveyed conflicting messages.[40] In his letter to Fritz of 23 February he thought four performances of *The Magic Flute* plus a Mozart orchestral concert would be an attractive (and financially the only viable) proposition and Fritz duly despatched a telegram of invitation to Toscanini's New York hotel; but Bing was worried by the size of Toscanini's likely fee and whether he would accept Glyndebourne's existing cast.

By the end of the first week of March, Bing felt 'driven mad with tension' by the absence of a reply from Toscanini and, in confidence, told Fritz he hoped to God that nothing would come of the invitation since he feared all hell would be let loose in Glyndebourne ['wir den Teufel und die Hölle ins Haus bekommen']. Frustrated by Toscanini's continued silence, Bing consulted Mase, recently in The Hague for the conductor's Residentie orchestra concerts; Mase was certain that Toscanini would not conduct any operas during 1938. Bing's letter of 24 March conveying this news to Fritz crossed with Fritz's to him of 25 March, curtly closing the matter: Fritz expected nothing more from Toscanini. But he failed to keep brother Adolf informed of events, with unfortunate consequences.

As later negotiations suggested, Fritz was doubtless annoyed about Toscanini's silence, but his initial approach to him was in itself rather curious: if Toscanini looked with disfavour on Fritz's *Magic Flute*, Fritz viewed Toscanini's 1937 Salzburg reading, part of which he heard on the radio, with equal disappointment. In any

[37] (1902–97) knighted 1971, British music administrator born in Austria, general manager Glyndebourne 1934–49, manager New York Metropolitan Opera 1950–72.

[38] GA, Eta Busch's letter to Bing, 21 February 1938.

[39] GA, Christie's letter to his wife Audrey Mildmay, 23 February 1938.

[40] GA, letters from Bing to Fritz Busch of 23 and 28 February, 7 and 24 March 1938 (also to Eta Busch of 21 March 1938); see also Greta Busch p. 150, who quotes from the letters of 23 February and 7 March.

event, it seems probable that Toscanini never received Fritz's invitation; his friendly and unconcerned demeanour when eventually he made his 1938 visit to Glyndebourne suggests that he was unaware of the previous plotting.

That visit, at John Christie's invitation, took place on 4 June.[41] Verdi's *Macbeth*, in its first professional British production, was performed that night; and afterwards Toscanini assured Christie that the world had no better Verdi conductor than Fritz Busch and that the chorus was 'the best little chorus' he had ever heard. To Fritz's son Hans Peter (then aged twenty-four and on the staff since 1935 as 'Assistant Producer') he remarked that his father 'conducted it as it must be conducted'. Christie ensured that Toscanini's enthusiasm was reported in newspapers throughout the land.[42] 'Before he came', he said – according to virtually every provincial newspaper in the country – 'he had learnt the score of *Macbeth* by heart in order to discuss it with Dr Busch. Toscanini said that Busch is the greatest of all Verdi conductors.' All good publicity for the Festival before Queen Elizabeth's promised visit, in which context these pardonable exaggerations were reported; unfortunately the death of her mother and the ensuing funeral arrangements prevented her attending.

Some sources suggest Toscanini found aspects of Carl Ebert's production too German (a growled '*tedesco*'), although such reservations seem unlikely, given his later praise for the whole affair and invitation to Ebert to produce the work in post-war Italy. Certainly his pleasure was not mitigated by Furtwängler's presence at the same performance. According to Gaisberg, Furtwängler (again in London for the Covent Garden *Ring* cycles) was invited by Ebert but, given the producer's stance towards the Nazi régime, from which Furtwängler on his Glyndebourne visits invariably carried fruitless messages to Fritz and Ebert,[43] it seems highly doubtful that Ebert ever issued such an invitation. Whatever the truth here, Furtwängler knew Toscanini was to be present and asked Gaisberg whether he should greet him: 'not unless you are dead sure he won't give you the cold shoulder', replied Gaisberg. Bing eventually deployed the opera house staff, among them Fritz's assistant Alberto Erede for Toscanini, Ebert for Furtwängler, with strict instructions to keep the two

[41]   Hughes 1965 pp. 131–2, Gaisberg p. 164, Ebert pp. 124–5.

[42]   Toscanini's and Furtwängler's visits on 4 June were reported in the *Times* and *Daily Telegraph* on 6 June 1938. Toscanini's comments, as reported by Christie, appeared in the *Evening News* on 10 June 1938 and were syndicated across the country's provincial press that day (cuttings in GA).

[43]   Ebert p. 125.

apart.[44] By such strenuous efforts Furtwängler was kept out of Toscanini's sight. A gossip columnist later reported that, while Toscanini applauded with an enthusiasm worthy of any amateur, Furtwängler did so with only a certain professional respect.[45]

Fritz had still not explained to brother Adolf his attitude towards any invitation to Toscanini to conduct at Glyndebourne but an ideal opportunity to do so was to be provided by their joint attendance at the first Lucerne Festival. Adolf was instrumental during 1938 in organising this Festival for the benefit of Toscanini and other musicians after Salzburg's takeover by the Nazi administration within Austria; Toscanini was to conduct one of the Festival concerts, a major attraction with a specially recruited orchestra for that concert led by members of the Busch Quartet. After Glyndebourne's 1938 season ended, Fritz travelled via Copenhagen to Lucerne to conduct the new Festival's inaugural concert and no doubt socialised with Toscanini and Adolf; even so, he again let slip the opportunity to discuss Glyndebourne affairs with his brother.

Eventually, after his return to Copenhagen Fritz wrote to Adolf on 5 September, apologising for his omission to notify him of the outcome of the February/March negotiations concerning Toscanini and Glyndebourne – 'the many people and my own worries about my work ... made me nervous', so he had neglected 'to take a restful walk with you' to explain his standpoint.[46] Fritz went on to detail his own role in heartfelt terms: 'Please be assured that I personally brought up, as best I could, all the arguments in favour of such an invitation [to Toscanini]. Again and again I also mentioned what you advised and your reasons for doing so.' He implored his brother not to take offence at Christie's ultimate decision against 'this tempting possibility'; they all knew that Adolf wished only the best for Glyndebourne and its future and he could surely be especially gratified in making Toscanini

---

[44] Alberto Erede, Italian conductor (1909–2001) a Weingartner pupil at Basle and at this time Glyndebourne's second conductor, later conductor of the Gothenburg Symphony Orchestra and prolific Decca recording artist. Carl Ebert, renowned opera producer (1887–1980), producer at Glyndebourne 1934–39 and later Glyndebourne's artistic director. Gaisberg's suggestion that Ebert invited Furtwängler is contrary to the thrust of Peter Ebert's memoir of his father: like Fritz Busch, who refused to meet Furtwängler at Glyndebourne (see Ch. 4 p. 99), Ebert left Germany in protest against the Nazi takeover and the previous year he had been as reluctant as Fritz to have any contact with Furtwängler (Adolf Busch vol. 2 p. 371). It is likely that there was more to the story of this invitation than Gaisberg disclosed. Hans Peter Busch (1914–96), operatic stage director, left Germany with his father in 1933, studied music in Geneva and Vienna and assisted Carl Ebert at Glyndebourne before the Second World War. He became a citizen of the USA in 1942. See further Ch. 10 p. 187 and Annex C p. 317.

[45] *Daily Telegraph* 6 June 1938.

[46] Adolf Busch vol. 2 pp. 384–5.

FIG. 28 TOSCANINI AND ADOLF BUSCH, SALZBURG, 1936

happy with his admirable organisation of the Lucerne concerts. The letter reads oddly – and not only in the light of subsequent correspondence and events: Fritz's assurances about his role were, at best, disingenuous, since according to extant correspondence he was both the initial prime mover and in the end the abrupt opponent of the invitation to Toscanini for the 1938 Glyndebourne Festival.

During his Lucerne stay Toscanini no doubt expressed to Adolf his pleasure at his brother's performance of *Macbeth* and the enveloping Glyndebourne atmosphere; and from Lucerne, still in ignorance of Fritz's views, Adolf, through his devoted attendant and Glyndebourne supporter Frances Dakyns, enthusiastically reopened the question of inviting Toscanini to conduct *The Magic Flute* and *Falstaff* at the 1939 Glyndebourne Festival. Likewise unaware of Fritz's expiatory letter of 5 September to Adolf, Bing wrote on 7 September to Fritz in Copenhagen and to Carl Ebert in Switzerland about this renewed proposal. 'Enormous advantages, enormous disadvantages, even risks', said Bing, and he discussed them all at length: in favour, the worldwide publicity and notable event in Glyndebourne's history; against, possible differences between Toscanini and Ebert – Glyndebourne's good fortune in having a conductor who recognised the importance of production values ought not to be jeopardised and any disagreement or walkout by Toscanini would result in adverse publicity around the world. Would Toscanini accept the little discomforts of Glyndebourne, and the orchestral players as they stood, without disturbing Glyndebourne's atmosphere? If he came in 1939 but not in 1940, would the house's reputation be lowered? These were but a few of the many considerations Bing laid before conductor and producer. Christie intervened with his own views, in part obviously reflecting discussions with Bing; his letter of 10 September to Fritz emphasised the virtues of Glyndebourne's production values as against Toscanini's possibly 'old fashioned' attitude: 'I personally think that you and Charles [*sic* – Carl Ebert] together are better than Toscanini and some little producer.' Innocently enough but too late, he asked Fritz to talk the matter through with his brother.

Ebert had in fact already been to Lucerne to discuss the issues with Adolf and Frances, probably before Adolf received his brother's letter of 5 September. In his reply to Bing on 9 September Ebert referred to 'our friend' (Frances) but *sub silencio* it is obvious that Adolf was included in his comments. The two of them were, said Ebert, incapable of viewing Glyndebourne as anything more than just another good festival theatre and regarded any opposition to Toscanini as imbecilic or, even worse, as fear of the competition. They failed to understand Ebert's explanation that a 'republic' and a 'dictatorship', each with its virtues, could not co-exist: the republic would 'kaput'. As to Bing's arguments, he (Ebert) was not personally concerned since no differences might occur between himself and Toscanini and, in any case, there were other producers who could be called on; but it would be regrettable if the views of Frances carried greater weight with Christie than those of Fritz, Bing and himself.

FIG. 29 ADOLF AND FRITZ BUSCH RELAX AT GLYNDEBOURNE

Fritz's reply to Bing on 10 September, just five days after his emollient letter of excuses to brother Adolf, was both categoric and brief. The matter of Toscanini and Glyndebourne was for him closed: a renewed invitation for 1939 was out of the question. Although his brother had in mind the best for Glyndebourne and for Fritz, his own view was, regrettably and finally, different; in any event, 'brotherly love' would not thereby be severed. He asked Bing to inform Christie that, so far as he was concerned, further discussion was superfluous. On 12 September Bing, summarising these letters in English for Christie's benefit, hastened to do so; and that, for the time being, was that.[47]

A recording session, a concert and a walkout

If Glyndebourne had no success in capturing Toscanini during 1938, HMV fared only a little better. It seems that Toscanini no longer opposed HMV recording his concerts, at least so far as concerned the Verdi *Requiem*, which from an early stage

---

[47] Letters here summarised and quoted in GA.

they were intent on committing to disc. In mid-April David Bicknell prepared a detailed chart of timings for the 78rpm sides, some 24–25 in number with allowances for dividing awkwardly long sides, based on timings made by HMV of Toscanini's Salzburg performance of the work on 14 August 1937.[48] Bicknell planned to use two recording machines with the sides fading at the end from one to another with a short overlap. He asked Collingwood's advice on the side divisions and the points of warning for the engineers to commence and fade up. All these preparations were in vain for, shortly before Toscanini's arrival in London, the Musicians Union unexpectedly stepped in to prohibit the recording, contrary to its previously expressed attitude.[49]

Luckily for posterity, without seeking permission from anyone (as Bicknell remarked three decades later), the BBC decided to record their own broadcast of the first performance on 27 May. The broadcast sound of this and other 1938 Festival concerts was enhanced by use of the new, superior television sound track.[50] For the recording the BBC used the Philips-Miller recording process on film, a system produced by Philips Lamps in Holland, which, since its first use by the corporation in 1937, provided high-quality playback of up to fifteen minutes on each reel. Together, these systems undoubtedly contributed to the superior sound of the *Requiem* as initially preserved.[51] Unfortunately, after completion of the BBC's post-

---

[48] EMI, Bicknell to Collingwood, 13 April 1938.

[49] EMI, Bicknell to Collingwood, 13 May 1938.

[50] In addition to their usual medium wave transmission, with limited high frequencies, for the 1938 Festival the BBC also broadcast the concerts using the sound track employed for their television transmissions since 1936. This effort to transmit improved sound quality was judged a success: see Jennifer Doctor & David Wright (eds.) *The Proms: A New History* London: Thames & Hudson 2007 p. 112.

[51] See EMI, Bicknell to Coveney, BBC, 15 September 1970, where Bicknell mentions the absence of consent for this recording and refers to the sound recording system as the Philips Light System. The system was invented in the USA by J. A. Miller, further developed by Philips in Holland and first marketed in 1936. The process involved recording on a 7mm film coated with gelatine and mercuric sulphide, cut with a vertically moving sapphire needle, and playing it back on a special machine. Beecham also arranged for the process to be used for recording some Covent Garden performances in this period: see Lucas pp. 238–9 and David Patmore 'Spools for spoils' *CRQ* Summer 2011 p. 54. For the BBC, as noted in the above text, the Philips film of the Verdi *Requiem* was transferred after the Second World War to acetates from which tapes were later made. For Walter Toscanini the Philips film was transferred to tape in 1954; this tape needed patching from lacquer discs at a later stage after the film was destroyed. Bicknell's view was that the distortion and other noise on the BBC tapes made the performance unusable but, according to Seth Winner, any such distortion on the high-grade tape transfer made for Walter Toscanini was 'curable'. That transfer was not used for the Testament or other issues, none of which is therefore in the best sound (see further Annex B p. 285). For the history of the Philips-Miller process, see the article by Professor Seán Street in the online Sound Journal of Bournemouth University: www.kent.ac.uk/arts/sound-journal/street002.html.

war programme to transfer these reels to acetate discs, they were destroyed as a fire hazard. Taped copies of these discs (of varying quality) were the basis for subsequent issues, including the Testament release authorised by the Toscanini estate.

HMV's disappointment over the Verdi was alleviated by the prospect of recording sessions lined up for 2 and 9 June, for the first time at the Abbey Road studios; but, perhaps to ensure matching acoustics for re-recording the finale of Beethoven's First Symphony, the venue for the first session was changed to the Queen's Hall, a wise decision as later events demonstrated. The scheduled works were, for 2 June, the Beethoven symphony's finale, the Overture to Rossini's *La scala di seta*, the Weber/Berlioz *Invitation to the Dance* and, an item to be added only if time allowed, Mozart's *Magic Flute* Overture; and for 9 June, Brahms's Second Symphony. All works save the Beethoven featured in Toscanini's programmes for the current Festival.

Gaisberg was now back in the picture and, emphasising the importance of the sessions to the company, asked Collingwood to ensure that he was present to assist the recording engineers in the control room to warn them in particular of impending fortissimos and the likely onslaught of timpani passages. He pointed to Beecham's recording of the Brahms symphony with timings of his sides for possible breaks, further explaining that, 'we will attempt to get Toscanini to accept our plan of stopping momentarily at the end of each stopping-place. The pause, however, must be of the briefest and for that reason we intend to have two pairs of machines; as one finishes the other will be running and ready for the cutter to go down on the wax.' Gaisberg evidently chose to overlook O'Connell's implicit warning to Palmer in April about RCA's adoption of continuous, unbroken recording methods in their March sessions with the NBC Symphony. A week later at the end of May, Palmer made his own requests for planned side-end breaks, warning that, given the duration of Toscanini's nine-minute concert performance (on 19 May), the Weber/Berlioz posed potential difficulties while Beecham's recording of the Rossini overture (also containing Handel's *Entry of the Queen of Sheba*) would not provide a suitable ground plan. But he, too, expected Toscanini to agree to short pauses between sides, as he had in October 1937.[52]

Next day, however, these expectations were dashed: on 1 June Toscanini communicated his insistence on performing the works straight through without pauses, as he had in his March recordings for RCA. This diktat posed problems for the

---

[52] EMI, Gaisberg to Collingwood, 23 May 1938; Palmer to Collingwood, 31 May 1938; Gaisberg to Collingwood, 1 June 1938. Beecham's LPO performance of Brahms's Second Symphony, recorded in March 1936 on Columbia LX 515–19; his LPO performances of Rossini's *La scala di seta* Overture and Handel's *Entry of the Queen of Sheba*, recorded in May 1933 on Columbia LX 255.

engineers. The pauses in the October 1937 sessions had enabled the recordings to be made direct on to matrices in HMV's standard series, but this course could not now be followed unless the works themselves contained natural musical breaks enabling the switch between turntables containing the waxes to be effected without loss of music. As Gaisberg noted, the engineers would therefore have to record as if at an actual performance and make transfers afterwards. 'Toscanini', he commented, 'feels that the break, even of a few seconds, upsets his tempi and as he is more concerned about this than the quality of the records, there is no danger in making transfers.'

Of the works to be recorded, only the *Magic Flute* Overture contained the requisite natural break permitting direct recording, before the mid-point fanfares. On the morning of 2 June, therefore, Toscanini rehearsed the items to be recorded in the Queen's Hall, during which discreet recording tests were made for balance and the like. The engineers then recorded this overture direct onto matrices in the 2EA series and in the result the work received the most perfectly balanced, natural sound enjoyed by the conductor in any pre-war recording (arguably throughout his recording career). The remarkable technicians responsible went undocumented but senior balance engineer Edward Fowler was no doubt in charge.

The other works lacked convenient musical breaks and the engineers therefore had to record them on Technical Test matrices using the method employed in Toscanini's first HMV session in June 1937; the material so recorded then had to be edited and transferred to standard matrices for issue. These dubbings were made after Toscanini's departure from London, on 13 June (the Beethoven and Rossini) and 14 June (the Weber/Berlioz). As Gaisberg pointed out, the sound quality was of secondary importance to Toscanini – which was just as well, since it suffered markedly from the transfer process. The Beethoven symphony's finale was least affected: its rapid tempo masked any sonic shortcoming other than the abrupt cut-off at the end of the first of the two sides. But in the other two pieces similarly abrupt cut-offs lost (like the *Pastoral*'s Andante) moments of musical substance, while legato passages among the woodwind were afflicted with a noticeable judder: oboe and horn solos by MacDonagh and Aubrey Brain in the opening Andantino of the Rossini were affected while the sound of Thurston's clarinet in the introduction to the Weber/Berlioz was marred beyond redemption.

As was by now becoming habitual, Toscanini's letter to Ada after the recording session complained that 'these sessions tire me more than rehearsals for concerts'[53] and he was therefore relieved to turn to rehearsals for the following evening's concert.

[53] ATL p. 335 (letter to AM, 2 June 1938).

The opening item was to be the Rossini overture just recorded, which Toscanini switched from its original place as opener for the last (Sibelius/Brahms) concert, sensing that it would not go well with Sibelius. Dissatisfied with MacDonagh's phrasing for the opening oboe phrases, overnight Toscanini wrote out corrected phrasing from memory,[54] a manuscript that MacDonagh later framed. The concert was to contain two of the greatest C major symphonies in the repertoire, Mozart's *Jupiter* and Schubert's Ninth, prefaced respectively by the Rossini overture and the Brahms *Liebeslieder* Waltzes, performed by the sixteen full-time BBC Singers accompanied by Britain's foremost duo pianists, Ethel Bartlett and Rae Robertson. Present at the final rehearsal on the day, Britten thought that 'Toscanini is worthy of such music' – he was referring to the two symphonies – 'the highest praise'.[55]

The next morning all the critics were delighted save, as to the Brahms, the *Times* ('magnificent but it was not Brahms') and, as to the Schubert, Cardus, who, obstinately alone, found it four-square. Everyone else thought it superb without qualification, even if a few of the tempos occasioned comment: 'convincing at all points', said Bonavia in the *Telegraph*, with 'moments of supreme beauty' in the Andante. The *Times* analysis of this performance was particularly close and acute. Toscanini solved the problem of the 'joins' between first and second subjects and elsewhere using less variation than usual, but 'his general method was to make a slight *ritardando* at the end of his exposition or development, and refrain from returning to *a tempo* immediately on entering the new section'. This method secured 'flexibility of rhythm and an increase of momentum'. In the finale's coda 'each time those four tremendous consecutive minims were pulled up just enough to increase their impact, but the intervening passages ... reverted at once to full speed'. The whole symphony gave the impression of a steady crescendo of energy, with the finale 'swept forward with fresh accessions of energy at each stage of its progress'. Newman, in the *Sunday Times* of 5 June, agreed fully but allowed most space for the *Jupiter* Symphony, which gave the impression that 'we were watching the music in the very process of composition, so lucid was it all, so inevitably did one phrase grow out of another'.

A few days later, on the morning of 9 June, Toscanini listened without enthusiasm to the results of his recording session of a week earlier; he seems, nonetheless, to have approved them, although the transfers of the test recordings had yet to be made. In the afternoon came his second recording session, located at Abbey Road (Studio 1), for which the Brahms Second Symphony was scheduled; but this was not to be. As he wrote to Ada later that day, after conducting less than twenty bars

[54]   Broadcast talk by Alex Nifosi.
[55]   Britten p. 473.

he left and went home (that is, to the Langham Hotel): 'my nerves couldn't take it' and, with the final rehearsal and concert on the following day, 'it's too much! I don't want to make records any more!'[56]

Gaisberg's memoirs corroborated Toscanini in every detail, if more diplomatically: he recollected a session 'arranged in our own studio ... When [Toscanini] arrived we detected dark clouds on his brow.' At first he declined to ascend the podium, but eventually did so and started to conduct; but he 'halted the musicians after twenty bars or so and said "I do not like the placing of the instruments and the acoustics ... If I conduct records today I shall not be able to conduct your concert tomorrow."' And with that he slipped away to the waiting motor.[57] Principal trumpet Ernest Hall (the orchestra's chairman) indeed warned the engineers that, seated as he and his colleagues were, Toscanini would be unhappy but was assured that, once in place, the Maestro would do just as they (the engineers) wanted – a foolhardy assumption: as soon as the instrumental sounds came from unaccustomed directions, that, said Hall, was the end of the session. Gaisberg and his colleagues were left to reflect that Toscanini, if rather drastic in his reaction, 'was right about the acoustics and the placing of the instruments'.

The sixth concert: HMV acts without delay

After delivering this salutary lesson, Toscanini duly undertook the final rehearsal and concert the following day. Again this contained two great symphonies in the same key, this time D major: the Second symphonies of Sibelius and Brahms. And

---

[56]   ATL p. 335 (letter to AM, 9 June 1938).

[57]   Gaisberg pp. 143–4. Bicknell's later account (Southall p. 24) had Toscanini ascending the podium, taking up his baton and looking around the studio, newly decorated for him. 'Then he dropped his hands to his head and said, "I couldn't possibly record in a dreadful hall like this", and with that he ran out of the studio into a waiting car and drove off.' Bicknell continued by commenting that those present suspected there might be 'a bit of trouble' and so Boult, who was also present, was able to step in for further work. Bicknell thought the whole incident was 'manufactured' by Toscanini because he did not want to record in Abbey Road, but wanted to record the Brahms symphony in the Queen's Hall, which was 'where we eventually did it'. Since Gaisberg's version closely corroborates both Toscanini's own, written at the time, and also Ernest Hall's account, it is to be preferred; on which basis, Bicknell's version misleads. Toscanini actually conducted the beginning of the work – he ceased when the orchestral layout was clearly not what he wanted. Boult was not standing by, at least for recording purposes: Sanders *Boult Discography* discloses no recording in 1938. Toscanini did not 'manufacture' the occasion nor want to record the Brahms in the Queen's Hall (no further sessions were scheduled): he did not want to record that day at all because of the following day's concert and his own exhaustion; the shortcomings (as he saw them) of the studio acoustics and orchestral layout precipitated his departure.

again he gave pleasure to a friend, programming as a surprise first item Scarlatti arrangements by Tommasini, who once more was in London for the Festival. Since Toscanini had performed the Brahms in London with the New York Philharmonic in 1930, interest centred on the Sibelius, which he first prepared during the preceding January for an NBC concert. Koussevitzky's much-praised performance of the work featured in the 1935 Festival, but Toscanini's approach, with tempos far closer to the authentic Robert Kajanus, differed markedly; indeed he thought Koussevitzky's 1935 Boston recording of the work 'scandalous' and 'destroys him as musician and interpreter'.[58] Precisely what precipitated this venom is not known; perhaps Koussevitzky's laboured tempos for the outer movements or his rewritten timpani part in the work's closing pages, which Sibelius himself disliked.

For all the differences between the two conductors in this work and Koussevitzky's undoubted prowess as a Sibelian, the critics found Toscanini's performance illuminating and idiomatic, as well as magnificently played. The *Times* on 11 June thought the first movement was built up with 'masterly assurance', the slow movement had 'just the right suppleness of rhythm' and the scherzo was 'a miracle of swiftness' with the trio 'beautifully poised' and 'magnificent tonal weight' given to the finale. Francis Toye in the same day's *Telegraph* found that 'all trace of Nordic bleakness had vanished; the music glowed with southern intensity', yet Toscanini's unflagging rhythm and clarification of textures 'left the music more revealed than usual'. Newman, in the *Sunday Times* of 12 June, thought the performance 'brought out with especial clearness and intensity the very essence of the work – its dramatic contrast of moods'.

Newman also thought the Brahms, the first movement in particular, 'a masterly piece of unity in diversity of mood'. For the *Times*, too, it was magnificent as a whole, with special praise for the third movement, which 'moved onwards in one rhythmic line. So exactly was the change to the 2/4 presto adjusted that there seemed to be no change of pace, but only a quickening of the movement.' But the overall impression was 'brilliant rather than genial' and the critic detected some raggedness in the 'hard-driven' finale, a 'sign that the orchestra, having given of its best throughout

---

[58] ATL p. 321 (letter to AM, 15 January 1938). Koussevitzky's first recording of the Second Symphony was made on 24 January 1935 (RCA Victor M 272, CD transfers including Pearl GEMM CDS 9408). Each outer movement outlasts Toscanini's by over a minute (Toscanini's Tempo andante second movement, however, is slower). Koussevitzky's second recording, made on 29 November 1950 (RCA LM 1172, CD transfer Naxos 8.111290), has a faster first movement. As to his rewritten timpani part, see *CRC* Summer 2010 pp. 6–7 (Edward Johnson). The Kajanus recording was made in May 1930 with an anonymous orchestra (probably the old RPO), issued on Columbia LX 50–54, various CD transfers including Finlandia 4509-95882-2.

these concerts, was showing a pardonable exhaustion in the final lap'. Judging by Toscanini's comments, the orchestra's exhaustion matched his own; but by the time this review was published, he was already on his way to Milan. The night before, Britten recorded in his diary, Toscanini was 'grand in lousy programme'.[59] Three days later that youthful diary ended.

After the debacle at the Abbey Road studios on 9 June, all was not yet lost to HMV. They took the precaution of recording on to test discs the BBC broadcast of the two symphonies on 10 June; and, having lost one Brahms Second, they were anxious to issue this one, as well as the Sibelius. As with earlier test discs, this batch had to be edited and transferred to the regular matrix series and the Transfer Room was booked for a series of sessions during late June and early July.[60] One of Gaisberg's last acts in furtherance of elusive Toscanini recordings while still in full harness – he retired in April 1939 – was to direct Collingwood to attend these sessions to supervise the editing of the dubbed discs; tricky work since the BBC had damped down several climaxes which required enhancement, particularly at the end of both symphonies.

HMV set great store by the results and the arrangements for securing Toscanini's approval of the finalised discs were exceptionally thorough and tactful. Toscanini was known to be resting on the Isolino in preparation for the first Lucerne Festival and there was therefore much debate as to how far the two sets of dubbed test press-ings of each work were to be transported.[61] Should they go no further than Milan or be taken on to Stresa (near Toscanini's island home) where electricity supplies were still reliable? Or, as in June 1937, should they go the whole distance to the Isolino? Initially Palmer chose Milan but, after consulting Mase, wisely abandoned this compromise for fear that the Maestro's journey there might be sufficient to upset him in advance of any audition. In July Palmer therefore asked HMV's Milan agents to request Carla to permit engineers to vet the Isolino's gramophone equip-ment in preparation for Toscanini's assessment of these 'important' records. A further factor in Mase's advice was doubtless his own plans for Georgina and himself to visit the Isolino, in response to an urgent telegram of invitation from Toscanini which gave evidence of their degree of intimacy: 'Come you will be received ad [*sic*] open arms Toscanini.'[62] Carla's (translated but signed) invitation followed: 'We will

[59] Britten p. 474.

[60] EMI, Gaisberg to Collingwood, 17 June 1938; Palmer to Collingwood, 24 June and 4 July 1938.

[61] EMI, Palmer to Passadoro, Milan, 11 and 20 July 1938.

[62] From Pallanza, 9 July 1938, in MA; Carla's letter, 8 July 1938, in MA.

be delighted to see you. We are looking forward to the pleasure of seeing you and Mrs Mase' – confirmation enough for Mase to arrange a motoring vacation across Europe ending in Stresa, which would give him the opportunity to carry a set of the test discs in his luggage as failsafe against breakage elsewhere.

The next stage was for Palmer to send a complete set of discs to the agents in Milan where he was to collect them. The other set was duly stowed away in Mase's luggage to be ferried to the Isolino. After picking up the test discs (still intact) in Milan, Palmer arrived in Stresa on 27 July and met Mase there the following day to plan their strategy. On 29 July Toscanini auditioned the discs in his island home with both Palmer and Mase in attendance; on 30 July he did so again, this time with Mase alone.[63] These joint and several efforts were in vain. Toscanini was interested to hear the discs but could not approve them. As Palmer put it, 'he is not sympathetic to the limitations of recording and expects absolute perfection, which is impossible'. Technically, Palmer later remarked, the records 'were excellent as the Maestro admitted' and he was not worried about a few coughs and other extraneous noises. But the playing fell short of the perfection he demanded of all the recordings he was to leave behind: it was in parts just not good enough, for which he mostly blamed himself – a legacy of the orchestra's exhaustion on which the press had commented at the time. Toscanini's remarks, Palmer continued, were scant enough consolation, but with him 'one cannot force the issue'.

The wholly negative outcome both of HMV's efforts to record at Abbey Road on 9 June and of their prolonged attempts to salvage the recording of the next day's concert no doubt forced them to lick multiple wounds; but at least they were now free to issue the completed recording of Beethoven's First Symphony. They promptly did so, followed over the next six months by issue of the other products of the session on 2 June. To assist in obliterating any unhappy memories of the Abbey Road session and the rejected concert recordings, in October Palmer wrote his one extant lengthy and flattering letter to Toscanini, emphasising HMV's good fortune for now and the future in having the opportunity to work with him. As for those rejected recordings, they had to wait more than half a century for their first official release which, at any rate as regards the Brahms symphony, made plain the wisdom of Toscanini's refusal to countenance contemporary issue: shortcomings in both the orchestral playing and the recording would almost certainly have drawn comment at the time.[64]

---

[63] EMI, Palmer to Berriman, Milan, 24 August 1938 and to Edward Wallerstein, RCA, 6 September 1938; Palmer to Toscanini, 12 October 1938.

[64] See further Annex B p. 286 and Annex C p. 340.

CHAPTER 8

1939: THE LAST LONDON MUSIC FESTIVAL

Getting back in peacetime

As early as March 1938 Toscanini proposed to Mase a 1939 BBC SO Beethoven/
Brahms cycle;[1] perhaps more realistically, during his 1938 visit he intimated to Boult
that he wished to set a seal on his London visits with a complete Beethoven cycle.[2]
Moreover he knew that in the BBC Chorus trained by Leslie Woodgate there was
material fit for the ultimate test, the *Missa Solemnis*. As noted in the preceding
chapter, at the Isolino on 30 July 1938 Mase was unsuccessful in gaining Toscanini's
approval for HMV's concert recordings; but on the same day, in his capacity as
Director of the London Music Festival, he did succeed in concluding an agreement
with Toscanini for a seven-concert Beethoven cycle in 1939, at an increased fee of
500 guineas (£525, today about £26,000) per concert. As usual, he later forwarded
it to the BBC for assignment and execution of its financial provisions.[3]

A few days later the Mase holiday on the Isolino came to an end, but not before
Carla donated one of her hats to their pet donkey Haiyu; as Georgina reported in
her letter of thanks to Toscanini, this offering was no sooner presented than
promptly eaten.[4] In a further measure of the growing intimacy between the conductor and his English friends, Georgina did not hesitate to address Toscanini in
remarkably familiar terms about their 'wonderful' holiday and how sad everyone
would be without him: 'but of course "everyone" doesn't love you quite so much as
we do, so we are saddest', their visit 'a beauty beyond forgetting'.

---

[1] BBCA, Howgill's memorandum, 31 March 1938.

[2] Boult 1973 p. 103.

[3] BBCA, Mase's letter to the BBC, 10 January 1939; the BBC to Mase, 16 January 1939. The
contract itself is in Mase's handwriting on his London Music Festival headed paper but signed by
Howgill for the BBC. Howgill was not present at the Isolino and presumably had pre- or post-
signed the document in London.

[4] Georgina Mase to Toscanini, 4 September 1938, ATC JPB 90-1 series L pt 1 folder L76E.

A few weeks later, in August 1938, the Toscanini entourage set off for Lucerne, where the single Festival concert to which the conductor was committed was increased by popular demand to two. Contingents of distinguished Italians crossed the border to be present and, after his return to Italy, Toscanini gave vent to his fury against Il Duce's new anti-Semitic policies on his tapped telephone. The consequent withdrawal of his passport was rescinded only after threats of a worldwide press campaign instigated by Toscanini's son Walter and his journalist friends. The conductor then left for his second NBC season knowing that thenceforward it would be too dangerous for him to return to his homeland; Italy did not see him again until his post-war return to La Scala. The loss of his home and his homeland were terrible deprivations for the conductor, whose homesickness figured largely in his correspondence for these years, but he bore it throughout as a sacrifice necessary for an unbending adherence to his anti-fascist principles. Fred Gaisberg, who as earlier chapters have demonstrated had every reason to limit his admiration for Toscanini, nonetheless took the view that 'no other musician, barring Pablo Casals, has paid so high a price for his convictions. It stamps him as one of the bravest of the brave.'[5]

The second NBC season was witnessed in part by Sybil Cholmondeley who, no doubt to her satisfaction, saw much of her beloved hero and his family in New York; she also received a radio from the head of RCA, David Sarnoff, who in 1937 had been instrumental in forming the orchestra. The series ended on 27 February 1939 and was followed by a single Washington concert with the orchestra in mid-March and five recording sessions, the first four of which completed the Mozart G minor Symphony and added Beethoven's Fifth Symphony and Rossini's *William Tell* Overture. The last session, which included Beethoven's Eighth Symphony, took place on 17 April. Four days later, without the customary

---

[5]   For these events, see Sachs 1978 p. 267 and Sachs 1987 pp. 229–32, reprinted with revisions in Sachs 1991. For Gaisberg's comments, see Gaisberg 'Toscanini' *Gramophone* June 1943 pp. 6–7. Gaisberg's cited comment, although sincerely meant, failed to take account of the even greater sacrifices of the Busch brothers, especially Adolf, who by exiling himself from Germany after 1933 lost two-thirds of his income and underwent a mental torture fully as severe as Toscanini's: see Potter pp. 538–40 and 542. Gaisberg's views and those of his contemporaries cited by Sachs contrast with recent, misconceived attempts to equate Toscanini's authoritarian attitude towards music-making at La Scala with Mussolini's violent suppression of democratic politics and connivance in the persecution of his political opponents: see e.g. Richard Taruskin 'The Dark Side of Modern Music' *The New Republic* 5 September 1988 pp. 28–34, a review of Sachs 1987, refuted by Sachs 1991 pp. 95–9; also Taruskin *Oxford History of Western Music: (Vol. 4) Music in the Early Twentieth Century* New York: OUP 2005 Ch. 13 'Music in a Totalitarian Society' p. 753. Taruskin's verdict on Toscanini here, 'no political resister', would have astonished Mussolini and everyone else at the time. For further comment on Taruskin's writings, see Frank 'Toscanini – myth and reality' *CRC* Winter 2006 pp. 10–14; see also Norman Lebrecht *The Maestro Myth* New York: Birch Lane Press 1992 p. 82, on which Frank comments in this *CRC* article and in Frank Ch. 4.

vacation in his now forbidden homeland, Toscanini prepared to board the *Queen Mary* for his London engagements.

Those engagements were but one element – albeit intended as the climax – of a London Music Festival designed by Mase as a co-ordinated display of cultural and musical events to showcase the capital's capabilities, extending from the third week in April to the beginning of June.[6] His committee of the musical great and good (called the Grand Council) obtained Royal patronage and, jointly with the Secretary of the Royal Philharmonic Society, Keith Douglas, Mase arranged for concerts and other functions in numerous venues in and around London. 'Never before has a musical event of such scope and comprehensive importance been planned for London, and, indeed, for the whole cause of British music and music-making' opined the Master of the King's Music, Sir Walford Davies, in the Foreword to the Festival Guide. 'The first aim', he continued, 'will be to attain, in every order of music presented, a standard of surpassing excellence.' That excellence was guaranteed by Queen's Hall events such as Beecham and the LPO in three favourite composers, Mozart, Sibelius and Delius, and Bruno Walter with the LSO in Mozart and Brahms, both with top price seats of ten shillings (50 pence, today some £25). At the Royal Albert Hall Fritz Kreisler, with Beecham and the LPO, was to perform the Brahms concerto, together with more Sibelius from conductor and orchestra; and elsewhere among a host of performers were the Léner Quartet with Léon Goossens and the Brains, Aubrey and Dennis, the Hungarian and Griller Quartets, and Joseph Szigeti, Myra Hess and Benno Moiseiwitsch. A special opening night for the Grand Opera Season at Covent Garden on 1 May was linked in with the Festival.

Mase planned the grand sequence of programmes to culminate in the Beethoven series, including the symphonies and *Missa Solemnis* conducted by Toscanini, with top price seats at 25 shillings (£1.25) rising to 35 shillings (£1.75, today over £85) for the Mass. There was only one doubt: was the international situation so precarious that Toscanini would cancel? With a cable sent to their North American correspondent in New York prior to his departure, the BBC sought to allay the doubts of the Toscanini entourage, giving assurances to the effect that, should war break out while he was in London, the BBC would take the utmost care of him.[7] Before Toscanini's arrival Mase further advised the BBC in the firmest tones that the conductor would not permit use of recordings of the concert performances for reproduction overseas; such recordings would require his approval.[8] Fortunately the prohibition on

6   Mase's plans were fully set out in his speech launching the Festival, the text of which is in MA.

7   BBCA, Howgill's telegram to New York, 20 April 1939.

8   BBCA, Mase to the BBC, 22 March 1939.

FIG. 30 OWEN MASE AND KEITH DOUGLAS PREPARE THE LONDON MUSIC FESTIVAL 1939

recording could not be fully enforced; survivals include private recordings of the Fourth and Fifth symphonies and fragments of *Coriolan* and the Seventh Symphony. Moreover, unlike the 1938 Festival, some transatlantic shortwave transmissions survived: the first part of the concert containing the Ninth Symphony (but not the symphony itself) and the first *Missa Solemnis*, the latter being broadcast also in France, Belgium, Italy, Switzerland, Norway and Poland. Nevertheless, relatively little seems to have survived of the first five concerts containing the cycle of symphonies.

The Beethoven symphony cycle: Cardus versus the rest

The first five of Toscanini's seven concerts included all the Beethoven symphonies along with various overtures and shorter works, with the two subsequent performances of the *Missa Solemnis* as a fitting climax to his series. Supplementing this cycle were two concerts conducted by Boult, one with Wilhelm Backhaus as soloist in the Third and Fifth Piano Concertos, the other with Solomon in the Fourth Concerto and Adolf Busch in the Violin Concerto; Szigeti was later substituted since Adolf was delayed in New York by illness.[9]

Toscanini disembarked at Southampton on 26 April and that evening was met at Waterloo station by Mase who, fortunately, was able to protect him from the worst effects of a crush of over-enthusiastic women intent on mobbing Hollywood star Spencer Tracy, arriving on the same train. The conductor was puzzled by this reception: 'some film star', Mase assured him.[10] The next day he was busy rearranging the sequence of works in the second half of his first concert on 3 May. He was pre-occupied thenceforth with his usual intensive rehearsals, but the press was more impressed by the fact that he had begged to be excused presentation to the King and Queen at the opening concert; a measure, many thought, of Toscanini's dedicated professionalism, for it was without precedent for the current monarchs to attend such a function. Boult felt obliged to speak to the King's Private Secretary, Sir Alexander Hardinge, about the conductor's request; Hardinge assured him that the King and Queen 'would of course not wish to have Toscanini's conducting capacities disturbed', a message duly conveyed to Mase. He in turn responded on 2 May that Their Majesties' understanding had greatly relieved Toscanini, who had spent a sleepless night over this vexed question.[11] Although his attitude during this episode was consistent with his refusal to receive continental royalty in Salzburg during 1935–37, it did not chime with his more permissive stance at earlier London concerts, when it seems he had allowed himself to be presented to British Royalty: in the interval of the first New York Philharmonic concert on 1 June 1930, when a vast contingent of the reigning family was present, and after the BBC SO concert of 28 May 1937, when he was presented to the Duke and Duchess of Kent.[12]

---

[9]   Adolf Busch vol. 2 p. 391 (letter to Fritz Busch, 20 June 1939).

[10] Reports in the *Daily Express* 27 and 30 April 1939.

[11] BBCA, Boult's memorandum of 2 May 1939; Mase's to the BBC, 2 May 1939 reporting Toscanini's 'immense relief'. Sir Alexander Hardinge (1894–1960) 2nd Baron Hardinge of Penshurst (1944).

[12] *Daily Telegraph* 2 June 1930 (see also Ch. 1 p. 22); the *Times* 29 May 1937.

Whatever the reason for Toscanini's revised stance, the absence of the star visitor from the Royal presence on the night of 3 May created difficulties for others in attendance – as did the unexpected behaviour of Royalty itself, as Boult was later to record.[13] According to his account, Toscanini diplomatically declined to be present when royalty arrived – 'No, no, thank you, I must be on the platform to play the 'ymn' (the National Anthem). Boult and senior BBC officials and their wives therefore stationed themselves outside the hall in readiness. What they had not bargained on was the early and unannounced arrival of the formidable Queen Mary (the late King's widow). She was detained in desultory conversation while hasty rearrangements were made to seat the enlarged Royal party; and when the King and Queen eventually arrived, the latter's greeting – 'Oh mother, how nice; I had no idea you were coming' – confirmed that 'Queen Mary's intentions had, for once, not been circulated as far as they should have been'. During the interval the Queen, greatly enjoying the concert, wanted to 'thank the great man' and intimated that she and the King would be happy to visit him in his dressing room (again, an unprecedented descent). But in that room Boult found a shirtless and breathless Maestro unable to receive them; so the orchestra's leader, Paul Beard, was despatched up to the Royal enclosure as substitute.

Fortunately this pantomime failed to distract Toscanini in the slightest and, as was by now customary, the majority of the press was unconstrained in its praise for the symphony cycle commencing that evening with the First and Second. In welcoming Toscanini's return, the *Times* on 4 May acclaimed 'performances magnificent in their breadth of treatment and their intensity of expression'. Particular qualities noted by this critic included the way in which the orchestra now sustained a note 'through the whole value of its length', for example at the outset of *Egmont*, and Toscanini's demonstration in the opening movements of both symphonies of the 'true meaning of the direction *Allegro con brio*'. In contrast, Cardus in that day's *Manchester Guardian* provided choice specimens of his caveats of which many more were to come: 'again we were made to feel that we were not attending a performance, but somehow hearing the music once and for all – *sub specie aeternitatis*, so to say'. Sometimes, he continued, 'Toscanini's uncompromising veracity compels us to crave – such is our weakness – for a yielding phrase, for a rhythm that is not driven logically onwards, for a melodic nuance which woos the impressionable senses'. Still, he concluded, 'it is all convincing and rare while it lasts'.

The cycle thereafter progressed sequentially with, however, the even preceding

---

[13] Boult 1973 pp. 103–4.

the odd numbers in each concert: Symphonies Nos 4 and 3, 6 and 5, 8 and 7. After the second concert on 8 May Capell in the *Telegraph* remarked that, while the orchestra played as if its life was at stake, some thought that it did not sound as brilliant as in the previous year. He supplied the answer: the Queen's Hall had just been reupholstered in an absorbent velvet, in place of the old 'smooth stuff which naturally reflected sound more readily'. This explanation was not good enough for Newman, who after the third concert on 12 May complained in the *Sunday Times* on 14 May that the orchestra had often been below its best during the cycle, 'some of the woodwind tone being thin and sour and the intonation faulty', and a week later reinforced these complaints after hearing the fourth concert on 17 May containing the Seventh and Eighth symphonies. Such recordings of the cycle as survive do not in general support Newman's strictures; indeed, as noted in more detail in Annex B,[14] these invaluable fragments suggest a virtuosity remarkable even by the standards obtaining in the following century and repeatedly praised at the time as 'magnificent' by, among others, the *Times*, Capell, Bonavia, Westrup and Turner.

Meanwhile, Cardus's reviews continued his self-confessedly lonely catalogue of reservations. After the second concert's Fourth and *Eroica* symphonies on 8 May, his *Manchester Guardian* review next day damned Toscanini's right arm, whose 'great wheel' never ceased: 'on and on we were driven; the rhythm beat into the brain. It was as though we were listening to music in the teeth of a wind.' Toscanini's constant staccato attack, if applied to music big enough to bear such treatment was 'impressive beyond anything I have heard in a concert-room'; Cardus instanced here the *Coriolan* Overture, which was 'a revelation; the music assumed a grandeur comparable with any composed by Beethoven' – thereby inverting the view he took of Toscanini's 'mechanical' performance of the work two years before, which in all probability differed little. But elsewhere, for example in the Fourth Symphony's opening movement, 'we moved onward in a magnificent streamlined car as soon as the signal showed the amber light'. As Cardus saw it, Toscanini's professional athleticism in this work contrasted with Beecham's bubbling spontaneity; he was clear about his preference.

Cardus did, however, find much to appreciate and he never left his readers in any doubt about, as he admitted, Toscanini's supreme stature. He thought the *Eroica*'s Adagio 'majestic and moving beyond mortal and temporal ideas' and, as his review on 15 May showed, he greatly enjoyed the third concert (12 May) containing the Fifth and *Pastoral* symphonies. The *Pastoral* had a 'rare beauty of tone,

---

[14]   See pp. 287–8.

phrasing and balance; the harmonies had a fullness seldom achieved by orchestras in this country'. As with other critical assessments of the sound Toscanini drew from his orchestra in the Queen's Hall concerts, these remarks convey a significant impression for subsequent generations of listeners, bearing in mind the sonic falsifications offered by so many of the conductor's later recordings. Cardus also noted that details in the orchestration known only from the score 'now came to natural musical life, all flowing along on the current of Toscanini's incomparable rhythm'. But the Fifth appealed less: although a 'magnificently musical performance', it was for him too highly organised, giving him 'no glimpse into Beethoven's forge'; so, if Toscanini's Beethoven was 'without doubt the most musically comprehensive of our time', it was hardly 'also the most poetically comprehensive'.

The surviving off-air recordings do not in general support Cardus's complaints about the rigidity and lack of humanity in Toscanini's general approach any more than they do Newman's criticisms of the playing. Many another review of the cycle discerned far more than Cardus's apparent preconceptions. The *Times* on 9 May commended the 'extraordinary energy' of the Fourth Symphony's first movement, part of a 'wonderful performance'; likewise the first movement of an *Eroica* which left an impression 'of a precision of rhythmic movement taut without becoming stiff', with a finale of 'immense spaciousness'. For Capell in that day's *Telegraph*, the *Marcia funebre* 'was of an unheard-of intensity'. In its review on 13 May, the *Times* virtually contradicted Cardus about the Fifth Symphony's first movement: 'the whole surged forward with an inevitable energy in which again the most vivid and the most subtle points of expression had space to make themselves realised within the span of the rhythm'. To similar effect was this critic's view of the *Pastoral*: 'With every detail so perfectly placed there is plenty of leisure to observe every beauty without having it pointed out ... Nothing escapes him but he does not expatiate on the view'. Bonavia, in his last review of a Toscanini concert in that day's *Telegraph*, came to similar conclusions, pointing to the rhythmic freedom in certain passages of the Fifth Symphony's Andante and to the beauty of tone in the *Pastoral*, particularly the 'lyrical singing tone' of the finale. Westrup, in *his* last review of a Toscanini concert in the *Telegraph* on 18 May, expounded at length on the many virtues of the Seventh Symphony: 'the sense of expectancy achieved by simple accuracy at the end of the slow introduction; the exact and constant value given to the dotted quaver and semi-quaver in the *Vivace* ... the final suggestion of bleak emptiness in the second ... and the hitting of 100 nails on the head in the finale'. The *Times* that day, if much shorter, was to identical effect about this 'performance of extraordinary exhilaration'.

Turner's last piece on Toscanini, in the *New Statesman* on 20 May, looked back at the first four concerts and once again heard what Cardus could not: under Toscanini 'the music unfolded before us correct and exact in detail but also in perfect proportion to a degree of clarity that no other conductor achieves'; but it was erroneous to ascribe this result to 'a mere scrupulous fidelity' to the text, for 'one of the amazing characteristics of Toscanini's conducting is the way in which he is almost continuously varying the tempo ... the ever-varying flame of Toscanini varies so sensitively that it is difficult to detect that it is varying at all. But this is what keeps it alive.' Summing up, Turner's ultimate verdict was that Toscanini had 'a pure and instantaneous comprehension of music such as has rarely occurred in history'.

Players also heard this 'ever-varying flame': Archie Camden, for one, later pointed out that, while Toscanini was 'credited with an unswerving rhythm' and never altering his beat, 'on the contrary, as one who played under him many times, I vouch for the fact that he frequently altered his beat to suit the music', although 'he never lost that fundamental rhythm'.[15] Fortunately, the manner in which the conductor accommodated Camden's last movement solo in the concert performance of the Fourth Symphony, subtly bending the tempo around him, was (as further detailed in Annex B) preserved, albeit in primitive sound, at Boult's behest.

If the reviews of this cycle were, on the whole, of an unalloyed enthusiasm, taken in the round they also disclosed an awareness of change in the nature of Toscanini's art: of some reduction in the breadth of his tempos, of an increasing tightness of grasp on symphonic structure by comparison with earlier seasons back to 1930. There were comments on, for example, the staccato attack in the first movement of the *Eroica* (the *Times*); the rigour of his rhythm, a product of the grip of his right arm which excluded charm in the Fourth's Adagio (Capell); and, later on, the disdain for pathos in the latter pages of the Ninth Symphony's first movement or for any hint of melting in its Adagio (again Capell). These characteristics were not felt by most critics to be shortcomings or limitations; merely the reverse side of the coin in interpretations which in their clear-eyed intensity led the listener closer to the composer's creative process than any others. Newman, in the *Sunday Times* of 21 May, summed up this reaction after hearing the Seventh and Eighth symphonies

---

[15]   Camden p. 95; see further p. 287. Turner's concert review here summarised came in the context of a review of Lawrence Gilman's book *Toscanini and Great Music* London: Bodley Head 1939, but he virtually ignored this hagiographic offering, of which the only valuable part is Sir Adrian Boult's Introduction. Turner's reference to Toscanini's 'flame' in this review was the final sputtering of his obsession about Schnabel's definition: see Ch. 1 n. 37. In the summaries of Turner's reviews in this and preceding chapters, I have not referred to the passages in which his arguments about these definitions figured so prominently.

in the fourth concert (17 May): 'seldom, even with Toscanini, has one had to such a degree the feeling that the conductor was simply the medium through which the composer was speaking ... everything in the scores was made crystal-clear, every phrase sprang into being as if instantaneously cast in the finest metal'.

In addition to these significant comments on the changing nature of Toscanini's approach, the reviews disclosed many details about his practice in performance which are not apparent from recordings. For example, Capell noted that in the *Eroica* Symphony there were four horns and doubled winds for the tutti and that in the fugato of the *Marcia funebre* – bars 133–40 – 'not Beethoven's third horn alone came in, but all'. Similarly, of the Eighth Symphony the *Times* noted that Toscanini used only the two horns as required by the score with a full body of strings – they were 'quite enough', especially in the Trio where their duetting was 'among the many moments of outstanding beauty'. But in the Seventh, said the *Times*, Toscanini added the second pair of horns; indeed Westrup noted that all the winds were doubled in this work and in both symphonies 'the result was an object lesson in balance'.

Last-minute changes were made to the programmes, affecting in particular the final concert of the symphony cycle. On 8 May Toscanini decided that the *Prometheus* Overture, originally scheduled to commence the programme containing the Ninth Symphony on 22 May, should start the concert on 12 May containing the Fifth and Sixth, so leaving time before the Ninth (in accordance with the BBC's strict time schedules) for both the Adagio and Allegretto from the *Prometheus* incidental music and the conductor's favoured string orchestra versions of the Vivace and Lento from the Quartet Op. 135. On the night, the latter movements were not liked by the *Times*, which thought them 'an act of violence which calls for protest'; they 'sounded poor and ... not very accurately played by the first violins' by the side of the 'brilliant' repetition of *Leonore No. 3*, which had also rounded off the first concert. Surviving off-air recordings of the first half of the concert on 22 May do, indeed, reveal a transcendent rendition of the overture but do not confirm the strictures about the quartet movements, of which other critics were more appreciative. Moreover, to the end of his life Newman chose Toscanini's recording of the Lento as his preferred statement of a particularly profound work, not because of the undoubted virtues of the performance, but because for him its significance was best conveyed by the larger forces: as he put it on the present occasion, the body of strings revealed 'depths of expression in Beethoven's music that is beyond the power of the finest quartet to plumb'.[16]

---

[16] See *Sunday Times* 6 July 1958: *The Ultimate Things*. Quotation from *Sunday Times* 28 May 1939.

As for the second half of the concert on 22 May, the Ninth Symphony as ever found Cardus pitted against all his contemporaries; for the first time he explicitly blamed Toscanini's age for the shortcomings he alone found. In the *Manchester Guardian* on 24 May, he suggested that, while the conception behind the performance was 'undoubtedly sublime', Toscanini would find only in heaven the orchestra 'able to give him all that he increasingly wants as, in his old age, he searches farther and farther and goes beyond poor mortal susceptibilities and weaknesses'. As in Toscanini's earlier Queen's Hall Ninth in November 1937, he found not only quick tempos, but a 'disdain of nuance ... while the great wheel revolves, sometimes metronomically'. The whole concert was, he thought, earthbound and the first movement 'lacked mystery ... the scherzo rattled on, chattered and bustled with no perceptible change of mood or tempo in the trio ... the Adagio was a masterpiece of logical connection in Toscanini's far-reaching control'. Cardus was allowed, indeed commanded by his editors to take at least six hundred words in his reviews and here, as in his other pieces on the cycle, he took full advantage of the space to indulge his isolated viewpoint, which with some apparent pride he denoted as being in an 'overwhelmed minority'.

Once more others heard with different ears, seemingly so contradictory as to persuade the reader that they were attending another concert altogether. Thus the *Times* on 23 May remarked on the 'amazing' way in which Toscanini kept the whole symphony 'at high tension from first to last without becoming hysterical at the climaxes', combining this achievement with 'his power of indulging in rubato without weakening the rhythm'. Of the first movement, 'he so carves out each phrase ... that there is no orchestral clatter. One hears every detail and it all contributes', while in the finale, 'though he requires a terrific energy ... he seems to avoid hustling the singers so as to make them inarticulate'. Capell in that day's *Telegraph* was, as ever, more idiosyncratic but hardly less enthusiastic: 'The supremely memorable thing about the evening was the wholeness of the effect of Toscanini's performance – the grasp which made, as never before, the finale the goal and fulfilment of it all.' If the first movement was urgent, this tempo 'made perfect sense' of passages which had often seemed awkward – Capell instanced the passage for alternate strings and woodwind near the end of the exposition (bar 138 onward). The scherzo was 'played as perhaps never before' and in the finale 'the noise was enough to send one's blood from the skin to the heart, as is right. But absolutely measured.' Whether this great majority of reviewers was enlightened or misguided – no recording survives to support either viewpoint – the enthusiastic endorsement of Toscanini's approach to the Ninth certainly conveyed to posterity the continued and extraordinary dominance of the conductor in contemporary critical esteem.

More entertainment

With Toscanini present in London for over a month, once more the burning question of how best to entertain him engaged the finest minds of the BBC in prolonged discussion before his arrival; and again senior personnel asked whether he should be approached direct rather than through Mase. In March Boult quashed this renewed suggestion, since any direct approach to Toscanini about entertainment would merely result in his discussing the subject with Mase; but he did take the opportunity to set out the Music Department's feelings about Mase.[17] He recalled that negotiations for Toscanini's re-engagement in 1936 were conducted by a number of different people within the BBC and in consequence so many misunderstandings occurred that Toscanini refused to come. The BBC, continued Boult, owed it entirely to Mase that Toscanini agreed to return in 1937: he undertook a most unpleasant job and achieved a result that he himself almost certainly could not have managed; moreover, Boult added, he doubted if anyone else could. On the other hand, Toscanini 'leans very much on Mase and Mase irritates us all by assuming a sort of proprietary right over the person of the Maestro, and an attitude of "what a good boy am I".' After firing off this internal salvo he urged that, whatever entertainment was arranged, programme organiser Julian Herbage should be present because planning future concerts was important and hitherto the BBC had been obliged to accept Toscanini's programmes without modification.[18] Herbage did attend the informal lunch ultimately given for Toscanini on 20 May at Pagani's, a famous restaurant in Great Portland Street close to the Queen's Hall and habitual haunt of generations of musicians;[19] as will be seen, he made good use of the opportunity.

After lunch at Pagani's Toscanini was due to rehearse Beethoven's Ninth Symphony for its performance on 22 May but an important engagement that evening meant that something had to give. As Boult testified, by the time of Toscanini's last visits, he had learnt to get the best out of the BBC orchestra by 'demanding a little less at a rehearsal and getting what he wanted at the show'; so he often finished a rehearsal early and occasionally cut one altogether.[20] On 20 May Mase drew the conductor's attention to the Festival event taking place that evening at Kenwood: Callender's Massed Bands were to play Handel's *Music for the Royal Fireworks*

---

[17] BBCA, Boult's memorandum, 7 March 1939.

[18] BBCA, Boult's memorandum, 4 May 1939.

[19] BBCA, BBC memorandum, 15 May 1939.

[20] Boult 1983 p. 91.

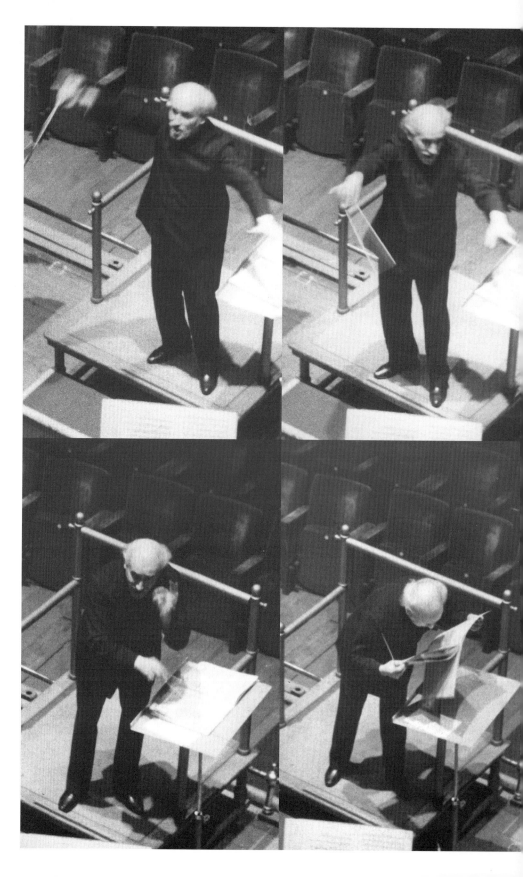

FIGS. 31–37 TOSCANINI REHEARSES
IN THE QUEEN'S HALL, OWEN MASE
LOOKS ON, 1939

followed (as the Festival Guide put it) by a 'GRAND DISPLAY OF FIREWORKS' including, in addition to various displays such as 'The Weird White Waterfall' and 'The Gigantic Pyramid of Revolving Fountains', a 'Grand Spectacular Set Piece' reproducing the 'MACHINE FOR THE ROYAL FIREWORKS' exhibited in Green Park in 1749 together with portraits of the current King and Queen. Toscanini loved fireworks and, after such a convivial lunch, had no hesitation in forgoing the rehearsal: the orchestra was astonished to learn from him that he was cancelling it because he was 'going to the fireworks' on Hampstead Heath. One rehearsal less was as nothing compared with Toscanini's enjoyment of the display, which in company with Mase and friends he watched 'with the enthusiasm of a schoolboy'.[21]

The Kenwood outing was not the only unusual Festival item to be enjoyed by Toscanini. On 9 May he attended the Prince's Galleries in Piccadilly (a Victorian entertainment hall) for an 'informal concert' of 'Folk Songs and Sea Shanties and other music of a convivial character' given by folk singer John Goss and the London Singers, where he was suitably amused by a rendering of Beethoven's *Metronoms-Kanon*.[22] More conventionally, he was present at Boult's second Beethoven concert on 21 May. On the evening after his first concert, 4 May, he attended Sadler's Wells ballet conducted by Constant Lambert, where the programme included *Checkmate* with music by Arthur Bliss. This was not Toscanini's first encounter with Bliss's music: he had heard the *Music for Strings* in Salzburg at a Vienna Philharmonic concert under Boult in August 1935. Bliss himself attended the rehearsals for the current Beethoven cycle and recollected Toscanini's 'vivid beat like a sword play in the air', the whole dedicated atmosphere leaving a profound impression. On his visit to the ballet Toscanini was for his part sufficiently impressed by the music for *Checkmate* to ask the composer to meet him at the Langham Hotel. He instantly put Bliss at ease with his question as he led him to a sofa, 'Tell me, Mr Bliss, – do you, as an English musician, think that I, as an Italian take the slow movements of Beethoven rather fast?' Conversation then flowed freely while Carla supervised tea.[23] For Bliss, Toscanini was both great and, unlike many of his colleagues, modest; but if his conversational starter suggested humility, it also provided evidence of his having read some of the concert reviews. In the end he did not conduct any of Bliss's music.

Outside Festival commitments, Mase and Georgina again entertained him and

[21] Mase *Memories*.

[22] See *Musical America* June 1939 (Edward Lockspeiser). The canon 'Ta ta ta ... lieber Maelzel' is now usually attributed to Anton Schindler.

[23] Bliss pp. 115–16. The other items on the ballet programme Toscanini attended were Lord Berners's *A Wedding Bouquet* and Walton's *Façade*. Sir Arthur Bliss, composer (1891–1975), appointed Master of the Queen's Music 1953; see further Ch. 9 p. 178.

FIG. 38 TOSCANINI, CARLA, GEORGINA AND OWEN MASE PREPARE FOR AN
EXPEDITION

his wife at their country cottage, the pastimes including a picnic in neighbouring
Chiltern beechwoods during which Toscanini declaimed extracts from the poems
of John Clare whose work he had discovered earlier that same day.[24] This love of
English literature was displayed only to intimates; the fabled memory was equally
evident both in public and in private.

Missa Solemnis – *and memories*

The crown of Toscanini's series, and of the Festival itself, was the two performances
of the *Missa Solemnis* on 26 and 28 May. London had, after all, experienced him
conducting all the symphonies save the Second and Eighth in earlier seasons; but

---

[24] See Mase's essay 'The Other Dimension', Ch. 11 p. 232. Almost certainly Georgina Mase drew
Toscanini's attention to the poet; the greater part of her published verse was about nature.

this was new. Unlike the Ninth Symphony, which Toscanini had first tackled complete in 1902, he did not take up the work until he was sixty-six (in March 1934 in New York) and the London performances were his first for nearly three years, the last having been in Vienna in November 1936. The forces were again the indefatigable BBC Chorus and Choral Society trained by Leslie Woodgate, with soloists Zinka Milanov, Kerstin Thorborg, Koloman von Pataky and Nicola Moscona seated immediately in front of the chorus. Denis Matthews, who attended both performances and the final rehearsal, recollected that rehearsal as having all the dedication of the performances themselves and later encountered Archie Camden who, exiting from the rehearsal, expressed his amazement at Toscanini's physical powers of endurance at the age of seventy-two.[25]

Surprisingly, Toscanini held much of the Bach B minor Mass in even higher regard than the *Missa*, although he never performed the former complete because of his uncertainty over the interpretation of Baroque works.[26] Nevertheless, the *Missa* sent him into verbal ecstasies similar to the Ninth Symphony's Adagio: of the Praeludio he remarked to Boult, 'it is so wonderful. I close my eyes when I conduct it – I close my eyes and then the organ comes in at the end and it is a light from heaven.'[27] He also expressed his acute anxiety about the danger of covering the solo violin in the Benedictus, consulting Boult as to whether he might even cut out the *sforzando* marking in the brass and timpani interjections. Furthermore, the work's stature was quite sufficient to induce in him an unusually severe fit of pre-concert nerves before the first of the two performances. As recounted by Boult, in the artists' room Toscanini seized him by the lapels of his coat, asking him to go on the platform of the packed hall to announce that 'we shall 'ave the concert next Tuesday' (the two performances were on a Friday and Sunday).[28] Boult had dazed visions of postponing the European and transatlantic transmission; but all was set to rights as Carla made her way to her seat as if nothing unusual were occurring and the imperturbable platform attendant Edgar Mays announced in stentorian tones, 'ready, thank you, Maestro'; upon which Toscanini meekly made his exit to the platform.

The performances were accounted triumphs by the press – although in the *Times* on 27 May not without significant qualifications. While its critic admired

[25] Matthews 1966 p. 73.

[26] ATL pp. 147–8 (letter to AM, 17 July 1933).

[27] Kennedy 1987 p. 186. See Ch. 6 p. 113 for similar thoughts on the Ninth Symphony's Adagio.

[28] Boult 1973 p. 104.

the symphonic coherence of the whole, and 'the conductor's incandescent fervour and iron discipline', those very qualities bore harshly on the chorus and more especially the solo voices. But many of these reservations related to what the critic saw as Beethoven's own miscalculations which Toscanini was seen as failing to mitigate – not a viewpoint to commend itself to later generations. In any event there were 'many singular beauties', the opening of the Kyrie never having sounded 'more noble' nor that of the Sanctus 'more profound'. Somewhat in contrast, Capell in that day's *Telegraph* noted that the soloists were encouraged to deviate from the strict letter of the score for the sake of expressivity and that Paul Beard's solo in the Benedictus had a 'liberty beautifully allowed'. In sum, Toscanini 'inspired in all the will to do or die' and, armed with the BBC Choral Society, achieved an 'extraordinary result' which in the Gloria 'piled mountain upon mountain'. Toscanini's consistent admiration for chorusmaster Leslie Woodgate was evident in his invitation to him to share the ovations. Commercial issue of the BBC's recording of the second performance's broadcast on 28 May now permits us to judge its supreme qualities for ourselves. After that performance London did not hear Toscanini again for thirteen years.

The impact remained. How could that be otherwise, after nearly thirty concerts conducted by Toscanini over the decade, culminating in the cycle by the symphonic composer whom he revered above all others? Nevertheless, relatively few attending the concerts left comments that conveyed the nature of this impact, while impressions of the conductor among succeeding generations of listeners have sometimes been unduly influenced by the sonic shortcomings of his later recordings. Moreover, although the exalted level of playing demanded by Toscanini left a permanent imprint on the collective minds of orchestras and listeners, the depredations of wartime conditions, as well as the added post-war competition from two new orchestras, the Philharmonia and Royal Philharmonic, took their toll on the BBC orchestra. A lengthy period of training under a succession of conductors was needed to replicate Toscanini's standards in the coming decades.

Among writers of the time, two, the supreme professional and the most eloquent player, must be allowed the farewell. Covering the Ninth Symphony and the *Missa Solemnis* in the *Sunday Times* on May 28, Newman once again, and for the last time, resorted to his ultimate paradox. The greatness of the music impressed itself on the listener 'from within the music itself', but not because Toscanini 'played the notes as written'; rather, 'in some mysterious way that utterly baffles analysis, Toscanini, while obviously accountable for the work sounding and shaping as it does ... gives us the grateful and comforting and unfortunately rare

Queen's Hall
Sole Lessees: Messrs. Chappell and Co., Ltd.

London Music Festival

Monday 14 June 1937 at 8.15 p.m.

FIFTH CONCERT

Symphony No. 40, in G minor (K.550)	MOZART
	1756-1791
Passacaglia in C minor	BACH-RESPIGHI
	1685-1750 1879—1936

INTERVAL

Iberia (Images, No. 2)	DEBUSSY
	1862-1918
Symphonic Poem En Saga (Op. 9)	SIBELIUS
	Born 1865
Marche Hongroise (La Damnation	
de Faust) (Op. 24)	BERLIOZ
	1803-1869

The B.B.C. Symphony Orchestra
Leader : Paul Beard   Organ : Berkeley Mason

CONDUCTOR : Arturo Toscanini

In accordance with the requirements of the London County Council:
I. The public may leave at the end of the performance or exhibition by all exit doors, and such doors must at that time be open.
II. All gangways, corridors, staircases and external passageways intended for exit shall be kept entirely free from obstruction, whether permanent or temporary.
III. Persons shall not be permitted to stand or sit in any of the gangways intersecting the seating or to sit in any of the other gangways. If standing be permitted in the gangways at the sides and rear of the seating, it shall be limited to the numbers indicated in the notices exhibited in those positions.

3

Queen's Hall
Sole Lessees: Messrs. Chappell and Co., Ltd.

London Music Festival

Wednesday 16 June 1937 at 8.15 p.m.

LAST CONCERT

God Save the King
ORCHESTRATION BY GERRARD WILLIAMS

Wagner
1813-1883

A Faust Overture
Preludes Acts I and III (Lohengrin)
Overture and Venusberg Music (Tannhäuser)
INTERVAL
Siegfried Idyll
Forest Murmurs (Siegfried)
Day-dawn and Siegfried's Journey to the Rhine
(Götterdämmerung)
The Ride of the Valkyries (Die Walküre)

The B.B.C. Symphony Orchestra
Leader: Paul Beard   Organ: Berkeley Mason

CONDUCTOR : Arturo Toscanini

In accordance with the requirements of the London County Council:
I. The public may leave at the end of the performance or exhibition by all exit doors, and such doors must at that time be open.
II. All gangways, corridors, staircases and external passageways intended for exit shall be kept entirely free from obstruction, whether permanent or temporary.
III. Persons shall not be permitted to stand or sit in any of the gangways intersecting the seating or to sit in any of the other gangways. If standing be permitted in the gangways at the sides and rear of the seating, it shall be limited to the numbers indicated in the notices exhibited in those positions.

3

Queen's Hall
Sole Lessees: Messrs. Chappell and Co., Ltd.

London Music Festival

THIRD CONCERT

Friday 27 May 1938 at 8.15 p.m.

Te Deum, for Double Chorus and Orchestra	VERDI
	1813—1901

INTERVAL

Requiem Mass, for Four Solo Voices,	
Chorus and Orchestra	VERDI

Zinka Milanov
Kerstin Thorborg
Helge Roswaenge
Nicola Moscona

The B.B.C. Choral Society
(Chorus Master: Leslie Woodgate)

The B.B.C. Symphony Orchestra
Leader: Paul Beard   Organ: Berkeley Mason

CONDUCTOR : Arturo Toscanini

In accordance with the requirements of the London County Council:
I. The public may leave at the end of the performance or exhibition by all exit doors, and such doors must at that time be open.
II. All gangways, corridors, staircases and external passageways intended for exit shall be kept entirely free from obstruction, whether permanent or temporary.
III. Persons shall not be permitted to stand or sit in any of the gangways intersecting the seating or to sit in any of the other gangways. If standing be permitted in the gangways at the sides and rear of the seating, it shall be limited to the numbers indicated in the notices exhibited in those positions.

3

Queen's Hall
Sole Lessees: Messrs. Chappell and Co., Ltd.

EIGHTH

Beethoven Concert

Friday 26 May 1939 at 8.15 p.m.

Mass in D (Op. 123)
(Missa Solennis)

Zinka Milanov
Kerstin Thorborg
Koloman von Pataky
Nicola Moscona

The BBC Choral Society
(Chorus Master: Leslie Woodgate)

The BBC Symphony Orchestra
Leader: Paul Beard   Organ: Berkeley Mason

CONDUCTOR : Arturo Toscanini

The Concert will be broadcast from 8.15 p.m. to 9.50 p.m.

In accordance with the requirements of the London County Council:
I. The public may leave at the end of the performance or exhibition by all exit doors, and such doors must at that time be open.
II. All gangways, corridors, staircases and external passageways intended for exit shall be kept entirely free from obstruction, whether permanent or temporary.
III. Persons shall not be permitted to stand or sit in any of the gangways intersecting the seating or to sit in any of the other gangways. If standing be permitted in the gangways at the sides and rear of the seating, it shall be limited to the numbers indicated in the notices exhibited in those positions.

3

FIGS. 39-42 A QUARTET OF PROGRAMMES

feeling that it is the composer himself who is talking to us without an intermediary'. The performances were 'stupendous – but stupendous in the composer's way in the first and last place'.

The BBC SO's principal viola Bernard Shore was also one of the most eloquent and perceptive commentators and some of his contemporaneous reflections in *The Orchestra Speaks* (1938) have already been noted. But it was his retrospective a decade later, similar in essence to but more explicit and straightforward than Newman's, that most fittingly serves as the final curtain to the chronicle of the BBC concerts. Of that 1939 series, he recollected, 'there remains an indelible impression of contact with Beethoven's very mind. The conductor's intensity and his relentless power and rhythm carried us through the colossal cycle with no intervention of an alien idiosyncracy between composer and orchestra; and Beethoven seemed to tower behind the conductor's shoulder like an almost invisible genie. The orchestra felt itself straining to the utmost of its power to respond to the demands that Beethoven himself seemed to be making through Toscanini.' The 1939 Festival, he observed, had been dreaded by the orchestra, promising an unrelieved endurance test; but instead, it 'became a steady crescendo of interest and power. It was an experience without which the orchestra of my time might never have measured the full grandeur of Beethoven so clearly.'[29]

Both retrospectives took as a matter of course the supreme architectonic power of Toscanini's performances, the 'frozen architecture' as Boult termed it; the obvious attributes required no emphasis. Instead, the writers evoked once more Toscanini's seeming power in the ears of his listeners at the time to penetrate the mind and heart of the composer at the instant of creation. That power was sometimes claimed again for others among later generations of great conductors such as Klemperer and Furtwängler, but not without accompanying controversy about aspects of their art such as choices of tempo and degrees of expressive liberty. By contrast, contemporary comment about Toscanini emphasised the absolute directness and absence of distraction in conveying the message, which nonetheless – as the summarised reception of the BBC concerts in preceding chapters has demonstrated – did not in the view of most critics preclude the constant suppleness of line and rhythm that brought the music to fullest expressive life. All these aspects of Toscanini's art, as demonstrated by his London-made recorded legacy, are more fully examined in Chapter 12.

---

[29] Shore 1949 p. 42.

Final recordings

Three days after the last concert Toscanini returned to the Queen's Hall for what proved to be his final pre-war recording sessions for HMV. As usual, Collingwood was in attendance for the two sessions, on the morning and afternoon of 1 June. The scheduled works were Beethoven's Fourth Symphony and three overtures, the first *Leonore*, *Coriolan* and *Prometheus*, a heavy programme for a single day, given that each movement of the symphony and each overture was to be played through twice to provide first and second takes. Nevertheless, the works were proficiently taken down by landline from the hall to Abbey Road. Two machines with a switch were used to secure proper side-breaks in the non-stop recording of complete works and movements lasting more than a single side; that comprised all the music save the single-sided *Prometheus* – and even that short work had a back-up recording on two ten-inch matrices for possible issue without coupling.

The next morning Toscanini visited HMV's new premises in Oxford Street and signed a wall plaque designed to take the signatures of their international artists. That afternoon he approved some RCA test pressings of the NBC Symphony recordings made before his departure for London, including Beethoven's Eighth Symphony (although the first side had to be re-recorded because of a flat clarinet solo near the start), the *William Tell* Overture and the two middle movements of Beethoven's Fifth Symphony. His approval of the Fifth's scherzo came after he compared his own with Furtwängler's recent Berlin Philharmonic recording which, as Palmer related to his RCA colleagues, caused Toscanini considerable amusement, doubtless stemming from Furtwängler's early anticipation of and exaggerated response to the *poco rits* near the start of the movement.[30] Then there was a party to attend, arranged by the orchestra in the small Queen's Hall, a unique occasion afforded no other conductor and a measure of the affection and respect in which the orchestra by now held him.[31] Seated at a small table, all players who wished to talk to him did so in turn while Sidonie Goossens (joint organiser of the

---

[30] EMI, Palmer to O'Connell, 2 June 1939. Furtwängler's HMV recording of Beethoven's Fifth Symphony made in Berlin, 8 October and 3 November 1937, DB 3328–32S, various CD transfers. The score's two *poco rits* near the beginning of the scherzo start at bars 7 and 17; Furtwängler starts these from bars 5 and 14, bringing the orchestra to a virtual halt by bar 17.

[31] Sidonie Goossens broadcast talk, Ernest Hall interview with the author, 1972. The date and year of this party cannot now be determined; but the players were not yet on such terms with Toscanini in 1937, while it is unlikely that they would have sought to duplicate Lady Ravensdale's party, at which the orchestra's principals were present, during the 1938 Festival (see Ch. 7 p. 133). Thus the most likely period was during or after the conclusion of the 1939 Festival.

FIG. 43 CARLA CONTROLS THE DRINKS: AN INTIMATE MOMENT, LONDON, 1939

party with violinist Jessie Hinchliffe) plied him with sherry; Carla forbade a third glass. Toscanini departed for Basle en route for Lucerne on 5 June.

The results of the 1 June sessions were sonically less successful than in previous years. Quite why that should have been is not clear, although the new upholstery mentioned by Capell may have posed acoustic difficulties in the empty hall. The expert balance engineer, Edward Fowler, was again present, yet the sound produced for these sessions, especially for the Fourth Symphony, was cavernous and in the lower frequencies often cloudy, with distantly balanced woodwind. The recording of the symphony's last movement was awkwardly switched midway through the sustained fortissimo at bars 118–19 and the last side was as a result marred by the music continuing prematurely in the run-in groove. The whole side therefore had to be transferred before it was fit for issue and it is ironic that this dubbing, made in the Abbey Road Transfer Room on 5 July, gave the sound a greater impact than the rest of the work.

Thereafter preparations to get Toscanini's approval went ahead.[32] In late July HMV sent out a specimen of their best gramophone to Switzerland for installation in the villa he had rented for the summer at Kastanienbaum outside Lucerne. Then Mase, on holiday for the Toscanini concerts in Lucerne (Gaisberg, too, was there), was followed on 4 August by Palmer; and, judging it impolitic to attempt anything before Toscanini's concert on 5 August, they waited until the next day to play the test discs to him. To their relief they obtained his approval for all the recordings with the exception of the *Coriolan* Overture. The approved discs were issued in Britain in October (*Leonore No. 1*) and December (the Fourth Symphony) when the country was already at war. *Prometheus*, for want of a coupling, had to wait until 1986. *Coriolan*, the masters of which were by then no longer extant, was saved only by a test pressing sent to New York during the war at Walter Toscanini's request; it has not survived. After Toscanini's departure from Switzerland the loaned gramophone found a place in a Basle showroom.

Aftermath – BBC plans

Despite the louring international situation at the time of Toscanini's Beethoven cycle, the BBC were already making plans for his return. After Herbage attended the lunch at Pagani's on 20 May, Toscanini invited him to his hotel the next day to discuss repertoire for a proposed London Music Festival in May/June 1940. On 24 May Herbage sent Toscanini a bundle of scores of English music discussed with him at their meeting. In his covering letter he asked him if he would wish to choose one or more for inclusion in the mooted Festival and the conductor signified his willingness to undertake the Third Symphony, *A Pastoral Symphony*, of Vaughan Williams; but BBC efforts in early June to tie him down to a contract failed because,

---

[32]   EMI, Palmer to Pinsker, Basle, 29 June 1939.

complaining of fatigue, he was unwilling to discuss the matter. It seems that on this occasion Mase was not involved in the negotiations and, significantly, they failed in their objective.

In early August Herbage informed Boult of his plans, appending programmes for six concerts based on his discussions with the Maestro; he commented in particular upon the Vaughan Williams symphony: 'I very much hope that Toscanini will still be in favour of the idea of the Vaughan Williams *Pastoral* [which] will be of much interest here.' One performance of the Verdi *Requiem* was planned for the Albert Hall, despite Toscanini's horror at its acoustics – did the conductor recognise that the performance was unlikely to take place? Whatever his private thoughts, he asked for an orchestra of 150 players and Herbage suggested the extras be recruited from the BBC's other orchestras (he mentioned the Theatre Orchestra and Empire Orchestra). The BBC Chorus was to be strengthened by the addition of the Royal Choral Society.[33] Other works in the programmes new to London audiences under Toscanini's baton included a concerto with Horowitz as soloist, Mozart's *Prague* Symphony, the Brahms Third and Schubert Second symphonies, Berlioz's *Harold in Italy*, Tchaikovsky's *Pathétique* Symphony and Strauss's *Ein Heldenleben*; all works he planned for, or had recently conducted with, the NBC Symphony.

Herbage then sent the draft programmes to Mase in Lucerne. On 15 August Mase reported that Toscanini had on 7 August signed a contract for the six concerts and agreed their dates, as well as the proposed repertoire (Vaughan Williams included) with a few amendments. For the Verdi *Requiem* he wanted Jussi Björling, who was to sing in his two Lucerne performances of the work on 16 and 17 August – he was clearly struck by the Swedish tenor. He also insisted that Brahms's Second Concerto should be substituted for Beethoven's *Emperor* Concerto, a work he conducted only once; he was to perform the Brahms with Horowitz in his final Lucerne concert on 29 August.[34] The complete programmes for May 1940 are set out at the end of Annex B. Boult then wrote to him remarking on the 'beautiful' performance

---

[33]   BBCA, Herbage's letter to Toscanini, 24 May 1939; BBC memorandum, 2 June 1939 recording Toscanini's unwillingness to discuss a contract; Herbage's letter to Boult with proposed programmes, 3 August 1939. The BBC Theatre Orchestra was formed in the 1930s and conducted by Stanford Robinson, renamed the BBC Opera Orchestra in 1949 and re-formed as the BBC Concert Orchestra in 1952. The BBC Empire Orchestra was formed in 1934 and gave live concerts under their conductor Eric Fogg (1903–39) on air late at night and in the early morning to reach appropriate radio stations around the world. Soon after Fogg's death it was disbanded and would therefore in any event have been unavailable in 1940.

[34]   This performance on APR 6001; Toscanini's personal tensions at the time, referred to at p. 176, are here evident in some exceptionally fast tempos.

of the *Requiem* he had heard on the radio from Lucerne and inviting him to contribute a few words about the BBC orchestra for a special booklet being prepared for the 1940 Festival to mark the tenth anniversary of Toscanini's first London appearance.

On 25 August Mase forwarded to the BBC the agreement for the 1940 concerts signed by Toscanini and himself; nine days later Britain was at war. It could have come as little surprise to Mase to be informed on 13 October that, because of the war, the BBC could not accept assignment of the contract. At his request the BBC returned the contract to him on 19 October.[35] So ended, for the duration of hostilities, any realistic possibility of hearing Toscanini conduct some musically diverse works, including a symphony by Britain's leading senior composer.

Glyndebourne finale

The BBC were not the only organisation urging Toscanini to return in 1940. As noted in Chapter 7, attempts to lure him to Glyndebourne, not merely as guest but as guest conductor, preoccupied minds over many months and with good reason: he greatly enjoyed his visits there and he loved the atmosphere, the dedication, the surroundings. The prolonged discussions and correspondence during 1938 were but a prelude to the more considered proposals in 1939 for a ten-day Verdi Festival before the start of the 1940 season, to include *Falstaff* conducted by Toscanini as well as a repeat of Fritz Busch's *Macbeth*.[36] With whom these proposals originated is not clear from surviving material, but the carefully elaborated plans bore the imprint of Bing's calculations.

On 9 July 1939 John Christie wrote to Toscanini enclosing outline proposals by Fritz and Erede.[37] 'I, personally', he said, 'should be delighted if you could see your way to accept: all of us would be more than pleased to welcome you and I hope that you would enjoy working here.' He deputed Erede to discuss the proposals with Toscanini in Lucerne and armed him with (Bing's) 'Detailed Instructions to Signor Erede for his Conversation with Maestro Toscanini, concerning the Verdi Festival at Glyndebourne in 1940'.[38] The 'Instructions' were indeed detailed as to dates: preceded by public dress rehearsals, *Falstaff* was to open on 29 April 1940, *Macbeth*

---

[35]   BBCA, letters/memoranda from Mase and the BBC on the dates specified.
[36]   Hughes 1965 p. 138.
[37]   Hughes 1965 pp. 147–8.
[38]   In GA.

the following night, with each to be followed by four further performances, the last on 8 and 9 May respectively; there was also a provisional schedule of rehearsals, for which Toscanini's presence would be required from 8 April onwards. He would be expected to accept the collaboration of the Glyndebourne staff, including Erede, who would act as prompter for *Falstaff*. His suggested fee would be £1000 for the five performances, representing about 20 per cent of the takings per night. The three names Toscanini, Busch and Ebert would be advertised with equal prominence. Everything would be done to satisfy Toscanini's wishes about the cast, but it was essential to know whether he would accept the orchestra personnel 'as engaged by Dr Busch'. As for lodgings, 'we shall try to find a comfortable villa in the neighbourhood of Glyndebourne', but details of Toscanini's requirements would be needed. This lengthy document continued with details of the proposed chorus, ballet and scenery, ending with the request for Erede to advise Toscanini 'of the special difficulties and limitations due to Glyndebourne's small organization and its position in the country'.

Erede met Toscanini in Lucerne on 13 July and that day he signalled his failure by telegram to Bing announcing that, after six hours of discussion regarding dates, there was no possibility of agreement.[39] Later he reported at greater length that, while Toscanini was pleased with Glyndebourne's atmosphere and was keen to conduct there, he could not spare sufficient time to rehearse and conduct five performances of *Falstaff*. The 1938 performance of *Macbeth* he attended was wonderful and he thought Fritz could do *Falstaff* just as well as he could himself. Years later Erede recollected how moved he had been to encounter two musicians so similar in their outlook and humility towards music as Fritz and Toscanini. Bing, however, maintained his reservations to the end: his ultimate verdict doubted that 'Glyndebourne was big enough to take either Toscanini's personality or his musical conceptions'.[40]

After the 1939 season there were no further performances at Glyndebourne until 1946. Still, the enforced pause in activities did not quite end Glyndebourne's attempt to engage Toscanini. At the war's end, Bing took the lead in persuading the Edinburgh authorities to establish a festival there, to commence in 1947. His success in that endeavour was followed by a turmoil of discussion about Glyndebourne's participation in the Festival and among many proposals Toscanini was once again

---

[39]   Only the telegram survives in GA; the rest reported in Grete Busch pp. 155–6, on which Hughes based his 1965 account, p. 148.

[40]   Rudolf Bing *5000 Nights at the Opera* London: Hamish Hamilton 1972 p. 63.

approached. In a telegram to Toscanini, then at La Scala, Christie explained Glyndebourne's plans for Ebert productions of *Macbeth* and *Figaro* in a three-week season at Edinburgh and asked, 'would you consider conducting season or *Macbeth* only'. But, even though Fritz Busch was at that time not there to conduct *Macbeth* 'as it must be conducted', the 79-year-old Maestro again declined.[41]

Toscanini's Lucerne negotiations with Mase and Erede took place around his festival commitments – six concerts and a performance of the *Siegfried Idyll* outside Tribschen (the villa in which Siegfried Wagner had been born and the work first played) – and against the background of an increasingly grim international situation. He was intensely homesick for Italy and the Isolino,[42] which he could not visit without risk to his life; and the imminent and inevitable slide into European war affected him deeply, persuading him that his prolonged Lucerne visit was a mistake. He envied those individuals, such as his brother-in-law Enrico Polo (a violinist in the Lucerne Festival Orchestra in 1938), who were able to erect mental barriers between their music and the outside world; he was incapable of such self-defence and, as he remarked in a letter to Ada, had no desire to hear music, much less to make it.[43] Those who could, among them Gaisberg, returned to London early and with relief. Toscanini did not leave Kastanienbaum for Bordeaux until 12 September, nine days after Britain declared war on Germany, having managed to secure berths on the S.S. *Manhattan*, scheduled to depart on 16 September.[44] For reasons that remain unclear, he seems to have endured an anxious wait of nearly a week as the wartime exodus from Europe gathered pace, eventually sailing with his wife on 22 September and arriving in New York on 1 October.[45]

[41]   Undated text of telegram and Christie's letter 14 November 1946 to Bing enclosing 'Toscanini's refusal' in GA. See also Hughes 1965 pp. 155–7, Ebert p. 180. Fritz Busch did not return to Glyndebourne until 1950. Some details of the circumstances surrounding this post-war invitation to Toscanini, as well as the text of his 'refusal', have not survived, possibly due to the wholesale clearance of old business records from some disused offices in the early 1960s.

[42]   ATL p. 355 (letters to AM, 8 and 23 June 1939).

[43]   ATL p. 358 (letter to AM, 25 August 1939). See also ATL p. 342 (letter to AM, 6 August 1938, referring to Polo).

[44]   ATL p. 359 (telegram to Wally di Castelbarco, 11 September 1939).

[45]   ATL p. 359 (telegram to Wally di Castelbarco, 22 September 1939), p. 364, (telegram to AM, 2 October 1939). Gaisberg, in his article 'Battistini and Others' *Gramophone* February 1944 p. 133 (and his article on Toscanini in the June 1943 issue), has him boarding the S.S. *George Washington*. Stravinsky, who was on the *Manhattan*, believed Toscanini to have been a fellow passenger on that vessel, although he did not see him; Walsh (Vol. 2 p. 103 and notes), however, cites evidence from the composer's mistress Vera (the following year to become his second wife) that, so crowded were all the cabins, Toscanini did not avail himself of his berth at night and 'instead paced the decks in a fury'.

CHAPTER 9

1940–45: WAR EFFORTS AND BEYOND

Exile

Once confined by war to the New World it was inevitable that, although Toscanini took no formal position in any of the various Italian émigré organisations, he should become an active figurehead of Italy in exile. Among other activities he drafted a Declaration published in *Life* magazine in September 1943 containing proposals for the future governance of Italy, which insisted on the need for the complete territorial integrity of the country and for future negotiations to be conducted with authorities untainted by association with fascism.[1] The Allies later ignored these demands with material consequences for the course of this narrative: in the timing of his return to his native country and in his visits to other countries that failed his tests. Mussolini's overthrow in July 1943, announced during an NBC Verdi concert on 25 July, saw him on stage clasping his hands and gazing heavenwards in thanksgiving, while in Milan La Scala's signboards were covered overnight with calls for his return. There were, however, grave impediments to overcome, even after cessation of hostilities. La Scala was partly devastated by Allied bombs; as a consequence of his personal influence, actively exercised, post-war Italy pursued its rebuilding as a priority. But in Toscanini's mind more substantial obstacles lay in Allied policy, which permitted negotiations with the monarch and others tainted by the defeated régime; to return in such circumstances would have compromised his principles, publicly stated in his *Life* Declaration. The situation changed only in February 1946, when Italy's post-war government announced a June referendum on the abolition of the monarchy.

---

[1] See generally Sachs 1991 pp. 88–93. Toscanini's 'Declaration to the People of America' appeared in *Life*, 13 September 1943.

1940–41: Sir Adrian requests the pleasure

Despite the obvious dangers of wartime transatlantic travel, as well as changes of venue and personnel in charge, the BBC constantly attempted to secure Toscanini's return to Britain throughout his period of exile. At the outset of war the orchestra and its management were evacuated to Bristol until June 1941, when devastation by enemy action forced a further relocation to Bedford for the duration of hostilities.[2] Boult was still both Chief Conductor of the orchestra and Director of Music but was answerable to a succession of Directors-General: Reith left in 1938 and among his several wartime successors the former Controller of Programmes Sir Cecil Graves occupied the post during 1942–44.[3] After a short period in a junior BBC position Arthur Bliss was appointed (at his own suggestion) Director of Music in April 1942, so relieving Boult of administrative and planning duties. In the spring of 1944 Bliss was succeeded by the tragically short-lived Victor Hely-Hutchinson.[4] All these top BBC personnel played an active role in seeking Toscanini's return, supported by others in senior management such as Controller of Programmes Basil Nicolls and his assistant Richard Howgill, who was himself appointed Director of Music in 1952.

If any invitation to Toscanini to visit wartime Britain appears in retrospect un-realistic, it did not seem so at the time, not least because of Toscanini's own warmth of attitude. Before the real bombing started Boult wrote him a chatty portrait of the orchestra's work in Bristol – 'a very poor substitute for the lovely Festival that we were planning with your cooperation' – hoping that by the following summer they could invite him to a peaceful London and 'pick up our old life again'.[5] A year later from Bedford Boult sent him greetings and some wartime programmes which elicited Toscanini's heartfelt telegram of thanks, dated 1 November 1941, in which he said Boult's greetings and love 'which I reciprocate, moved me to tears. I remember every one of you dear friends. I follow you with love sympathy admira-tion.' He wanted to be with them to work and share everything: 'I embrace you all – Sursum corda [lift up your hearts] and we will win.'[6] Whether or not disingenu-

---

[2]   See Kenyon pp. 155 and 168.

[3]   For the appointment of Graves and others here mentioned, see Kenyon pp. 172–3.

[4]   (1901–47) composer and music administrator, joined the BBC in 1926, succeeded Sir Granville Bantock as Professor of Music at Birmingham University 1934–44, after which he was appointed BBC Director of Music until his early death.

[5]   BBCA, Boult's letter to Toscanini, 23 May 1940.

[6]   BBCA, Toscanini's telegram, 1 November 1941 (also reproduced in Jerrold Northrop Moore *Music and Friends – Letters to Adrian Boult* London: Hamish Hamilton 1979 p. 137); Boult's reply, 3 November 1941.

ously, Boult took this message at face value, replying, 'we loved getting your cable and are thrilled to think that you would wish to be with us. We long to make music with you again.' This immediate response was but a prelude to his New Year's telegram of good wishes to Toscanini and Carla, to which he added effusively, 'all my colleagues feel an irresistible desire to ask if you would consider visiting England this summer. We and all our countrymen would be overjoyed if such were possible. To make music with you again would be of untold inspiration to us all.'[7] Toscanini did not, it seems, reply at that stage.

1942–44: Of flying-boats and fees

By early August 1942, apparently at the suggestion of Boult and Sir Henry Wood, more direct proposals were under discussion with the Washington embassy for Toscanini to conduct two concerts in Britain, including Shostakovich's Seventh, *Leningrad* Symphony, of which he had given the American premiere on 19 July.[8] News of these plans undoubtedly reached Toscanini for he was reported to have declared that nothing would have given him greater joy; only the mode of transportation, by bomber, put him off – a misunderstanding by the embassy, since the intention was to offer him civilian Clipper-class flying-boat travel.

Perhaps it was just as well that Toscanini declined this opportunity to conduct the *Leningrad* Symphony in London: unlike his New York premiere, Wood's London premiere in June,[9] the first performance in the West, was met by a critical response ranging from the disappointed (most critics) to the vitriolic (Newman). Critical opinion, however, mattered little: what moved the upper echelons of the BBC in their seemingly strange, almost wonderland efforts to secure Toscanini's return to wartorn London was the pressure of contemporary musical politics. In particular some made a strong case for the propaganda potential of Toscanini's presence at a time when the Berlin Philharmonic under Furtwängler and Karajan were at the behest of the Nazi régime on tour in neutral and occupied Europe.[10]

---

[7]   BBCA, Boult's telegram, 29 December 1941.

[8]   BBCA, H. G. Nicholas, Ministry of Information, letter to Nicolls, 13 August 1942, containing the text of the embassy's telegram and commenting on the proposals.

[9]   With the BBC SO at the Maida Vale Studios on 22 June 1942 and at a promenade concert in the Albert Hall on 29 June 1942: see Fairclough pp. 275–6.

[10]   BBCA, minute from Seymour de Lotbiniere, BBC Director of Empire Programmes, 29 December 1941, referring to this factor and to the Berlin Philharmonic's tour to Lisbon; Nicholas to Nicolls, 13 August 1942. Furtwängler conducted in occupied Copenhagen and Prague, Karajan in Paris and elsewhere.

In this spirit of the times, it becomes rather less surprising that BBC management reacted to Toscanini's reportedly reluctant rejection in August 1942 by offering a series of concerts in September/October, with transportation of the Maestro and his entourage by flying-boat. Director-General Graves, then visiting the United States, was charged with negotiations but eventually and with reluctance decided not to pursue the invitation: the Clipper-class flying-boat service could not cope with such sudden and large demands. As he put it in a subsequent report, 'we could get him over but there was no guarantee of getting him back, and it was not possible to transport his retinue at short notice'. Besides, the wear and tear of such a trip would weigh heavily on a person of Toscanini's age and 'we would want to prolong his conducting life, while a trip like this might shorten it'.[11] NBC's Vice-President John Royal confirmed this line to Boult: Toscanini was most anxious to come over but, after careful consideration by everyone, he decided it would be unwise, a conclusion Boult by then shared.[12] Still, the BBC, including the orchestra, were buoyed by constant messages of support from the Maestro – 'saluti tanti augurii' (literally, 'welcome so many [good] omens') ended one delivered by Barbirolli in June 1942 – to all of which Boult was meticulous in responding with hopeful post-hostility expectations ('most happy to get your lovely message' etc.).[13]

One firm rejection might have been thought sufficient to settle the matter for the duration; but the next BBC overture commenced almost immediately after the last, a measure of Toscanini's stature and the perceived value his presence would bring to wartime Britain. It was Graves himself who, while rejecting the autumn 1942 proposals, suggested a London Music Festival with Toscanini in April/May 1943. Promptly fleshing this out, Howgill thought fees should be suitably generous: for eight concerts, up to £1000 (today, over £35,000) per concert – a phenomenal sum for wartime Britain. Herbage urged concerts in

[11] The principal documents are BBCA, Nicolls's letter to Nicholas, 19 August 1942; Graves's cable to the BBC, 22 August 1942; Howgill's memorandum of a transatlantic telephone conversation with Graves, 24 August 1942; Graves's cable to the BBC, 1 September 1942, and memorandum dated 22 September 1942 after his return from the USA. The Boeing 314 Clipper-class flying-boats were used by PanAm's transatlantic service from 1939; BOAC (British Overseas Airways Corporation) took delivery of three in 1941, modified for extra range and used in January 1941 to transport Churchill back from the USA. Their restricted number and seat availability explain the doubts about transporting Toscanini and his entourage.

[12] BBCA, Royal's letter to Boult, 9 September 1942; Boult's reply, 11 September 1942.

[13] BBCA, Boult's memorandum, 22 June 1942, listing Toscanini's telegraphed messages, mostly in response to New Year or birthday greetings, dated 1 November 1941 (quoted in the text), 1 January 1942, 3 and 14 April 1942 to Barbirolli in New York, delivered by Barbirolli while visiting Britain. Boult replied to this last message on 22 June 1942.

Liverpool and Glasgow as well, which Bliss thought impractical, given 'the difficulties and hardship of travel for so old a man'.[14]

These proposals foundered on the issue of costs about which, in October 1942, Graves took the precaution of consulting Cyril Radcliffe KC, Director-General of the Ministry of Information.[15] Radcliffe, later demarcator of divided India and Pakistan and one of Britain's most distinguished Law Lords, advised elegantly that, since no issue of principle was involved, the real question was 'does the national interest really require the presence of Toscanini in this country at the cost of this amount of exchange, of which we can never have enough? I do not know by what process the equation in these matters is determined, but my private feeling would make me reluctant to agree.' No-one else outside the BBC supported getting Toscanini to Britain at this price. A similar proposal the following year, stemming from a Washington embassy report that Toscanini would like to broadcast from England, eventually ran into the sand, on this occasion because, when proposals were actually put to him, he declined on grounds of fatigue.[16]

That invitation finally settled the issue: efforts to get Toscanini back to Britain ceased until peace returned to Europe. But in a curious move which again demonstrated the high value placed upon him for morale and propaganda purposes, Clement Fuller, the BBC's European Service Correspondent, wrote to Walter Toscanini in January 1944 requesting a BBC interview to be recorded with Toscanini for broadcast to Europe in which the conductor would be asked his views on Furtwängler's recent concert in Sweden (on 8 December 1943 when he conducted Beethoven's Ninth Symphony). Fuller proposed a dual interview, in Italian for broadcast to Italy and in English for broadcast to the rest of Europe, the objective being to encourage people in the occupied territories. Toscanini would speak in New York but his voice would be recorded in London.[17] Correspondence apparently petered out after further enquiries by Walter.

---

[14] The principal documents are BBCA, Graves's memorandum, 22 September 1942; Howgill's memorandum, 2 October 1942; Herbage's memorandum, 2 October 1942, with manuscript comment by Bliss dated 4 October 1942; Graves's letter to Radcliffe, Ministry of Information, 14 October 1942; Radcliffe's letter to Graves, 17 October 1942; Graves's memorandum to R. W. Foot (co-Director-General), 27 November 1942.

[15] Cyril (Lord, later Viscount) Radcliffe (1899–1977) Director-General, Ministry of Information from 1941, Chairman, Indian Boundary Commission June–August 1947, appointed a Law Lord in 1949.

[16] BBCA, Washington embassy's cable to Ministry of Information, 1 January 1943; Bliss's memorandum, 25 January 1943; Herbage's memorandum, 8 March 1943; Nicolls's memorandum, 7 December 1943; embassy's cable, 14 December 1943.

[17] Letter of 24 January 1944 in ATC, further details in David Hamilton's lecture.

To a degree the BBC compensated for the many frustrated invitations here outlined (the correspondence and internal memoranda were voluminous) by their Sunday morning broadcasts of recordings of some of Toscanini's weekly NBC concerts. Toscanini was aware of these retransmissions and from New York specially requested that the BBC contact Mase to make sure he heard them. This enabled Mase, home by chance on leave from wartime service, to hear the Loeffler-Gershwin concert of 1 November 1942, rebroadcast in Britain three months later. Mase was touched by the conductor's solicitude even if he could have wished for a different choice of music.[18]

1940–45: Siren songs reach a receptive ear[19]

Naturally Mase was prominent among the many correspondents who, in addition to Toscanini's friends within the BBC, strove to maintain contact with him as the European conflict took hold of British lives. First among communicants though he was, his wife Georgina had to take over the letter-writing after July 1940, when he rejoined the armed forces in which he had served in the Great War. She was lavish with news, photographs and other gossip, including among much else kind remembrances to Toscanini from Henry Wood, who with his family was housed temporarily in the Mase cottage, and detailed descriptions of pet donkey Haiyu's trials, tribulations and eventual demise. Her constant requests for their 'darling Maestro' to write were answered first by his son Walter who, at Carla's insistence, responded in a lengthy letter to Georgina, assuring her that 'our hearts are near to you'.[20] At last came Toscanini's telegram to Mase at the end of December 1941: 'Often thinking of you with friendship and love today our souls are with you more than ever.'[21] Some two years later Georgina was thrilled to view (and Mase was 'desolate' to miss) Toscanini's film made in 1943 for the American Office of War

---

[18] The concert comprised Loeffler's *Memories of My Childhood*, Creston's *Choric Dance No. 2*, Gould's *Lincoln Legend* and Gershwin's *Rhapsody in Blue*. Mase's letter to Toscanini, 14 February 1943, ATC JPB 90-1 series L pt 1 folder L110A.

[19] This section is based on the following letters: Owen and Georgina Mase to Toscanini, 18 July 1940; Georgina Mase to Toscanini, 16 August, 22 September and 20 October 1941, 21 March 1943 and 5 June 1944; Sybil Cholmondeley to Toscanini, 29 November 1940, 6 May 1941, 1 January and 28 March 1943. These letters are in ATC JPB 90-1 series L pt 1 folders L88H and I, L93D and E, L110B and C, and L118B. See also Stansky pp. 251–2.

[20] 22 November 1940 in MA.

[21] 28 December 1941 in MA.

Information,[22] a copy of which was made available to Sybil Cholmondeley in 1944 and shared by her with Georgina; as Georgina added, 'I often see Sybil who deserves love and admiration for her work'.

That work figured prominently in Sybil's own letters to Toscanini, for neither she nor Yvonne Rothschild was to be outdone in written reminders of devotion. Sybil's stream of news, all on Admiralty notepaper, reported her important efforts to organise many thousands of women recruits for the navy.[23] One of her first letters remarked that Mrs Mase was coming to lunch 'from that nice cottage in the country where you have had some peaceful days'; evidently the devotees found strength in mutual support. Sybil, too, listened to the BBC rebroadcasts of the NBC concerts 'on the radio given me by David Sarnoff in 1939'.

Toscanini's reaction to this deluge from quarters both welcome and less welcome can be guessed from his equivocal response to similar missives in earlier years, noted at the end of Chapter 6. Moreover, he was on his own admission a reluctant correspondent, much given to oversight when it suited him. But none of these downsides affected the fundamental warmth of feeling he retained both for Britain and for his British friends, as is shown by his brief wartime cables to Boult and Mase. What moved him most was the very fact of Britain's wartime resistance to European forces which for him represented the embodiment of evil – at a time when the USA was not yet a participant in the conflict. So strong were his feelings that, when at the end of July 1940 his son Walter persisted in identifying all of Britain's alleged wrongdoings, his father 'called him a bastard and sent him out of the house' for a couple of months: 'England is fighting to save Europe from slavery, the subjection that threatens it. That is enough to make me love her.' In the letter to Ada dated 11 August 1940 from which the foregoing graphic quotes are extracted,[24] Toscanini forwarded a clipping from the *New York Herald Tribune* of 1 August 1940 containing a quotation from Garibaldi dated 1854: 'If ever England should be so circumstanced as to require the help of any ally, cursed be the Italian who would not step forward in her defence.'

Toscanini clearly had the Garibaldi quotation in the forefront of his mind at this

---

[22]   Containing performances with the NBC SO of Verdi's *La forza del destino* Overture and *Hymn of the Nations* filmed in Studio 8H on 8 and 20 December 1943, included in RCA DVD 82876 582429.

[23]   From November 1939 Sybil Cholmondeley was Chief Staff Officer to the Director of the Women's Royal Naval Service. In 1945 she was appointed Superintendent of the WRNS until 1946, when she was awarded the CBE for her war work.

[24]   ATL p. 375, containing also the Garibaldi text in Sachs's commentary.

FIG. 44 TOSCANINI AND FRIEDELIND WAGNER, BUENOS AIRES, MAY 1941

time for, in response to Sybil Cholmondeley's stream of correspondence, he sent her a signed photograph of himself with a note which, among other encouraging words, included this same quotation. Her prompt and grateful reply on 29 November 1940 assured him that his photograph was the only one on her desk – 'it has taken a war for you to send one to me of your own accord – a heavy price, but still!' Further, 'I showed your quotation from Garibaldi to Winston – of course he knew it well but he seemed pleased to see it again *and* from you.' Toscanini's strenuous efforts to get Friedelind Wagner released from wartime internment, which included various messages to foreign ambassadors in London including the American Joseph Kennedy, were also doubtless familiar to Churchill, who eventually gave the signal for her freedom in March 1941.[25] Two months later Toscanini met her again in Buenos Aires.

Toscanini's wartime British correspondents displayed at least one feature in common: their fulsome expressions of love for him in terms of uninhibited effusiveness. 'Wherever I go', wrote Mase in July 1940, 'Georgina and I will carry with us always the undying affection we bear for you and great pride and gratitude that we were honoured (*are* honoured with) your affection in return'. Georgina solo outbid her husband: in August 1941, her letter apostrophised him fervently – 'O Maestro darling, what wouldn't we give' to see him, signing off with 'bushels of love' – and was followed only a month later by another letter containing 'a large hug Maestro dear, and then another'. Her unrestrained language did not abate: in March 1943, thanking Toscanini for his Brahms Third Symphony on the preceding Sunday (a BBC rebroadcast of his NBC concert of 20 December 1942),[26] 'the loveliest I have ever heard', Georgina concluded with 'my undying gratitude for the loveliness you give us and my love for the person you are'.

If it were possible, Sybil Cholmondeley surpassed all competitors. Her news of Churchill in November 1940 ended with professions of undying love: 'I think of you *so* much and with such love and affection'. In January 1943 she again assured Toscanini that, leaving aside her own sons who were absent on war service, he was 'the first and most beloved friend I look forward to seeing ... Please think of me sometimes – I need to feel that I have your affection. All my devoted love'. Only two months later another letter ended 'always your dear kindness to me and my deep affection which grows stronger as these years go by – *All my love*'.

Although the extravagant language of this correspondence may now read a little strangely, it provides vivid evidence of the love and friendship the conductor inspired at the time, as also the particular warmth of his interaction with British friends who, it seems, freely shed a customary reserve in his presence. Responses from Toscanini himself were few and far between, but the family amanuensis Margherita De Vecchi[27] was kept busy in acknowledging the constant messages from what their writers emphasised was a deprived and much injured capital. Whatever his views on these effusions, the correspondence, along with the cajolery

[25] See Carr pp. 219–20, ATL p. 376 (letter to AM, 14 August 1940).

[26] The programme also included the *Haydn* Variations; the symphony issued on Music & Arts CD 995.

[27] See ATL p. 120.

emanating from the BBC, at least kept alive in Toscanini's memory the undoubted pleasures of his pre-war London visits and help explain the positive frame of mind with which he addressed post-war invitations urging his return.

1945: Mase, and realism, return

As soon as the war was over, and even before the BBC orchestra returned from Bedford to London in September, Owen Mase reappeared, asserting his proprietorial claims to represent Toscanini's interests. He was engaged throughout much of the war in distinguished war service, first as a founder member of an RAF regiment guarding airfields and later, among activities in several countries, devising new methods of aircraft recognition, for all of which he received the OBE (as he proudly informed Toscanini).[28] Re-entering the world of concert management soon after hostilities ceased, he was soon Managing Director of the Music, Art, and Drama Society, with offices in Park Lane, and involved himself with operatic seasons mounted at various London theatres. In early September 1945 he wrote to the BBC about a lengthy cable he had received from Toscanini explaining why he could not come to London in 1946:[29] he was expected in Italy in December 1945 to reopen La Scala in February 1946, dates later confirmed by NBC's Music Division Manager, Samuel Chotzinoff, in a cable to the BBC's new Director-General, William Haley.[30] Mase's reply to Toscanini expressed both his sorrow that he could 'not have the joy of running concerts with you in England next year' and his joy at the expected return to Italy. But the time was not ripe for that return and in early April 1946, citing uncertainty about his La Scala dates, Toscanini responded with a regretful but definite negative to an 'alluring', even 'sentimental' cable from Mase (the adjectives were Hely-Hutchinson's) again inviting him to conduct in London.[31]

---

[28] The author's conversation with Peter Agrell, 16 December 2008, and see Lewis p. 73.

[29] BBCA, Mase's letter to Kenneth Wright, Deputy Director of Music, 3 September 1945. Mase's reply to Toscanini, 18 September 1945, in MA.

[30] BBCA, Chotzinoff cable to Haley, 22 March 1946. (Sir) William Haley (1901–87) Director-General of the BBC 1944–52, editor of the *Times* 1952–66.

[31] BBCA, Hely-Hutchinson memorandum to Herbage, 4 April 1946, recording a conversation with Mase.

1 9 4 6 – 5 1 : L A S C A L A

Return to La Scala

In the spring of 1946 Toscanini was standing by in New York in readiness for his long-awaited return to Milan. His informant there was Fritz Busch's son, Hans Peter, then serving with the occupying forces in north Italy and appointed at the war's end to take charge of all musical activities in the city for the Allied Military Government, including in particular La Scala.[1] One of his noteworthy activities, close to Toscanini's heart, was soliciting funds for the rebuilding of the theatre with assistance from, among others, the Maestro's elder daughter, the 'charming' Wally; the cable to her father elicited a gift of one million lire. Further, Hans Peter organised immediate post-war La Scala concerts with politically clean conductors (too few, he remarked); he personally drove some of the most eminent exiled Jewish musicians back from the Swiss border – men such as Vittorio Veneziani, the famed La Scala chorusmaster on whose re-engagement Toscanini insisted; and he established and chaired the committee to run La Scala which in turn chose Antonio Ghiringhelli as the theatre's commissioner, later its general director.[2]

Despite the evident dynamism of Hans Peter, delays in completing La Scala kept Toscanini in New York for some months early in 1946. Eventually he received the information both political and material for which he had been waiting. In mid-April he was assured that a referendum on the monarchy would take place in June and was also sufficiently reassured about the progress of La Scala's reconstruction by an invitation to return sent by Hans Peter. Thereupon he flew to Geneva where

---

[1]   Information about Hans Peter Busch's activities in his letter of 6 June 1945 from Milan to his parents, in GA. As to Toscanini's donation to La Scala, see ATL p. 403. Wally di Castelbarco lived in Italy during the war until November 1943 when, to avoid imminent arrest, she escaped to Switzerland with her daughter Emanuela. She returned to Milan at the end of the war before travelling to New York: see ATL pp. 396 and 404.

[2]   See further Sachs 1978 pp. 288–9.

FIG. 45 TOSCANINI GREETS HIS AUDIENCE, LA SCALA, 11 MAY 1946

he landed on 22 April and, travelling through the night, arrived the following day at his villa at Ripalta Guerrina, near Crema. Although forty kilometres from Milan, this old farmhouse, purchased by Carla with her husband's earnings in the 1930s, had to serve as his base, since neither his Milan home in the Via Durini nor the Isolino was ready for occupation.[3] Until the first of his concerts, which reopened La Scala on 11 May, he was occupied in inspecting the reconstruction (he first entered the theatre towards the end of April), reconstituting the orchestra and arranging programmes, all in company with Ghiringhelli. So far as he could, Toscanini insisted upon the righting of those wrongs by the fascist government that lay in his power to order, such as the re-engagement of all Jewish musicians who could be contacted.

Toscanini's seven opening concerts between 11 May and 26 June, so far as recordings have preserved them, bore all the marks of this exceptional outburst of energy which revitalised the conductor in his eightieth year. No doubt this renewed vitality was in part stoked by his delight at the liberated populace's unconstrained enthusiasm for his return, the extraordinary efforts made to complete the resurrected La Scala on time and the devotion of his musicians. It was underpinned by his joy on returning from a prolonged exile that vindicated his decades of opposition to arbitrary and undemocratic rule as well as his pride in his principles and his own brand of nationalism. For whatever reasons, his performances seemed revivified, particularly by comparison with some NBC Symphony concerts during the latter days of the war when an audible constriction of musical arteries perhaps reflected his frustrated mood at the fate of Europe and his own country. Now the powers heard in pre-war recordings of the BBC and early NBC years returned in full force, together with a greater breadth and a sheer exhilaration in music-making rarely encountered in his surviving legacy. Yet for all this flowering, here too Toscanini was intent on righting wrongs or at least teaching his audiences a lesson in musical history: although his opening concert consisted solely of Italian music, his others included works by composers, Gershwin and Kabalevsky among them, impossible to programme under fascism.

To London?

Toscanini's return to Italy precipitated a frenzy of activity within the BBC. Could he be induced to conduct their orchestra in London? The BBC girded all senior management loins to that end in an effort unparalleled since Mase's transcontinental

---

[3]   For a detailed account of Toscanini's return to La Scala, see Sachs 1978 pp. 289–92.

trips in 1936. In mid-May 1946 Director-General William Haley, Chief Conductor Boult, Director of Music Hely-Hutchinson and even the Italian ambassador's wife all wrote to Toscanini in Milan strongly urging him to conduct for the BBC.[4] In particular Boult, with his personal connection with the Maestro, explained his changed position as Chief Conductor of the orchestra and Hely-Hutchinson's appointment as Director of Music, adding his 'greetings and cordial invitation to come to us, which I very much hope you see your way to accept'. The fusillade of letters prepared the way for Hely-Hutchinson himself, who travelled to Milan on 18 May to persuade the conductor to accept the BBC's invitation. At the time of his visit Leslie Perowne, later director of BBC light music, was colonel (and by all accounts a highly persuasive force) in charge of the British Army forces radio network in northern Italy; he acted as liaison with the Toscanini family and arranged for Hely-Hutchinson to visit their home on 20 May.[5]

The visitor was kindly received on this, his one face-to-face meeting with Toscanini; also present were the conductor's son Walter, by then taking the principal share in managing his father's affairs, Carla and Ghiringhelli. Hely-Hutchinson's report of the meeting and the rest of his six-day visit gave his colleagues a detailed and absorbing portrait of Toscanini, of his music-making at La Scala during this first post-war visit, and of the context in which the Maestro was then operating.[6] Toscanini, genial and friendly throughout, made clear his desire to conduct 'the dear BBC Orchestra' again but referred to his heavy NBC commitments and his efforts on behalf of La Scala; he also complained of his age.

Hely-Hutchinson's verdict was that in his music-making the 'old man' was in 'terrific form'. Toscanini invited him to the rehearsals on 21 and 22 May for the concert in La Scala on 23 May, which was a 'typical Toscanini hotch-potch' of Kabalevsky's Overture *Colas Breugnon*, Brahms's Third Symphony, Gershwin's *An American in Paris*, Respighi's *Fountains of Rome* and Debussy's *La Mer*.[7] At rehearsals he witnessed the conductor 'gradually impressing on the orchestra the

[4]   BBCA, Boult's letter to Toscanini, 13 May 1946; Haley's and Hely-Hutchinson's letters to Toscanini, 16 May 1946; letter also from 'Signora Caradini' referred to in Hely-Hutchinson's report dated 29 May 1946.

[5]   Leslie Perowne (1906–97) was until 1956 BBC producer of various popular music programmes including *Desert Island Discs* (1942) and *Down Your Way* (1946).

[6]   BBCA, Hely-Hutchinson's letters to Toscanini, 30 May 1946, and to Mase, 31 May 1946 (which refers both to Toscanini's 'terrific form' and to the BBC's intention to negotiate with him direct) and his memoranda, 29 May 1946 (his detailed account of the visit) and 31 May 1946 (about difficulties in finding a London concert venue).

[7]   The Brahms, Gershwin and Debussy are preserved in ATC, LT-107873.

right way to play Brahms', done 'with practically no explanation, but simply by force of personality'. On 21 May they tackled the work in 'the Italian style – with a great deal of attack and verve, but without the broad *sostenuto* which is the first essential for Brahms'. The next day 'they got considerably nearer the right style', while at the concert they gave a 'really magnificent performance', which, despite minor blemishes, was 'quite splendid'. Indeed, the most striking feature of the concert was how Toscanini managed to make 'a not very good orchestra play superlatively well', particularly in the superb Respighi and Debussy – although Hely-Hutchinson noted that the orchestra was somewhat thrown by Kabalevsky's cross-rhythms and that both conductor and orchestra fell short stylistically in Gershwin. The orchestra's weaknesses stemmed from the very process of its re-formation: some players could not be re-employed for political reasons while others had not returned from national service; thus the balance of 'old hands' had to be complemented by whichever players, mostly old, happened to be available. Nevertheless, said Hely-Hutchinson, it was the sheer force of Toscanini's personal prestige and influence that had ensured rebuilding of La Scala's auditorium and reconstitution of the orchestra as national priorities.

Hely-Hutchinson saw Walter on several occasions, including an appointment on his last morning when Walter apologised for his lateness: he had been detained in conversation with his father after the concert until 5am – 'so much', remarked Hely-Hutchinson, 'for his old age!' But despite the friendliness of the family, despite the pleasures of rehearsals and concert-going, despite the opportunity to make the announcements himself for a transmission of part of the concert relayed via the British Army network on the BBC Light Programme, he came away on 24 May virtually empty-handed. He did, as he thought, have the assurance of Toscanini and Walter that the BBC could continue to negotiate direct with them rather than through Mase, whom they described as a friend rather than an agent; and on his return he promptly informed Mase of the BBC's intention to negotiate without intermediary.[8]

That move was premature, for Toscanini's assurance, if kindly meant, was quite empty: Mase was even then arranging the conductor's visit with La Scala's orchestra to the Royal Opera House, Covent Garden, as part of a Paris/London tour at the conclusion of his Milan concerts. Mase's principal difficulty, which also confronted Hely-Hutchinson in his Milan negotiations, lay in finding an adequate hall in war-

---

[8] BBCA, Hely-Hutchinson's memorandum to Herbage, 6 June 1946, directing BBC negotiations via Walter Toscanini.

torn London. Ever since the beloved Queen's Hall was the victim of direct hits by
German bombs in 1941, there existed, as Hely-Hutchinson remarked, an 'atroc-
iously tight situation'; hence Mase's choice of Covent Garden which was free for the
one chosen night of 3 July. By mid-June Toscanini's programme was settled: the
Kabalevsky overture, Brahms's Fourth Symphony, *La Mer*, two dances from *William
Tell* and Strauss's *Tod und Verklärung*, all save the Brahms included in the Milan
concerts. The same programme was to be given in Paris at the Théâtre des Champs-
Élysées on 30 June.

Initially, taking Toscanini's assurance at face value, the BBC made efforts directly
through Walter to invite his father to conduct their orchestra during his London
visit.[9] Walter's categoric telegram to Hely-Hutchinson on 18 June ended such hopes:
'Father's commitments and necessary rest period make it impossible for him to
accept other, extra concerts – sorry, greetings.' Hely-Hutchinson's letter the following
day asking if Toscanini would nonetheless lunch or dine 'with us in Broadcasting
House' went unanswered. After this rebuff the corporation were content to settle
for a broadcast of the concert from Covent Garden. They contracted direct with
Mase for the home, European and overseas transmissions and for recording the
concert for subsequent overseas broadcast.[10] They concluded arrangements, too,
for balance tests to be carried out during the rehearsal, to take place at 5pm on 2
July; an 'atrociously tight schedule' as Hely-Hutchinson again remarked, but the
need for such precision of timing will become apparent.[11] On 19 June all BBC
programmes for the Home Service during the evening of 3 July were cleared in
readiness for this hugely anticipated event.[12]

Enter EMI again

EMI were as keen as the BBC to mark Toscanini's visit and David Bicknell, now in
charge of classical recordings for the HMV label, liaised about repertoire with the
company's Italian affiliate, La Voce del Padrone, and with Mase, who had the ear of

[9]   BBCA, Howgill's memorandum to Hely-Hutchinson, 14 June 1946; Hely-Hutchinson's letter
to Walter Toscanini, 15 June 1946; Walter Toscanini's telegram to Hely-Hutchinson, 18 June 1946;
Hely-Hutchinson's letter to Walter, 19 June 1946.

[10] BBCA, BBC letter to Mase, 21 June 1946, covering the contract for the broadcast (fee of £500)
and a contractual letter for the recording (fee of £125); Mase's reply to the BBC in his capacity as
Managing Director of the Music, Art, and Drama Society, 24 June 1946.

[11] BBCA, Hely-Hutchinson's memorandum to the BBC's concert manager W. W. Thompson, 31
May 1946.

[12] BBCA, Joanna Spicer's memorandum, 19 June 1946, setting out arrangements to broadcast
from Covent Garden.

the Maestro about practical arrangements for recordings. Recording the concert on 3 July would pose no problem: Toscanini did not object and the company were particularly keen to capture *La Mer*. Nor did he raise objections to a further recording session; indeed, cabling from Milan, La Voce del Padrone informed Bicknell that after the concert Toscanini was content to record any of a specified list of works which included, in addition to the Brahms Fourth Symphony and *Tod und Verklärung* already in the concert programme, Brahms's Third Symphony, Respighi's *Fountains of Rome* and Gershwin's *An American in Paris*, all of them featured in the concert attended by Hely-Hutchinson at La Scala. Up to that point Toscanini's expansive mood encompassed even the despised recording process. There were, however, problems in arranging any recording session. Toscanini would almost certainly decline to record at Abbey Road, as the experience of June 1938 had shown, but London was desperately short of suitable venues. Covent Garden itself was occupied that week by the Ballet Theatre (later the American Ballet Theatre) from New York; the Scala orchestra's rehearsal on 2 July and the concert on 3 July were to take place in the intervals of the Ballet Theatre's rehearsals but the ballet company's opening night was on Thursday 4 July with further performances on each subsequent night. With difficulty Bicknell arranged for two recording sessions to take place there on the mornings of 5 and 6 July.[13]

Bicknell cabled these arrangements to La Voce del Padrone on 22 June with the further suggestion that at each session one major work be played through with very short pauses for recording breaks to allow switching from one machine to another, a procedure which would revert to the recording practice of the Queen's Hall sessions in October 1937. The plans, said Bicknell, were 'designed to tire the Maestro as little as possible, and to provide him with familiar surroundings'; Mase agreed them and cabled Toscanini recommending their acceptance, while Bicknell applied to RCA for permission to record the conductor. Despite concerns in Milan over the British consular office's delay in providing visas for the orchestra's passage to London, all seemed set fair.[14]

On 24 and 26 June Toscanini conducted his last two concerts at La Scala, both containing Beethoven's First and Ninth symphonies, of which the first was relayed from Italy by the BBC. Preparations then went ahead for the orchestra to entrain for the Paris concert on 30 June.[15] Neither that nor the London concert took place.

---

[13]   EMI, La Voce del Padrone's telegram to Bicknell, 13 June 1946; Bicknell's to La Voce del Padrone, 22 June 1946.

[14]   Barblan p. 299.

[15]   A copy of the lavish programme for the Paris concert, printed on 29 June 1946, is in ATC JPB 90-1 series L pt 3 folder L132C.

UNDER THE AUSPICES OF THE MUSIC, ART, AND DRAMA SOCIETY

Toscanini

conducts the Orchestra della Scala, Milan

(One hundred and twenty players)

from the Royal Opera House, Covent Garden

7.30
Overture: Colas Bruegnon.........................*Kabalevsky*
Symphony No. 4, in E minor........................*Brahms*
Three Symphonic Sketches: La Mer...........*Debussy*

9.15
Dances from William Tell...........................*Rossini*
Death and Transfiguration...........................*Strauss*

FIG. 46 THE CANCELLED CONCERT AT COVENT GARDEN: THE *RADIO TIMES* ILLUSTRATION

At the end of June Toscanini learned that the Allies had decided to cede a small part of Italian territory (the villages of Briga and Tenda) to France. The train for Paris with some orchestra members already standing by was due to depart that very afternoon but an incensed Maestro cancelled the tour: the Allies had failed to respect Italy's territorial integrity and for Toscanini – as could have been foreseen from his 1943 Declaration – the cancellation was an inevitable consequence. Ghiringhelli tried unsuccessfully to change his mind and then announced to the press Toscanini's decision to cancel 'in agreement with the City Council and the entire La Scala Directorate', a decision caused not by 'injured nationalism' but confirming 'the Italian's state of mourning for these new humiliations'. The plans of Mase, the BBC and Bicknell were set at naught although, after Mase had sold 2800 tickets from the one hundred thousand applications, it was reported that Toscanini offered to reimburse him his £500-worth of refunding expenses.

Later on, after attending the substituted La Scala Orchestra visit to Lucerne described below, Mase reported to the BBC the conductor's regret at having to cancel the London concert, which he was compelled to do because of pressure of public opinion in Italy against France.[16] This antagonism, said Toscanini, made it impossible for the orchestra to travel either to France or across France to England, an explanation perhaps disingenuous if not also ingenious. But he was more than ready to try to arrange a London visit on his way to open La Scala as an opera house at Christmas 1946 (a reference to his unfulfilled plan to conduct *Otello* there),[17] provided his contract in New York left sufficient time. In the event, the NBC schedule made such a visit impossible,[18] further tentative plans ran into the sand[19] and, finally, Toscanini's cable to Mase at the time of his eightieth birthday in March 1947 regretted that 'advancing years' made a European visit impossible that year. With characteristic sentiment, Mase's letter to Boult found 'the cable ... so sad and his moving greetings in it made me feel very humble and thankful for his dear friendship'; he expressed grave doubts about seeing Toscanini again, an assessment soon to be proved too pessimistic. Toscanini's cable virtually extinguished hopes of a London visit for the rest of the decade, although there were tentative discussions involving Chotzinoff and Mase to that end during 1948; they came to nothing.[20] The conductor did not, however, forget his British friends: Newman gratefully received food parcels from him in May 1947 while Mase and Georgina went to stay with him in Milan during December 1948.[21]

To Lucerne instead

After the Paris/London cancellation in June 1946 HMV were once more left to recover from shattered expectations. All was not lost. The Lucerne authorities, with still vivid memories of Toscanini's Festival visits in 1938 and 1939, acted quickly to invite him and La Scala's orchestra to perform there instead; all parties quickly reached agreement. Orchestra and conductor travelled north on 4 July for two

---

[16] BBCA, Wright's memorandum to Hely-Hutchinson, 10 July 1946, recording a conversation with Mase.

[17] See Sachs 1978 pp. 291–2.

[18] BBCA, BBC memorandum, 2 August 1946, reporting Mase's telephone call.

[19] BBCA, Wright's memoranda, 6 September 1946 and 24 January 1947.

[20] The extensive correspondence is in BBCA, including Mase's letters to Boult, 17 March 1947, and to the BBC, 18 March 1947; Edward Lockspeiser's memorandum, 14 April 1948; Wright's memorandum, 19 April 1948; Mase's letter, 23 June 1948.

[21] Letters Newman to Toscanini, 24 May 1947; Georgina Mase to Toscanini, 12 December 1948, in ATC JPB 90-1 series L pt 1 folders L135C and L139A.

FIG. 47 TOSCANINI ARRIVES IN LUCERNE, JULY 1946, WITH MANAGER WALTER
STREBI AND CRITIC ALOYS MOOSER, WALTER TOSCANINI PART HIDDEN

concerts in Lucerne's Kunsthaus on 5 and 7 July. The programmes were demanding:
on 5 July the programme originally intended for London; on 7 July extensive selec-
tions by Beethoven and Wagner. If the circumstances – wounded Italian pride and
sudden cancellations – might have been expected to have had an adverse effect on
Toscanini's mood at the time, the concerts themselves suggested otherwise: he
seems to have been in an exceptionally relaxed frame of mind. The performances,
so far as recordings of them have surfaced, disclose an interpretative approach
rarely encountered at that stage of his career, with characteristic power and intensity but also a breadth of tempo and flexibility reaching back to the style of the early
Philharmonic years.

The concerts were triumphant successes for the 79-year-old conductor and the orchestra he had trained. The extensive coverage in the French and German language press was summed up by the foremost Swiss French-language critic (Toscanini's friend in early mountaineering exploits), Aloys Mooser, in *La Suisse* on 10 July 1946: 'Il demeure aujourd'hui comme hier, l'interprète inspiré et universel des grands maîtres.'[22] Yet more significant were the letter and telegram sent by a frail colleague to Toscanini from a Swiss lakeside resort some 90 miles south-west of Lucerne: 'Honoured Maestro, Dear Friend', began Richard Strauss in his letter of 2 July, written at the Hotel Beau-Rivage, Ouchy-Lausanne, while recovering from an operation, 'to me it is a great joy that one of my works [*Tod und Verklärung*] will, under your master baton [Meisterstabe], make a small contribution to the rehabilitation of the beautiful Scala where my operas have seen so many wonderful performances. At the same time it is a great sorrow to me that this time I cannot greet you personally.' He regretted that a heavy cold confined him to his 'asylum' and begged pardon, therefore, for extending his warm thanks and best wishes for Toscanini's well-being by letter. He also sent greetings and thanks to the 'excellent' orchestra, signing off with 'continued admiration and most cordial greetings'. And after the first broadcast, in a telegram dated 7 July signed by both Pauline and Richard Strauss, came the message: 'Begeistert und zu Tränen gerührt.'[23]

EMI were fully alert to this Swiss expedition. Bicknell made arrangements for the technicians of Zürich radio, who were responsible for broadcasting the concerts, to record the performances on their behalf on to acetate discs. The discs were sent to Abbey Road and a panel including Bicknell and Walter Legge sat in judgement on the results. Where the panel thought there was any prospect of being able to utilise the acetates, they were allocated serial numbers in the Technical Test series and transfers made of their contents to the standard matrix series in February and March 1947, using techniques similar to those employed in the transfer of Toscanini's BBC SO performances of Brahms and Sibelius in June 1938. Transfers were not possible in all cases: Zürich radio failed to capture *La Mer* altogether, while the acetates of the Brahms Fourth were considered too noisy to transfer.

Of the works transferred (listed in the Discography, Annex A), the EMI panel thought the results very mixed. Some were technically satisfactory: Kabalevsky's

---

[22]   R. Aloys Mooser, Swiss writer (1876–1969), critic for *La Suisse* 1909–62: 'He remains today as yesterday, the inspired and universal interpreter of the great masters.' The reviews are collected in ATC JPB 90-1 series L pt 2 folder L130Q.

[23]   'Enraptured and moved to tears'. Strauss's letter and telegram in ATC JPB 90-1 series L pt 1 folder L129B, with English translation of the letter. Strauss was then living in Baden outside Zürich but in April 1946 had undergone an operation in Ouchy-Lausanne to remove his appendix.

Colas Breugnon Overture, the *Meistersinger* Prelude and the *Lohengrin* Preludes to Acts 1 and 3. The other transfers were not thought good enough for issue; but copies of every transfer, whether judged good or bad, were at Walter Toscanini's request sent to RCA for Toscanini's assessment (not all, it seems, arrived at Riverdale).[24] None was approved and it was over half a century before a few of HMV's efforts (as distinct from poor quality amateur recordings derived from the broadcasts) were released in an isolated issue by the specialist British label APR. Among those few was the *Tod und Verklärung* that had so moved its composer and his wife, hailed now in reviews as one of the greatest performances of the work captured on disc;[25] but the balance of these concert recordings was left under wraps.

Later EMI La Scala recordings: August 1951

After his Lucerne visit, Toscanini returned to La Scala for further discussions before setting out for New York on 16 August 1946. He did not return to La Scala until 1948 when, for the Boito anniversary concert on 10 June, he conducted the Prologue and Act 3 of *Mefistofele* together with Act 3 and Part 2 of Act 4 of *Nerone*, the last occasion on which he participated in a fully staged opera performance. At an early stage Toscanini consented to a recording session at which HMV were to record the extracts from *Mefistofele*. Later he decided to cancel the session, but the performances on 10 June were broadcast (relayed also on the BBC's Third Programme) and recorded by Italian Radio on acetate discs. Shortly afterwards, Bicknell travelled to Italy and with Walter Toscanini auditioned the *Mefistofele* extracts, which they thought sufficiently promising to be worth transferring.[26] After months of delay, Italian Radio consented to lend some of them to HMV; three acetates were sent to Abbey Road, identified as the 'Finale', Prologue Parts 1 and 2, and the Vocal Scherzo, and were transferred to the standard matrix series in the usual way in January 1949. The remaining acetates were expected but never arrived. Bicknell thought the

---

[24] EMI, Bicknell to Constance Hope, RCA, 27 May 1947. Walter Toscanini's later correspondence with EMI lists some, but not all, of the transfers as being in his collection. Copies of the complete recordings are now in ATC.

[25] See APR 5538. Economics dictated a choice confined to those recordings for which complete sets of pressings had already been made: see the Discography, Annex A. Among reviewers, David Patmore (*International Record Review*, June 2000) wrote, 'the crowning glory is the Strauss: Toscanini secures a reading of unparalleled eloquence and power, the climax truly overpowering and transcendental'. See also Dyment *CRQ* Summer 2011 p. 39. Other items in varying sound quality are in M&A CD1027, Archipel ARPCD 0536 and Immortal Performances IPCD 1016–2.

[26] EMI, Bicknell to Constance Hope, RCA, 31 January 1949.

results, while technically unimpressive, captured the excitement of a great occasion but the test copies sent to Walter for his father's approval of a possible commercial issue elicited, as usual, a negative response. Later unofficial issues of the radio acetates confirmed the accuracy of Bicknell's assessment.[27]

EMI played no part in the recording or transfer of Toscanini's remaining concerts with La Scala's orchestra in 1949, 1950 and 1952. There were, however, two other recordings of note. On 26 June 1950 Toscanini conducted the first of two performances of the Verdi *Requiem* at La Scala (preceded as usual by the *Te Deum*) with which, despite the participation of distinguished soloists including Renata Tebaldi and Cesare Siepi, he was extremely dissatisfied. The BBC recorded the Italian radio transmission for a later broadcastwhich apparently never took place;[28] the recording seems not to have survived, although recordings of the performance have been issued from other transcriptions.

The final chapter in EMI's collaboration with Toscanini took place in 1951, when his only post-war studio recordings with the Orchestra of La Scala were made in unusual circumstances. In February 1951 he broke off his NBC broadcast season because of ill-health and a month later flew to Milan to be with Carla, whose health was in terminal decline.[29] He was with her until her death on 23 June and his grief and mental state thereafter caused others to doubt whether he would conduct again; he himself was quite sure he would not. He was prevailed on to move from Milan's summer heat to the Isolino where he began to recover. Months before he had considered a request to make some recordings with the Orchestra of La Scala which would benefit the Casa di Riposo 'G. Verdi', a retirement home for musicians whose welfare was a cause dear to him. The request was now renewed and Toscanini travelled back to Milan in early August to conduct in conditions of great secrecy the works he chose for the purpose both of benefiting the Casa and of testing his own powers of renewal.

The chosen works were the Overture to Verdi's *I vespri siciliani* and the Preludes to Acts 1 and 3 of *La Traviata*. La Voce del Padrone, with their central office in Milan and in immediate charge of recordings, initially contented themselves with plans for conventional short-play recording despite the introduction elsewhere of tape recording; their difficulty lay in transporting one of the rare and bulky tape machines into the theatre. Bicknell was determined to overcome these obstacles.

---

[27]   E.g. Standing Room Only SRO 802–03.

[28]   BBCA, Peggy Miller, BBC European Liaison Office, cable to Pizzini, RAI, 29 June 1950. Most sources indicate a single (broadcast) performance, but see Ch. 11 p. 204.

[29]   For the events of February–August 1951, see Sachs 1978 pp. 300–1, Marek pp. 261–2.

Fully aware of the significance of the sessions and the fraught circumstances surrounding them, he made plans for a musical supervisor and recording engineers of sufficient calibre with the best current equipment. On 16 July he wrote to R. Degoy, in charge of the Milan office, suggesting that the best intermediary between Toscanini and the engineers would be his trusted protégé Guido Cantelli, whom Bicknell had got to know and respect during the preceding year.[30] He enclosed a letter to be passed to Cantelli, further intimating to Degoy that no payment be offered since 'the honour and glory of helping Toscanini should be its own reward'. Bicknell's letter to Cantelli set out the circumstances and EMI's particular desire for success, given that Toscanini had not made any studio recordings with La Scala since the introduction of electric recordings (Bicknell was probably unaware of certain early tests).[31] 'We are sending from London the most up to date recording apparatus and an experienced engineer, and I would be very much obliged if you would act as artistic supervisor at these sessions.' Bicknell conceded that this was an exceptional request, but it was justified in view of Cantelli's special relationship with Toscanini and the importance of the occasion. Degoy informed Bicknell on 20 July that Cantelli had agreed to the request; and not just one EMI engineer but three were on hand: Arthur Clarke, Barry Waite and Horace Hack.[32]

On 10 August Degoy reported in detail to Bicknell about the events of the preceding days. Rehearsals for the sessions began on the afternoon of 6 August, the orchestra being prepared by Argeo Quadri.[33] With much trouble, the local personnel managed to transport the tape equipment in to the studio 'at the very last minute' and the recordings were therefore made both on tape and direct to wax. To guard their secrecy, the two sessions on 7 and 8 August commenced at 9pm, both lasting over two hours.[34] The *Vespri* Overture was recorded at the first session, with three takes of the first side and a single one of the second. In the second session two takes were recorded of the Prelude to Act 1 of *La Traviata* and three

---

[30] Full texts in Bennett p. 181; see further Ch. 11 p. 210.

[31] It seems that Toscanini made a few test recordings in Milan Conservatory which were rejected and destroyed: matrices CD 4895 on 5 November 1927 (part of Wagner's *Tannhäuser* Overture) and CD 4964–65 on 12 December 1927 (a Rossini overture), all identified in EMI's ledgers as 'tests for Mr Toscanini's approval'; see Dyment *CRQ* Summer 2011 p. 39.

[32] Identified courtesy Malcolm Walker.

[33] Italian conductor (1911–2004) conductor at the Vienna State Opera from 1957.

[34] Details of these sessions and EMI processing in EMI, Degoy's letter to Bicknell, 10 August 1951; Bicknell's to George Marek, RCA, 10 August 1951; and Bicknell's to Alan Kayes, RCA, 7 November 1951.

of the Prelude to Act 3.[35] 'Maestro Cantelli was present all the time and did not compliment musicians or engineers until after completion of the work.' Toscanini himself was 'very pleased' with the orchestral playing and sound quality of the play-backs. As Degoy put it, 'everybody was of the opinion that rarely did the Orchestra of the Scala play better than on this occasion'. After this experience Toscanini knew he was capable of returning to New York for the next NBC season.

Subsequently the masters were processed in Milan and the tapes sent to London for further work on them. On Toscanini's instruction the Adagio from the third take of the *Vespri* Overture's first side was dubbed onto the Allegro of the second take; a manuscript comment in EMI files suggests that these manipulations were effected on tape by the EMI technicians present on the spot on the afternoon of 8 August, before the *Traviata* session. These manifold efforts were, however, in vain since eventually Toscanini rejected all the recordings for issue. By error, for which EMI apologised profusely at the time to RCA, stampers for the *Traviata* preludes slipped out to Brazil, where the single 78rpm disc containing them was issued by the local branch of RCA Victor. Forty years later EMI (somewhat sotto voce) issued the *Vespri* Overture and the *Traviata* Act 3 Prelude in CD collections of La Scala-based historic vocal recordings.[36] They show Toscanini at full and seemingly undiminished strength, the *Vespri* Overture in particular being a brilliantly realised performance – a fitting close to EMI's series of studio recordings with the Maestro.

---

[35] See the Discography, Annex A.

[36] *I vespri siciliani* in EMI 'La Scala edition' vol. 1, *La Traviata* Prelude to Act 3 in vol. 2: see the Discography, Annex A.

1 9 5 1 – 5 2 : R O Y A L F E S T I V A L H A L L [1]

The Festival of Britain concerts

For six years after the end of the war London had no purpose-built concert hall and, as noted in Chapter 10, that void caused acute difficulties for those attempting to arrange Toscanini's abortive visit and recordings in 1946. Plans for a modern hall on the south bank of the Thames were, however, drawn up in the late 1940s as part of a site for a festival to take place in the spring of 1951, named by the sponsoring Labour government the Festival of Britain. Hence the title Royal Festival Hall, which was perpetuated despite the premature demolition of other structures surrounding it, following elections in October 1951 that brought in a new government determined to expunge positive memories of life under its predecessor.

In 1950 the hall's commissioning authority, the London County Council (LCC), appointed Owen Mase as its Concerts Adviser for the new hall, in effect its programme planner wielding the authority to solicit bookings and determine priorities

---

[1] Although nearer in time than the events of earlier chapters, there is no single, unified or chronological account of the attempts to bring Toscanini back to London to conduct at the Festival Hall. The only substantial documentation about the first attempt, on the opening of the hall in 1951, is in BBC files and the report by Owen Mase dated July 1950 reproduced in this chapter. As to the invitation to conduct the Philharmonia, much is missing particularly from the perspective of Mase who, acting as Concerts Adviser to the LCC and the Festival Hall management, and in substance as Toscanini's agent in London, effectively took the lead in getting agreement from all parties. There are, however, three accounts by Walter Legge (1906–79), impresario and EMI's recording producer for the Columbia label, another of Gaisberg's former assistants: his article in the *Times*, 27 December 1975, 'The Birth of the Philharmonia'; the edited version of this article in Schwarzkopf pp. 96–9; and the interview with John Amis in *Gramophone* June 1990, 'Legge on Toscanini', which supplements both. There is valuable material also in Gorlinsky and Osborne 1998, while the most balanced account of the Philharmonia episode is in Pettitt pp. 56–8 and 60–3. Once Toscanini was inside the hall, Parikian is the fullest and most reliable source. The account in this chapter draws on all the sources mentioned, together with documents in BBCA, ATC and MA, noted individually below.

among the various orchestras and other organisations competing to appear. From the outset Mase made clear that only one conductor, Toscanini, was fitted to start the hall's life and he had no difficulty in persuading the management to agree: opening concerts conducted by the world's most famous maestro would secure its future as the country's most prestigious concert venue. In March the hall's prospective general manager, John Shove, contacted the BBC to notify them of the LCC's intention to promote concerts conducted by Toscanini immediately following the hall's ceremonial opening.[2] Initially the BBC suspected Shove's motives, voicing the suspicion that he wished to take the glory for sponsoring something more brilliant than anything in the upcoming Festival.[3] Within a short time, however, the BBC accepted that a series with Toscanini, who would no doubt wish to conduct their orchestra, was both appropriate and feasible.[4] At Mase's instance they discussed repertoire with the hall's management, all parties favouring in particular Beethoven's Seventh Symphony, *La Mer*, *Daphnis et Chloé* (the second suite), and some Vaughan Williams, at that stage the Fifth Symphony and the *Tallis* Fantasia.[5]

It was time to bring in the principal participant. Mase was, as always, on the friendliest terms with Toscanini and informed him in the spring of 1950 of the hall management's wishes. Toscanini showed great interest in the project for the new hall and wanted especially to mark his visit by conducting a major British work. By then Mase must have felt the contemplative Fifth of Vaughan Williams to be less likely to engage the conductor's interest than the composer's latest symphony, the Sixth, composed in 1944–47 and premiered by Boult in April 1948 with the BBC orchestra. Mase therefore sent him the score of this work, at that time as yet unrevised by the composer. After studying the score, Toscanini pronounced himself keen to conduct it. Following his transcontinental tour of the USA in May and further recording sessions in early June, Toscanini returned to

---

[2] BBCA, Murrill, Assistant Head of Music, memorandum, 6 March 1950. Herbert Murrill (1909–July 1952) composer and organist, Assistant Director of Music from 1946, succeeded Steuart Wilson as Director of Music in 1950, a post he occupied until his premature death.

[3] BBCA, Murrill's memoranda, 6 and 7 March 1950.

[4] BBCA, Steuart Wilson's letter to Shove, 3 April 1950. Sir Steuart Wilson (1889–1966) tenor and music administrator, was appointed Director of Music in 1948, succeeding Kenneth Wright, acting Director since Hely-Hutchinson's death in March 1947, who resumed his previous post as Assistant Director. Wilson's first and major act was to force Chief Conductor Boult into premature retirement; in 1933 Boult had married Wilson's ex-wife who divorced him on grounds of cruelty. See Kenyon pp. 214–29 for the saga of Boult's replacement by Sir Malcolm Sargent and Wilson's part in it.

[5] BBCA, memorandum of meeting at Yalding House, 13 April 1950, present: Shove, Mase, Wilson, Murrill, Thompson.

Milan on 17 June and started rehearsals immediately for Verdi's *Te Deum* and *Requiem* at La Scala. On 24 June Mase travelled to Milan both to assess the 83-year-old conductor's continuing fitness for the planned London concerts and to discuss with him programmes and dates. Mase's report to Shove dated 5 July 1950 went into such detail on what he found and heard that the relevant parts must be set out in full:[6]

> I arrived in Milan on Sunday, 25th June, and Maestro Toscanini made contact with me quickly and I went to dinner with him that night. We had interesting conversations on the state of music and artistes in various countries and had some preliminary talk over his coming visit to London in 1951.
>
> On Monday I attended his rehearsal of the Verdi Requiem at the Scala Theatre and the actual performance in the evening. At [Ghiringhelli's] party afterwards, which lasted until 4am, there was general conversation on music and I was able to give a number of prominent Italian musicians news about our Royal Festival Hall. They asked many questions and were very interested in the project.
>
> On Tuesday I had the first of several conversations with Dr Ghiringhelli. He has had great struggles undoubtedly in getting the Scala on its feet again, but his difficulties with the Government, reconstruction and the reorganisation seem to have been mostly overcome, and the Scala now has progressed very much from its hopeless position after the war. The orchestra is now very good, the chorus good, the general arrangements are running smoothly and they have a school which promises to be flourishing.
>
> On Tuesday evening there was the second performance of the Verdi Requiem.[7] This was not so good as the first performance because the singers were, I think, tired. Tebaldi, the soprano, has a lovely voice, but is not yet altogether satisfactory in this kind of work. She has had more experience in opera. The mezzo soprano [Cloë Elmo] was indifferent, certainly not as good as our own Kathleen Ferrier. The tenor [Giacinto Prandelli] was adequate and the bass (Siepi) was good. They were the

---

[6]   In MA; the omitted paragraphs relate in the main to some of Mase's conversations with Ghiringhelli, Cantelli and others concerning future engagements which did not take place.

[7]   Mase's report makes clear that there were two performances on successive evenings, 26 and 27 June. One of them, stated to be that of 26 June, was issued on CD IDIS 345–46. Despite Mase's adverse comments on some of the soloists, all four worked with Toscanini on a number of occasions.

best that Toscanini could get together. The chorus was good, but, I think, should have been a little bigger. It was only 115. Maestro Toscanini afterwards in conversation agreed with me about this – that it might have been up to 150 with advantage. The orchestra was very good and the whole performance was, of course, lit with that amazing incandescence which is so typical of Maestro Toscanini's performances. After this second performance there was another party which lasted until 3.30am. This party was at Maestro Guido Cantelli's house and I was very interested to meet and make friends with this young conductor of thirty who is outstanding and of whom Toscanini says 'he will, I feel sure, be my true successor'. You will remember Toscanini took him to America to conduct with him the NBC orchestra.

Toscanini was himself the life and soul of both these parties. Although 83 years old he conducted these two consecutive performances of the enormous work and had a great party after each one, without any apparent diminution of energy – a very remarkable man – and I know no other conductor of any age who would not have shown considerable signs of wear and tear.

Wednesday I spent largely with Toscanini and we finished up the final draft of his programme for us in London next Spring. He has finally decided that he wants to open the hall with the Beethoven Ninth Symphony. This great song of brotherhood he feels is absolutely right for the occasion and also provides that mise-en-scene necessary for a great occasion with its chorus, orchestra and soloists. He agreed to do the three programmes that we want and they are as follows:-

First Concert – April 30th, 1951
   Beethoven Symphony No. 1
   Beethoven Symphony No. 9

Second Concert – May 2nd, 1951
   Kabalevsky Overture "Colas Breugnon"
   Vaughan Williams Symphony No. 6
   Strauss Don Juan
   Debussy La Mer

Third Concert – May 4th, 1951
   Beethoven Fantasia for Piano, Orchestra and Chorus
   Beethoven Symphony No. 9

He particularly wanted to do an important English work in one of the concerts and he chose, quite rightly I think, the latest symphony of our most famous composer, Vaughan Williams. He has not yet played it but he has seen the score which I sent him previously, likes it and already practically knows it. I am sure his decision to do this work will receive hearty appreciation in this country.

On Thursday ... I also had a further talk with Maestro Cantelli ... [who] at thirty years of age, impressed me very much. We talked much music and he is a fine musician and very honest. I have not yet heard him conduct but we shall have the opportunity of hearing him in London in the Autumn of this year after he finishes at the Edinburgh Festival ...

On Friday, I saw nearly everybody again to say goodbye and caught the night train.

I talked about Maestro Toscanini's fees for the three concerts.[8] On the last occasion he came to London for me he was paid £800 a concert. That, of course, was in 1939 before the war. His fee in America at the moment is £1200 a concert. I am glad to say that I was able to arrange with him to come and do these three concerts for us at a total fee of £2500. I naturally told him how much we appreciated his consideration of conditions in England.

I am sure that the visit was extremely worth while in addition to being absolutely necessary from the point of view of arranging programmes with Toscanini. Renewal of old contacts and making fresh ones, which can now be followed up from time to time, will I am sure, prove of very great value from the point of view of music in the Royal Festival Hall in the future ...

When the hall's opening ceremony was later postponed from 29 April to 3 May the dates for the three concerts were changed to 4, 6 and 8 May.[9] As was to be expected in the light of the history of the conductor's London performances, Toscanini insisted on performing with the BBC orchestra alone. This restriction was hardly appropriate for a hall which was to be host to all London orchestras, including the LPO, LSO and (eventually) Beecham's RPO, particularly when the orchestra for the ceremonial opening was to be drawn from all of them. Toscanini's reduced fee was, however, a factor which was appreciated. Kathleen Ferrier was con-

---

[8]   As noted in Ch. 8 p. 150, Toscanini's fee for each 1939 concert was £525; Mase here presumably adjusted the amounts to take account of inflation and corresponding US$ rates.

[9]   BBCA, Murrill (now Head of Music) memorandum setting out full programmes and dates, 27 September 1950.

tracted as mezzo-soprano for the Beethoven Ninth Symphony[10] and Solomon engaged for the Fantasia.[11] As on so many previous occasions, all seemed set fair, notwithstanding Beecham's intermittent noises off.[12]

Shortly after Mase's return from Italy on 1 July he sent the BBC a preliminary rehearsal schedule for the concerts which, despite his assurance that not all sessions would be needed, caused some consternation by its length and absence of free time for the orchestra.[13] But the BBC were somewhat mollified by Toscanini's insistence, conveyed by Mase, that Leslie Woodgate should be in personal charge of choral training, a measure of his high opinion of him; this praise was 'highly appreciated' and the BBC realised that they had to be 'liberal' in such matters as rehearsal time. By the end of the year negotiations were complete: the orchestra was to be made available without charge for the three concerts promoted by Shove, but the hall management would be responsible for the conductor's fees, including those for broadcasting and recording the concerts.[14]

Meanwhile, in a letter dated 14 July[15] Mase sent Toscanini a copy of Vaughan Williams's revised score of the Sixth Symphony 'in replacement of the earlier version which you [already] have. The scherzo', he continued, 'has been extensively altered and there are alterations in the other movements also'. He concluded, 'I am glad you liked Kathleen Ferrier as mezzo for the Beethoven Ninth'. Four weeks later Toscanini sent a telegram to Mase with his suggestions for all four soloists in the Ninth: Erna Berger, Ferrier, Giacinto Prandelli and Italo Tajo, to which Mase responded with his assurance that he would contact all of them to ensure they were free.[16]

In October Toscanini returned to New York for his 1950/51 NBC season suffering persistent trouble from a knee joint; he had also learned that 'his' Studio 8H was to be converted into a television studio and that his concerts were to be moved, not to Carnegie Hall as he wished, but to the Manhattan Center, the harsh

---

[10] See Christopher Fifield (ed.) *Letters and Diaries of Kathleen Ferrier* Woodbridge: Boydell & Brewer 2003/2011 p. 167, and Fifield 2005 pp. 288 and 293–4. The latter source states that this engagement was confirmed in mid-1950 but cancelled as Ferrier's illness progressed in March 1951, by which time it was in any event clear that Toscanini himself would not appear.

[11] Referred to in BBCA, W. L. Streeton, BBC Head of Contracts, memorandum to Murrill, 5 October 1950; Moiseiwitsch substituted at the concert: see n. 21 below.

[12] Lucas p. 326.

[13] BBCA, Mase's letters to Murrill, 22 September 1950, and to the BBC, 30 January 1951; Murrill's letter to Mase, 27 September 1950.

[14] BBCA, Streeton's letter to Shove, 19 December 1950; Shove's letter to Streeton, 2 January 1951.

[15] ATC JPB 90-1 series L pt 1 folder L151C.

[16] Toscanini's telegram, 11 August 1950, and Mase's reply, 24 August 1950, in MA.

acoustics of which he loathed. Angered and in pain, he cancelled his autumn broad-casts and did not resume work with the NBC Symphony until January 1951; the four concerts he then conducted were given in Carnegie Hall without an audience.[17]

Toscanini's several months of enforced leisure in late 1950 gave him the oppor-tunity for further study of the Vaughan Williams symphony. Walter Toscanini asked EMI to send his father a copy of Boult's LSO recording of the work, originally made at Abbey Road in February 1949. Toscanini respected Boult's Classically disciplined approach to music-making and had witnessed him conduct one of the composer's greatest non-symphonic orchestral works, *Job – A Masque for Dancing*, in the Vienna Philharmonic's Salzburg concert of August 1935. EMI duly despatched the set of 78rpm discs, which by this date included Boult's February 1950 re-recording of the revised scherzo. The degree of Toscanini's absorption in the work may be gauged by his annotations of the unrevised score originally received from Mase with the revisions of the final version sent by Mase in July and the changes he heard in the set of discs from HMV.[18]

These elaborate preparations were, however, destined not to bear fruit. The events of February–August 1951 recounted in Chapter 10 – Toscanini's ill-health, Carla's fatal illness – were by then unfolding and one of their casualties was the cancellation of Toscanini's participation in the new hall's three opening concerts. On 14 February 1951 Walter sent Mase a message explaining that, because of a recurrent ailment and increasing stiffness in Toscanini's left knee which was injured 'years ago' and was now depriving him of his freedom of movement when conducting, he had been forced to cancel the last two concerts with the NBC Symphony. He continued with the inevitable news: 'Doctors have ordered him to give up all his future engagements for an indefinite period. It is very sad that these circumstances will forbid him to appear at the London Festival.'[19] Mase immedi-ately asked him to reconsider, suggesting that Toscanini conduct just the first and third concerts; but all was in vain and by 21 February the BBC were aware that Toscanini had cancelled.[20]

---

[17] See Sachs 1978 p. 299, Frank p. 101 and Meyer pp. 321–6.

[18] The two scores are in ATC (f.A251 and f.I121a, with an additional copy of the unrevised score, f.B146), the first version with Toscanini's annotations, the revised version unmarked. Boult's recording of the Sixth Symphony with the LSO, recorded 23–24 February 1949, the scherzo re-recorded 15 February 1950, HMV C 3873–76; both versions on Dutton CDBP 9703.

[19] Walter's letter and Mase's undated reply in MA.

[20] BBCA, Wellington (Controller Home Service) memorandum, 21 February 1951, stating that the LCC (Mase) was 'not yet wholly certain that Toscanini will not now be coming in May but there can be little doubt that this is so'.

FIG. 48 TOSCANINI'S TELEGRAM TO OWEN MASE, 4 MAY 1951

With the sole substitution of Brahms's *Academic Festival Overture* for the Kabalevsky, the three programmes were left intact but with Sir Malcolm Sargent conducting (on revised terms)[21] in place of Toscanini, who by the time the concerts took place was attending the terminally ill Carla. For the second and last time London was deprived of the opportunity of hearing him conduct a symphony by Britain's most eminent living composer. How he would have interpreted the Sixth's stormy start or the louring fanfares of its second movement would never be known; that he had studied and solved such problems in his mind's ear cannot be doubted. Deeply distressed though Toscanini was by his wife's condition, he found the opportunity to send a telegram to Mase on 4 May, the day of what was to have been his first concert, regretting once more his cancellation, applauding Sargent's engagement (he had welcomed him to the NBC for four concerts in 1945) and wishing the occasion great success. Mase's telegram in reply reported the great success of the concerts, tempered only by deep regret that Toscanini could not be there.[22]

---

[21] BBCA, Streeton's memorandum to Murrill, 19 March 1951; Murrill to Assistant Head of Music, 28 March 1951; Shove's letter to Streeton, 9 April 1951. In Sargent's *Choral Fantasia* Moiseiwitsch was the soloist; in his Ninth Symphony, Elisabeth Schwarzkopf, Gladys Ripley, William Herbert and Norman Walker.

[22] Toscanini's telegram courtesy Donald Dean to whom Mase gave it in 1967; Mase's reply, 4 May 1951, in MA.

Renewed overtures – and disaster averted

As Mase's report made clear, his Milan visit in June 1950 was not limited to contact with Toscanini. The two post-Requiem parties he attended brought him into contact for the first time with Toscanini's protégé Guido Cantelli, only three months before the thirty-year-old conductor's first visit to Britain with the company of La Scala, when his conducting as De Sabata's deputy was enormously admired.[23] The impact of his concert performances that September in Edinburgh and London led imme-diately to his first EMI recordings with the Orchestra of La Scala under David Bicknell's supervision; and once under contract to EMI, an invitation to conduct Walter Legge's Philharmonia Orchestra soon followed. Cantelli's debut with that orchestra in the now fully functioning Royal Festival Hall took place on 30 September 1951, the first of five concerts followed by some fraught recording

sessions. Throughout his 1950 and 1951 visits, and in all his later visits until 1956, Cantelli was faithfully and sensitively shepherded by Mase, who saw in him, as did many others, the anointed successor to Toscanini; so much so that, after discussions with Mase in October 1951, the BBC's Director of Music Herbert Murrill thought he was transferring his interest in Toscanini to the 'brilliant young' Cantelli who seemed to rely on Mase's advice 'as Toscanini has apparently bidden him to do.'[24]

FIG. 49 OWEN MASE, c.1950

[23] In Edinburgh (Usher Hall) Cantelli conducted concerts on 5, 6, 7 and 9 September 1950, in London 22 September (Covent Garden) and 25 September 1950 (Albert Hall); his recording sessions were on 23 and 26 September (Abbey Road, Tchaikovsky Symphony No. 5, issued HMV ALP 1001).

[24] BBCA, Murrill's memorandum to BBC concert manager, 25 October 1951. Mase acted inform-ally in assisting Cantelli but never as an agent. Cantelli's earliest contacts in Britain were with concert promoter Julian Finzi; later Gorlinsky acted as Cantelli's agent: see Bennett pp. 168 and 176.

Cantelli's first Philharmonia concerts coincided in time with Toscanini's resumption of activity with the NBC Symphony following his experimental La Scala sessions in August recounted in Chapter 10, with recording sessions and concerts commencing at the end of September 1951. In December came Cantelli's three NBC concerts, interspersed with a series of Toscanini's recording sessions which produced some of his finest late performances, including the *Enigma* Variations and Beethoven's First Symphony. At last Cantelli had the opportunity to tell Toscanini in person of his experiences with the Philharmonia and to urge on him that here was an orchestra truly worthy of his attention. Toscanini was aware of the Philharmonia's reputation from recordings but wanted to experience personally something of the orchestra's quality before committing himself further. Throughout the following months he was in contact with Mase who, on behalf of the LCC and the Festival Hall together with their agent Sandor (S. A.) Gorlinsky, was intent on redeeming Toscanini's promise to visit London once more – this time, after Mase's discussions with Cantelli, to conduct the Philharmonia. Gorlinsky, too, had attended the 1950 Verdi *Requiem* at La Scala and by early 1952 was in negotiation with Toscanini on terms, advising him that he would have the opportunity to hear the Philharmonia in Italy later in the year.

Walter Legge's plans had made that possible. In late 1951 he arranged a five-country European tour for the Philharmonia to take place during May and June 1952 under the leadership of Herbert von Karajan. Jane Withers, initially Secretary and later Managing Director of the Philharmonia Orchestra, filled out and concluded details of the tour. Karajan was interested in furthering his career with this first-rate orchestra, which would give the opportunity to visit Berlin, otherwise effectively closed to him while Furtwängler headed the Philharmonic. Legge, as the orchestra's impresario, needed to display its prowess in furtherance of his own and EMI's interests, to develop its public persona – and, as a principal subtext on the Italian leg of the tour, to attract Toscanini to London again to conduct it.

The timing of the Philharmonia's tour seemed to fit well with Legge's plans. Following the conclusion of his 1951/52 NBC season, Toscanini flew back to Milan at the beginning of May for his customary vacation. As a result of his contacts with Mase, Cantelli and Gorlinsky, he was no doubt aware of Legge's designs on him. It seems, however, that Legge's activities in furtherance of his strategy to capture Toscanini commenced, ostensibly at least, in ignorance of the concurrent efforts of Mase and others with the same aim in view; either that, or Legge was aware of those efforts but chose to attempt to take sole charge. Whatever may have been the extent of Legge's knowledge, by the tour's end outright disaster was barely averted – as will be seen, by Mase exercising yet again his well-honed diplomatic skills.

Outwardly the Italian leg of the tour proceeded more or less according to plan, if with some unexpected complications. The orchestra was due to play two concerts at La Scala on 19 and 20 May at which it was expected Toscanini would be present; but in Turin on 15 May, only one hour before the orchestra's concert there was due to begin, Toscanini's daughter Wally di Castelbarco telephoned Legge to explain that her father could not be present at La Scala, but would be listening to the broadcast from Turin. Legge relayed this to Karajan and the orchestra, imploring the latter to give of its utmost to an unprecedented degree. Perhaps because of this very admonition, which added to the strains of the by now much-travelled musicians, the concert was not among the orchestra's best.[25] Nevertheless, when Legge telephoned Wally after his arrival in Milan, she assured him that her father had heard the broadcast and was 'very interested'.

The Philharmonia's first La Scala concert on 19 May was a triumphant success and on the afternoon of 20 May, only hours before the second concert, Wally asked Legge to tea to meet her father. Legge and his partner (later wife) Elisabeth Schwarzkopf sat with her over tea from 4pm for over three hours awaiting the arrival of Toscanini, who Wally was afraid would not appear because of a slight cold. At 7.30pm Legge signalled their departure to dress for the 9.15pm concert, an announcement that seemingly precipitated Toscanini's entrance; Legge thought he must have been listening outside. The conductor began the conversation by remarking that he was too old to undertake concerts with a new, strange orchestra and continued by cross-questioning Legge: did he know Ernest Newman (two decades earlier Legge had indeed been a Newman protégé)? Had he heard Newman's broadcast talk marking his (Toscanini's) eighty-fifth birthday? Which records did he play? Legge mentioned *La Traviata*. Did he (Legge) like it? Legge answered with characteristic bluntness, not much – to the consternation of Wally and Schwarzkopf. Why didn't he like it? Because it sounded rushed with tempos too fast. What authority had he for that? A lifetime's experience in trying to discover what was past practice in matters of tempo and phrasing, answered Legge. Toscanini disappeared, only to return with a bundle of test discs including *La Bohème* and some Wagner, asking Legge to let him know within a day what he thought of them. And with that, he thanked him for coming, making no further mention of the Philharmonia.

After the second, triumphant concert, and in the course of packing for an

[25] The concert included Handel's *Water Music* Suite, Stravinsky's *Jeu de cartes* and Brahms's First Symphony; 'by the orchestra's usual standards the concert was decidedly below par': Osborne 1998 p. 322.

overnight journey by car to Zürich en route for the next concert in Vienna, Legge received a further message from Wally requesting his immediate attendance on her father. On arrival at his house Legge was confronted by the Maestro and in addition by a dozen aged men whom he realised intuitively were Toscanini's contemporaries in La Scala's orchestra of old; they had heard the concert and reported on it to Toscanini. After greeting him briefly, Toscanini announced that he was not too old to conduct the Philharmonia and that he would come to London in July and August for a series of concerts. What programmes should he do? Thereupon, Legge asked for six programmes for orchestra alone (he had no chorus worthy of Toscanini) including both standard repertoire and lesser known works such as Sibelius's Fourth Symphony which, from private tapes, he knew Toscanini did supremely well.[26] Toscanini agreed this scheme without demur. Legge then departed, with Dennis Brain at the wheel, for a slippery and dangerous drive to Zürich, from where he telephoned Jane Withers with firm instructions to book the Festival Hall for six concert evenings during the summer months, widely spaced over a number of weeks; he also cabled Walter Toscanini in New York to inform him that he had booked his father for the concerts.

Jane Withers was unable to book the hall as instructed, primarily because between the BBC and the hall management there existed an understanding that, during the annual season of Henry Wood Promenade Concerts held at the Albert Hall from mid-July to mid-September, the Festival Hall would not permit rival bookings; and in this the hall proved immovable. Withers telephoned Legge in Vienna and he was forced to inform Wally of his lack of success. After the tour's end in Berlin, Legge returned to London empty-handed.

Legge's actions in (it seems) unwittingly crossing the paths of Mase and Gorlinsky very nearly wrecked any chance of getting Toscanini back to London. Walter Toscanini was well aware of his father's by then limited powers of endurance and was opposed to his undertaking the heavy schedule agreed with Legge; before long he widened his opposition to the whole London venture. Mase had already advised the LCC that they would be wise to secure a more limited commitment from Toscanini and it took his always expert diplomacy (which apparently included

---

[26]   In the *Times* article (see n. 1) Legge refers also to Berlioz's *Symphonie fantastique*, a work which Toscanini never conducted complete and which it is highly unlikely he would have agreed with Legge; this reference is omitted in Schwarzkopf. Legge's subsequent journey to Zürich is described and illustrated in Stephen Gamble and William Lynch *Dennis Brain: A Life in Music* Denton, Texas: University of North Texas Press 2011 pp. 81 and 94–5, but the authors are under the mistaken impression that he was to meet Toscanini there.

a visit of his own to Milan to smooth the passage with Toscanini)[27] to persuade Walter that a London engagement consisting of only two concerts would be within his father's capacity to undertake.

A contract and a journey – at eighty-five

With Walter Toscanini's agreement gained, negotiations continued without further incident and by 23 June Gorlinsky was able to tell the BBC that he had 'signed up' Toscanini to appear with the Philharmonia at the Festival Hall to conduct all four Brahms symphonies in two concerts, on 29 September and 1 October.[28] Gorlinsky's part of the contract was not forwarded to the family until 5 July when Mase wrote to Wally enclosing the agent's signed document which detailed contractual and financial terms, specifying fees of £1786 (that is, $5000 now over £40,000) per concert.[29] Mase assured Wally that Gorlinsky would personally arrange details of payments to her father's best advantage when visiting Italy later that month and would check with her the family's requirements for accommodation and 'anything needed for comfort and happiness while you are all here. This will be my own especial care as always. As the contract says', concluded Mase, 'I shall also personally direct everything about the concerts so that Maestro will know that everything shall be in accord with his desires.'

These comprehensive plans, executed by Mase in close conjunction with the hall's agent, left Legge with no room for manoeuvre. Whether Gorlinsky's contract was actually signed by Toscanini before Legge's resumed efforts aimed at engaging him is not disclosed by available documentation – and, since Toscanini was contracted to conduct Legge's orchestra, that order of events seems unlikely. But whatever the precise sequence, Legge later complained that 'all the Festival Hall would give me was two dates', without adverting to the history; and when at last he had the opportunity to explain the position personally to Toscanini in Milan, the latter thereupon, somewhat to Legge's discomfiture, responded that he would indeed come for two concerts and would conduct a cycle of the major orchestral works of

---

[27] In his *Times* article Legge refers to 'at least two' visits by unidentified 'messengers' to see Toscanini at some stage during the summer of 1952. It is almost certain that Mase went, since he would have been the only person with whom Toscanini would have consented to negotiate; furthermore, Toscanini's readiness to come on the already agreed dates later suggested by Legge indicates that the dates had been under discussion beforehand, presumably between Mase and Toscanini. The other 'messenger' was undoubtedly Gorlinsky who, according to Mase's letter to Wally of 5 July described in the next paragraph, visited Italy in mid-July to finalise arrangements with Toscanini.

[28] BBCA, Gorlinsky's letter to the BBC, 23 June 1952.

[29] ATC JPB 90-1 series L pt 1 folder L155E, with contract signed by Gorlinsky.

Brahms – not Legge's favourite composer. Toscanini's response certainly suggested that he knew very well only two concerts to be on offer, that he had already agreed the dates and that he had worked out, with Mase and Gorlinsky, what he wanted to conduct before Legge approached him again. It was therefore settled between all interested parties that Toscanini would now return to London, for concerts promoted jointly by Legge's Philharmonia Concerts Society, the LCC and Gorlinsky. Originally the concerts were to include only the four symphonies and *Haydn Variations*, but Gorlinsky later suggested the addition of the *Tragic* and *Academic Festival* overtures of which the former was eventually agreed. This late addition was to have unfortunate consequences at the first of the two concerts. At all events, the programmes and dates were settled and the contract concluded, after which Toscanini departed for New York to undertake two summer broadcasts and several recording sessions in July and August before returning again to Milan.

As soon as Gorlinsky notified the BBC that he had signed up Toscanini, the corporation sprang into life to obtain the broadcasting rights. Relaying the two concerts was an expensive business (£1100 per concert, all but £200 of the fee destined for the conductor) but agreement was reached with Gorlinsky without qualm or delay.[30] More hazardous were negotiations for televising them, an attempt into which the BBC put much effort, since they were fully aware that Toscanini's visit was an event of 'unique importance' and likely to be his last.[31] Anthony Craxton, television's head of outside broadcasts, scouted the hall in detail and reserved camera positions in the balcony, behind the orchestra (with special 'hides' to be built to disguise the cameras' presence) and in the regular announcer's box at the side; no extra lighting would be needed. All this effort was in vain: in August Mase, and later Gorlinsky, told the BBC that Toscanini did not wish to have the concerts televised.[32]

Despite this setback, the BBC were amenable to Mase's request for a rehearsal session at their Maida Vale studios on 27 September, when the hall would be unavailable; he knew that Toscanini would not rehearse in any of the recording studios in London. Hermann Scherchen, a great admirer of Toscanini, was due to rehearse the BBC orchestra at Maida Vale in the morning for an evening studio broadcast that day, but the afternoon was vacant and duly booked for Toscanini and

[30] BBCA, Streeton's letter to Gorlinsky, 9 July 1952; Gorlinsky to Streeton, 11 July 1952. However, the broadcasting contracts were not exchanged until September: BBCA, BBC to Gorlinsky, 16 September 1952; Gorlinsky to the BBC, 22 September 1952.

[31] BBCA, Kenneth Wright's memorandum, 10 July 1952; Gorlinsky's letter to Streeton, 11 July 1952; Craxton's memorandum, 30 July 1952; Streeton's memorandum to Wright, 6 August 1952, about a telephone conversation with Mase.

[32] BBCA, Mase's letter to Streeton, 22 August 1952; Gorlinsky's letter to Streeton, 26 August 1952.

the Philharmonia.[33] It remained only to finalise arrangements for the Europe-wide relays of the concerts, which the BBC completed in early September,[34] and to engage the services of Sir Adrian Boult for a brief interval talk during the second concert, to be recorded at the hall to ensure that he did not miss any part of the programme; the arrangement with Boult was concluded only three days before the first concert.[35]

No concerts at the still young hall had been awaited with such enormous expectation. But were Toscanini's powers still undimmed? What standard of music-making could London audiences expect of the 85-year-old? The events recounted in Chapter 10 and earlier in this chapter – the physical disabilities and the mental afflictions attendant on Carla's illness and death – took their toll at the time but, to all appearances, Toscanini's recovery had been complete. Moreover, his 1951/52 season with the NBC Symphony was longer than usual and he had led more recordings and televised broadcasts – exceptionally demanding, since he hated the TV lights – than in any other season.

There were, however, signs for those with ears attuned suggesting that Toscanini's powers were operating less consistently than in earlier years. The majority of performances still conveyed his unique qualities – the characteristic drama, passion and precision combined with that still unexampled architectural sweep and assurance. Some, such as the Brahms Fourth Symphony at the Carnegie Hall benefit concert on 22 December 1951 and the *Tod und Verklärung* broadcast on 8 March 1952, displayed in addition a sheer breadth of vision redolent of the Maestro's palmiest days. But others at times provided evidence of a less assured grasp than hitherto, suggesting that Toscanini was delivering with less power and with a technique less able than before to control the finest details of ensemble. Among several possible examples, two may be noted because they were included in whole or in part in RCA's officially issued recordings: the Beethoven Seventh

---

[33] BBCA, Norman Fulton (assistant to Head of Music) memorandum of telephone request by Mase, 30 July 1952; Fulton's letter to Mase, 1 August 1952.

[34] BBCA, Bush House (headquarters of the BBC's Overseas Service) memorandum, 3 September 1952: the concert on 29 September was broadcast by NWDR (Hamburg), RAVAG (Vienna), INR (Brussels), VARA (Hilversum, pt 2 only). The concert on 1 October was broadcast by NWDR, RAVAG, RTF (Paris), INR, VARA (pt 1 only).

[35] BBCA, Acting Controller Home Service memorandum, 28 August 1952; P. Crossley-Holland (Home Service Music Organiser) memorandum to Alec Robertson, 12 September 1952; T. H. Eckersley's memorandum, 26 September 1952, emphasising that, while Boult's talk was to be recorded, none of the music should be. It is, however, likely that the concerts were recorded by both the BBC and Legge/EMI.

Symphony broadcast on 10 November 1951, part of which was used in the final product of the previous day's recording session, and the Fifth Symphony broadcast and televised (to the conductor's visible and obvious discomfort) on 22 March 1952. But the most audible example of this variability occurred in the first, faltering fortissimo near the start of Beethoven's Ninth Symphony during Toscanini's final broadcast of the season, 29 March 1952, when his perennial dread of the opening movement apparently caused a momentary paralysis of judgement in this, his last concert performance of the work.

Following the 1951/52 season, Toscanini's vacation in Italy seemingly banished all fatigue, of which there was no trace in his summer NBC broadcasts and recording sessions during July and August. Further, back in Milan again after these summer exertions, he conducted what was to prove his final concert with the Orchestra of La Scala, a long, arduous but magnificently conceived and executed programme of Wagner excerpts. The Philharmonia concerts fitted neatly between that concert on 19 September and the first NBC concert of the 1952/53 season on 1 November. There was, then, every expectation that London would hear the fabled Toscanini of old as preserved in the memory of so many pre-war concertgoers.

In London Gorlinsky made elaborate arrangements in preparation for the Maestro and his entourage. A ticket ballot was held in which over sixty thousand applications were made for the six thousand tickets; as he remarked, he arranged to be on holiday on the day booking opened, to avoid the chaos. He ensured in advance that the hall doors would be locked to exclude all outsiders from rehearsals. He warned photographers to avoid flashes on Toscanini's arrival. And he advised Toscanini and his entourage to travel direct from Milan by a two-engined British aircraft rather than by a four-engined American aircraft, which would have entailed a change in Paris. In this last he was let down: the aircraft with everyone aboard left Milan on 22 September but developed engine trouble, forcing it to land at Geneva for an unscheduled overnight stop. As a result Toscanini arrived a day late and with a slight cold; anxious newspaper bulletins followed the diagnosis and care of London specialists. Nevertheless, in a reversal of all his old habits, on landing Toscanini expressed himself happy for photographers to take as many shots as they wished. Further, when eventually – sore throat alleviated – he arrived at the hall for the first rehearsal on 26 September, he was concerned over the wellbeing of the queue waiting to greet him in the rain (hoping also to purchase standing tickets) and, according to Gorlinsky, invited them into the rehearsal.

Whose memory was reliable about this last incident? Gorlinsky's account contrasts with the *Daily Telegraph* on 27 September, which reported that for this

FIG. 50 TOSCANINI ARRIVES AT LONDON HEATHROW, SEPTEMBER 1952

rehearsal 'the closest substitute for an Iron Curtain which London can provide' descended on the hall itself: all doors leading to it were locked, special passes were necessary even to use the lift to other parts of the building and staff were instructed to absent themselves. Whatever the truth here, virtually all newspapers spotlit the very visible three-day queue that attracted Toscanini's attention, with instant celebrity and full photographic treatment for those heading it.

Six rehearsals, then five

Six rehearsals were scheduled, all but the one at Maida Vale in the hall. According to some accounts (including Karajan's), Karajan had already rehearsed the orchestra in all four Brahms symphonies in preparation for Toscanini, although when and where remain unstated.[36] Certainly the players took Karajan's advice to be in their places beforehand, ready tuned, and on 26 September at 2pm were duly and punctually seated with Mase inspecting them in anticipation of Toscanini's arrival. In fact the conductor had arrived with Guido Cantelli half an hour ahead of time to check the orchestra's seating and, while waiting, was introduced by Cantelli to the leader Manoug Parikian, who was struck by his nervous, diffident manner – all the symptoms of old in meeting a strange orchestra for the first time.[37] This shyness extended to his acknowledgement of the orchestra's applause in greeting; but, as Parikian remarked, 'as soon as he raised his baton he was a different man': 'one felt that it was inevitable that one should play the music the way he wanted'. Parikian, and indeed the orchestra as a whole, were surprised to find him, contrary to his reputation, so genial, kind and patient. Only once was there a flare-up, a trace of the reputed fire, which immediately had the desired response; for much of the time the voice was so quiet that it demanded careful listening, perhaps a legacy of his recent throat infection. Back-desk players found difficulty in hearing many of his remarks, mostly concerning matters of tempo, which he often addressed simply to the front desks. But his ability to project what seemed just the right tempo to the players, as well as an inner pulse which dictated exactly how the music should be phrased, seemed entirely unimpaired by age.[38]

Thereafter the rehearsals advanced without adverse incident, so efficiently

---

[36] Osborne 1998 p. 336, Osborne 1989 p. 70.

[37] Manoug Parikian (1920–87) Istanbul-born violinist, leader of the Philharmonia Orchestra 1949–57.

[38] See Sanders, note for Testament issue of these concerts SBT 3167, quoting Alexander Kok, deputy principal cellist of the Philharmonia.

FIGS. 51–52 TOSCANINI IN REHEARSAL WITH THE PHILHARMONIA
ORCHESTRA, WITH (in Fig. 52 below) MANOUG PARIKIAN

indeed that one of them was cancelled (although documentation is lacking, probably the one located at Maida Vale) and another finished early, contrary to Cantelli's wish that the full time be expended; the old man knew better and was the better psychologist. Nevertheless, rehearsals were tailored precisely to the needs of each work as the conductor required: the Second Symphony had only a single run-through, an achievement of which Karajan was proud to boast on several occasions afterwards, since some had expected Toscanini to be ready to stop for expected difficulties in the finale.[39] By contrast, the Third demanded hours of attention to achieve the correct balance.

At the conclusion of initial rehearsals Toscanini felt the weight of string tone to be insufficient, a possible consequence of the hall's dry acoustics. Extra string desks, including violinists Hugh Maguire, Neville Marriner and Felix Kok as well as cellist Ambrose Gauntlett (from BBC days) were drafted in to supplement the Philharmonia's already full complement. But he had no complaints about the players themselves; indeed, he remarked to Legge in the interval of the first rehearsal that 'the man who cannot make music with this orchestra has no right to stand before an orchestra'. It was also a pleasure for him to encounter again favoured artists from pre-war days, such as clarinettist Frederick Thurston, from 1949 until November 1953 principal with the Philharmonia, of whom he said, 'that is a great artist! He plays with the accents of a human voice.'[40]

Several pleasing events during the course of rehearsals had a wider significance. To the orchestra Toscanini recounted incidents occurring in the course of the First German Brahms Festival (Erstes Deutsches Brahms-Fest) in Munich in 1909 when he witnessed the composer's favourite conductor Fritz Steinbach conduct all the major orchestral works. During his own rehearsal of the *Haydn* Variations he paused to remember Steinbach's account of the fifth variation, which was carried off with such brilliance that the audience immediately burst into applause, asking for a *bis* which was granted forthwith.[41] And Toscanini's handling of it in rehearsal, rapid, light and miraculously pointed, drew spontaneous applause from the players – at

---

[39]   Osborne 1989 p. 70, Osborne 1998 p. 336. Toscanini expected to stop in two places in the finale of the Second Symphony but found this unnecessary, according to a conversation between Osborne and Massimo Freccia: ibid. p. 336.

[40]   Legge p. 125.

[41]   As to Fritz Steinbach and Toscanini's Munich visit, see Sachs 1978 p. 109 and Annex C p. 303. Parikian refers to Steinbach in Monte Carlo but this was a misunderstanding of Toscanini's reference to Munich (in Italian, Monaco). Fritz Steinbach is to be distinguished from his brother Emil (1849–1919), a competent but uninspired Wagner specialist who conducted at Covent Garden in 1893.

which he asked for a *bis* purely for his own pleasure. Steinbach came up again in conversation with Legge, for Toscanini recollected especially his conducting of the Third Symphony, which he himself sought to emulate but on his own admission forever in some respects failed to match. Nevertheless, Legge thought Toscanini's performance of this work the finest of anything he had ever heard, a substantial compliment given that he heartily disliked it.[42]

Two concerts: 'the most successful visit ever'

All should have been well for the first concert on 29 September. The programme book, lavish for the period, displayed in colour Rietti's famous 1933 portrait of the conductor on its cover.[43] Its contents included contributions from the current critical fraternity; Colles, Bonavia, Lambert and others had gone but here once more were Cardus, Capell, the *Times* critic Frank Howes and newcomers such as William Mann, all analysing Brahms, and there was also an essay on Toscanini himself by Owen Mase (listed as 'Personal Direction for Arturo Toscanini').[44] A special ramp was built for the aged conductor up to the podium. The hall was expectant as never before, full of celebrities, royalty and those lucky in the ballot. Three hundred standing places had been filled from a queue waiting up to three days for the privilege.

Backstage shortly before the start, Parikian had to lead Toscanini through the National Anthem, the need for which in the general excitement had been over-looked; he had not had occasion to conduct it since 1939. This disturbance was no doubt responsible for Toscanini's failure to remember that the programme was to commence with the lately-added *Tragic Overture*; his downbeat for the First Symphony was met by the two (typically focused) chords of the overture, which for one second discomposed him. A moment's slackness was audible before he gathered himself for the succeeding onslaught. At the time only Cantelli and the orchestra realised what had happened. Toscanini apologised in the interval to Cantelli and Parikian but their reassurances failed to mollify a sad conductor who was only too conscious of the fallibilities of age.

After the overture, Toscanini's interpretation of the First Symphony bore all his typical imprints, as well as some new freedoms such as momentary but thrilling

[42] Legge p. 163. 'Toscanini's handling' etc.: as recounted by Thomas Heinitz, present at this rehearsal, to the author in the 1980s.

[43] Arturo Rietti (1863–1943) Italian portrait painter; the painting is in the Museo Teatrale alla Scala, Milan.

[44] See p. 283.

FIG. 53 TOSCANINI IN THE ROYAL FESTIVAL HALL WITH GUIDO CANTELLI AND
PHILHARMONIA PRINCIPALS: left to right, MAX SALPETER (JOINT LEADER),
CECIL JAMES (BASSOON), UNIDENTIFIED (part hidden at rear), CANTELLI,
FREDERICK THURSTON (CLARINET, half-hidden by Cantelli); JAMES BRADSHAW
(TIMPANI, at rear), HERBERT DOWNES (VIOLA, part hidden by Toscanini),
DENNIS BRAIN (HORN), MANOUG PARIKIAN (JOINT LEADER), JAMES EDWARD
MERRETT (DOUBLE BASS)

rhetorical pauses in the *poco sostenuto* introduction. But perhaps because of the concert's opening contretemps, the playing throughout this symphony also betrayed more than the usual crop of nervous entries, most crucially, because most exposed after three movements of silence, errors of omission and commission by the first trombone in the introduction to the last movement. The errors 'crucified' Legge even though he was expecting something of the kind: the selfsame player's loss of confidence at rehearsal sufficed to warn Legge to bring in the LSO's principal as cover for him.

In both the First Symphony and in the Second, which closed the first concert, other instrumental glories among the Philharmonia's principals, notably Dennis Brain's horn, went far to expunge the memory of the trombone's shortcomings. Seduced by Brain's ease, flexibility and unique sound, Toscanini allowed his solos in the last movement of the First Symphony and the coda of the Second's first movement to linger momentarily in wonderment and magic. Brain in turn experienced Toscanini's magical powers of suggestion.[45] At one point where the horns are tempted to anticipate a crescendo and often do so, he was conscious of Toscanini's hand flickering as if to say 'take care!' although no obvious gesture was visible: it was a mere tremor, sufficient in the conductor's high-voltage concentration to convey the needed warning. At the conclusion of the first half Toscanini stumbled in his descent from the podium but, with only a momentary caesura in the applause, he was steadied by Parikian's strong bow arm; and at the end of the concert the audience stood and cheered. As he always did, Toscanini motioned the orchestra to stand before acknowledging the applause. He returned three times before signalling to Parikian to lead the players off.

If there were weaknesses in these performances, most critics were unaware of them; all commented on the unimpaired vigour of the 85-year-old conductor and none was sparing of praise. The *Times* on 30 September noted the characteristic 'saturated' sonority drawn from the Philharmonia (once more an assessment at odds with much of Toscanini's recorded legacy) and the 'tremendous' tension of the First Symphony's opening movement. Summarising his response, the critic thought Toscanini commanded 'boundless admiration for music so perfectly executed, so alive, so majestic', the product of 'a mind so uncompromising, so aristocratic'. Capell in that day's *Telegraph*, found that 'high tension and robustness of spirit characterised everything', with 'brilliant clarity'. He compared the Second Symphony with his memories of it with the New York Philharmonic in 1930:

---

[45] Matthews *Records and Recordings* p. 18.

this performance was more 'unbuttoned', with the finale's first forte now an 'unmitigated fortissimo'.

Cardus in the same day's *Manchester Guardian* thought the First Symphony 'superb in musical flow, shapeliness, and a forgetive and plastic energy which moved onward, moulding periods and phrases in its course, to an end foreseen in the first bar's beginning'. Each movement had its tribute from this critic, while the Second Symphony was described simply as 'magnificent, ripe and full-throated'. It seemed as if Cardus had forgotten his pre-war animadversions, but no: on 1 October he retracted much of his praise, now confessing to a 'certain disappointment' with the interpretation of the First Symphony and the finale of the Second, because Toscanini made Brahms 'move along at some discomfort to the composer's natural gait'. There was much more, providing evidence of the critic's somewhat sentimentalised view of the composer; but Toscanini was 'still a magician in tone production: nobody else can draw from an orchestra the Toscanini resonance, his balanced sonorities'.

By general agreement, the second concert on 1 October was less afflicted with nerves, although the feather-light fifth *Haydn* Variation, fine as it was, failed to repli-cate the miracle heard at rehearsals. The performance of the Third Symphony was very different from the over-studied, sluggish affairs heard a month later in an NBC concert and (still more listless) recording session; its high point was a third movement Romanza characterised by Parikian as 'sublime and unforgettable', which Toscanini 'approached ... with such loving care, shaped the phrases with such ten-derness, that it stirred the depths of human feeling'. The Fourth maintained this new found freedom and revived memories of his extraordinary handling of the work in his first concerts with the BBC orchestra in 1935. Firecrackers let off during the passacaglia by what the press described as 'hooligans' on the roof were audible in the hall but did not affect Toscanini's concentration. Those responsible remained unidentified, as did their motives; some thought it was retaliation by fascist remnants against Toscanini's principled stand in years gone by, but that explanation has never been confirmed.

At the concert's conclusion the expected standing ovation terminated after Toscanini's third reappearance, when Mase came forward with a message for the excited crowd: 'the Maestro sends you his love – he knows that you will understand'. Still, fatigued though he was, among those Toscanini received after the concert was a group of young people, from Norway, Trinidad and London, representing the standees who had waited throughout the three days. They gave him a laurel wreath wound round with the Italian flag, a presentation which earlier in his career would probably have evoked scorn ('I am not a ballerina'); now, he was sufficiently moved by the gesture to thank them personally.[46] Later, four players were summoned to his dressing room, among them Dennis Brain and flautist Gareth Morris. Both commented on his kindly humanity and his 'sweet smile, almost countrified' for them and for Parikian as, during the concerts, he helped Toscanini to the rostrum; but the sweetest smile, it is said, was reserved for Brain himself.[47] The subsequent celebratory supper at Toscanini's hotel, the Savoy, on the other bank of the river Thames opposite the hall, found him undiminished in enjoyment in a company that included Legge and Schwarzkopf, with Chaplin, Olivier, Walton and their spouses.[48] In conversation with Legge, Toscanini assured him of his wish to return; further, had he been ten years younger he would have wished to re-record his repertoire, subjected (according to Legge) to Legge's critical gaze.[49]

The critics, too, were happy, their reaction confirming and augmenting the views expressed after the first concert. The *Times* on 2 October thought that, by avoiding over-elastic rhythm, each movement of the symphonies 'emerged massive and strong even though at white heat. Sentimentality he eschews like the plague'; and 'in this superhuman quality of mind, his detachment from the purely subjective ... he belongs to the world of heroes rather than of ordinary men'. In that day's *Telegraph* Capell's deputy, Martin Cooper (soon to take over from him), singled out several movements including the 'intensely dramatic but never theatrical' passacaglia of the Fourth, concluding that 'this was a concert of wonders'.[50] Reservations about the first concert were forgotten by Cardus, for whom the Third Symphony was 'as gracious in its yielding periods as it was firm and reliant in its commanding ones', the whole work 'beautifully shaped with every part vital and related to the whole'; the Fourth was even more magnificent, displaying 'autumnal beauty in all the movements, with a superb climax'. For this last review of a Toscanini concert, Cardus expressed unalloyed pleasure in place of his uneasy prewar mixture of ecstasy and strictures.

The Sunday press provided the longer view. The *Observer*'s Eric Blom, delivering his verdict on 5 October in characteristically elegant and discriminating prose, thought that, outwardly, Toscanini's conducting was the 'calmest', the most

---

[46] *Daily Telegraph* and *News Chronicle* 2 October 1952. For an earlier instance of Toscanini's refusal to accept bouquets etc., with his accompanying imprecations, see Potter p. 683 (Lucerne Festival 1938).

[47] Pettitt 1989 p. 122.

[48] According to Olivier's account of this occasion, Toscanini (uncharacteristically) spoke little and ate nothing: *Confessions of an Actor* London: Weidenfeld & Nicholson, 1982 p. 151.

[49] Schwarzkopf p. 98.

[50] Martin Cooper (1910–86) assisted Capell from 1950 and took his place in 1954.

'uneventful' of all – there was virtually nothing to see at all, since he offered no visible guidance to the music: 'he reserved everything for those with ears and musical minds – and there he was prodigally generous ... nothing could have been more musical, nothing more revealing and satisfying'. Almost in spite of himself, Toscanini 'impressed the immensity of his genius' on the musically aware, making 'nothing of Brahms's weaknesses ... and everything of what is truly impressive and magnificent'.[51]

It was, however, the 84-year-old Newman in the *Sunday Times* who provided the most eloquent summing up, *multum in parvo*, passing to a new generation of readers all that Toscanini had meant to him. He was 'lost in amazement at such a display of intellectual power and imaginative fire from a man of eighty-five'. In analysing the multiple constituents characterising Toscanini's art, he lauded the 'magical clarity' throughout, the 'exquisite balance' between every part, the combined 'beauty and strength in the melodic and rhythmic lines, with their manifold inflections and nuances, their subtle cadences, as natural as breathing'. But enveloping all the performances, he pointed especially to the 'unity and totality' of the conception of each work, and the feeling that 'the vast whole is implicit in each of the innumerable parts, and every part a necessary constituent of the whole'. In the Third Symphony in particular he felt that for the first time he was 'seeing the whole from the inside', a feeling repeated at a 'hundred points' in both concerts. It was, for him, a summation of the interpreter's art which rejoiced him beyond words: 'the music as the composer had put it on the paper was being transmitted to us through a mind and a temperament that saw and re-lived it all as he must have done'.

Throughout Toscanini's visit Mase and Cantelli were ever present, the young conductor tending in particular the orchestral seating and every comfort the old man might require and, at rehearsals, following closely all the details of Toscanini's interpretations from the scores. One player characterised it as a father and son relationship, the younger clearly adoring the older man, the latter realising that, at the end of his own career, there was one in his own mould to carry on. Toscanini's son Walter was left to field press enquiries, such as the request from the *Daily Express* for his father's views on the new hall. Walter replied that his father 'has expressed his great appreciation of the Royal Festival Hall of which he has formed a very high opinion. He hopes authorities in other countries and cities may be moved to emulate the LCC's fine achievement'; diplomatic indeed in the face of widely held views about its acoustic shortcomings.[52]

---

[51] Eric Blom (1888–1959) was music critic of the *Observer* from 1949 and editor of the fifth edition of *Grove's Dictionary of Music and Musicians*.

[52] Texts of the *Express* inquiry about the Festival Hall and Walter Toscanini's reply in ATC JPB 90-1 series L pt 1 folder L155A.

FIG. 54 TOSCANINI WITH GRANDDAUGHTER EMANUELA DI CASTELBARCO, AT
HEATHROW BEFORE DEPARTING FROM LONDON, 4 OCTOBER 1952

In the days remaining to him after his concerts, 2 and 3 October, Toscanini spent time at the rehearsals for the first of Cantelli's six Philharmonia concerts on 5 October, observing intently his handling of Beethoven's Seventh Symphony from ten rows back in the stalls, consulting closely with him in the intervals and conversing with orchestra members. He wanted, he told them, to continue their association and to record with them. No such recordings were ever made. On the evening of 4 October Toscanini boarded his overnight plane for New York where his penultimate NBC season awaited. It had been 'the most successful visit ever made to London by a foreign conductor'; but London never saw him again.[53]

Envoi

If many realised that this was a valedictory visit, others continued to make multiple attempts to induce him to return. Barely three months after Toscanini's departure Legge visited the USA to try to secure a London concert from him to be broadcast during the week celebrating the coronation of Queen Elizabeth in June 1953, but in mid-January he was forced to report failure to the BBC. Walter Toscanini felt it would be unfair to the BBC to commit his father at his age so far ahead to a concert of such importance.[54] It was probably during this visit that, at a party given by Toscanini, he remarked to Legge and Schwarzkopf that, in thinking back over his career, the happiest event was the rehearsal of Brahms's Second Symphony with the Philharmonia: 'I stopped only once, and that was to tell the oboe [Sidney Sutcliffe] to play with exactly the same *espressivo* – ma *in tempo*. For the only time in my life I was simply a musician making music with other musicians.'[55]

These flattering words tempted Legge to press further invitations, despite Walter Toscanini's resistance. A few days after Legge's report to the BBC, the Philharmonia sent a telegram, obviously drafted by Legge, urging Toscanini to reconsider his decision not to return, because his absence would be considered by those unaware of the actual situation as 'adverse criticism of our ability to satisfy those standards

---

[53] 'The most successful visit', *Evening News* 4 October 1952.

[54] BBCA, Legge's letter to C. Holme, BBC Assistant Controller of the Third Programme, 19 January 1953; Holme's reply, 27 January 1953.

[55] Quotation from Schwarzkopf p. 99. In the *Times* article (see n. 1) Legge says this interchange occurred 'four or five years' after the Philharmonia concerts, which cannot be right (Toscanini would not have been permitted visitors such as Legge during 1956 and he died in January 1957); but also incorrect was the corrected reference, in Schwarzkopf, to his eighty-fifth birthday party, since Toscanini was already eighty-five at the time of the Philharmonia concerts (he celebrated his eighty-sixth in New York in March 1953). The most likely time was therefore during Legge's New York visit to the Toscanini home in January 1953.

which we have learned from you. We beg you to come again to give us the opportunity of showing you how we have profited by the lessons you gave us in the two short times that we had the honour of working for you last year.' It seems this transparent chop-logic went unanswered, as did a further letter from Legge to Walter in January 1954 asking that Toscanini conduct the Philharmonia at the Lucerne Festival later that year.[56]

Meanwhile, following Legge's report to the BBC in January 1953, the BBC orchestra's conductor Sir Malcolm Sargent, apparently with Mase's advice, asked Toscanini if he would be willing to conduct the orchestra in London. In his letter of 5 February Sargent spoke of everyone longing to see him again in England: 'I am writing to you to express the wishes of the BBC and of course my own ... I did so want you to know how greatly we long for your presence here and how much we shall appreciate it.' There was no direct reply but a few weeks later, at the end of March 1953, Toscanini replied (as he always did, sometimes in his own hand) to the last of the regular cables sent by the BBC's Music Department as birthday greetings: 'your old friend thanks you warmly for your thought of him'.[57] On 4 April 1954 Toscanini conducted his last concert, returning only for two days of recording in June. There was further desultory talk of his returning to London once more and, indeed, Bicknell addressed RCA on the subject with the aim of recording several Beethoven symphonies with the Philharmonia, pointing to the unsatisfactory standard of the RCA recordings made just a few years before – but, as with all these proposals, sensible or otherwise, the answer was silence: it was too late.[58]

Mase now performed his last service for the retired Maestro. Redrafting the article that had originally appeared in the Philharmonia's concert programme of September/October 1952 for the circumstances of Toscanini's retirement, he provided the June 1954 issue of the *Gramophone* with an elegant essay entitled 'The Other Dimension', full of insight and personal memories – a fitting farewell to the conductor's sixty-eight years on the podium:

[56] Telegram dated 21 January 1953 and Legge's letter of 5 January 1954, also expressing disappointment that Toscanini would not conduct the Brahms *Requiem* at his (final) concert on 4 April 1954, with Schwarzkopf as soprano soloist, in ATC JPB 90-1 series L pt 1 folder L161H. Toscanini's plans for performing the Brahms *Requiem* were dropped in favour of a programme of Wagner excerpts.
[57] Sargent's letter of 5 February 1953 in ATC JPB 90-1 series L pt 1 folder L166C; Toscanini's greeting in BBCA, cable from Toscanini to the BBC, 30 March 1953. In reply to the Music Department's greetings cable on his eighty-first birthday, Toscanini's handwritten reply dated 25 April 1948 was, 'Grateful for your kindness. I thank you very cordially. Arturo Toscanini' (in BBCA).
[58] EMI, Bicknell's letter to George Marek, RCA, 20 July 1954.

At the end of a Beethoven concert at Queen's Hall, London, on a May evening in 1939 the 'capacity' audience was slowly making its way out. Inside, at the close, the scene had been unforgettable; it seemed that the people would never leave; all had been on their feet trying to express with hand and voice the admiration and emotion which filled them to over-flowing. Now, as they left, one might have expected excitement to show itself in animated conversation, the buzz of talk in the crowd to be even greater than usual, but in all its history the crowded foyer had never been so quiet. Played as it was that evening the *Eroica* had seized the hearers' hearts and minds afresh and, consciously or instinctively, most of them were silent, as if fearing that words could only disturb the new vision glowing within them.

Later that night I asked a friend, a well-known musician of long exper-ience, what there had been in that performance of an old work which had so opened a new world. He thought for a while and said: 'He showed us another dimension.' I think he expressed, as far as words can express, what Arturo Toscanini had done for us, what he has done for thousands wherever he has been.

In another of that memorable series of concerts was Beethoven's Sixth Symphony. It goes without saying that Toscanini knew every note; it would be hard to reckon the number of its performances by the finest orchestras under his direction. The first rehearsal for this concert was fixed for ten-thirty one morning and he had asked me to have breakfast with him. On arriving at nine I found him hard at work on the score. He had been working on it since six. As always, he was faithful to his own creed: 'Every time you play anything it must be for the first time.'

He once told a young colleague: 'You must not conduct a piece until the notes have marched off the paper and come alive in your head and heart.' He himself has invariably obeyed that injunction. Howard Taubman says in his recent biography: 'You get the feeling, after watching Toscanini over the years, that he is possessed by the music. In him there seems to sing an ideal version of every voice and every instrument, and his unremitting purpose as a conductor is to make the living sound correspond to the song that surges in his brain.'

That is true, but the song surges in brain *and* heart. It is in both that the music has 'come alive'. Through deep study of the score, through toil of mind and spirit, there seems to be reborn in him the joy and pain that poss-essed the composer at the creation of the work. Then, at rehearsal, with relentless integrity and consuming passion, he will strive not only to secure from each and all the meticulous accuracy without which the composer is betrayed, but to awaken and weld into one whole each individual player's spiritual and personal participation in his own artistic vision. He himself gives all he has and the players must do the same. The letter and the spirit – he insists on both. Nothing less will do. His demand can be ruthless.

This all-inclusive absorption of the music undoubtedly explains in part his astoundingly exact and tenacious memory. Those of us who know him well, however, know that memory to embrace much besides music. Beauty and sincerity, wherever met, find ready entry into the storehouse of his mind. On one occasion I saw his attention drawn, for the first time, to the poems of John Clare. For perhaps twenty minutes he turned the pages of this early nineteenth-century rural poet, occasionally giving small exclamations of appreciation. In the afternoon, while having picnic tea in a Chiltern beechwood, he recalled his morning's pleasure, quoting from memory considerable passages from several of the poems that had touched him by their direct and simple beauty. This he did in a language foreign to him. How many could have done it even though English were their native tongue?

Sincerity – this is the touch-stone he applies to the work of the composer. He applies it equally to his own presentation of the work in performance, that performance which appears so wonderfully spontaneous that it is difficult for the hearer to imagine the long and devoted labour unsparingly given before such seeming spontaneity could be achieved.

What Paul Valéry says regarding a different art is as surely applicable to music:

'Le spontané est le fruit d'une conquête. Il n'appartient qu'à ceux qui ont acquis la certitude de pouvoir conduire un travail à l'extrême de l'exécution, d'en conserver l'unité de l'ensemble en réalisant les parties et sans perdre en chemin l'esprit ni la nature.'[59]

Now, at the age of 87, Arturo Toscanini has decided to lay down his baton. We are for ever in his debt. Retiring to his beloved Italian home he takes with him the affectionate admiration and gratitude of musicians and music-lovers the world over.

Let us be thankful that by means of a number of fine recordings we can, in some degree, recall in sound many of the unforgettable experiences his incomparable musical vision and integrity have given us and so share with him again that 'other dimension'.

[59] 'Spontaneity is the fruit of a conquest. It belongs only to those who have achieved that certainty which enables them to carry a work through to its absolute completion, to preserve the unity of the whole while realising each part and without losing on the way either its essential spirit or nature.' (Translation, as published in the *Gramophone*, presumably by Mase himself.)

Exits

The principal actors in this narrative began to make their final exits soon after Toscanini's retirement. The conductor himself made a last, long visit to Italy from June 1954 to February 1955; throughout he nursed plans to conduct once more but all, as before, came to naught. Back in New York he spent a period of reflective retirement, working when he could in approving his earlier broadcast performances for issue by RCA. He died at his home in Riverdale on 16 January 1957.

Among Toscanini's British friends he was much missed, especially by Ernest Newman. A parcel of records from Toscanini in 1955 elicited Newman's reply to Walter Toscanini asking that he give him most affectionate greetings, 'from myself more particularly the assurance that I can never thank him sufficiently for all he has taught me and all he has meant to me in my musical life'.[60] The parcels from Walter continued until Newman's death in 1959.

Owen Mase retired as LCC Concerts Adviser in 1953. He won high commendations from the LCC for his efforts but, with the development of the orchestras' own managements and the full calendar of hall events now assured, his post terminated with his retirement. Mase continued to assist Cantelli during his London visits and often functioned as go-between with Bicknell in the latter's sometimes frustrated efforts to secure the young conductor's commitment to recording sessions.[61] With the tragic death of the 36-year-old conductor in November 1956, Mase saw all hope of a direct continuation of the Toscanini tradition expire and he virtually retired from musical life. He was not, however, forgotten by the Toscanini family: correspondence with Walter continued on several occasions over the years, the frequency tapering off as time passed; the last letter from Walter was dated 1966, five years before his death.[62] As he did with Newman, Walter regularly supplied Mase with Toscanini's newly approved recordings as they appeared – but they remained largely unplayed. Nevertheless, while Georgina was alive Mase was willing to reminisce at length about his experiences with Toscanini and was generous with mementoes. To the foremost British collectors of Toscaniniana in the immediate post-war generation, Stuart Pollard and Donald Dean, he was both patient and friendly; when the latter visited Mase's cottage at Waterbeach near Cambridge, he

---

[60]   Letter 28 May 1955 and letters from Vera Newman, the last dated 10 July 1959, in ATC JPB 90-1 Appendix series L pt 1 folders L205A and C.

[61]   Bennett p. 180, also ibid. pp. 187 and 212.

[62]   Six letters from Walter dating from 24 January 1957 to 1966 in MA. As to Mase's later career, see Lewis p. 78. Further details courtesy Donald Dean and Peter Agrell.

was presented with one of the Maestro's batons used with the Philharmonia.[63] Mase's principal concern at the time, however, was Georgina's health and after her sudden death in 1967 he withdrew from all such contacts until his own death in 1973.

Some of the actors prominent in the narrative of Toscanini's association with London had by then already died; Fred Gaisberg, for example, passed away in 1951 just one week after a jovial lunch with one of his successors, David Bicknell.[64] Bicknell himself left EMI in 1971 and lived in quiet retirement with his wife, violinist Gioconda De Vito, until his death in 1988.[65] All the other principal actors survived into extreme old age. Collingwood, after countless years' service to EMI, also retired in 1971 and died in 1982, aged ninety-five; his fellow student at Oxford, Sir Adrian Boult, followed a few months later in early 1983, aged ninety-three. Sybil Cholmondeley's passion did not, it seems, outlast the war: her final extant letter to Toscanini, chastising his failure to answer her correspondence, dates from October 1944;[66] whether they met after the war has not been recorded. Sybil continued to pursue her many cultural interests for several decades, as Dowager Marchioness after the death of her husband in 1968. Among much else, she completed the renovation of Houghton where she lived during her last years.[67] Her death in 1989, just short of her ninety-sixth birthday, severed the last intimate British link with Toscanini's memorable seasons in London half a century earlier.

[63] Information courtesy Donald Dean. As to Stuart Pollard, see *Recorded Sound* 76, October 1979 p. 116 (obituary by the author).

[64] Moore p. 242.

[65] See further Martland p. 166.

[66] Letter of 21 October 1944, ATC JPB 90-1 series L pt 1 folder L118B.

[67] See Stansky Ch. 8.

CHAPTER 12

THE LONDON RECORDINGS – A STUDY IN STYLE

An interpretative traversal: its character and origins

Toscanini's extensive legacy of recordings remains, including those made in London during the years 1935–39. The latter have their distinctive qualities, as this chapter attempts to demonstrate. But as Toscanini's era recedes in time, as living witness vanishes and as judgement relies (sometimes with malice aforethought) upon select-ive recordings made in his final years, the perception of Toscanini's special attributes has over succeeding generations undergone a change, and not for the better. Retro-spectively some commentators have transmuted the conductor into the very figure Newman and Constant Lambert always, and rightly, insisted he was not – the apostle of 'objectivism' and 'literalism', forever pitted against, as some current proponents would again have it, the intuitive thrust of his polar opposite, Wilhelm Furtwängler.[1] Toscanini would not have recognised himself in such straitjacketed, simplistic terms; his constant concern was to approach as near as possible to the composer's creative process as revealed in every particle of the score. The correct appreciation of the notes, and everything entailed by that in terms of tempo and phrasing, was but the end of the beginning, the springboard for realising with all the passion at his command the composer's intentions in sound – as he himself put it, 'my ideal dream ... is, to come as close as possible to expressing the author's thoughts'.[2]

Such elementary truths, self-evident to most observers at the time of Toscanini's first visit to London in 1930, have since lost some of their currency. Few would now recognise the portrait of the pre-war conductor painted by Cardus at the time of Toscanini's death, in which he maintained that 'once upon a time ... it was

---

[1] For further comment on this misconception see e.g. Sachs 1991 p. 145, Frank p. 248 and the articles cited in Ch. 1 n. 15.

[2] ATL p. 132 (letter to Baron Hans Paul von Wolzogen, 5 August 1931).

Weingartner who represented a classic objectivity in conducting, while Toscanini was made the rallying-ground for young musicians eager for freedom of utterance and liberty to go adventuring among the masterpieces. We respected Toscanini's scrupulous regard for the blueprint of a composition, the authentic and published score; but we were [also] conquered by the passion of Toscanini that went into his conducting, the singing line, the Italianate nuances and flavours.'[3] This tribute, if over-colourful and given to exaggeration, highlights the interpretative distance traversed by Toscanini during the twenty-two years spanned by his London concerts.

What was the nature of that stylistic change? Why did it evolve in the way it did? And where, in the spectrum of that evolution, should the London recordings be placed? What, if any, were their special qualities? The period before the Second World War is often loosely referred to as Toscanini's prime, his performances of the time somewhat different in style from his later NBC years. Yet, as demonstrated in Chapter 8, critical reaction to the BBC SO's 1939 Beethoven cycle gave evidence of the development of Toscanini's approach since his first visit with the Philharmonic: some increase in pace, a lessening flexibility, a more consistently cutting attack. By that date he had been on the podium for over fifty years and had been conducting the great German classics, Beethoven, Schubert and Brahms among them, for more than four decades. Schubert's Ninth Symphony was in his first orchestral concert in 1896, the Beethoven First, *Eroica*, *Pastoral*, Seventh and Eighth symphonies (and the Adagio of Bruckner's Seventh) joined his repertoire during 1896–98 and in 1898 he gave the first performances in Italy of Brahms's Second and Fourth symphonies at the Turin Exposition. Over such a time span Toscanini's approach could hardly have avoided extensive change and development although, in the absence of recordings from the first half of his career, precisely how he performed such works at the turn of the twentieth century is in some degree inevitably speculative.

Despite the absence of documentation in sound, there is enough evidence to suggest that the stylistic approach of Toscanini's last years with the BBC SO represented a relatively advanced stage in his development as a symphonic conductor: a late flowering rather than the zenith, if zenith there was. Consider first some of the written evidence. In 1944 Toscanini remarked to B. H. Haggin that early in the century he had heard Hans Richter conduct Beethoven, the *Eroica* in particular,[4] and felt obliged to model his approach to this German music on that of the acknowledged German masters – a contrast to his attitude to Felix Mottl described in Chapter 1. A

---

[3]   Evan Senior (ed.) *The Concert Goer's Annual No. 1* London: John Calder 1957 p. 83.
[4]   Haggin 1959 p. 48.

survivor of Toscanini's tours with the newly reconstituted La Scala Orchestra in 1920–21 described how at that date his conducting of Beethoven still subscribed to the approach of some German conductors in its broad flexing of tempos and emphatic declamation of the opening bars of Beethoven's Fifth Symphony.

By 1930 the *Times* was noting his steady, straightforward (but supple) approach to rhythm and tempo in his Queen's Hall *Eroica*. Shortly afterwards Richard Strauss, as noted in Chapter 1, although lauding Toscanini's Beethoven performances above those of all his juniors, remarked on his relative neglect (as Strauss saw it) of the romantic side of the composer's musical character. Evidently Toscanini's evolving approach was by then already leaving behind much that was overtly romantic in gesture; but surviving timings of his *Eroica* from Berlin on the Philharmonic tour (discussed in detail below) show a continuing breadth of tempo which by all accounts had diminished in his last London performance of the work in 1939.

Toscanini's first recordings date from that era of 'broad flexing of tempos' in Beethoven, pre-electric recordings made during the 1920–21 La Scala Orchestra tour of North America at an exact mid-point in his career. Although these recordings include the finales of the First and Fifth symphonies, the two performances disclose few secrets: the performance of the First's finale is similar to many later ones, while the Fifth's retains minor changes of tempo between first and second subject material ironed out within the next decade.

The Philharmonic years (1926–36) are by comparison prolific and provide tangible evidence of Toscanini's stylistic evolution up to that point, particularly in Beethoven's symphonies. Survivors include two complete Beethoven Fifths (1931 and 1933); two Sevenths, one incomplete (1933), the other RCA's famous recording (1936); and almost complete performances of the First, Fourth, Sixth, Eighth and Ninth symphonies, all save the 1935 *Pastoral* from broadcasts during his last Philharmonic season.[5] So far as these sometimes dim recordings permit reliable judgement, the architectonic assurance and dramatic power of all Toscanini's Beethoven are present throughout these accounts in their customary splendour; but they also retain a breadth of tempo and a solidity of pacing combined with a

---

[5]   La Scala Orchestra finales of the First Symphony, rec. 30 March 1921, Victor 74690, and Fifth Symphony, rec. 24 December 1920, Victor 74769–70, various CD transfers including RCA GD 60315. For the two Philharmonic versions of Beethoven's Fifth Symphony, see Ch. 3 p. 57. Beethoven's Seventh Symphony aircheck 16 April 1933 has circulated only unofficially. The RCA Seventh Symphony rec. 9 and 10 April 1936, was issued first as RCA Victor M 317; numerous transfers include RCA GD 60316. The airchecks of Symphonies Nos 1, 4, 8 and 9 from February/March 1936 were issued to Toscanini Society subscribers in the late 1960s on ATS 1016–24; Nos 8 and 9 also on Pristine Audio PASC 117 (No. 9) and PASC 128 (No. 8). The *Pastoral* Symphony aircheck, 30 March 1935, is in ATC only.

constant suppleness of detail, qualities which were less to the fore by the time of his last BBC SO performances and were less noteworthy still during later NBC years. This tendency towards increased velocity and austerity of approach was certainly by no means consistent: it did not run in a straightforward line during the documented second half of his career and there were many exceptions, byways and backward glances between one performance and another; but, taken overall, there can be no real dispute that changes of the kind described did occur.[6]

Various reasons have been advanced for this quite rapid stylistic development in the late 1930s. Some have attributed it to Toscanini's ceasing to conduct opera on stage after his seasons at the Salzburg Festival during 1935–37; his concentration on the symphonic repertoire thereafter led to the progressive elimination of dramatic flourishes in his interpretations. This explanation would be more convincing if there were any parallel in the similarly non-operatic years 1931–35, but surviving evidence does not support the thesis. In any event, during the second half of the 1930s elements of the sheerly dramatic continued to feature in Toscanini's performances as much as they did in earlier years. Again, according to another explanation Toscanini's dissatisfaction with his performances was stoked by his study of recordings made of his earlier broadcasts. Certainly, he sometimes listened to his NBC broadcasts particularly when, as was the case with Brahms's Third Symphony, he had difficulty in solving particular interpretative problems. But the most noticeable change in his interpretative approach took place during 1936–39 (coincident with his later BBC visits), largely before recordings of his broadcasts were available to him.

In truth, the principal reason for this change seems to have been the constant study and restudy of the scores to which Toscanini subjected himself every time he prepared them, supplemented by much thought and omnivorous reading. His career from the 1920s onward was forever punctuated by his conversational announcements that, at last, he had found the courage to take the 'correct' tempo for this or that work. If at the start of his career the great German conductors sometimes provided a guide to the way forward – Toscanini was usually too assured and original in mind merely to model himself on others – already by the second decade of the twentieth century he found Karl Muck's approach to the German classics in Boston 'terrible', his tempos in Beethoven's First Symphony 'so slow'.[7] His summing up, 'Muck was Beckmesser of conductors', was by no means fair, but

[6]   Frank Ch. 4 has a detailed examination of the variations and inconsistencies in the development of Toscanini's approach to some major works in his repertoire, and of the thinking behind that approach.

[7]   Haggin 1959 p. 50.

was evidence of the degree to which he reacted increasingly against traditions of performance seemingly without justification in what Beethoven wrote or meant. And if in early days he swallowed Wagner's advice whole, for he had read and absorbed virtually all his published prose works, in the last phase of his career (the post-BBC SO era) only subtilised traces, a mere suggestion of tempo flux, remained in many performances by comparison with previous decades. Furthermore, by then Toscanini took the view that all the great German exponents performed much of their music at the wrong tempos,[8] a conclusion consonant with more recent research and performance practice.

Beside Toscanini's constant study and thought, other factors contributed to the stylistic change of the late 1930s. As Harvey Sachs has pointed out, Toscanini possessed 'in unusually small measure ... the talent for being happy ... Toscanini's speciality was dissatisfaction. He was dissatisfied with his artistic accomplishments, with himself as a human being, with his destiny, with other people, and indeed with the way in which the world had been put together. He was dissatisfied when he was working, but he was even more dissatisfied when he was not working.'[9] As the 'low, dishonest decade' advanced, and particularly as it drew to its end, there was much to stoke, not merely Toscanini's perpetual dissatisfaction, but a righteous anger. Although he was by no means politically sophisticated, during the late 1930s he saw with greater clarity than most of his contemporaries the coming and inevitable breakdown of European order. The threat of disintegration affected him profoundly, inducing in him, as noted in Chapter 8, acute depression and even an aversion to making music during the months in Switzerland that followed his final BBC SO concerts.

Throughout this period his one great consolation was his passionate affair with Ada Mainardi. Time and again he told her of the inspiration for his work he gained from their love, of how she 'would have been proud' of him on account of particular performances (an example is given in Chapter 4) and of how he was, indeed, thinking of her during them. So long as it lasted, he regarded his affair with Ada as the source of extra and continued vitality wherewith to fight the infirmities of old age. There can be little doubt that the cares and pressures of a terrible world and this passionate affair both contributed, whether or not at a conscious level, to the character and stylistic development of Toscanini's performances of the late 1930s. The distinction in this context of the BBC SO recordings is the principal theme of this chapter but, first, contemporary echoes of the Philharmonic tour's concerts in London demand further attention.

[8]   Ibid.
[9]   ATL p. xx.

The Philharmonic tour's London concerts, June 1930: the Eroica *on trial*

'Once upon a time', wrote Cardus: not the opening of a fairy-tale, but his recollection of the New York Philharmonic-Symphony Orchestra in London – his memory, for example, of the Brahms Second Symphony enchanting listeners in the Royal Albert Hall on 1 June 1930 with 'phrasing songful and elastic'. All that remains now are those memories and the responses set down in words under the spell cast at the time, for nothing more tangible has come down to us of the fabled performances which introduced Toscanini to London audiences. A somewhat misty idea of a few items may be gathered from the series of recordings undertaken in Carnegie Hall by the Philharmonic in February–April 1929. Of the items later played in London, Haydn's *Clock* Symphony and the Scherzo from Mendelssohn's incidental music to *A Midsummer Night's Dream* demonstrate the already extraordinary results of Toscanini's training;[10] and their repetition on tour – the Haydn was also played in, among other places, Paris, Vienna and Berlin – no doubt further polished the ensemble.

These few works aside, we are left only with the descriptions salvaged from contemporary reviews; some of these have been summarised in Chapter 1 and speak for themselves. With a sidelong glance at the third *Leonore* Overture, only the *Eroica* Symphony needs further detailed attention, because the evidence suggests that, certainly in the latter work, Toscanini's approach at that time differed substantially from any complete recording that survives. The two works were played respectively in the first and last of Toscanini's London programmes, also in his Berlin Philharmonie concerts on 27 and 28 May 1930, less than a week before their London hearings; and, although Toscanini's performances never precisely duplicated one another, it is unlikely that the performances in the two cities differed more than marginally. Alfred Wallenstein remembered the Berlin *Eroica* as a performance in which 'everything went right – when every player in the orchestra was just right, and the balance and the sound and everything'.[11] The witness of Klemperer and Richard Strauss has already been quoted in Chapter 1 and, significantly, Bruno Walter, Klemperer and Erich Kleiber were among the most enthusiastic members of the audience on both nights. As one observer put it, 'the impartial recognition of that perfection on the part of those three great conductors is superior to any critical comment'.[12]

---

[10] Haydn Symphony No. 101, rec. 29 and 30 March 1929, first issued in Victor M 57 (7077–80), CD Naxos 8.110841; Mendelssohn Scherzo, rec. 30 March 1929, first issued in Victor M 57 (7080), CD Naxos 8.110844.

[11] Haggin 1967 p. 183.

[12] Quotation from Heinrich Strobel, in Sachs 1978 p. 201.

The sole dissenting voice was, it seems, Wilhelm Furtwängler's. His private Note-books, in their detailed appraisal of Toscanini's Berlin concerts, show him critical of virtually every performance and in particular of the *Eroica* Symphony and the *Leonore No. 3* Overture. For example, he found excessive flexibility in the *Eroica*'s first movement, particularly in the woodwind second subject material which, he avers, was so retarded that it got Toscanini into difficulties in accelerating back to the basic tempo; indeed, the alternate militancy and embarrassed sentimentality throughout the movement he characterised as nothing but 'tuttis and arias'.[13] The Adagio was too slow for a proper *Marcia funebre* and was again sentimentalised at critical points. As for *Leonore No. 3*, Toscanini failed to signal a crucial change of mood and key in its slow introduction and commenced the Allegro in tempo rather than easing into it from the preceding bars. And much, much more.

Our concern here is not whether Furtwängler's assessments were valid, on which views will differ: those who favour his approach to the Beethoven canon will applaud, while others will not recognise his description of Toscanini's operation. The crucial issue is whether Furtwängler so closely and accurately described what he heard that his critique of those Berlin performances assists now in reconstructing what London audiences heard in the Queen's Hall just one week later. In this analysis we are fortunate to have, not only other contemporary observations, but exact timings of that Berlin performance of the *Eroica* from the (later destroyed) recording made of it by the Reichs-Rundfunk[14] which, for purposes of comparison, may be placed alongside those of the famous recording of October 1939 drawn from the live NBC Symphony cycle of October–December:

	28 May 1930	28 October 1939
I	14:37	13:36
II	19:18	16:19
III	5:32	5:19
IV	12:01	10:38

[13] Furtwängler pp. 40–6. As presented in the English translation, the comments at pp. 43–4 of the Notebooks about the 'excessive retardation' of the woodwind second subject of the *Eroica*'s first movement are seemingly attributed to the second movement; but it is apparent from the context that Furtwängler must be referring to the first. Moreover, contemporary comment made much of Toscanini's undeviating pulse in the *Marcia funebre* by comparison with his coevals, which would render attribution of Furtwängler's comments to that movement nonsensical: see further Ch. 4 p. 92.

[14] *Schallaufnahmen des Deutschen Rundfunks 1929 bis 1936* p. 483: catalogue in the British Library. The numbers of the destroyed shellac discs were 855–68.

From the foregoing figures it is not difficult to conclude that, with the exception of the scherzo, the Berlin *Eroica* was substantially more expansive than the 1939 recording, exceptionally so in the *Marcia funebre*. Toscanini's very slow tempo in that movement during the Philharmonic years is confirmed by the single, surviving fragment of his *Eroica* from Stockholm in December 1933, which, with about two minutes' worth of music missing from that movement, still extends over seventeen minutes. Nothing 'sentimental' in change of pace or other detail is audible there, but what about the first two movements three years before? In his pioneering *Toscanini and the Art of Orchestral Performance* (1956), Robert Charles Marsh's observations about the 1939 performance were not dissimilar to Furtwängler's in 1930: he thought it contained 'too many Italian elements that don't belong in Beethoven, fugues whipped up like the long, accelerating climaxes of Rossini overtures, chords like falling blows, violent and unexpected compression and expansion of phrases'.[15] But the individual and exceptionally dramatic character of that performance was probably much influenced by the earlier mentioned stresses operating on his mind: the terrible world situation, his relationship with Ada, more problematic as the European conflict broadened, as well as the challenge of renewing and re-gathering his interpretative vision just six months after his last Beethoven cycle with the BBC orchestra.[16] Moreover, what we now hear of the NBC performance is also a product of the notoriously dry, close recorded sound ('one of the most hideously aggressive sounds that ever emanated from a gramophone')[17] that influences the way in which the music is perceived.

In any event, Marsh thought the features of the 1939 performance he found inappropriate would not have been present in performances dating from the Philharmonic era and, to judge by extant Philharmonic Beethoven recordings (many of them unavailable when he wrote), that conclusion is almost certainly correct: these earlier performances, unfortunately not including an *Eroica* among them, strongly suggest a formal restraint in relation to major tempo fluxes without the sudden changes of gear perceived by Marsh in the 1939 performance. Furthermore, Toscanini's earliest complete recording of the *Eroica* to have been preserved, dating from less than a year before the one discussed by Marsh, is perhaps less idiosyncratic

---

[15] Marsh p. 85.

[16] ATL pp. 364–5 (letter to AM, 30 October 1939). Toscanini severed his relationship with Ada Mainardi in 1941 and wrote to her only once after the war: ATL pp. 383 and 411.

[17] Matthews *Records and Recordings* p. 18. The recording was first issued on RCA Victor M 765 (17852–58S), HMV DB 6058–64S. Of various CD transfers attempting to improve the sound, the RCA version on GD 60269 did not make use of first-grade NBC broadcast material, unlike the most recent issue, Sony 88697916312–23.

in character,[18] while all contemporary observations about the Philharmonic tour performances, other than Furtwängler's, point in the same direction; for example, the *Times* assessment mentioned above.

As to the retarding of the first movement's principal woodwind subject, Toscanini long agonised over the passage and his recorded performances suggest his solution equated closely with Furtwängler's own (albeit at a faster overall tempo), a halfway house between, at one end of the spectrum, the virtually non-retarding Erich Kleiber and Fritz Busch and, at the other, the romantic indulgence of some earlier German conductors exemplified among surviving recordings by Hans Pfitzner. Moreover, according to Spike Hughes,[19] resident in New York in early 1933, Toscanini did not at that time alter the tempo at all for this passage, which in any event, as Hughes correctly pointed out, he handled with extreme restraint by comparison with Weingartner – whom elsewhere Furtwängler lauded as the outstanding Classicist of his younger days.[20] As for the *Marcia funebre*, the *Times*, as mentioned in Chapter 1, commented in particular on the Queen's Hall performance's superb vitality and evenness of rhythm, pointing to the conductor's 'genius' in handling 'those critical points where one subject is joined to another and any little check or hesitation will destroy the continuity of the music'. Recalling the performance in the *Musical Times* as late as August 1935, critic Roger Fiske remarked that, 'the whole movement gained in intensity and depth at the slower tempo'.

Collectively, critical comments (other than Furtwängler's alone) suggest that, while the London *Eroica* in 1930 was consistently more expansive than any of Toscanini's NBC performances, its fluctuations of tempo were less marked than those of the 1939 performance. In the first two movements the rhythm was no doubt supple throughout, as contemporary comment indicates, but tempo fluctuations were very probably modest in character. Certainly no other contemporary musician or commentator discerned any trace of sentimentality.

The recorded history of Toscanini's performances of *Leonore No. 3* is rather different since there exists a Carnegie Hall concert aircheck from the Philharmonic period, dating from his penultimate concert as their principal conductor on 26 April 1936.[21] It discloses a performance of greater breadth and flexibility than any

---

[18]   NBC SO broadcast, 3 December 1938, on Music & Arts CD 1134.

[19]   Hughes 1959 p. 41; Pfitzner's *Eroica* Symphony recording issued in 1929, Polydor 66939–44, Naxos CD 8.110910. As to Pfitzner's approach, see further Annex C p. 316.

[20]   Walter Jacob, ed., *Felix von Weingartner, Ein Brevier*, Weisbaden/Antwerp: Heine Spett 1933 p. 32.

[21]   Guild GHCD 2344.

of his later ones and, in keeping with the Viennese classical tradition long established by such native Austrians as Weingartner and Franz Schalk (although at
tempos notably slower than theirs), Toscanini treats the Allegros precisely as they
did.[22] Furtwängler's interpretative preference here seems to have originated in one
of Mahler's many innovations.[23]

On all available evidence it is difficult to avoid the conclusion that Furtwängler's
criticisms examined here, a typical cross-section of his comments generally, at the
very least greatly exaggerated what he heard for his own purposes. Although his
comments were doubtless valid for him and apt to describe his own agenda for performing the two works, fellow musicians, critics and audiences across Europe all
reached very different conclusions. On the basis of similar recorded and written
evidence summarised in preceding chapters, parallel conclusions may be drawn
about Furtwängler's criticisms of the other Philharmonic performances he heard,
somewhat detailed in the case of Toscanini's approach to Haydn, Strauss and
Debussy but, for reasons suggested hereafter, cursory and dismissive as to his performances of Brahms.[24]

The 1935 concerts: the Brahms Fourth and a stylistic detour

Toscanini's later visits to London produced more tangible recordings of his concerts,
the extent of which is detailed in the Discography, Annex A. In particular Fred
Gaisberg's persistence recounted in Chapter 3 was responsible for the most important segment of the London recorded concert legacy, a more or less full documentation in sound excellent for its date of the first four concerts Toscanini conducted
with a British orchestra, the BBC concerts in June 1935.[25] Precisely how in 1930
Toscanini conducted that perennial test of a conductor's long-spanned vision and
musicianship, the *Eroica* Symphony, must remain to some degree speculative. Fortunately, how he conducted just five years later that other paradigmatic test, the
Fourth Symphony of Brahms, at a time when contemporary comment suggests that
he was still in his late prime as a symphonic conductor, can be assessed in the BBC

---

[22]   Weingartner recorded *Leonore No. 2* in 1938 (Columbia LX 712–13); Schalk recorded *Leonore
No. 3* in 1928 (HMV D 1614–15).

[23]   Henry-Louis de La Grange *Mahler* (vol. 1) London: Gollancz 1974 p. 257.

[24]   Furtwängler mentions Haydn's *Clock* Symphony, the Brahms *Haydn* Variations, *La Mer* and
Tod und Verklärung: see Notebooks pp. 40–6.

[25]   HMV issue numbers for the discs made from these concerts and for the recording sessions
1937–39 are given in the Discography, Annex A.

SO performance undisturbed by the abrasive aural eruptions accompanying many unofficial airchecks of his Philharmonic broadcasts in that period.[26]

This performance of the Brahms Fourth is of exceptional significance, not only in the way it illuminates aspects of Toscanini's general stylistic approach at the time but in its possible reflection of the approach of a great conductor whom Toscanini explicitly acknowledged as a direct influence on his own work, Fritz Steinbach. The previous chapter noted Toscanini's absorption of Steinbach's approach during the Munich Brahms Festival in September 1909 as well as his homage to Steinbach as late as his Philharmonia rehearsals in 1952. The depth and sincerity of that influence is unquestionable. Toscanini's Munich experience stimulated his lapidary but expressive postcard to his brother-in-law Enrico Polo: 'Brahms is great, Steinbach marvellous [meraviglioso]'. Toscanini's insight was put to practical use in September 1911 when Steinbach came to Turin to conduct Brahms's Second Symphony. In preparation for Steinbach's arrival, Toscanini rehearsed the orchestra in that work and, after playing it through with them, Steinbach remarked, 'I have nothing to do. Who is your conductor?' Toscanini himself quietly recounted this anecdote to Furtwängler when on 16 June 1924, after a La Scala concert in Zürich, the latter berated him (in what Rudolf Serkin, who witnessed the incident, described as violent and embarrassing terms) for mishandling the symphony.[27] Toscanini would perhaps have been less polite had he been aware of recent Berlin comment criticising Furtwängler for taking un-Brahmsian liberties in this very work.[28]

It is easy to understand why Toscanini was so impressed with Fritz Steinbach and why he cited the latter's implicit approval when confronted by Furtwängler. Throughout Europe in the early years of the twentieth century Steinbach held the reputation as the foremost conductor of Brahms, with the composer's imprimatur for his performances, a background of which Toscanini would have been fully aware. Characteristic of Steinbach was an implacable sense of rhythm combined

---

[26] These shortcomings can be cured, as shown by Pristine Audio's transfer of the Beethoven Ninth Symphony of 8 March 1936, PASC 117.

[27] Robert Jacobson *Reverberations: Interviews with the World's Leading Musicians* New York: William Morrow 1974 p. 203, cited by Haggin 1984 p. 227 (without attribution) and Potter pp. 350–1. This performance of Brahms's Second Symphony was for Serkin an 'incredible revelation' (ibid.). Adolf Busch was with him and relayed his impressions in a letter to Fritz (see Annex C p. 319) and no doubt later told his brother of the exchange between Toscanini and Furtwängler; hence its inclusion (without reference to the latter) in Fritz Busch p. 48, where Fritz mistakenly refers to the work in question as the *Haydn* Variations. The orchestra rehearsed by Toscanini for Steinbach was assembled for the Turin International Exposition in 1911; Toscanini himself conducted four concerts: Sachs 1978 pp. 115–16.

[28] See Shirakawa p. 49 and Annex C p. 316.

with a flexible pulse and minute attention to nuancing of detail, attributes which would have appealed to Toscanini in his younger days. Steinbach's style is further examined in Annex C.

Precisely how much influence Steinbach's approach had on Toscanini's Brahms in his younger years, let alone in the 1930s, can never be known. It would be unrealistic simply to claim that, since the BBC Brahms Fourth is the work of a master conductor and admirer of Steinbach still in his prime, it therefore reflects closely what Toscanini heard in Munich a quarter of a century before. Fritz Busch's comments on Toscanini's Oxford performance of Brahms's First Symphony noted in Chapter 4 are warning enough against any such rush to judgement. Moreover, the lengthy *Times* article examined in Chapter 2, reflecting on Toscanini's performance of Elgar's *Enigma* Variations in the 1935 concert series, remarked that those who could remember how Richter, then Steinbach, Nikisch, Weingartner, Furtwängler 'and now Toscanini' handled the symphonies of Brahms, could trace the process of individual interpretation producing a gradual revision of the estimate of Brahms.[29] If the highest estimate was given to interpreters most faithful to the text, 'nonetheless if we could be given an absolutely accurate record of the Meiningen Orchestra's performance of the Symphony in E minor which Brahms found completely satisfactory, there can be little doubt but that we should receive something of a shock at the difference between it and those which we think of as being most Brahms-like today'.

Yet with all necessary qualifications, there can be no doubt about some degree of a Steinbach imprint on the 1935 recording. Steinbach's score markings, as handed down to us, are in substantial measure adverted to here.[30] Still more reliable than these markings is the witness of other distinguished musicians, such as Adrian Boult, for whom Steinbach was one of the greatest conductors and (notwithstanding the claims of Richter) without real rival in Brahms. Boult notated his score of the Fourth's passacaglia with Steinbach's manifold tempo modifications;[31] and the tempo relationships and proportioning of the movement in his finest recorded performance (LPO 1954) and Toscanini's (BBC SO 1935) mirror each other in almost uncanny fashion, particularly in the latter variations. Such an exact meeting of minds, which in both performances results in unsurpassed structural clarity and remarkably vivid characterisation of each variation, cannot be ascribed merely to coincidence or to

[29] In the *Times* 8 June 1935; see further Ch. 2 p. 44.
[30] See Annex C pp. 344–6.
[31] See Dyment 'Boult' *CRC* p. 40 (text of Boult's interview with the author, September 1972) and Annex C p. 305.

the two conductors' exceptional musical penetration: the common influence is plain to hear. The conclusions here outlined are detailed further in Annex C.

Naturally this Fourth is also refracted through the lens of Toscanini's overwhelming personal vision; and at least as significant as the putative Steinbach influence in assessing the stature of the performance is the degree to which as a whole it illuminates the conductor's own performance practice at the time. Turner wrote of the 'ruthlessly musical rendering' he heard in this performance; even so (and this does not in any way contradict Turner's verdict), what is most striking is the continual subtle flexibility of pulse, in which scarcely a single phrase is conducted in precisely the same tempo throughout. Especially in the Andante, now barely noticeable, now slightly more marked, the changing pulse makes for musical shapes very different in character from Toscanini's later style. No doubt this interpretative approach also set formidable problems for the players: the pizzicato lower strings must have clung to every inch of the beat to follow with such precision the extraordinary fluctuations in that movement's bars 30–5. Indeed, to revert to the speculative Steinbach shadow, this performance of the whole movement might in itself serve as a checklist of the characteristics attributed to that master. Nevertheless, it is only if one consciously adverts to these fluctuations that they become noticeable, since here and throughout the work they follow with complete understanding the implicit character of the musical material, its alternate intensification and relaxation; hence the impression conveyed of absolute architectural integrity and certainty of purpose.

It was doubtless this understanding, this supreme equipoise of intellect and emotion matched by the sheer physical impact in sound drawn from Toscanini's orchestra, that compelled the *Times* critic, as noted in Chapter 2, to describe this performance as 'a hundred per cent solution of the music, the "how" and the "what" are made one'; in consequence, 'the absorption of the listener in the nature of the thing so created is whole and complete'. These comments led Denis Matthews to protest on behalf of the claims of other valid interpretations of the Fourth;[32] he surely had in mind, among others, Bruno Walter, whose recording of the work with the same orchestra made just a year before is also absorbing and almost as convincing. Walter's headlong but very pliable scherzo, for example, differs fundamentally from Toscanini's thunderous, albeit flexible, deliberation or Weingartner's loftily imperturbable but relatively sedate LSO recording of 1938. Nevertheless it

---

[32] Matthews 1982 p. 68. For details of Walter's recording, see p. 327. Weingartner's recording was made at Abbey Road on 14 February 1938, issued on Columbia LX 705–09, EMI CD CHS 764256-2.

would be unrealistic to claim that, with his occasional rushes of blood to the head, Walter conveys a vision of the work as wholly integrated as Toscanini's.

With such superhuman demands in terms of flexibility, clarity and power, it was inevitable that, at that stage of Toscanini's relationship with the orchestra, the playing would betray its share of accidents and first- (and second-)night nerves. For some listeners that lack of polish adds its share of spontaneity; for other, mostly American, commentators it is viewed as a substantial disadvantage by comparison with the finest NBC performances such as that of 27 November 1948, which has a corresponding breadth and superior finish.[33] Again, in repeated observations to the author, B. H. Haggin judged the BBC SO performance uncharacteristic by comparison with the incomplete aircheck of the New York Philharmonic performance on 15 March 1936. It is true that in the latter the fluctuations of tempo in the Andante and scherzo are less marked and the opening movement's ensemble superior. But even if Haggin was correct, the BBC SO performance is all the more valuable in illuminating a still earlier interpretative approach, probably stimulated by the orchestra's remarkable responsiveness which in their studio performances, as noted hereafter, encouraged the spontaneous release of Toscanini's deepest feelings about the works recorded. That view is supported by the characteristics of another Philharmonic aircheck of the first three movements conducted by Toscanini only six weeks before his arrival in London: they are less inflected and, in the first movement, tighter in tempo than the BBC SO performance.[34]

It is, however, undeniable that the BBC orchestra's execution falls short of perfection and in minor respects the recording itself falsifies Toscanini's intentions. The triangle in the scherzo is barely audible and, more crucially, the oboe, usually plangently forward in Toscanini's characteristic orchestral textures, almost completely evades the microphone; thus its brief standout at bars 17–18 in the first movement (a signal feature of his performances) fails to make its usual mark.[35]

For all these shortcomings, overall the performance demonstrates more explicitly than any other the nature of Toscanini's art as it stood in the mid-1930s, in the period before the influences discussed earlier in this chapter perceptibly

---

[33] See e.g. Frank's comments on the 1948 NBC performance: notes for its EMI/IMG release, CD 72435629392.

[34] Concert of 17 April 1935, recording made available courtesy Seth Winner, as also the incomplete performance of 15 March 1936.

[35] In Toscanini's swifter performances of the first movement (e.g. the NBC SO broadcasts of 11 February 1939 and 28 October 1945, and also the RCA recording of 3 December 1951) the oboe phrase is taken strictly in tempo, whereas in his more expansive versions (10 January 1943, 27 November 1948 and 22 December 1951) he lingers momentarily.

changed that art in the following years. The Brahms symphony is not alone in this respect and in some of that first BBC season's performances the playing is more completely achieved, notably in the terrifyingly elemental *La Mer*. Other performances in the 1935 series have their own virtues: the Wagner excerpts of a sustained loftiness and earth-shaking intensity; the wonderfully pliable Mendelssohn Nocturne with Aubrey Brain a matchless soloist; and the acutely drawn *Enigma* Variations of overpowering emotional warmth. The two performances of Beethoven's Seventh Symphony are also formidable examples of concentrated firepower, even if in that work the Philharmonic recording of the following year must be handed the ultimate prize for discipline and polish. But the Brahms symphony remains an unrivalled experience for its intellectual grasp and emotional penetration of every corner of the score and for the conductor's overarching projection of a supreme masterpiece of symphonic logic. In the work's recorded history, this performance's combination of passion, majesty and compelling sense of inevitable progression has never been matched.

The 1937–39 concerts

HMV were unable to record any of the concerts during subsequent seasons. All too little survives from the 1937 London Music Festival because of Toscanini's ban on both live recordings and shortwave transmissions, fortunately lifted as to the latter for the two choral concerts of 30 October and 3 November that year. In terms of sound quality, the finest survivors from these later festivals stem from recordings made either by the BBC of its own broadcasts (the Verdi *Requiem* of 27 May 1938, the *Missa Solemnis* of 28 May 1939) or by HMV of BBC broadcasts (the Second symphonies of Sibelius and Brahms, 10 June 1938). All these performances have outstanding qualities save, perhaps, the Brahms Second Symphony which, for reasons given in Chapter 7, suffers audibly from the wear and tear of concert conditions. But all told, these recordings have their analogues in superior sound in other contemporary versions by Toscanini with the NBC Symphony Orchestra, in particular the Verdi and Beethoven choral works in performances dating respectively from November and December 1940, which are marginally more expansive in approach. The specific qualities which inform the foregoing BBC SO performances are detailed in the list of concert programmes at Annex B, but they do not require extended notice here.

    Similar observations apply for the most part to the other surviving off-air recordings circulating through unofficial channels, which derive from three principal sources. First, there are a few private recordings professionally made from BBC broadcasts within Britain; these include the Beethoven Ninth Symphony of 3 November 1937 and the Beethoven Fourth and Fifth symphonies from the complete cycle of May 1939. These recordings were, it seems, made at the instance or with the co-operation of the BBC orchestra's conductor Sir Adrian Boult, and the quality, while tolerable to the enthusiast, is poor by the standards of the time. Secondly, there are some private recordings made by amateurs from BBC broadcasts within Britain; with the exception of the items from the Leech Collection in the British Library's Sound Archive, these are few in number and poor in quality.[36] Although most of the Leech Collection items enjoy superior sound, their fragmentary character and discontinuity rob them of a great deal of their value. Finally, there exist a number of recordings made abroad from shortwave broadcasts; these include recordings made in the USA of the Brahms *German Requiem* of 30 October 1937 and the Beethoven Ninth Symphony of 3 November (the latter duplicating the professional recording mentioned above), as well as parts of two concerts in the 1939 Beethoven cycle and the first of the two performances of the *Missa Solemnis* in that cycle dated 26 May 1939. Other shortwave recordings from 1938 come from various European venues. The sound quality of these broadcasts is variable and subject in most cases to the serious fading and distortion which accompanied reception of shortwave transmissions; and, while some works were captured complete, others (among them the Feuermann *Don Quixote* of 23 May 1938 noted in Chapter 7) suffer some discontinuity.

The majority of the mostly poor-sounding survivors outlined in the preceding paragraph need not be examined here; all, including items in the Leech Collection, are detailed in Annex B. Three items do, however, demand attention because of the unique quality of the performance, or of a particular light thrown on Toscanini's approach. First, in sound which survived the shortwave transmission relatively intact (part of it is also in the Leech Collection), the Brahms *Tragic Overture* which preceded the *German Requiem* in the concert on 30 October 1937 shows Toscanini at the peak of his form. The orchestra responds with a precision in all departments that it was seemingly unwilling or unable to give at the recording session of this work only five days before. The conductor's demonic concentration and the freedom

[36] Kenneth Leech (1892–1995) trained as a mechanical engineer working on the railways; he was also a composer, but is best remembered for his work as an amateur sound recordist, most notably for having cut some 1200 discs from BBC radio broadcasts between 1935 and the early 1960s; the collection is now in the British Library Sound Archive, where the content has been transferred to tape/CD-R. He had only one machine and all material recorded is therefore subject to side breaks. See further, Foreman.

with which he felt able to express himself in matters of phrasing and tempo throughout – the generosity, for example, in response to Brahms's frequent *dolce* and *espressivo* markings – all mark this performance as superior to the HMV recording, a lesson in the virtues of live recording and the inhibitions and limitations which, for Toscanini at the time, recording in studio conditions entailed.

Secondly, as noted in Chapter 6, the Adagio of Beethoven's Ninth Symphony evoked a particular response in Toscanini's imagination – Elysium, a visitation from on high and so on. Rarely, however, is that reflected in what we hear in his recordings of the movement, sometimes because close microphoning ruins the perspective undoubtedly present in the hall (the NBC Symphony performances of February 1938 and December 1939),[37] sometimes because of the relative short-comings of the all-important solo woodwinds which, as Spike Hughes observed of RCA's 1952 NBC recording, were incapable of rising to the heights of the BBC orchestra's equivalents: few orchestras could.[38] While the rough sound of the best existing source of the BBC performance of the Ninth Symphony on 3 November 1937 makes the first two movements something of a trial to the ears, the distinctive sounds of the BBC SO principals in the Adagio, notably Thurston's clarinet and MacDonagh's oboe, sing out clearly with great individuality from the prevailing murk and convince the sympathetic listener that Toscanini had indeed seen the light. 'In paradiso' he urged the orchestra in rehearsing this movement; and, as Bernard Shore so aptly put it, by contrast with Bruno Walter's warmth of feeling, here was the quietest, subdued tenderness, with restraint and an other-worldly character in which the conductor's detachment provided the maximum contrast with the violence of the first two movements.[39]

Finally, a few months later, in the concert of 3 June 1938, Toscanini conducted a performance of Mozart's *Jupiter* Symphony about which Hughes again wrote at length, recalling the alternate majesty and lyricism of the opening bars, the tender-ness of the second subject, the electric crackle of energy ending the first movement, the unending cantabile of the Andante and the shimmer of the minuet. But he treas-ured most his recollection of the finale, a 'miracle of music-making about which there is virtually nothing to be said to those who never experienced it', an 'immortal instance of the [fish] that got away'.[40] Fortunately the performance survives in prim-itive sound and differs so perceptibly from Toscanini's later renditions as to

---

[37] Music & Arts CD 1135 and CD 1203.
[38] Hughes 1959 p. 94.
[39] Shore 1949 pp. 48–9.
[40] Hughes 1959 pp. 165–7.

command attention, despite the obscuring noise and fading of a poor shortwave transmission. Hughes's memory was reliable in every respect, so indelible was the impression; but not even his eloquence could convey fully the first movement's unique combination of grandeur and songfulness, in which the hairs-breadth rubato of the second subject arrests the heart – but by not one whit the music's inevitable forward motion. As for that elusive finale, Klemperer's 1954 Philharmonia recording[41] approaches Toscanini's elevation, Szell in his Cleveland recordings his technical perfection and clarity, but the sheer elation, a product of the intensity of line – every line – is Toscanini's alone. All four movements capture Toscanini's spontaneous approach to Mozart less than two years before his more obviously drilled but still immensely impressive performance in April 1940, the earliest version with the NBC Symphony.[42] Like the *Tragic Overture*, the recording should be made available for wider study irrespective of sonic considerations.

The HMV recordings

If Toscanini rejected the live HMV recordings of 1935 and 1938, he did approve most products of his Queen's Hall 'studio' recording sessions dating from 1937–39 and it is those, therefore, by which he deserves to be judged. But his correspondence at the time of the sessions in October 1937 and June 1938 provides vivid evidence both of his disillusionment with the recording process even with the ever-responsive BBC orchestra in the almost ideal acoustics of the hall, and of a fatigue and head pains that sapped his energy far more than concert rehearsals. His mood during the sessions, as shown by the letters, appears to have had audible effects on the results. He first complained of fatigue on 25 October 1937 after recording Beethoven's First Symphony and the *Tragic Overture*. Recorded at the end of a day strenuous for both conductor and orchestra, the morning of which was spent in rehearsing the first movement of the Ninth Symphony (as noted in Chapter 6, always problematic for Toscanini), the *Tragic Overture* discloses obvious signs of wear. Horn blips (bar 43 and elsewhere), errant string ensemble (209–10) and some suspect brass intonation contrast with the above-noted concert performance of 30 October, the conductor at his most incandescent, which was virtually immaculate. Beethoven's First Symphony, which started that afternoon session, also suffered: the opening pizzicato chords were by no means unanimous as, many years later,

---

[41] On Testament SBT 1093.
[42] 20 April 1940, Music & Arts CD 833, reissued by Pristine Audio.

Stravinsky waspishly remarked in commenting on Toscanini's famed precision,[43] while the finale had to be re-recorded in 1938. Recording that finale and a few other short works on 2 June 1938 tired him out and by 9 June his nervous exhaustion caused him to abort that day's recording session: his reserves, as well as his patience, were at their lowest ebb.

Such a degree of distraction makes the conductor's overall achievement during the sessions all the more remarkable. Some American commentators have compared the results unfavourably with the celebrated New York Philharmonic recordings of 1936. No doubt, given the lung-power and polished perfection displayed by those performances, there is some justification for these observations; but there must have been other qualities compelling Toscanini to claim the BBC orchestra as among the finest, if not the very best, with which he had worked. The essence surely lay in the players' flexibility and immediacy of response which, while fulfilling the conductor's usual demands for architectural clarity and intensity of vision, also enabled his deepest feelings to emerge with a degree of spontaneity and freshness not encountered so consistently elsewhere in his recorded legacy. The *Pastoral* Symphony, for all the enforced brief pauses made during the October 1937 sessions when most of the work was recorded, is unsurpassed for what one recent annotator called its 'wonderful fluidity and spontaneous ease of expression' that gives an 'overriding impression of wonder and enchantment' driving to the inmost heart of a work which Toscanini loved perhaps more than any other of the symphonies.[44] Achieved principally by a subtle flexibility of pulse, shaping of phrase and a remarkable variety of attack, these attributes in themselves bespeak a supreme level of technical skill on the part of both players and conductor.

To analyse such skills further risks destroying the magic; but the attempt was nonetheless made in 1949 by the BBC orchestra's former principal viola, Bernard

---

[43] See Stravinsky's comments on the performance of this work in Robert Craft *Stravinsky in Conversation with Robert Craft* (including *Conversations with Igor Stravinsky* and *Memories and Commentaries*) London: Penguin 1962 p. 239. Since Stravinsky's observations about the opening chords of Beethoven's First Symphony do not fit Toscanini's NBC SO recording, it must be assumed that the comments refer to the BBC SO recording. As noted in the Reception section of the Discography, Annex A p. 275, Peter Hugh Reed, in reviewing this set for the *American Music Lover*, thought the opening lack of unanimity an illusion created by the hall acoustics and the limitations of the recording equipment; but heard through modern equipment, this seems doubtful. In his 1936 autobiography Stravinsky gave unstinting praise for Toscanini's preparation of his (Stravinsky's) works for performance at La Scala in 1926 (see Norton ed. 1962 pp. 129–30). The change to scarcely veiled vituperation, as recorded by Craft, came only after composer and conductor quarrelled about Beethoven during a transatlantic voyage. See further, Sachs 1978 pp. 179–81, Taubman p. 305 and Walsh (Vol. 1) pp. 429–30.

[44] See Naxos CD 8.110877 (notes by Ian Julier).

Shore.[45] He observed that, when Toscanini first prepared the *Pastoral* with them for the concert of 2 June 1937, he poured infinite labour into the first movement's exposition; little surprise, then, that the peculiar sense of wonderment is there from the very opening bars. Toscanini insisted on the violas' first note being clearly audible – 'if nobody 'ears, the melody has no beginning' – the violins playing *a tempo* until the pause in the fourth measure. Here an unmarked diminuendo was matched by a similarly unmarked, momentary and breathtaking drop to pianissimo at bar 15, the better to enhance without exaggeration the subsequent crescendo leading to the entrance of the oboe. At bar 67, instead of the customary and obvious *luft-pause*, Toscanini laboured to achieve a 'perfect dovetailing' of the quavers between first and second violins and cellos, asking the violins, Shore observed, 'to sing with a natural expression, while he kept the accompaniment down so that these two bars of undulating quavers were handed over clearly and smoothly between the departments' – an effect 'quite entrancing' instead of the usual 'dull kind of churning accompaniment'.

The great crescendos of the development, continued Shore, again started pianissimo rather than the marked piano, with the orchestra under Toscanini's 'broad rhythmic beat strongly swinging over the barlines, instead of the usual heavy rhythm, bar by bar'. At the climaxes (bars 179–82 and 225–8), in each phrase Toscanini's beat fractionally anticipates expectations, the sudden ferocity suggesting momentarily the driving, rhythmic powerhouse of nature itself at work: a pantheistic vision that surely reflected Beethoven's own beliefs. And so the magic is created throughout the work by the subtlest and purely musical means, enhanced, particularly in the Peasants' Merrymaking, by the remarkable BBC SO wind principals. After some three-quarters of a century the sympathetic listener may still discern that empathy, that insight which persuaded so many witnesses of his BBC concerts that the conductor was awakening the music in the very mind of the composer at the instant of creation.

For all these wonders it would be idle to pretend that this recording of the *Pastoral* Symphony represents perfection in every way. The first movement is shorn of its repeat, invariably present in Toscanini's later concert performances, while in the Andante violin trills are also shorn of their turns, to blunt effect. Shore's account of rehearsals[46] illuminates both these problematic aspects and also confirms that the repeat in the recording was omitted for reasons of timing. At one rehearsal the orchestra was in doubt as to whether there was to be a repeat and, for once,

---

[45]   In Shore 1949 pp. 50–68.
[46]   Shore 1949 pp. 53 and 59n.

Toscanini himself was undecided. 'I have always Da capo until now, but I think I may be wrong. For the balance of the movement perhaps it is best we make it. Yes, we will go back!' As for those violin trills and turns, once more Toscanini himself seemed doubtful and said, 'First violins – I know Beethoven did not write a turn, but I don't think I like it cut off. Try, just try, bitte for me now! Try it with turn! – Ah bene, bene! It is more natural.' And that was how he decided it should be played. It is not clear whether the latter incident occurred during rehearsals for the performance in June 1937 or May 1939; if it was during the latter, this dating would explain the omission of turns in the 1937 recording. In any event, both examples illustrate Toscanini's musically intuitive, rather than literal or historically driven, solution to such problems.

These shortcomings barely detract from the genius of the *Pastoral*, where the qualities of responsiveness and spontaneity typify the BBC orchestra's HMV recordings. Examination of them all would be tedious; let the following examples stand for many, commencing with one embodying the finest sound that the engineers could provide at the time. The introduction to the *Magic Flute* Overture is usually little more than a call to attention followed by the few bars of transition to the Allegro. After the forthright but finely weighted opening fanfares, that transition in Toscanini's 1938 recording unfolds unique subtleties, which start with the little violin triplet in the third bar landing featherlight on the first, hushed chord in the fourth; and each subsequent bar, precisely balanced and delicately touched in the strings, brings a succession of magical sounds moving inevitably to the mysterious modulations heralding the Allegro. The main body of the overture, when at last it arrives, has a clarity matched only by Václav Talich in his live performance of June 1954 and a pace exceeded (among historic recordings) only by Richard Strauss in 1929, with an easy mastery of rhythm and dynamics that surpasses both.[47]

Further examples are legion in the Beethoven recordings; three must suffice, commencing with two from the Fourth Symphony, the last extended work Toscanini recorded with the BBC orchestra. Some have judged this performance as a whole inferior to Toscanini's earlier BBC SO recordings and also his other versions of this work;[48] but although the recorded sound is unsatisfactory, the players' keynote qualities again mark it out, despite the relatively strict adherence to tempos typifying

---

[47] The Talich recording on (CD) Supraphon SU 3829-2, the Richard Strauss on (78) Decca CA 8106, Polydor 66826, various CD transfers, e.g. Dutton CDBP 9785. Some recent conductors, with orchestras playing on period instruments, far exceed the pace of the cited performances, e.g. Akademie für Alte Musik, Berlin/René Jacobs, Harmonia Mundi HMC 902068–70.

[48] See e.g. Biddulph WHL 008–09 (notes by Harris Goldsmith) and *CRC* Winter 2007 p. 85 (review of Toscanini's 1939 NBC SO Beethoven cycle by Harris Goldsmith).

Toscanini's style at this late date in his collaboration with the orchestra. Take first the introduction which, while never losing its pulse, seemingly suspends time, a universe in microcosm nowhere to be found in other conductors' performances and vitiated in Toscanini's later NBC versions (October 1939 and February 1951) by glaring recorded sound quality. This remarkable sound world is conjured through precise balances, with a fully audible and singing bass line allied to imperious control of the slow, arching phrases that move inexorably to the transition to the Allegro. Extraordinary again is the perfect dovetailing of strings and wind in the scale passages near the close of the second movement Adagio, where the interplay is not merely technically seamless, as if rendered by a single instrument, but borne aloft in a single curve perfectly reflecting the implicit character of the music. A precisely similar result is achieved with utmost spontaneity in the scale passages for the strings ending in woodwind and string phrases near the start of *Leonore No. 1*, where players recollected the intensive rehearsing needed to produce the miracle.[49]

In all the BBC SO recordings, Toscanini's fabled clarity, intensity of vision and architectural integrity may be taken as read. Over and above such bedrock, expected characteristics, however, the foregoing examples demonstrate how the orchestra's immediacy of response drew forth special qualities from their conductor. Further, they aptly illustrate Newman's penetrating observation that 'Toscanini does more than merely reproduce the score. He reproduces it with an exquisite sense of what the music means – the shape of a phrase, the colour of a tissue and so on ... what Toscanini made [the passage] mean, by the subtlest nuance of curve and intensity is beyond description: and he made us feel that that, just that, was what Beethoven intended it to mean.'[50]

The remarkable calibre of the BBC SO winds emphasised throughout this appraisal is highlighted again in the final example, Rossini's *La scala di seta* Overture, in which the striking individuality and responsiveness of the orchestra's famed principals – at the date of recording in June 1938 Robert Murchie, Frederick Thurston, Terence MacDonagh, Aubrey Brain and Archie Camden – eclipse their contemporaries on both sides of the Atlantic; and Toscanini's uninhibited but easeful exploitation of their virtuosity reaches us impeded only by the faulty dubbing passed for publication.

---

[49] Broadcast talk by Alex Nifosi.

[50] *Sunday Times* 21 June 1937; Newman's musical example was the ten-times repeated phrase at bar 153 of the *Egmont* Overture which he heard Toscanini rehearse at the end of December 1935 and perform on 1 January 1936 at Monte Carlo, referred to in Ch. 3 p. 65.

Such compromises were part of the price for capturing Toscanini on the wing. His reaction to the recording process during these sessions suggests that HMV, and posterity, were fortunate to secure as much as they did. Despite immense advances in orchestral technique over the last seven decades, Toscanini's honing of an orchestra already disciplined to an exceptional degree assures the immortality of these performances. They can be heard today without the indulgence often required for other orchestral recordings of the time and, through them, the conductor's unique powers and perception in his late prime shine undimmed.

DISCOGRAPHY OF EMI RECORDINGS 1935–51

INTRODUCTION

Scope

A discography containing only the basic data about Toscanini's HMV sessions during 1937–39 would be meagre indeed; it would cover barely a couple of sheets – but it would reflect a mere tithe of EMI's endeavours. From Chapter 3 onwards, the narrative of those endeavours demonstrates the efforts of the major record-making company in Europe to follow the twists and turns of a pre-eminent artist who hated recording; to placate and please him with the object of securing enough music in the grooves to meet the clamour of demand from an impatient, record-buying public. Recording sessions were one aspect of the effort. Another aspect was the elaborate preparations to make live recordings of some of the concerts. Yet another was the equally elaborate aftermath of so many sessions, live and 'studio', taking place in the Abbey Road Transfer Room with the aim of producing a final product for the Maestro's approval. Without a full picture of all these activities, a discography would mislead.

Furthermore, EMI's efforts continued after the Second World War. Fully expecting to record Toscanini and the Orchestra of La Scala on their aborted visit to London in July 1946, EMI had instead to fall back on the Zürich Radio acetates of the substituted Lucerne concerts. Where judged fit for transfer, these discs were subjected in the Transfer Room to the same processing as some of the pre-war BBC SO live recordings and with the same aim: securing Toscanini's approval of them for issue. In this endeavour EMI failed, as they did with their less enthusiastic efforts on behalf of his Boito anniversary concert at La Scala in 1948. Finally, as recounted in Chapter 10, Toscanini's 'studio' La Scala recordings in August 1951 had a major input from Abbey Road, with the tapes being processed at Hayes. All this work merits inclusion in a complete listing of EMI recordings. The discography therefore contains the recording sessions, live concert recordings by EMI, and details of the processing in the Abbey Road Transfer Room, all of these activities integrated by date in a single listing. Other BBC SO concerts transmitted by the BBC and released in authorised and unofficial LP and CD transfers, together with shortwave and other recordings, professional and amateur, are noted in Chapter 12 and Annex B.

The discographical information is followed by a reception study, in substance the reviews which met the 78rpm issues in Britain, the country of first issue, where the pre-eminent organ of professional opinion was the *Gramophone*. Selecting this journal's opinions was not straightforward, since all the relevant reviews were the work of one man, W. R. Anderson (1891–1979), whose style was, by today's conventions, idiosyncratic and whose method often adopted a side-by-78-side scheme of comment on the work and/or recording which it would be irrelevant for today's reader to follow. Short passages extracting the reviews' essence are presented here in chronological order of publication in the *Gramophone*, reflecting also the date of issue by HMV. For comparative purposes, extracts are also presented from contemporary issues of the *American Music Lover* (from 1944 *American Record Guide*), whose reviewer, except where noted, was its founding editor Peter Hugh Reed (1892–1969). Reviews also appeared in London daily papers and other journals but were relatively uninformative.

Technical details, arrangement and key

All Toscanini/BBC SO/HMV recordings were made on the 2EA, 0EA or 2ER matrix series; 2 signifies the 12-inch matrices, 0 the 10-inch, EA the HMV studio recordings made in England, ER the HMV mobile van recordings.[1] But blocks of 2EA and 0EA matrix numbers (among them all Toscanini/BBC SO 2EA/0EA matrices) were also allocated to the Abbey Road No. 4 Machine Room whenever the room received landline transmissions from external locations such as the Queen's Hall, and to the Abbey Road Transfer Room where, in Toscanini's case, material recorded on TT test matrices was dubbed onto the 2EA matrix series. An obvious example of these differing series and allocations is provided by the 1937 *Pastoral* Symphony which was recorded on 2ER matrices, since it was a product of Queen's Hall sessions in October 1937 transmitted to the mobile van, save for the Andante on 2EA matrices dubbed from TT test matrices recorded during Toscanini's first Queen's Hall 'studio' session the previous June. Another clear example of the different matrix series is provided by the three short works, together with the finale of Beethoven's First Symphony, recorded on 2 June 1938. All these works are in the 2EA series, but the *Magic Flute* Overture's matrix numbers are in a different block from the others, which were dubbed from TT test matrices, because it was recorded from the hall direct onto 2EA matrices the numbers of which were already allocated *en bloc* to such landline transmissions from external locations.

The TT (Technical Test) series, which were not meant for commercial issue, were used for events when start/finish/recording levels etc could not be determined

---

[1] The 'Lancia mobile unit' was a purpose-built body on a two-ton Lancia chassis equipped with a complete recording system and was used extensively in a great variety of recording locations from Glyndebourne to La Scala: see Southall pp. 20–1.

in advance. Typically these included live events, such as the annual ceremony of Trooping the Colour (on TT2466), during which it was impossible to make preliminary 'test' discs to determine correct placement of microphones and maximum and minimum recording levels for the wax. The tests were recorded on standard 14-inch waxes; the extra inches at the margin permitted cutting the lead-in grooves and enabled engineers to mark the matrix, take, session date and other data, in preparation for later transfer. One or more TT numbers were allocated for a complete event, but the 'take' numbers attached to each TT were, it seems, not consecutive; thus, for example, the test 'takes' used for the BBC broadcast concert of 10 June 1938 (below), follow no observable sequence. The Zürich radio recordings of the two 1946 Lucerne La Scala Orchestra concerts made on vinyl acetates by the Swiss engineers were treated by EMI as TTs and allocated TT numbers.[2]

The discography is chronological in order of the *initial* recording date of each work, after which follow *all* subsequent recording and/or transfer dates, as applicable, for that particular work. It falls into two parts – the 1935–39 recordings made with the BBC Symphony Orchestra in the Queen's Hall, London, and those of 1946–51 with the Orchestra of La Scala, Milan, made at various locations, as stated. Takes approved by Toscanini and used for 78rpm issue are in **bold**. Symphonic movements are denoted by Roman numerals. The names of recording session producers and recording engineers, where known, can be found at the appropriate places in the main narrative.

Issue details (which do not claim to be comprehensive) follow the recording details of each work: 78rpm (78), followed by 45rpm extended-play (EP), 33rpm long-play (LP) and compact disc (CD).[3]

Issue key:
78 DB, DBS (single-sided) *HMV (UK) 12-inch red label series*; 15000 *RCA Victor (USA) 12-inch series, with M (manual)/AM (slide automatic)/DM (drop automatic) coupling*

EP WCT *RCA Victor (USA)*; 7RQ *La Voce del Padrone (Italy)*

LP ALP, XLP, E, EH, EX *HMV (EMI, UK)*; SH *World Record Club (EMI, UK)*; LCT *RCA Victor (USA)*; Sera. *Seraphim (Angel, USA)*; QJLP, QALP *La Voce del Padrone (Italy)*

CD CDH *EMI (UK)*; SBT *Testament*; BBCL *BBC Legends*; WHL *Biddulph*; APR *Appian*; CDEA *Dutton*; IN *Iron Needle*; ARPCD *Archipel*; GHCD *Guild*

---

[2] If TTs were available, superior transfers could be made of the relevant works (or parts of works). Their whereabouts is, however, not known and it seems probable that they are no longer extant.

[3] Most of the BBC SO recordings have also been issued on the Italian label Grammofono 2000; as re-equalised and inferior dubbings of EMI transfers (LP and CD), they are not listed here.

DISCOGRAPHY

BBC Symphony Orchestra in the Queen's Hall, London

CHERUBINI Anacréon – Overture
Public concert 3 June 1935[4]
Pt 1   2EA1787-1-1A
Pt 2   2EA1788-1-1A
Pt 3   2EA1789-1-1A
CD: BBCL 4016-2, West Hill Radio Archives WHRA-6046

BRAHMS Symphony No. 4 in E minor
Public concerts 3 and 5 June 1935
I   Pt 1   2EA1790-1-1A-2
I   Pt 2   2EA1791-1-1A-2
I   Pt 3   2EA1792-1-1A-2
II   Pt 1   2EA1793-1-1A-2
II   Pt 2   2EA1794-1-1A-2
II   Pt 3   2EA1795-1-1A-2
III   Pt 1   2EA1796-1-1A-2
III   Pt 2   2EA1797-1-1A-2
IV   Pt 1   2EA1798-1-1A-2
IV   Pt 2   2EA1799-1-1A-2
IV   Pt 3   2EA1800-1-1A-2
Takes 2 rec. 5 June.
LP: ATS 1008 (5 June)
CD: CDH 7697832, WHRA-6046 (from both performances)

WAGNER Götterdämmerung – Siegfried's Death and Funeral Music
Public concerts 3 and 5 June 1935
Pt 1   2EA2201-1-1A-2-2A
Pt 2   2EA2202-1-1A-2-2A
Pt 3   2EA2203-1-1A-2-2A
Takes 2/2A rec. 5 June.
CD: CDH 7630442, WHRA-6046 (5 June)

---

[4] All four 1935 concerts were relayed by landline to the Machine Room.

ELGAR Variations on an Original Theme, 'Enigma'
Public concert 3 June 1935
Pt 1   2EA2204-1-1A
Pt 2   2EA2205-1-1A
Pt 3   2EA2206-1-1A
Pt 4   2EA2207-1-1A
Pt 5   2EA2208-1-1A
Pt 6   2EA2209-1-1A
Pt 7   2EA2210-1-1A
Pt 8   2EA2211-1-1A
Pt 9   2EA2212-1-1A
21 June 1935, Transfer Room
Pt 2 from 2EA2205-1: 2EA2205-2 (to reduce volume)
LP: EH 2913451
CD: CDH 7697842, GHCD 2384, WHRA-6046

WAGNER A Faust Overture
Public concert 5 June 1935
Pt 1   2EA2216-1-1A
Pt 2   2EA2217-1-1A
Pt 3   2EA2218-1-1A
LP: ATS 1008
CD: CDH 7630442, WHRA-6046

WAGNER Parsifal – Prelude to Act 1 and Good Friday Music
Public concert 5 June 1935
Pt 1   2EA2219-1-1A
Pt 2   2EA2220-1-1A
Pt 3   2EA2221-1-1A
Pt 4   2EA2222-1-1A
Pt 5   2EA2223-1-1A
Pt 6   2EA2224-1-1A
Pt 7   2EA2225-1-1A
Pt 8   2EA2226-1-1A
4 July 1935, Transfer Room
Pt 5 from 2EA2223-1: 2EA2223-2 (to cut last note)
Pt 6 from 2EA2224-1: 2EA2224-2 (to cut first note)
CD: CDH 7630442, WHRA-6046

GEMINIANI Concerto Grosso in B minor, Op. 3 No. 2
Public concert 12 June 1935
Pt 1   2EA2248-1-1A
Pt 2   2EA2249-1-1A
Pt 3   2EA2250-1-1A
WHRA-6046

BEETHOVEN Symphony No. 7 in A
Public concerts 12 and 14 June 1935
I   Pt 1   2EA2251-1-1A-2-2A
I   Pt 2   2EA2252-1-1A-2-2A
I   Pt 3   2EA2253-1-1A-2-2A
II   Pt 1   2EA2254-1-1A-2-2A
II   Pt 2   2EA2255-1-1A-2-2A
II   Pt 3   2EA2256-1-1A-2-2A
III   Pt 1   2EA2257-1-1A-2-2A
III   Pt 2   2EA2258-1-1A-2-2A
IV   Pt 1   2EA2259-1-1A-2-2A
IV   Pt 2   2EA2260-1-1A-2-2A
Takes 2/2A rec. 14 June.
LP: E 2909321 (in EX 2909303) (14 June)
CD: BBCL 4016-2 (12 June), WHRA-6046 (14 June)

DEBUSSY La Mer
Public concerts 12 and 14 June 1935
I   Pt 1   2EA2261-1-1A-2-2A
I   Pt 2   2EA2262-1-1A-2-2A
II   Pt 1   2EA2263-1-1A
II   Pt 2   2EA2264-1-1A-2-2A
III   Pt 1   2EA2265-1-1A-2-2A
III   Pt 2   2EA2266-1-1A-2-2A
Takes 2/2A and II Pt 1 takes 1/1A rec. 14 June (II Pt 1 not rec. 12 June).
LP: EH 2913451
CD: CDH 7630442, CDH 7697842, WHRA-6046 (from both performances)

ROSSINI Semiramide – Overture
Public concert 12 June 1935
Pt 1   2EA2267-1-1A
Pt 2   2EA2268-1-1A
Pt 3   2EA2269-1-1A
CD: SBT 1015, IN 1355, WHRA-6046

MOZART Symphony No. 35 in D, K385 (Haffner)
Public concert 14 June 1935

I	Pt 1	2EA2273-1-1A
I	Pt 2	2EA2274-1-1A
II	Pt 1	2EA2275-1-1A
II	Pt 2	2EA2276-1-1A
III		2EA2277-1-1A
IV		2EA2278-1-1A

CD: BBCL 4016-2, WHRA-6046

MENDELSSOHN A Midsummer Night's Dream – Nocturne and Scherzo
Public concert 14 June 1935

Pt 1	2EA2279-1-1A
Pt 2	2EA2280-1-1A
Pt 3	2EA2281-1-1A

CD: SBT 1015, WHRA-6046

BEETHOVEN Symphony No. 6 in F (Pastoral)
Recording session 17 June 1937[5]

I and II TT5241-1(?) to 7

21 June 1937, Transfer Room

| I | Pt 1 from TT5241: 2EA3582-1 |
| I | Pt 2 from TT5241: 2EA3583-1 |

22 June 1937, Transfer Room

II	Pt 1 from TT5241: 2EA3585-1
II	Pt 2 from TT5241: 2EA3586-1
II	Pt 3 from TT5241: 2EA3587-**1**

24 June 1937, Transfer Room

| I | Pt 3 from TT5241: 2EA3584-1 |

14 July 1937, Transfer Room

| I | Pt 1 from TT5241-5 and 6: 2EA3582-2 |
| I | Pt 3 from TT5241-6 and 7: 2EA3584-2 |

16 July 1937, Transfer Room[6]

| II | Pt 1 from TT5241: 2EA3585-**2** |
| II | Pt 2 from TT5241: 2EA3586-**2** |

CONTINUED ON FOLLOWING PAGE

---

[5] Details of the number of test takes made at this session, and which movements were recorded on which takes, have not survived, save as noted in the Transfer Room session of 14 July. The documented test take numbers from that session suggest that I and II may have been recorded in reverse order but such numbering is not conclusive, as shown by the miscellaneous sequencing of the TT 'takes' of the BBC broadcast, 10 June 1938 (below).

[6] On 29 June at the Isolino Toscanini heard and approved several June transfers; he presumably approved these July transfers of II during his London visit in October/November 1937.

Recording session 21 October 1937[7]
I	Pt 1	2ER231-**1**-1A
I	Pt 2	2ER232-**1**-1A
I	Pt 3	2ER233-**1**-1A
II	Pt 1	2ER234-1-1A
II	Pt 2	2ER235-1-1A
II	Pt 3	2ER236-1-1A
III	Pt 1	2ER237-1-1A
III	Pt 2 and IV	2ER238-1-1A
V	Pt 1	2ER239-1-1A
V	Pt 2	2ER240-1-**1A**

Recording session 22 October 1937
II	Pt 3	2ER236-2-2A-2B-3
III	Pt 1	2ER237-**2**-2A
III	Pt 2 and IV	2ER238-2-**2A**
V	Pt 1	2ER239-2-**2A**
V	Pt 2	2ER240-2-2A[8]

78: Album 295 (DB 3333–37, auto DB 8369–73), M 417 (14707–11), AM (14712–16), DM (16472–76)
EP: WCT 70
LP: E 2909311 (in EX 2909303), ALP 1664, SH 112, in BBC4001, LCT 1042, Sera. 6015, QJLP 107
CD: EMI/IMG 72435629392s, Naxos 8.110877, WHL 009, Sony 88697916312–72

BEETHOVEN Symphony No. 1 in C, Op. 21
Recording session 25 October 1937
I	Pt 1	2ER241-1-1A-2-**2A**
I	Pt 2	2ER242-1-**1A**
II	Pt 1	2ER243-1-**1A**
II	Pt 2	2ER244-1-**1A**
III		2ER245-1-1A-2-**2A**
IV	Pt 1	2ER246-1-1A
IV	Pt 2	2ER247-1-1A-2-2B

Recording session 2 June 1938
| IV | (Pts 1 and 2) TT5257-7-8 |

13 June 1938, Transfer Room
| IV | Pt 1 from TT5257-7: 2ER246-**2** |
| IV | Pt 2 from TT5257-8: 2ER247-**3** |

78: Album 315 (DB 3537–38, DBS 3539, DB 3540, auto DB 8520–21, DBS 8522, DB 8523), M 507 (15383–87, with Brahms's *Tragic Overture*), AM (15388–92), DM (16179–83)
EP: WCT 49
LP: E 2909301 (in EX 2909303), SH 134, LCT 1023, Sera. 6015, QJLP 106
CD: Naxos 8.110854, WHL 008, CDEA 5004, IN 1310, 88697916312–72

---

[7] Recording sessions 21, 22 and 25 October 1937: for these sessions the 'plain number' takes were relayed from the hall to the Machine Room, the 'A' takes from the hall to the mobile van recording unit.

[8] The date for take 2 of 2ER240 is missing but it was presumably recorded at this session.

BRAHMS Tragic Overture
Recording session 25 October 1937
Pt 1   2ER248-1-1A-2-**2A**
Pt 2   2ER249-1-1A-**2A**
Pt 3   2ER250-1-1A-2-**2A**
78: DB 3349–50 (side 4: Beethoven's Symphony No. 1 III), M 507 (15386–87, with Beethoven's Symphony No. 1)
EP: WCT 49
LP: XLP 30079, Sera. 6015, Sera. 60150, QJLP 106
CD: CDH 7697832, Naxos 8.110877, WHL 009, 88697916312–72

MOZART The Magic Flute – Overture[9]
Recording session 2 June 1938[10]
Pt 1   2EA6654-**1**
Pt 2   2EA6655-**1**
78: DB 3350, 15190
LP: XLP 30079, Sera. 6015, Sera. 60150, QJLP 106
CD: Naxos 8.110877, WHL 008, IN 1355, Andante 1982, 88697916312–72

ROSSINI La scala di seta – Overture
Recording session 2 June 1938
TT5257-3-4
13 June 1938, Transfer Room
Pt 1 from TT5257-3: 2EA5754-**1**
Pt 2 from TT5257-4: 2EA5755-**1**
3 February 1948, Transfer Room
Pt 2 from 2EA5755-1: 2EA5755-**2**-3[11]
78: DB 3541, 15191
LP: XLP 30079, Sera. 60150
CD: Naxos 8.110877, WHL 009, 88697916312–72

---

[9] A manuscript entry on ledgers, absent in the recording books, says 'from TT5257' (like the Rossini and Weber items recorded at this session) but, although probably also recorded on TTs, they were not used: (i) these matrix numbers belong to the block allocated for *direct* recording onto wax (see the introduction to this Discography); (ii) the trace of the preceding chord followed by a prolonged silence at the start of side two indicates that it *is* a direct recording – this would have been eliminated in any dubbing; (iii) the sound does not suffer from the defects of the dubbed transfers (see Ch. 7 p. 144).

[10] The recording machine for this session was, according to the recording sheets, located in the Long Dressing Room in the Queen's Hall; presumably this was the location for the machine at other sessions during 1937–39.

[11] Transferred from library copy of take 1 pressing following shell damage.

WEBER orch. BERLIOZ Invitation to the Dance
Recording session 2 June 1938
TT5257-12-13-14
14 June 1938, Transfer Room
Pt 1 from TT5257-12-13: 2EA5756-**1**
Pt 2 from TT5257-13-14: 2EA5757-**1**
78: DB 3542, 15192
LP: XLP 30079, Sera. 60150
CD: Naxos 8.110877, WHL 009, 88697916312–72

SIBELIUS Symphony No. 2 in D
Public concert 10 June 1938
TT5258-1, TT5260-2-3, TT5258-3-4-5-6-7, TT5260-8-9, TT5258-8-9-10
22 June 1938, Transfer Room[12]
Pt 1 from TT5258-1:   2EA5769-1
Pt 2 from TT5260-2-3:   2EA5770-1
Pt 3 from TT5258-3:   2EA5771-1
Pt 4 from TT5258-4-5:   2EA5772-1
Pt 5 from TT5258-5-6:   2EA5773-1
Pt 6 from TT5258-6:   2EA5774-1
Pt 7 from TT5258-7:   2EA5775-1
27 June 1938, Transfer Room
Pt 8 from TT5260-8-9:   2EA5780-1
Pt 9 from TT5258-8-9:   2EA5781-1-2
Pt 10 from TT5258-9-10: 2EA5782-1
6 July 1938, Transfer Room
Pt 2 from TT5260-2-3:   2EA5770-2
Pt 8 from TT5260-8-9:   2EA5780-2
Pt 9 from TT5258-8-9:   2EA5781-3
Pt 10 from TT5258-9-10: 2EA5782-2
CD: CDH 7633072

---

[12] Transfer Room sessions 22, 27 June and 6 July 1938: individual movements of the two symphonies are not documented.

BRAHMS Symphony No. 2 in D
Public concert 10 June 1938
TT5259-1, TT5261-2, TT5259-3, TT5261-3-4-5-6-7-8, TT5259-9-10, TT5261-10
22 June 1938, Transfer Room
Pt 1 from TT5259-1:   2EA5759-1
Pt 2 from TT5261-2:   2EA5760-1
Pt 3 from TT5259-3:   2EA5761-1
Pt 4 from TT5261-3-4: 2EA5762-1
Pt 5 from TT5261-5:   2EA5763-1
Pt 6 from TT5261-6-7: 2EA5764-1
Pt 7 from TT5261-7:   2EA5765-1
Pt 8 from TT5261-7-8: 2EA5766-1
Pt 9 from TT5259-9-10: 2EA5767-1
Pt 10 from TT5261-10: 2EA5768-1
6 July 1938, Transfer Room
Pt 10 from TT5261-10: 2EA5768-2-3
CD: SBT 1015

BEETHOVEN Symphony No. 4 in B flat[13]
Recording session 1 June 1939
I   Pt 1   2EA7959-2-**3**
I   Pt 2   2EA7960-**2**-3
I   Pt 3   2EA7961-2-**3**
II   Pt 1   2EA7962-1-**2**
II   Pt 2   2EA7963-1-**2**
III   2EA7964-**1**-2
IV   Pt 1   2EA7965-**1**-2
IV   Pt 2   2EA7966-1-2-2A
5 July 1939, Transfer Room
IV   Pt 2 from 2EA7966-2A: 2EA7966-**3**-4
78: Album 334 (DB 3896–99, auto DB 8733–36), M 676 (16325–28), AM
(16329–32), DM (16333–36)
LP: E 2909301 (in EX 2909303), ALP 1598, SH 134, Sera. 6015, QALP 10227
CD: Naxos 8.110854, WHL 008, CDEA 5004, IN 1310, 88697916312–72

BEETHOVEN Coriolan – Overture
Recording session 1 June 1939
Pt 1   2EA7967-1-2
Pt 2   2EA7968-1-2
Unissued, 'rejected by artist'.

---

[13] Each movement of Beethoven's Fourth Symphony was, it seems, performed twice for the two sets of recorded takes. There seem also to have been third takes of the first movement preceding the two which were recorded, but no documentation of them survives; probably they were used as balance etc. tests during Toscanini's rehearsal at the start of the morning session. One side only, the second side of the finale, has an additional 'A' take, used for the transfer on 5 July 1939, but there is no explanation for this solitary addition.

BEETHOVEN Leonore Overture No. 1
Recording session 1 June 1939
Pt 1   2EA7969-1-**2**
Pt 2   2EA7970-1-**2**
78: DB 3846, 15945
EP: WCT 65, 7RQ 275
LP: E 2909321 (in EX 2909303), ALP 1598, XLP 30079, LCT 1041, Sera. 6015,
Sera. 60150, QALP 10227
CD: Naxos 8.110854, WHL 009, CDEA 5004, IN 1310, 88697916312-72

BEETHOVEN The Creatures of Prometheus – Overture
Recording session 1 June 1939
2EA7971-1-2
0EA7972-1, 0EA7973-1[14]
LP: E 2909311 (in EX 2909303)
CD: WHRA–6046

Orchestra of La Scala, Milan (various locations, as stated)

KABALEVSKY Colas Breugnon – Overture
Public concert 5 July 1946, Kunsthaus Lucerne
TT5T1-2
25 February 1947, Transfer Room
Pt 1 from TT5T1-2: 0EA11668-1
Pt 2 from TT5T1-2: 0EA11669-1

BRAHMS Symphony No. 4 in E minor
Public concert 5 July 1946, Kunsthaus Lucerne
Recorded but not transferred

[DEBUSSY La Mer
Public concert 5 July 1946, Kunsthaus Lucerne
Not recorded]

ROSSINI William Tell – Act 1 Passo a sei, Act 3 Soldiers' Dance
Public concert 5 July 1946, Kunsthaus Lucerne
TT5T11-12
25 February 1947, Transfer Room
Pt 1 from TT5T11: 0EA11670-1
Pt 2 from TT5T11: 0EA11671-1
26 February 1947, Transfer Room
From TT5T12: 2EA11672-1-2
3 March 1947, Transfer Room
Pt 1 from TT5T11: 0EA11670-2[15]

---

[14] The two ten-inch matrices, both destroyed, were presumably back-ups, perhaps to be used if no coupling was available. Although not issued until 1986, there is no evidence that 2EA7971 was rejected by Toscanini.

[15] Second transfer made, the first having been 'lost at factory'.

STRAUSS Tod und Verklärung, Op. 24
Public concert 5 July 1946, Kunsthaus Lucerne
TT5T13-18
28 February 1947, Transfer Room/Studio 3*
Pt 1 from TT5T13-14: 2EA11691-1
Pt 2 from TT5T14-15: 2EA11692-1*
Pt 3 from TT5T15:   2EA11693-1
Pt 4 from TT5T16:   2EA11694-1
Pt 5 from TT5T16-17: 2EA11695-1
Pt 6 from TT5T17-18: 2EA11696-1
CD: APR 5538

BEETHOVEN Egmont – Overture
Public concert 7 July 1946, Kunsthaus Lucerne
TT7T1-2
3 March 1947, Transfer Room
Pt 1 from TT7T1-2: 2EA11704-1
Pt 2 from TT7T2:   2EA11705-1

BEETHOVEN Symphony No. 1 in C
Public concert 7 July 1946, Kunsthaus Lucerne
TT7T3-8
28 February 1947, Transfer Room
Pt 1 from TT7T3:   2EA11697-1
Pt 2 from TT7T4:   2EA11698-1
3 March 1947, Transfer Room
Pt 3 from TT7T5:   2EA11699-1
Pt 4 from TT7T6:   2EA11700-1
Pt 5 from TT7T6-7: 2EA11701-1
Pt 6 from TT7T7-8: 2EA 702-1
Pt 7 from TT7T8:   2EA11703-1
19 March 1947, Transfer Room[16]
Pt 3 from TT7T5:   2EA11699-2
Pt 4 from TT7T6:   2EA11700-2

BEETHOVEN Leonore Overture No. 2
Public concert 7 July 1946, Kunsthaus Lucerne
TT7T9-11
5 March 1947, Transfer Room
Pt 1 from TT7T9:   2EA11706-1-2
Pt 2 from TT7T10:   2EA11707-1
Pt 3 from TT7T10-11: 2EA11708-1
Pt 4 from TT7T11:   2EA11709-1
CD: APR 5538

---

[16] Second transfers made, TT7T5 lost in the process.

WAGNER Lohengrin – Prelude, Act 1
Public concert 7 July 1946, Kunsthaus Lucerne
TT7T13-14
27 February 1947, Transfer Room
Pt 1 from TT7T13:   2EA11684-1
Pt 2 from TT7T13-14: 2EA11685-1
Pt 3 from TT7T14:   2EA11686-1
CD: APR 5538

WAGNER Lohengrin – Prelude, Act 3
Public concert 7 July 1946, Kunsthaus Lucerne
TT7T15
27 February 1947, Transfer Room
From TT7T15: 2EA11687-1
CD: APR 5538

WAGNER Tannhäuser – Overture & Venusberg Music
Public concert 7 July 1946, Kunsthaus Lucerne
TT7T16-21
26 February 1947, Transfer Room
Pt 1 from TT7T16-17: 2EA11673-1
Pt 2 from TT7T17:   2EA11674-1
Pt 3 from TT7T18:   2EA11675-1
Pt 4 from TT7T18-19: 2EA11676-1-2
Pt 5 from TT7T19-20: 2EA11677-1
Pt 6 from TT7T20:   2EA11678-1
Pt 7 from TT7T20-21: 2EA11679-1
19 March 1947, Transfer Room
Pt 7 from TT7T20-21: 2EA11679-2-3

WAGNER Die Meistersinger von Nürnberg – Prelude, Act 1
Public concert 7 July 1946, Kunsthaus Lucerne
TT7T22-23
28 February 1947, Transfer Room
Pt 1 from TT7T22:   2EA11688-1
Pt 2 from TT7T22-23: 2EA11689-1
Pt 3 from TT7T23:   2EA11690-1

BOITO Mefistofele – Prologue & Act 3[17]
Public performance (staged) 10 June 1948, La Scala, Milan
21 January 1949, Transfer Room(?)
Pt 1   2EA13552-1
Pt 2   2EA13553-1
Pt 3   2EA13554-1

---

[17] The singers were Cesare Siepi (Mefistofele), Giacinto Prandelli (Faust) and Herva Nelli (Margherita) with the Chorus and Orchestra of La Scala, Milan. Excerpts from the Prologue – including the 'Vocal Scherzo' and Finale – were transferred from broadcast disc recordings. While surviving documentation does not identify the location of transfer, virtually all such transfers were made in the Transfer Room.

VERDI I Vespri Siciliani – Overture
Recording session 7 August 1951, La Scala, Milan[18]
Pt 1   2BA7813-1-2-3
Pt 2   2BA7814-1
CD: CHS 7648602, (USA) CDHC 64860

VERDI La Traviata – Prelude, Act 1
Recording session 8 August 1951, La Scala, Milan
2BA7815-1-2
78: Brazilian Victor 886-5000

VERDI La Traviata – Prelude, Act 3
Recording session 8 August 1951, La Scala, Milan
2BA7816-1-2-3
78: Brazilian Victor 886-5000
CD: CHS 7648642

RECEPTION

Beethoven: Symphony No. 6
Gramophone vol. 15, December 1937 p. 289
The exhilaration never fails in this long-phrased performance. ... The music seems to come with even more than its usual directness of speech ... It is the beautiful sense of proportion that always most strongly remains with you after hearing most of Toscanini's performances ... [Never] does a symphonic slow movement drag.

[II] The volume of tone is big. I thought it so when I heard in Queen's Hall the First and Ninth. ... Clear articulation is the best help to understanding one can have. That is where Toscanini scores again. He never 'throws away' a phrase ... Every little figure is full-shaped. The clarity of the design is paramount. ... The light and shade ... is an important element of the conductor's management.

[V] This is beautifully launched. ... A whole-hearted work, then, open-heartedly performed (the ingenuousness hiding the subtlety) and open-tonedly recorded.

American Music Lover vol. 3 no. 10, February 1938 p. 379
The *Pastoral* has long been one of Toscanini's most admired musical re-creations. He shapes this music with consummate artistry ... No-one sustains the clarity of the design of this music like Toscanini, but Toscanini's veritably uncanny sense of proportion is one of the familiar features of his music-making ...

Toscanini plays the 'By the Brooklet' movement with rare finesse; one can almost hear him admonishing the players to keep the music 'singing'. His light and shade

---

[18] Recordings on 7 and 8 August 1951 made on disc and tape by La Voce del Padrone, supervised by Guido Cantelli and EMI Abbey Road engineers; see further Ch. 10 p. 199.

have been more delicate in the concert hall, but they are not by any means lost in the recording. The festival and the storm are never exaggerated by Toscanini, they are integral parts of the pastoral journey, not featured parts. The finale, which is so often misinterpreted, is given a noble reading by the Italian maestro ...

The recording here is less imposing than the domestic ones made of Toscanini's performances. The wide range of dynamics, which is an essential part of this conductor's extraordinary playing, has not been realized here. His miraculous *pianissimi*, admittedly often ineffectual in a recording and a broadcast, are 'stepped up' here and his magnificent *fortissimi* are similarly 'stepped down' ... The breaks in the recording have not been as well chosen as they were in the domestic recording of the *Seventh* but it cannot be honestly said that any of the above definitely lessens our pleasure in the conductor's superb reading of the *Pastoral*.

Brahms: Tragic Overture
Gramophone vol. 15, March 1938 p. 425
The impetuosity here seems more intense than in Beecham's recording, and the phrasing has a swift, light quality that is characteristic of this conductor ... There is flexibility in the second theme. In the middle section, one can mark an orchestra not yet fully used to the conductor's phrasing demands. This was always to be noted during Toscanini's visit ... There is bound to be some tiny discrepancy, to the sensitive ear, when a man of exceptional power of domination comes along, a man who lives in and for subtle phrasing. I like the playing, though, for it does reach the drive of human affairs, and avoids any extreme note of fury ... [Of the Beethoven First Symphony scherzo on the fourth side] The same all-through style shines here even more noticeably. The trio dances on lighter toes than I think I have heard it before. The players achieve quite a *tour de force*. There is so little emphasis that everything stands out in noonday sunshine.

American Music Lover vol. 5 no. 1, May 1939 p. 13
Toscanini takes the overture faster [than Beecham's LPO recording of March 1937, Columbia LX 638–39], driving the opening, for example, much harder than Beecham. The latter's pace is closer to Brahms's marking, which is *allegro non troppo*. Toscanini indulges in quite a bit of *rubati* here. His anticipation of the slower marking of the middle section of the overture ... is no more in keeping with the composer's intentions than is his avoidance of its romantic implications. The poetry of the tranquil mood [from bar 264] is masterfully conveyed by Toscanini. One can almost see his finger on his lips urging the players to keep the tone soft and mellow. Of the two recordings, that of Toscanini has the edge on that of Beecham.

Beethoven: Symphony No. 1

Gramophone vol. 16, September 1938 p. 153

Some of the best pleasure herein is the pussy-foot-ness of it, with which the conductor makes exceedingly apt play – its moments of ease and of intense energy, that contrast so charmingly. The articulation, as always with this conductor, gives the fullest point to the latter quality ... When little things are happening how quietly they are done; the *scale* of doing is always so right.

[II] Here the work's leisurely spirit comes in best. On the slow side? I think so ... but it doesn't drag, as Mr X, at the same speed, infallibly would.

[III] Here everybody is on the toes, without ostentation. The middle section sounds a shade hurried in the strings ...

[IV] The zest is strong ... The size of the playing is not allowed to droop, for the sake of being natty in the second subject, as the way of some is. ... Congratulations to the band in its reaching home in such good shape, and to the recorders on catching so much of Toscanini's authentic essence of Beethoven.

American Music Lover vol. 5 no. 1, May 1939 p. 13

Toscanini has a way with last movements quite unlike anyone I know ... The elation, the animation and the buoyancy of the last movement here are caught and conveyed as in the Haydn symphony [No. 88], but with the added joy of a richer and more lifelike reproduction ... No-one plays this music ... quite as he does. Even Weingartner's sterling performance fails to convey the full essence of Beethoven as Toscanini does ... The recording of this work is good. In our estimation the lack of unison in the opening chords is a trick of recording, the overtones of the strings apparently being caught sooner than those of the wind instruments. The same thing happens in Weingartner's recording ...

Rossini: La scala di seta – Overture

Gramophone vol. 16, October 1938 p. 198

The music rather oddly sounds as did the works I heard Toscanini conduct in Queen's Hall – as if the microphone were getting at them a bit, even before (you knew) that were possible. For such full-bosomed music the method is all right, as to colour, but I am not convinced that some of those solo wind bits need to be recorded so very fulsomely, or that passage work of this type is the British orchestra's high-flight. The record is gay, indeed, but it all sounds a bit overdone, as to *empressement*, and slightly heavy in attack. It doesn't strike me as one of the best of Toscanini's recordings.

American Music Lover vol. 4 no. 9, January 1939 p. 332

[Beecham's] and Toscanini's performances offer some interesting points of contrast. Toscanini is somewhat brusquer and more highly vitalized in his performance, while Beecham, though not lacking in precision, makes more of the inner rhythms and the melodic curves of the music ... Toscanini's predilection for setting forth music in long lines makes for greater virtuosity in performance ... The recording of both orchestras is resonant and full, with the edge for slightly better reproduction going to the Toscanini disc.

Weber orch. Berlioz: Invitation to the Dance
Gramophone vol. 16, December 1938 p. 282
The recording makes much of the wind tone, giving the effect of an acoustically slightly geared-up studio ... The give and take of the phrasing, the attention to precision of articulation, always delight me ... It is in the slighter orchestration that I like best the mere tone; in the bigger washes of colour, I do not find quite so high a pleasure ... The *tour de force* is in order, and I do not grumble if the force be shaped for the strongest and heftiest instrument's rejoicing, as I think this is.

American Music Lover vol. 5 no. 2, June 1939 p. 58
Toscanini unquestionably loves this music ... His precision here is welcome. His dynamics are widely contrasted, more so than is usually the case ...

Mozart: The Magic Flute – Overture
Gramophone vol. 16, March 1939 p. 424
Here is the fullest degree of power consistent with quality that I care for, with just a shade faster pace than I think gives perfect articulation ... With all the brilliance that the pace and the conductor's personal force inspire, I have a tiny impression that the players felt rushed. The lightness is certainly attained, but the dignity inherent in the woven writing seems not so surely caught. [The review concluded with a reference to the 'tiny ghost note in the pause at the start of side 2', proof of the direct-to-disc recording; see note 9 above.]

American Music Lover vol. 4 no. 7, November 1938 p. 253 (Nathan Broder)
This overture ... now receives its greatest performance under the baton of the incredible Toscanini. No matter how often we hear this conductor each fresh reading brings back his familiar virtues with the impact of new miracles. Not the least of these miracles is the supreme clarity of his orchestra, which allows us to hear things we never heard before in familiar compositions. Here the golden tone of the brass in the famous chords, the beautifully molded phrases of the unhurried woodwinds above an electric basic rhythm, the crisp precision of the strings express everything written and implied in Mozart's score in a manner that throws new light on the overture. The recording is very good. This disc belongs in every record library.

Beethoven: Leonore Overture No. 1

Gramophone vol. 17, October 1939 p. 195

We get the operatic attack and scent, which makes the recording notable. How fresh and vital it sounds – partly Toscanini's doing, but much more Beethoven's.

American Music Lover vol. 6 no. 1, May 1940 p. 22

It will not be necessary to recommend this work to the Toscanini fans, but to those who are not attracted to a recording by the magic of a name only, it might be well to say – do not miss this disc ...

Beethoven: Symphony No. 4

Gramophone vol. 17, December 1939 p. 252

Here is a resounding [recording]. [I] I do not think the BBC wind quite the best: it seems slight and pale, against their strings. The composer's godlike energy ... swings the movement along like the universe itself. That long passage, with the drums, leading to the return of the first theme, after the development, is one of the best excitements ... One of the things I most admire about this movement and in the slow one is the way in which the ball is kept rolling ... [III] My only doubt is about the time given to the wind in the Trio. They don't feel quite happy: they don't perfectly get all the notes timed ... [IV] How excellent are the doings early on the last side ... Those succeeding gusts of wind are given full power. The conductor shows fine style in reserving strength for the best places. It sounds almost as if the recorders had lent a hand too, on this [dubbed] side. The virility and flexibility of the strings is especially praiseworthy here. A grand recording.

American Music Lover vol. 6 no. 3, July 1940 p. 88

In the midst of distressing news in a war-torn world, Toscanini's beautifully articulated reading of the opening adagio of this symphony ... comes as a welcome note of benignity and compassion. And with the entrance of the allegro vivace we are transported into a world without ominous shadows, a world of sunlight and geniality. Toscanini takes the Adagio considerably faster than most conductors, yet his tempo does not destroy but rather enhances its cantabile characteristics. There is a beautiful flow to the music, the sort of thing we have come to expect from this conductor ... In the scherzo and the finale Toscanini's fine phrasing and accentuation are admirable. ... Two points of digression from the written score offer conclusive proof that Toscanini does not always observe to the letter the composer's directions: one is the accelerando he makes in the climax of the second movement and the other is a ritard utilized in the latter half of the finale. ... Mechanically this set is far from perfect; there is a suggestion that it was made in a performance uninterrupted for the breaks. These latter are abrupt and often ill chosen. The quality of the tone is on the whole good, but not quite up to the highest standards of English recording.

The strings come through excellently, but the woodwinds are not as forward in tone as they might be and, as in the latter part of the adagio, the balance is faulty; here the clarinet is obscured. Despite the above criticism, this recording is eminently worthwhile ...

THE CONCERTS 1930–52: PROGRAMMES AND RECORDINGS

Toscanini's London concert programmes are here set out in chronological order, each followed by a note on any extant recordings with an estimation of their significance in the context of Toscanini's recorded legacy as a whole. The planned programmes for cancelled concerts, including his 1940 series, follow.

All the BBC SO concerts, other than the concert in Oxford on 8 June 1937, were broadcast, and all commenced at 8.15pm, with the exception of those on 30 October 1937 (8.30pm) and 28 May 1939 (3pm). The BBC required that all concerts had an interval except the Brahms *Requiem* on 30 October 1937 (no interval) and Beethoven's *Missa Solemnis* on 26 and 28 May 1939, when Toscanini was persuaded to make a mid-work pause for five minutes only. The 1935 and the 1937, 1938 and 1939 series were broadcast on the National Service, save for the following broadcasts on the Regional Service:[1] 28 May, 4 and 14 June 1937; 23 and 30 May 1938; 12 and 26 May 1939. Both 1952 Philharmonia concerts were broadcast by the BBC.[2]

In addition to the works listed below, the British National Anthem was customarily performed at the first and last concerts of a series and also when royalty was present (indicated with an asterisk by the dates below). The American anthem was also played during the 1930 European tour of the New York Philharmonic-Symphony. Both anthems were therefore conducted by Toscanini on 1 and 4 June 1930. He would also have conducted the British anthem on 14 June 1935; 26, 28* May, 8 and 16 June 1937; 3 November 1937*; 19 May and 10 June 1938; 3 May* and 28 May 1939. The anthem was performed and recorded at both Philharmonia concerts, on 29 September* and 1 October 1952.

New York Philharmonic-Symphony Orchestra, Sunday 1 June 1930, Royal Albert Hall
Rossini L'italiana in Algeri – Overture
Brahms Symphony No. 2 in D
Wagner Tannhäuser – Overture and Venusberg Music
Beethoven Leonore Overture No. 3
Recordings None known.

---

[1] For the distinction between the two services, see Ch. 4 n. 11.

[2] See Ch. 11 p. 215.

New York Philharmonic-Symphony Orchestra, Monday 2 June 1930, Queen's Hall
Haydn Symphony No. 101 in D, 'Clock'
Elgar Variations on an Original Theme, 'Enigma'
Debussy La Mer
Mendelssohn A Midsummer Night's Dream – Nocturne and Scherzo
Wagner Tristan und Isolde – Prelude and Liebestod
Recordings None known.

New York Philharmonic-Symphony Orchestra, Tuesday 3 June 1930, Royal Albert Hall
Eugene Goossens Sinfonietta
Strauss Tod und Verklärung
Franck Les Éolides
Mussorgsky orch. Ravel Pictures at an Exhibition
Recordings None known.

New York Philharmonic-Symphony Orchestra, Wednesday 4 June 1930, Queen's Hall
Beethoven Symphony No. 3 in E flat, 'Eroica'
Brahms Variations on a Theme of Haydn
Bach orch. Respighi Passacaglia and Fugue in C minor, BWV582
Wagner Die Meistersinger von Nürnberg – Prelude to Act 1
Recordings None known, but see Chapter 12 page 240.

BBC Symphony Orchestra, Monday 3 June 1935, Queen's Hall
Cherubini Anacréon – Overture
Brahms Symphony No. 4 in E minor
Wagner Götterdämmerung – Siegfried's Death and Funeral Music (Act 3)
Elgar Variations on an Original Theme, 'Enigma'
Recordings The concert was recorded by HMV; for details and issue numbers, see Annex A. Part of *Nimrod* is in the British Library Sound Archive Leech Collection (Leech 122, cat. 30B 5712). The performances are examined in Chapter 12 and, as to the Elgar, in Chapter 2.

BBC Symphony Orchestra, Wednesday 5 June 1935, Queen's Hall
Wagner   A Faust Overture
          Parsifal – Prelude to Act 1 and Good Friday Music (Act 3)
          Götterdämmerung – Siegfried's Death and Funeral Music (Act 3)
Brahms Symphony No. 4 in E minor
Recordings See Annex A and Chapter 12.

BBC Symphony Orchestra, Wednesday 12 June 1935, Queen's Hall
Geminiani Concerto Grosso in B minor, Op. 3 No. 2
Beethoven Symphony No. 7 in A
Debussy La Mer
Rossini Semiramide – Overture
Recordings See Annex A and Chapter 12.

BBC Symphony Orchestra, Friday 14 June 1935, Queen's Hall
Mozart Symphony No. 35 in D, K385, 'Haffner'
Debussy La Mer
Mendelssohn A Midsummer Night's Dream – Nocturne and Scherzo
Beethoven Symphony No. 7 in A
Recordings See Annex A and Chapter 12.

BBC Symphony Orchestra, Wednesday 26 May 1937, Queen's Hall
Corelli arr. Geminiani Concerto Grosso in D minor, Op. 5 No. 12, 'La Follia'
Busoni Rondó Arlecchinesco (*solo tenor, Heddle Nash*)
Ravel Daphnis et Chloé – Suite No. 2
Beethoven Coriolan – Overture
Brahms Symphony No. 1 in C minor
Recordings None known.

BBC Symphony Orchestra, Friday 28 May 1937, Queen's Hall
Elgar Introduction and Allegro
Cherubini Symphony in D
Tommasini Il carnevale di Venezia
Berlioz Roméo et Juliette – La Reine Mab, Scherzo
Wagner Die Meistersinger von Nürnberg – Prelude to Act 1
Recordings The Elgar is in the Leech Collection (Leech 509, cat. 30B 6024). The recording is almost complete, with short gaps before 10 and 24 (Novello), but the sound is severely distorted; the performance is both more finished and more freely spontaneous than Toscanini's only other recorded performance, with the NBC Symphony on 20 April 1940.

BBC Symphony Orchestra, Wednesday 2 June 1937, Queen's Hall
Rossini L'Italiana in Algeri – Overture
Beethoven Symphony No. 6 in F, 'Pastoral'
Brahms Variations on a Theme of Haydn
Strauss Tod und Verklärung
Recordings The Leech Collection contains a substantial segment of *Tod und Verklärung* (Leech 509–11, cat. 30B 6024–26) amounting to about half of the work, in reasonable sound. The excerpts include the pages covering the final and greatest climax of the 'transfiguration' and confirm the shattering power of this orchestral build-up described in Chapter 4. The *Haydn* Variations were also recorded privately off-air; the sound is poor and side breaks miss a substantial quantity of the work, including the whole of the second variation. Nevertheless, the recording confirms that Toscanini's tempo for the fifth variation was indeed faster than, say, that of the Philharmonic recording of the preceding year; also that the *Siciliano* seventh variation was exceptionally gracious and yielding, an approach that Toscanini replicated only in the NBC Symphony performance of 21 February 1948.

BBC Symphony Orchestra, Friday 4 June 1937, Queen's Hall
Vivaldi Concerto Grosso in D minor, Op. 3 No. 11
Shostakovich Symphony No. 1 in F
Beethoven Symphony No. 3 in E flat, 'Eroica'
Recordings None known.

BBC Symphony Orchestra, Tuesday 8 June 1937, New Theatre, Oxford
Rossini L'italiana in Algeri – Overture
Beethoven Symphony No. 6 in F, 'Pastoral'
Brahms Symphony No. 1 in C minor
Recordings None known.

BBC Symphony Orchestra, Monday 14 June 1937, Queen's Hall
Mozart Symphony No. 40 in G minor, K550
Bach orch. Respighi Passacaglia and Fugue in C minor, BWV582
Sibelius En Saga
Debussy Images – No. 2, Ibéria
Berlioz La Damnation de Faust – Marche hongroise
Recordings Off-air recordings of the Debussy and Sibelius, both complete save for side-end interruptions, are poor in sound quality with the noisy surfaces of worn acetates. Sufficient is audible, however, to confirm the views of the critics quoted in Chapter 4: these performances are as fine as, if not finer than, any other recording of the two works left by the conductor.

BBC Symphony Orchestra, Wednesday 16 June 1937, Queen's Hall

Wagner   A Faust Overture

Lohengrin – Preludes to Acts 1 and 3

Tannhäuser – Overture and Venusberg Music

Siegfried Idyll

Siegfried – Forest Murmurs (Act 2)

Götterdämmerung – Dawn and Siegfried's Rhine Journey (Prologue)
(arr. Toscanini)

Die Walküre – Ride of the Valkyries (Act 3)

Recordings The whole concert, including the National Anthem, was recorded off-air; the sound is remote and poor in quality and, while the sympathetic acoustic of the Queen's Hall is evident, in the circumstances the performances, characteristic though they appear to be, add little to what is available in greatly superior sound elsewhere, such as the 1935 BBC SO Wagner excerpts and the New York Philharmonic Wagner recordings of 1936. The two *Lohengrin* Preludes are also in the Leech Collection in superior sound (Leech 520, cat. 30B 6028).

BBC Symphony Orchestra, Saturday 30 October 1937, Queen's Hall

Brahms   Tragic Overture

Ein Deutsches Requiem

BBC Choral Society (chorusmaster Leslie Woodgate); soloists Isobel Baillie (soprano), Alexander Svéd (baritone)[3]

Recordings The complete concert was transmitted on shortwave by NBC to the United States where it was recorded; the shortwave sound has the expected limitations but is reasonably audible and, in the overture, clear with relatively little of the usual fading. The *Requiem* is yet more broadly paced than the 1943 NBC Symphony performance, markedly so in the second movement. As to the *Tragic Overture*, see Chapter 12 page 250. Parts of both overture and *Requiem* are in the Leech Collection (Leech 566–69, cat. 30B 6056–57). The excerpt from the overture is from bar 264 to the end, from the *Requiem*, two short extracts from two movements; all are in adequate sound.

---

[3] Isobel Baillie (1895–1983) soprano; Alexander Svéd (1906–79) Hungarian baritone; Leslie Woodgate (1902–61) choral trainer and conductor. The *Times* commented on Toscanini's adherence to the German text but his next and final performance, with the NBC SO on 24 January 1943, used an English translation which, as may be inferred from the *Times* review, was also the norm in Britain at that time.

BBC Symphony Orchestra, Wednesday 3 November 1937, Queen's Hall
Beethoven   Symphony No. 1 in C
                  Symphony No. 9 in D minor, 'Choral'
BBC Choral Society (chorusmaster Leslie Woodgate); soloists Isobel Baillie (soprano), Mary Jarred (mezzo-soprano), Parry Jones (tenor), Harold Williams (bass)[4]
Recordings The Ninth Symphony was transmitted on shortwave by NBC but the surviving recording in ATC is dim and poor. It was also recorded privately from the BBC broadcast by the 'Memphis Recording Company' from an address in Wigmore Street close to the offices of Sir Adrian Boult, the BBC's Director of Music. Eventually this recording was passed to the British Institute of Recorded Sound, predecessor of the British Library Sound Archive, and issued by Music & Arts (CD 1144). The sound, if superior to other off-air recordings of Toscanini's BBC SO concerts made in 1937, is rough by contemporary standards. Part of the second movement, in good sound, is also in the Leech Collection (Leech 569, cat. 30B 6057); this extract cuts the first bar but includes the scherzo with part of its repeat, stopping short of the trio. The finale aside, the performance is one of Toscanini's less expansive, consistently faster in the first three movements than the RCA recording of 1952. In particular, the first movement is pushed at some points to the very limit of the players' capacity, although there are moments of flexibility, such as the hush at the start of the development and elsewhere in response to woodwind solos, not encountered in Toscanini's later performances. The Adagio is examined in Chapter 12 page 251. The finale's opening recitatives are of unexampled freedom; thereafter each successive exposition of the main theme (that of the violas with the counterpoint of Archie Camden's unmistakable bassoon) has that peculiarly weightless ebb and flow of which Toscanini alone held the secret, while as usual here the strings sing with the uniquely *dolce* yet tactile quality that fascinated other conductors. Although the overall timing of this movement is within seconds of the RCA recording, there are subtle differences of pacing within it: a slower Alla marcia and orchestral fugue but some faster subsequent sections with more expressive emphases. As a whole the finale's force and eloquence is superior to the RCA recording, helped by some incisive brass playing and the large, highly disciplined chorus.

BBC Symphony Orchestra, Thursday 19 May 1938, Queen's Hall
Mozart The Magic Flute – Overture
Beethoven Symphony No. 4 in B flat
Vaughan Williams Fantasia on a Theme by Thomas Tallis
Weber orch. Berlioz Invitation to the Dance
Smetana Ma vlást – Vltava (Moldau)
Recordings National Anthem only (Symposium 1253).

---

[4] Mary Jarred (1899–1993) mezzo-soprano; Parry Jones (1891–1963) tenor; Harold Williams (1893–1976) Australian bass-baritone.

BBC Symphony Orchestra, Monday 23 May 1938, Queen's Hall
Bach Brandenburg Concerto No. 2 in F
Soloists Paul Beard (violin), Robert Murchie (flute), Terence MacDonagh (oboe),
Ralph Clarke (clarinet)
Strauss Don Quixote
Soloists Emanuel Feuermann (cello), Bernard Shore (viola)
Beethoven Symphony No. 5 in C minor
Recordings The first half (possibly also the second) was recorded from its shortwave
transmission. Cetra LP issues of the last two items are reported but unverified. For
the performances of the Brandenburg Concerto and *Don Quixote*, see Chapter 7
pages 127–30. The Beethoven was picked up by an amateur recorder from the BBC
broadcast but what has survived is not adequate to assess the performance in detail
because of constant groove-jumping and missing passages.

BBC Symphony Orchestra, Friday 27 May 1938, Queen's Hall
Verdi   Four Sacred Pieces – Te Deum (*solo soprano, Sybilla Marshall*)
                Requiem
BBC Choral Society (chorusmaster Leslie Woodgate); soloists Zinka Milanov
(soprano), Kerstin Thorborg (mezzo-soprano), Helge Roswaenge (tenor), Nicola
Moscona (bass)[5]
Recordings The *Te Deum* was recorded only on shortwave transmission. The
Requiem was recorded by the BBC and has been issued in several versions: (LP)
ATS 1108–09, (CD) Iron Needle IN 1415–16 and (with the approval of the
Toscanini estate) Testament SBT2 1362, none in the best sound quality; see further
Chapter 7 and note 51. The performance is identical in overall timing to the 1951
RCA recording (a mix of dress rehearsal and live performance) but it is altogether
more powerful and assured, in detail more flexible; it benefits also from the out-
standing contribution of the BBC orchestra's woodwind line-up. Further, with the
possible exception of Roswaenge, the soloists (including the still young Moscona)
are superior. These advantages place the performance on an equal footing with the
NBC versions of 23 November 1940 and 26 April 1948.

BBC Symphony Orchestra, Monday 30 May 1938, Queen's Hall
As 27 May.
Recordings None known.

---

[5]   Zinka Milanov (1906–89) Croatian soprano; Kerstin Thorborg (1896–1970) Swedish mezzo- soprano;
Helge Roswaenge (1897–1972) Danish tenor; Nicola Moscona (1907–75) Greek bass.

BBC Symphony Orchestra, Friday 3 June 1938, Queen's Hall
Rossini La scala di seta – Overture
Mozart Symphony No. 41 in C, K551, 'Jupiter'
Brahms Liebeslieder Walzer, Op. 52
BBC Singers with Ethel Bartlett, Rae Robertson (pianos)[6]
Schubert Symphony No. 9 in C
Recordings The first half was recorded virtually complete on shortwave transmission; the Mozart symphony is discussed in Chapter 12 page 251. The Schubert was recorded by an amateur from the BBC broadcast and has parts missing from all movements. Nevertheless, enough remains with sufficient sound to disclose it as the finest of all Toscanini's many extant statements of the score. The tempos and general approach do not differ substantially from the aircheck of Toscanini's performance in his final concert as principal conductor of the New York Philharmonic on 26 April 1936 (which is more relaxed than the overly tense first NBC broadcast of 8 January 1938). However, the suavity of the orchestral palette and the typical spontaneity of feeling that pervaded Toscanini's work with the BBC orchestra – the extra oiling of the joints and the natural changes of pace in the finale (features seized upon by the *Times*, as noted in Chapter 7 page 145) – mark this out from other versions; so, too, do the contributions of Aubrey Brain's horn, MacDonagh's oboe and Thurston's clarinet in the second movement, and their joint contributions to the Trio.

BBC Symphony Orchestra, Friday 10 June 1938, Queen's Hall
Scarlatti arr. Tommasini The Good-Humoured Ladies – Ballet Suite
Sibelius Symphony No. 2 in D
Brahms Symphony No. 2 in D
Recordings The Tommasini was recorded in poor sound from the BBC broadcast; for the Sibelius and Brahms recordings, see the Discography, Annex A, and the account of HMV's efforts to secure their contemporary release in Chapter 7. While the performances of the two symphonies are characteristic, they are not superior to more clearly recorded contemporaneous NBC performances. In particular, the Brahms is perhaps the least distinguished of Toscanini's several preserved performances: occasional rough playing in the finale causes it to sound rushed and some of the phrasing in the outer movements ends abruptly or (as recorded) garbled. As recounted in Chapter 7, the two works were recorded by HMV on test discs from the BBC broadcasts and then transferred. Especially in the Brahms, the dubbing cramps and clouds the sound and introduces a disturbing flutter in virtually all woodwind solos – where most of the performance's virtues lie.

---

[6]   Ethel Bartlett (1900–78) pianist; Rae Robertson (1893–1956) pianist.

BBC Symphony Orchestra, Wednesday 3 May 1939, Queen's Hall

Beethoven   Egmont – Overture
                 Symphony No. 1 in C
                 Symphony No. 2 in D
                 Leonore Overture No. 3
Recordings None known.

BBC Symphony Orchestra, Monday 8 May 1939, Queen's Hall

Beethoven   Coriolan – Overture
                 Symphony No. 4 in B flat
                 Symphony No. 3 in E flat, 'Eroica'
Recordings The Fourth Symphony was recorded, probably professionally and from the BBC broadcast. While the sound is rough, enough survives to assess the performance. Save in the scherzo, the performance differs only in detail from the recording of 1 June. However, the players in the live Adagio second movement occasionally sound overpressed; with the extra rehearsal for the recording, on 1 June they seem fully at home with Toscanini's tempo. By contrast, Archie Camden's bassoon solo in the finale is accommodated in the live performance a shade more comfortably than in the recording. The scherzo in this live performance has a winged fleetness not present to the same degree elsewhere in Toscanini's or any other performances, with the possible exception of Weingartner's LPO recording (13–14 November 1933, Columbia LX 274–77, Naxos CD 8.110956). A recording of this *Coriolan* in good sound, commencing halfway through the development, is in ATC, LT-109813. Had this been complete, it would have been the Toscanini performance of choice: the playing of what remains is superb while the mastery of the transition into the second subject in the recapitulation, and also the slight relaxation in the final bars, typify the spontaneity of Toscanini's music-making with this orchestra.

BBC Symphony Orchestra, Friday 12 May 1939, Queen's Hall

Beethoven   Die Geschöpfe des Prometheus – Overture
                 Symphony No. 6 in F, 'Pastoral'
                 Symphony No. 5 in C minor
Recordings The Fifth Symphony was recorded, probably professionally and from the BBC broadcast. The sound quality, if marginally superior to the Fourth Symphony recorded in the preceding concert, is rough but permits adequate assessment of the performance. It differs in no marked fashion from the NBC performances of 1939 save for the remarkable impulse of the final peroration, taken at Toscanini's most furious pace; the playing here achieves an incandescent concentration. Furthermore, the perspective of the Queen's Hall and some of the solo

woodwind make for a different qualitative impact: those in the Andante have a freedom and tonal bloom not to be heard in most of their NBC counterparts, while Aubrey Brain's horn in the third movement enters with spectacular boldness.

BBC Symphony Orchestra, Wednesday 17 May 1939, Queen's Hall

Beethoven   Leonore Overture No. 1
                     Symphony No. 8 in F
                     Symphony No. 7 in A

Recordings Extracts from the Seventh Symphony's two middle movements are in the Leech Collection (Leech 816, cat. 30B 6206) in fine sound. The Allegretto is complete save for fifteen bars from 153. Toscanini starts this movement at virtually the same tempo as his 1936 Philharmonic recording but moves it forward more noticeably as the dynamic level builds; generally, there is a greater freedom of tempo. The woodwind intonation is exact and euphonious, contrary to Newman's observations about this and other concerts in the cycle, noted in Chapter 8. The scherzo extract ends at bar 180. Like the NBC performance on 18 November 1939, the tempo is swifter than in 1936, the rhythmic pointing of the winds even finer – evidence of the meticulous response that Toscanini secured from the BBC SO throughout the cycle.

BBC Symphony Orchestra, Monday 22 May 1939, Queen's Hall

Beethoven   Die Geschöpfe des Prometheus – Adagio & Andante quasi allegretto
                     (*solo cello, Ambrose Gauntlett*)
                     String Quartet No. 16 in F, Op. 135 – Vivace & Lento (arr. Toscanini)
                     Leonore Overture No. 3
                     Symphony No. 9 in D minor, 'Choral'

BBC Choral Society (chorusmaster Leslie Woodgate); soloists Isobel Baillie (soprano), Margaret Balfour (mezzo-soprano),[7] *Parry Jones (tenor), Harold Williams (bass)*

Recordings A shortwave recording of the first half, commencing two minutes from the end of the *Prometheus* excerpt, is in ATC, LT-109814. The Vivace from Op. 135, placed first, is superbly played (contra the *Times* report – see Chapter 8 page 159) while the Lento, at over nine minutes, is the broadest and most elevated in feeling of all Toscanini's preserved performances. *Leonore No. 3* is faster than the commercially issued NBC Symphony performance of 4 November 1939, the final pages in particular being played at speed, but the orchestral playing, especially the winds including Aubrey Brain's horn, is spectacularly fine.

---

[7] Mary Jarred was originally announced but her place was taken by Margaret Balfour, mezzo-soprano (*c.*1892–1961); see also n. 4.

BBC Symphony Orchestra, Friday 26 May 1939, Queen's Hall
Beethoven Missa Solemnis

BBC Choral Society (chorusmaster Leslie Woodgate); soloists Zinka Milanov (soprano), Kerstin Thorborg (mezzo-soprano), Koloman von Pataky (tenor),[8] Nicola Moscona (bass)

Recordings A recording of the shortwave transmission in poor sound is in ATC, LT-109815. The exceptionally long wait from the commencement of the broadcast to Toscanini's entrance lends credence to Boult's story of the conductor's acute attack of nerves recounted in Chapter 8. The poor quality of sound precludes detailed assessment of the performance, but certain details, such as the extremely precise and forceful trumpet fanfares in the *Dona nobis pacem*, do stand out.

BBC Symphony Orchestra, Sunday 28 May 1939, Queen's Hall
As 26 May.

Recordings Recorded by the BBC and issued on (CD) BBCL 4016-2. One of the principal themes in the critical reception of Toscanini's BBC concerts outlined in Chapters 2–8 is the perception of his stylistic change during the few years (1935–39) in which they took place – an increased tautness of pace and sharpness of attack and some reduction in flexibility of detailed shaping of the phrase, characteristics which were to become still more evident in some of his subsequent NBC perform-ances. In no other instances are those changes so pronounced and so obvious as in the two performances of the *Missa Solemnis*, the first dating from 26 April 1935 with the New York Philharmonic,[9] a few weeks before Toscanini's first concerts with the BBC SO, and this BBC SO version which marked Toscanini's departure from London before the outbreak of the Second World War. The change in his approach is clear from the timings of the work's sections and the total timings:

	26 April 1935	*28 May 1939*
Kyrie	11:40	9:54
Gloria	18:21	16:28
Credo	19:15	17:42
Sanctus	18:15	17:19
Agnus Dei	16:34	16:15
Total	84:05	77:38

[8] (1896–1964) Hungarian tenor; see also n. 5.

[9] With the Schola Cantorum, soloists Elisabeth Rethberg, Marion Telva, Giovanni Martinelli and Ezio Pinza, organ Pietro Yon. Various unofficial versions of this recording in execrable sound have circulated over many years. The author is fortunate to have a version taken direct from the original discs in what was at the time Walter Toscanini's collection, in clear and pitch-corrected sound capable of founding reliable observation of the performance's tempo and other characteristics.

The earlier performance is essentially contemplative, broadly paced and extremely inward in its reflective pages, although all vigorous sections bear the unmistakable Toscanini imprint. He is, however, to a minor extent hampered by a choir less than ideally flexible or focused in sound. The later performance is leaner than the more broadly paced NBC performance of 28 December 1940 and in timing quite close to the NBC broadcast concert of 28 March 1953, which preceded Toscanini's RCA recording spread over 30, 31 March and 2 April (this recording was in parts yet more swift than the preceding concert performance, notably in the opening *Kyrie*). However, the control and concentration in the BBC SO version are absolute and the choral singing markedly superior to the 1935 and 1940 performances, with contributions from soloists of equivalent stature. Furthermore, by comparison with the two 1953 versions, some of the inwardness characteristic of the 1935 performance – the end of the *Kyrie*, the opening of the *Sanctus*, to take but two of many examples – is still notably present. These elements, combined with the natural Queen's Hall acoustic and Paul Beard's solo in the *Benedictus*, make this arguably the preferred statement among Toscanini's preserved performances. However, the recorded sound is somewhat clouded with limited upper frequency response, which dulls the effect especially in the martial passages in the *Dona nobis*. Furthermore, the balance does not favour the woodwind, a factor which obscures some details characteristic of all Toscanini's performances, such as the long woodwind lines (bar 7 onwards) of the *Kyrie*. In sum, the full impact of Toscanini's approach to the *Missa Solemnis* can only be appreciated by hearing several versions, of which the BBC SO performance must surely be one of the most favoured.

Philharmonia Orchestra, 29 September 1952, Royal Festival Hall
Brahms　　Tragic Overture
　　　　　　　Symphony No. 1 in C minor
　　　　　　　Symphony No. 2 in D
Recordings See below.

Philharmonia Orchestra, 1 October 1952, Royal Festival Hall
Brahms　　Variations on a Theme of Haydn
　　　　　　　Symphony No. 3 in F
　　　　　　　Symphony No. 4 in E minor
Recordings Recordings of both Philharmonia concerts stemming from the BBC broadcasts have been released in several versions, on LP (by the Toscanini Society in the USA and Cetra in Italy) and on CD (among them Hunt 524). The recording of the concerts (including both performances of the National Anthem) made under the direction of Walter Legge for EMI was released with the approval of the Toscanini estate on Testament (CD) SBT 3167. The recorded quality, at its best in

the Legge version, has a dull and typically tight-textured early Festival Hall sound, greatly inferior to RCA's studio sound for the 'official' recordings of the early 1950s: any refulgence emanates from the efforts of the Philharmonia and Toscanini. That there is refulgence is undeniable. The liquid sound of Thurston's clarinet is balm whenever it appears, while Dennis Brain's horn and Gareth Morris's flute stop the heart in the introduction to the First Symphony's finale. But there must be some doubt about whether Toscanini was on top form. In May 1952 the 85-year-old conductor declared himself too old to take on a new, strange orchestra and only later changed his mind (see Chapter 11 page 213). Although some have suggested that these performances are superior to Toscanini's RCA records, there is enough evidence to support the view that his first opinion about his age and abilities was correct and that, leaving aside the undoubted sense of occasion, this, his last Brahms cycle, did not as a whole measure up to the NBC cycles of 1942–43 and 1948. Toscanini's first-night nerves are obvious, not only in the memory lapse afflicting the *Tragic Overture* and the trombone's reciprocal attack of nerves in the First Symphony's finale (see Chapter 11 page 222), but in occasional racing tempos which result in some smudging of the orchestral response (at least as recorded), notably in the overture. In only a small minority of movements does Toscanini's approach possess a greater breadth than the equivalents in his RCA recordings. The Allegretto of the First Symphony loses some of its *grazioso*, so eagerly does it press forward; so also in the corresponding movement of the Second Symphony, which is deprived of the unique combination of affection, subtle inflection and incisiveness heard in the RCA recording of 1952, as well as the NBC performance of 1938 examined in Annex C. The Third Symphony is a special case, for the RCA recording, made a few weeks after these concerts, is notoriously a listless, probably over-studied failure. The Festival Hall rendition displays much of the vigour and thrust of Toscanini's many earlier concert recordings, but his nervousness still shows through in the orchestral response: the unexpected accelerando at bar 65 of the first movement, first time round, which seems almost to throw the players, and the premature entry of the lower strings at bar 100 of that movement. However, most of this movement goes well and there are wonderful passages later on: the Andante and Allegretto have a spontaneous lyricism, subtly and constantly flexible within tightly controlled limits. There are, in addition, many magnificently achieved pages throughout the concerts. Working with such a flexible instrument as the Philharmonia stimulates in Toscanini a sometimes fresher response than is to be heard in his studio recordings. Unforgettable passages include the striking caesura in the introduction to the First Symphony (bar 25), the overwhelming build-up leading into the recapitulation of that movement, the magic of Dennis Brain again in the coda of the Second Symphony's first movement. Virtually the whole of the Fourth Symphony is vintage Toscanini, the most consistently achieved of the performances. Within the parameters of timings differing only by seconds from the 1951 NBC studio recording, it exhibits an expressive profile which, if less generous than the BBC SO performance of 1935, is certainly reminiscent of it. There is great Brahms in this cycle even if, for Toscanini's finest efforts, one must look elsewhere.

PROGRAMMES OF CANCELLED CONCERTS

In August 1939 Toscanini agreed the following programmes for six concerts with the BBC Symphony Orchestra in 1940 but, because of the outbreak of war involving the United Kingdom on 3 September 1939, they did not take place. For further details, see Chapter 8 page 172.

Friday 17 May 1940, Queen's Hall
Weber Oberon – Overture
Brahms Symphony No. 3 in F
Debussy Prélude à l'après-midi d'un faune
Elgar Variations on an Original Theme, 'Enigma'

Wednesday 22 May 1940, Queen's Hall
Wagner Der fliegende Holländer – Overture
Berlioz Harold in Italy (*solo viola, Bernard Shore*)
Schubert Symphony No. 2 in B flat
Rossini William Tell – Overture

Wednesday 29 May 1940, Royal Albert Hall
Verdi   Four Sacred Pieces – Te Deum
         Requiem (*soloists Zinka Milanov, Kerstin Thorborg, Jussi Björling, Nicola Moscona*)

Wednesday 5 June 1940, Queen's Hall
Mozart Symphony No. 38 in D, K504, 'Prague'
Debussy La Mer
Strauss Ein Heldenleben (*solo violin, Paul Beard*)

Wednesday 12 June 1940, Queen's Hall
Smetana The Bartered Bride – Overture
Vaughan Williams Symphony No. 3, 'A Pastoral Symphony' (*soloist Isobel Baillie*)
Tchaikovsky Symphony No. 6 in B minor, 'Pathétique'

Wednesday 19 June 1940, Queen's Hall
Mozart Don Giovanni – Overture
Brahms Piano Concerto No. 2 in B flat (*soloist Vladimir Horowitz*)
Schubert Symphony No. 9 in C

In July 1946 Toscanini was to have conducted one concert in London with the Orchestra of La Scala, Milan; this was cancelled for reasons given in Chapter 10 page 194.

Wednesday 3 July 1946, Royal Opera House, Covent Garden
Kabalevsky Colas Breugnon – Overture
Brahms Symphony No. 4 in E minor
Debussy La Mer
Rossini William Tell – Passo a sei (Act 1) & Soldiers' March (Act 3)
Strauss Tod und Verklärung

In May 1951 Toscanini was to have conducted the BBC Symphony Orchestra as part of the first series of concerts in the Royal Festival Hall but, for reasons given in Chapter 11 page 208, his place was taken by Sir Malcolm Sargent.

Friday 4 May 1951, Royal Festival Hall
Beethoven　　Symphony No. 1 in C
　　　　　　　　Symphony No. 9 in D minor, 'Choral' (*soloists Erna Berger, Kathleen Ferrier, Italo Tajo, Giacinto Prandelli*)

Sunday 6 May 1951, Royal Festival Hall
Beethoven　　Fantasia in C for piano, chorus and orchestra (*Solomon, piano*)
　　　　　　　　Symphony No. 9 in D minor, 'Choral' (*soloists as 4 May*)

Tuesday 8 May 1951, Royal Festival Hall
Kabalevsky Colas Breugnon – Overture
Vaughan Williams Symphony No. 6 in E minor
Strauss Don Juan
Debussy La Mer

ANNEX C

BRAHMS AND TOSCANINI: AN HISTORICAL EXCURSUS

THE STEINBACH CONUNDRUM

The problem stated

No observer or listener, nor anyone familiar with the copious literature about Toscanini, can fail to be aware of his fierce independence of spirit and of his devotion to every aspect of the score as written – 'come scritto' – a devotion manifest in virtually all of his recorded legacy. Nevertheless, one theme emerging from the narrative in this book which may tend to affect perceptions of Toscanini's literal adherence to the score – an adherence frequently modified in practice – is the presence of various influences, certainly in the early stages of his career, which were absorbed into his musical bloodstream in his approach to the great Austro-German works to which, from the outset, he was determined to give as much weight as his native Italian repertoire.

If, as the opening chapter suggests, Toscanini's approach to Wagner took due note of the achievements of such luminaries as Hans Richter and Karl Muck, it was the Brahms performances of the composer's favoured conductor, Fritz Steinbach, which throughout his career drew Toscanini's most explicit praise. Chapters 11 and 12 detail Toscanini's tributes to Steinbach's Brahms, which he absorbed at the Munich Brahms Festival in 1909, and the latter chapter also examines in outline the characteristics of Steinbach's style which appear to have left an imprint on Toscanini's landmark performances (as there evaluated) of Brahms's Fourth Symphony in the Queen's Hall on 3 and 5 June 1935.

Unusually for him, Toscanini was to the end of his career quite open about the influence Steinbach had on his approach to Brahms; so, too, were other great conductors who knew Steinbach's performances, among them Adrian Boult and Steinbach's foremost conducting pupil, Fritz Busch – Classicists all who adjured excess. Such a degree of unanimity among these noted Brahms interpreters may well provide obvious clues about Steinbach's style, yet no effort has hitherto been made to assess whether any Steinbach imprint may be traced in their recorded performances. Current scholarship has instead concentrated on two other threads of evidence.[1] First, attention has centred on Steinbach's annotations of the scores of

---

[1] See Musgrave & Sherman Ch. 10, Walter Frisch 'In Search of Brahms's First Symphony: Steinbach, the Meiningen tradition, and the recordings of Hermann Abendroth'.

the Brahms symphonies, as transcribed and compiled after his death by the otherwise little-known conductor Walter Blume – a work, it must here be noted, dedicated to Fritz Busch. The substance of these annotations has in some degree been observed in certain performances, notably in the Brahms recordings conducted by Sir Charles Mackerras.[2] Secondly, some commentators have called in aid the recorded Brahms interpretations of Steinbach's successor in Cologne, Hermann Abendroth, as providing a significant indication of Steinbach's approach, since, in the view of those commentators, they pay close regard to Blume. Abendroth's emphatic and sometimes (to current ears) exaggerated tempo shifts – the polar opposite in style of the eye-witness conductors already mentioned – are therefore proposed as suggestive evidence in the search for Steinbach's performance practice. Again, at least one contemporary conductor, Sir John Eliot Gardiner, has taken account of Abendroth's recordings in his own performances of the Brahms symphonies.[3]

There are obvious difficulties about the evidential approach taken to establish the Steinbach style described above. Quite how Blume came to set down his observations and the degree to which they reflect Steinbach's practice is unclear. Why did Blume dedicate his work to Fritz Busch? And what was the link, if any, between Abendroth and Steinbach? Would Toscanini, Boult and Fritz Busch have accorded Steinbach such veneration if they had witnessed Abendroth-style extremes in the matter of tempo manipulations? Of immediate relevance to the assessment of Toscanini's London performances, do the plentiful expressive effects in his 1935 Queen's Hall Fourth Symphony, found to such a degree in none of his other recorded performances, signify a backward look towards the Steinbach model or are they just a 'sport', reflecting the feelings of the moment?

The Steinbach problem – how, indeed, did he perform Brahms, with what degree of freedom, and how closely did his successors and admirers cleave to his performance practice – is too obvious to require further explication. Given the contradictory pointers summarised above, it is also in need of re-examination. The answers, if they can be determined with sufficient precision and reliability, may substantiate the conclusions outlined in Chapter 12, somewhat tentative in their context, about the central importance of Toscanini's London performances of the Fourth Symphony there described. Precision requires a detailed examination of all relevant strands of both documentary and recorded evidence, which provides

---

[2] Symphonies Nos 1–4, *Academic Festival Overture*, Variations on a Theme of Haydn, Symphony No. 1, alternate second movement, Scottish Chamber Orchestra conducted by Sir Charles Mackerras with notes and CD interview, Telarc CD 80450.

[3] In an interview broadcast on BBC Radio 3, 20 September 2008, Gardiner even suggested a master-pupil relationship between Steinbach and Abendroth. Gardiner's recording of Brahms's Third Symphony, Soli Deo Gloria SDG 704, particularly its first and third movements, suggests close regard for Abendroth's approach; but, as will be seen from the analysis at p. 342 below, Abendroth is here remote from Steinbach's practice. See further Walter Frisch, n. 1 above.

the bulk of what follows. First, however, an overview is required of what Brahms himself expected from his conductors.

Brahms and orchestral performance: what did he want?

Recent research has brought together and analysed many sources of information about the performance characteristics of both Brahms himself as conductor and the conductors he favoured.[4] Problems stem from the interpretation of this ample material; any summary is liable to reflect the predilections and ultimate intent of the writer rather than the copious and often contradictory indications to be found in the sources. What follows is therefore illustrative with a bare minimum of comment.

From the mass of seemingly conflicting data about Brahms's preferences in the performance of his orchestral music, one factor is constant, namely, his abhorrence of unfelt, sloppily rehearsed run-throughs. Hans Richter with the Vienna Philharmonic were here too often the guilty parties: the composer was on occasion known to have deliberately avoided Richter conducting the First Symphony and to have walked out of one of his metronomically inclined performances of that work.[5] Yet Richter could also rise to the occasion with a properly prepared presentation as he did at the premiere of the Second Symphony[6] and then, as Boult observed to the author, fundamentally his straightforward grasp of the large design had the composer's confidence.[7]

Did Brahms therefore welcome any thoroughly prepared, sincerely felt performance with impartial approbation? Certainly, he seems to have approved a very wide range of interpretative styles. He was fully appreciative of Bülow's amply nuanced, precisely prepared and drilled performances at Meiningen. After initial suspicion of Weingartner as a notorious Wagnerite, Brahms was also enthusiastic about his 1895 performance of the Second Symphony with the Berlin Philharmonic in Vienna: 'I am delighted with the way my piece was reflected in your head.'[8] Later he said Weingartner conducted 'quite splendidly' and the performance was 'quite

---

[4] See in particular Musgrave & Sherman Chs 4, 8, 9, 10 and 13.

[5] Musgrave & Sherman Ch. 8, Robert Pascall & Philip Weller 'Flexible tempo and nuancing in orchestral music: understanding Brahms's view of interpretation in his Second Piano Concerto and Fourth Symphony' pp. 232 and 234, citing Charles Villiers Stanford *Pages from an Unwritten Diary* London 1914 pp. 201–2 and *Interludes: Records and Reflections* London 1922. See also Fifield 1993 pp. 468–9, where the second extract from Stanford is set out in full, and Richard Heuberger *Erinnerungen an Johannes Brahms* ed. Hofmann, Tutzing: 1996 pp. 58, 88 and 147.

[6] Fifield 1993 p. 138, citing and translating Hanslick's review in the *Neue freie Presse*, 3 January 1878. Brahms was also enthusiastic about Richter's handling of Bach's *St Matthew Passion*: Avins p. 620.

[7] Dyment *CRC* Spring 2003 p. 40.

[8] See Weingartner 1937 pp. 221–2, the German text in *Lebenserinnerungen* vol. 2 pp. 62–3. See also Dyment 1976 p. 27 for Weingartner pupil Stewart Deas's literal translation quoted here of Brahms's words 'Ich freue mich wie sich mein Stück in Ihrem Kopfe gespiegelt hat'.

wonderful'; and the uncluttered but spontaneous freshness of the young Weingartner showed Brahms one secure way forward for his music in the future.[9] But in the next year he expressed equal delight at Nikisch's performance of the Fourth Symphony in Leipzig:[10] 'impossible to hear it better done' was the composer's verdict, with Nikisch the 'perfect' conductor of works 'about which he is enthusiastic (and my symphonies are among these)'; yet Nikisch's poetic abandon was at the opposite pole from Weingartner's sobriety.

Nevertheless, not all stylistic approaches were equally acceptable to the composer. To a degree Brahms resisted the elaborate didacticisms of Bülow, objecting to his constant, premeditated manipulation of tempos, often punctuated by unmarked pauses – 'if I had wanted this, I would have written it in.'[11] True, he was at loggerheads with Bülow at the time of this remark, but it strikes home nonetheless. Weingartner, who on one occasion in Hamburg in the late 1880s saw both Brahms and Bülow conduct in the same concert, commented on the composer's 'restrained movements and broad conceptions [ruhigen grosslinigen Bewegungen]' as against the 'mercurial unrest [quecksilberartigen Unruhe]' of Bülow, even though at the time he failed to understand the Fourth Symphony he witnessed in Brahms's hands.[12] Brahms himself warned of the dangers of exaggeration in performance if too much attention were paid to his supplementary, pencilled-in score instructions which he later withdrew.[13] Such instructions were, he thought, necessary only at the stage when conductors were learning to 'feel' the expressive requirements of this new language cast in Classical form. The correct route should reject, as Brahms put it, a 'free artistic' performance style. 'The so-called

---

[9] Brahms to Simrock, *Brahms Briefwechsel* Berlin, vol. 12, 1919 ed. Kalbeck, translation Avins p. 726.

[10] *Letters of Clara Schumann and Johannes Brahms 1853–1896* ed. Litzmann (Longmans, 1927) p. 295. See also Brahms's letter to Simrock in similar terms, Avins p. 730.

[11] Musgrave & Sherman Ch. 8 (Pascall & Weller) p. 230 citing Kalbeck *Johannes Brahms* vol. 3 (Berlin, 1904–14) p. 495. Walker p. 308 throws doubt on Kalbeck's reliability generally, but the cited quotation has not, it seems, been called into question; see also n. 12. For a balanced assessment of Kalbeck's reliability, see Avins p. 3 n. 3.

[12] Weingartner 1937 p. 165, *Lebenserinnerungen* vol. 1 p. 311. Typically, the translated paragraph is half the length of Weingartner's original, omitting all mention of his failure to appreciate the Brahms symphony at the time. Walker pp. 364–6, in a sustained attack on Weingartner's credibility and stature, maintains that he was motivated purely by revenge in his remarks about Bülow after 1887, following their acute differences in that year over the interpretation of Bizet's *Carmen* in Hamburg. However, his book does not examine Bülow's style in any detail or refute the examples which Weingartner gave of what, in his opinion, were Bülow's distortions (e.g. in the *Egmont* and *Coriolan* overtures and the Eighth and Ninth symphonies in *On Conducting* Dover pp. 12–18). The witness of, among innumerable contemporaries, Brahms himself is sufficient confirmation of Weingartner's stature while Walker's view (ibid.) that Weingartner's style was characterised by 'self-effacement to the point of redundancy' and that his Beethoven recordings give 'the whole text and not much more than the text' takes insufficient account of his recorded legacy: see e.g. pp. 92 and 243 above.

[13] See Musgrave & Sherman Ch. 8 p. 224 and p. 344 below.

FIG. 55: HANS VON BÜLOW IN 1886

elastic tempo is not a new discovery', wrote Brahms in 1880 to his young friend
George Henschel, 'and to it, as to many another, one should attach a *con discrezione*.'[14]

---

[14] George Henschel *Personal Recollections of Johannes Brahms* (Boston, 1907) pp. 78–9; this letter is not
reproduced in the English publication by his daughter Helen Henschel, containing correspondence from
Brahms, but is included in Avins p. 559, from which this translation is drawn.

In the context of these apparently irreconcilable stylistic divergencies, Steinbach's performances achieved a special distinction in the eye (or ear) of the composer: they avoided what some saw as Bülow's exaggerations but delivered the world of flexibility and nuance envisaged by Brahms if his orchestral music's expressive thrust was to be most fully realised. Just how much flexibility and nuance has, however, been the subject of much debate and clarifying this crucial issue requires a renewed assessment, not only of contemporary evidence, but also of the career and stylistic affinities of the various authenticist witnesses, conductors and others. In the following pages the witnesses are described in rough chronological order with the exceptions of Alexander Berrsche and Walter Blume, whose importance lies now in the documentary evidence they left to posterity.

DOCUMENTARY EVIDENCE

Alexander Berrsche

This fine critic (1883–1940), a pupil of Max Reger, wrote for the *Augsburger Postzeitung* (1907–12) and the *Münchener Zeitung* (1912–40). With other essays, his writings were collected posthumously in *Trösterin Musika*, an 800-page volume published in two editions, the first in 1942 (Callweg, Munich), the second in 1949 (Hermann Rinn, Munich). The latter added items on musicians *verboten* in 1942, including Mahler, Walter and the Busch brothers; the references hereafter are to the page numbers of this edition. Berrsche's vantage point in Munich means that some desirable names are missing – Abendroth, Toscanini and the Brahms performances of Weingartner and Fritz Busch – and there is an excusable focus on those with posts in Munich during his time, such as Franz Fischer, Hans Pfitzner and Hans Knappertsbusch.[15] Nevertheless, Berrsche's detailed comments on the Brahms style of those conductors he did hear are invaluable, in particular his descriptions of the first conducting witness, Fritz Steinbach.

Fritz Steinbach

A pupil of the Leipzig Conservatory and of Nottebohm in Vienna, to whom Brahms recommended him after he first met the young student in 1875, Fritz Steinbach

---

[15] Franz Fischer, conductor at the Munich opera from 1879, Generalmusikdirektor of Bavaria after the death of Mottl but relinquishing the post when Walter was appointed in January 1913: Riding and Pechevsky, p. 103 (see also Ch. 1 n. 10). Hans Pfitzner was appointed Senator of the German Academy, Munich, in 1925 and was a life member of the Munich Academy of Music 1927–34. Hans Knappertsbusch (see further p. 320) was, in succession to Walter, music director of the Bavarian State Opera in Munich 1922–36.

(1855–1916)[16] went on to study in Karlsruhe with Brahms's friend Otto Dessoff and, on Bülow's recommendation, became assistant Kapellmeister in Mainz before succeeding that master (and his interim successor Richard Strauss) as Kapellmeister of the Meiningen Hofkapelle in 1886. Steinbach owed this post to Brahms's recommendation and he maintained the closest relationship with the composer until shortly before the latter's death. He took every opportunity to observe him at work and it is probable that his own Brahms performances were influenced by this thorough study.[17] Brahms regularly visited Meiningen to hear the repertoire, including his own works, rehearsed and conducted by Steinbach, to his

FIG. 56 FRITZ STEINBACH IN 1890, LITHOGRAPH BY ANTON KLAMROTH

profound satisfaction. To take but one example, in January 1891 his Fourth Symphony conducted by Steinbach moved Brahms so much that he asked for it to be repeated. Steinbach toured with the Meiningen orchestra from 1897 onwards, always promoting Brahms, and their visit to London in 1902 produced some superlative critiques for the five concerts.[18] Here were the four Brahms symphonies

---

[16] See Herta Müller's entry in the *New Grove Dictionary of Music and Musicians* 2nd ed. vol. 24 pp. 334–5 and her more detailed treatment in Müller; see also Potter pp. 1118–19.

[17] See Musgrave & Sherman Ch. 8 (Pascall & Weller) p. 242 citing Kalbeck *Johannes Brahms* vol. 4 2nd ed. (Berlin, 1915) p. 81. Steinbach was promoted to Generalmusikdirektor in 1893 and Intendant in 1896.

[18] *Musical Times* vol. 43 December 1902 p. 819 (concerts 17–21 November 1902); but see Grierson pp. 104–5 for the discord among London critics of which the visiting Meiningen Orchestra was an unwitting victim. Walker p. 332 takes the view, shared by no other writer, that under Steinbach Bülow's 'marvellous machine ... began slowly to unwind'. The cited *Musical Times* review stated that Bülow established the orchestra's fame and under Steinbach 'that fame has not in any way diminished'. The orchestra was disbanded in 1914 soon after the resignation on health grounds of one of Steinbach's successors, Max Reger, its conductor 1911–14, under whom in 1913 the orchestra was still 'remarkable for precision and clarity': W. J. Turner *Music and Life* London: Methuen 1921 'Max Reger' p. 82, quoted in Potter p. 172.

FIG. 57 STEINBACH IN HIS COLOGNE PERIOD

'rendered with such life and impulse, with such a spirit of romance, that one felt their power in a quite unaccustomed degree; the conductor seemed to be recreating rather than giving a rendering of the music'. By 1903, when Steinbach took over the Cologne Conservatory and Gürzenich Orchestra, this dominating musician, outwardly prickly but inwardly warm-hearted, was recognised throughout Europe as the foremost exponent of Brahms's orchestral music.

Steinbach's tenure in Cologne consolidated his position and launched him in conquest of fresh territories as guest conductor – with the London Symphony Orchestra as a regular guest until 1914,[19] Italy, Russia, France, Spain, throughout German-speaking Europe and New York. Only in the last was success limited: 'not of the stature of Weingartner or Safonov' pronounced *Musical America* in March 1906 and, while Steinbach was praised for a superb Elgar *Enigma* Variations with the New York Philharmonic, his Brahms Second Symphony was judged 'too slow' save in the last movement. However, New York had only recently

---

[19] For Steinbach's first concert with the LSO on 15 December 1904 (Beethoven's Overture *Leonore No. 2*, Bach's Brandenburg Concerto No. 3, Beethoven's Violin Concerto (Zimmerman) and Brahms's Fourth Symphony) see Scholes p. 393 and Kennedy 1987 p. 226. For some of his later concerts, see the following issues of the *Musical Times*: vol. 53 April 1912 p. 258 (concert of 18 March 1912 including Beethoven's Overture *Leonore No. 3*, Brahms's Fourth Symphony and Adolf Busch's London concerto debut in the Brahms concerto) – see also p. 305 and n. 27 below; vol. 53 December 1912 p. 805 (two concerts, the first on 28 October 1912 including Schubert's Symphony No. 8, Adolf Busch in the Beethoven concerto – this notice referred in error to the Brahms concerto – and Brahms's First Symphony, as to which see further p. 335; the second concert on 11 November 1912 including Mozart's Symphony No. 40); vol. 55 January 1914 p. 45 (23 November 1913 including Brahms's Fourth Symphony, 'a memorable interpretation', and Mozart's Symphony No. 39; and 24 November 1913 including the *Eroica* Symphony and other works); vol. 55 March 1914 p. 188 (9 February 1914 including Beethoven's Symphonies Nos 2 and 6 and the Brahms concerto with Huberman). For a further description of Steinbach's Brahms and its impact on London audiences, see Pearton p. 32.

heard Weingartner twice conduct that work and his unusually swift rendition was later to be criticised on that account by one of Steinbach's most fervent admirers, Adrian Boult.[20]

The German Brahms Festival witnessed by Toscanini at the Königliche Odeon, Munich during 10–14 September 1909, one of many such festivals organised by Steinbach between 1895 and 1913, was one of the peaks of Steinbach's career.[21] For it he brought together members of his former Meiningen Orchestra and the Munich Tonkünstlerorchester, with some distinguished soloists. Steinbach's favourite composition pupil Adolf Busch (hereafter Adolf) played in the first violins.[22] On travels such as this Steinbach never carried his Cologne parts for the Brahms symphonies since, as he later remarked to Adolf, 'we [sic – presumably his librarian and himself] have not written anything special in them'.[23] Such insouciance was a measure of his technique, which astonished Tovey at Meiningen in October 1900: 'the most amazing conductor I ever dreamt of. Flies into three pieces with a strong electric spark at the *fortissimos*, but never loses clearness or lets the orchestra mistake his meaning.'

Steinbach's position was unchallenged until in mid-1914 scandal enveloped him. A female Conservatory pupil accused him of improper behaviour; the whole incident, if it ever happened, was, for Steinbach, a misunderstanding. Nevertheless, he felt obliged to resign all his Cologne posts and fled initially to Vienna where for a time he and his wife occupied Adolf's then vacant apartment.[24] With the onset of war, he moved over the border to Munich, but recurrence of a serious heart ailment prevented him from re-establishing himself fully. According to his copious correspondence with Adolf, he had a mere couple of unpaid charity events in Munich, including Brahms's First Symphony on 24 October 1914 and another concert on 9 November; but he complained of poor orchestral standards and eventually gave up conducting there. There followed a few engagements in other centres, including Frankfurt and Karlsruhe, the odd triumph in Berlin. Pathetically he complained to Adolf of penury and poor health; from early December 1915 until his death in August the following year he was too ill for any musical activity. As Adolf summed up the post-Cologne years, Steinbach was 'condemned to inactivity'; he attempted to console his mentor, but his career was finished.[25]

---

[20] See Kennedy 1987 p. 87.

[21] See Scharberth p. 54. According to Müller p. 115, about a half of Steinbach's former Meiningen orchestra served in the Festival orchestra, amounting therefore to some 20–25 players out of its total complement of 48.

[22] Potter p. 105.

[23] Adolf Busch vol. 1 p. 86. As to Tovey's remarks, see Grierson p. 84. Donald Francis Tovey (1875–1940), foremost British critical writer of his day, composer, conductor and pianist, was on this occasion at a festival for the unveiling of a Brahms memorial, a photograph and further details of which are in Müller p. 107.

[24] Adolf Busch vol. 1 p. 97; as to Steinbach's fall, see also Potter p. 181.

[25] For references to Steinbach's post-Cologne concerts, his illness and death, see Adolf Busch vol. 1 pp. 107, 115, 128, 139, 142, 145, 150, 156 and 171.

The characteristics of Steinbach's approach to Brahms were vividly detailed by Berrsche in his notice of the 1909 German Brahms Festival in Munich:

> There is a shaping of the large line without any neglect of the smallest detail, there is a loving cultivation of details, without for a moment losing sight of the relationship with the whole. Thus we can once again see what phrasing means, where and how slurs and caesuras are placed, how the differing groups of instruments play out and balance against each other, how great climaxes are planned and how, through dynamic and agogic refinements, a melody attains declamatory power. Through the whole execution flows the pulse of a strict, intensely musical rhythm, which is the unmistakable distinguishing mark of a true and complete master musician ... Steinbach ... achieved directly through his iron rhythm a thrilling and irresistibly overwhelming effect (276–7).

In his obituary of Steinbach, Berrsche wrote of the 'great expressive power of the cantilena, the dynamic shading, the absolutely plastic phrasing and the rarely used but so natural rubato' (590–1). For Berrsche, when Steinbach died, Brahms died a second time; he was *the* Brahms conductor with whom all successors stood to be compared – and were almost always found wanting.

Steinbach was not, however, a mere Brahms specialist. Under his baton Bach Passions flourished, his Beethoven Ninth Symphony was a speciality lauded by Boult and Fritz Busch, his friend Reger featured prominently (in world and Cologne premieres) as latterly did Mahler, Korngold and Braunfels. Contemporary comment makes clear that in the pre-Brahms repertoire he adhered to Classical ideals in the line of Hans Richter, if with greater animation and imagination. There was none of the far-flung abandon of a Nikisch and, indeed, the Viennese-born composer Hans Gál remarked that while Steinbach 'was an excellent conductor in the Classical line', he was 'a little stiff compared with Nikisch, who was a little too loose and relaxed. They were absolute opposites.' Gál's impression is corroborated by another eye-witness, Florizel von Reuter, who pointed out that even Steinbach's Brahms conceptions 'stressed the rugged side of the ... symphonies', although 'he never disregarded the lyrical element completely'.[26] Again, although strongly distancing himself from negative comments about Steinbach, Fritz Busch quoted others who decried his performances as militaristic and unvaried. Contemporary critical comment confirms the overall impression of an animated Classicism: witness the *Times* view of his Beethoven and Brahms with the LSO in 1912,

---

[26] Gál quotation, Potter p. 67 (his interview with the composer in 1979). Reuter quotation, Florizel von Reuter *Great People I Have Known* Waukesha: Freeman 1961 pp. 79–80, quoted in Potter p. 1118.

which stressed the unique 'longsightedness' and 'perfect perception of the proportions' of his interpretations.[27]

As Boult described Steinbach to the author, although his conducting method was, as Tovey hinted, rather more demonstrative than the relative minimalism of Richter and Weingartner, his interpretative approach was in the tradition of the former: 'I heard performances of the Brandenburg Concertos and the Ninth Symphony of Beethoven which were absolute models for me.' Only in Brahms did he 'let himself go a little more'; so Boult's own score of the Fourth's passacaglia, annotated on a hearing of Steinbach, contained 'up to ten different tempo markings' in the course of it. Steinbach 'wasn't always doing that, but he certainly did in that movement express himself very freely'.[28] Nevertheless, Boult was adamant that Steinbach's style contrasted sharply with those of Nikisch and Furtwängler. This view, expressed in his old age, was consistent with his remarks in 1906 about Nikisch's 'irresistible reading' of Brahms's First Symphony, which nonetheless made him wish for 'a dose of Steinbach to make me see straight',[29] and his further assessment in 1922 of Furtwängler's Beethoven Ninth Symphony in Leipzig, when 'sometimes one felt it was in danger of falling to pieces, but one must not compare it with the monumental performances of Richter and Steinbach'.[30]

It seems clear enough that, very flexible though Steinbach was in conducting Brahms, that flexibility usually operated within circumscribed limits. Steinbach's approach, consistent with his standing in the Brahms circle, eschewed the extravagances of those who followed in the footsteps of Wagner's conducting practice: until the twentieth century adherents of Wagner and Brahms occupied separate camps, whether as performers, composers or critics.

Felix Mottl

The truth of the last statement is exemplified[31] in the career and musical affinities of Felix Mottl (1856–1911). From his earliest musical days immersed in Wagner,

---

[27] The words Fritz Busch used were 'militärisch' and 'undifferenziert'; see Fritz Busch p. 48 (English translation not here followed). His reference to Steinbach's Beethoven Ninth, p. 57. The *Times* comment on Steinbach's performance of the *Leonore No. 3* Overture in the LSO concert of 18 March 1912, quoted in Potter p. 140; see n. 19.

[28] Dyment *CRC* Spring 2003 pp. 40–1.

[29] Kennedy 1987 p. 34.

[30] Kennedy 1987 p. 86.

[31] Another example is Hermann Levi (1839–1900), an early champion of Brahms whose friendship with him was shattered by, among other factors, his entry into the Wagnerian orbit. Thereafter his Brahms performances lacked both conviction and success: see Frithjof Haas *Zwischen Brahms und Wagner: Der Dirigent Hermann Levi* Atlantis Musikbuch-Verlag 1995 pp. 165 and 196–214. Avins proposes other reasons for this breach: Walter Frisch and Kevin Karnes (eds.) *Brahms and his World* 2nd ed. Princeton 2009 'Brahms the Godfather' pp. 41–56 at p. 52; also Avins pp. 473–5. See also n. 105 below concerning Anton Seidl.

FIG. 58 FELIX MOTTL IN 1895

he felt little sympathy with his conducting teacher Otto Dessoff at the Vienna Conservatoire. Although Dessoff did his best for Liszt and Wagner in his programmes
as conductor of the Vienna Philharmonic (from 1860 to 1875), he was known first
and foremost as a propagandist for Brahms, of whom Mottl had no understanding,
then or later.[32] Nor could he warm to Dessoff's mere formal proficiency, which
lacked a 'spirit of love'. When Mottl was summoned by Wagner to Bayreuth, where
as a member of the so-called 'Nibelungen-Kanzlei' he acted as stage conductor for
the first *Ring* cycles in 1876, his Wagnerian immersion and hero-worship were
total; so much so that, after his appointment as Hofkapellmeister in Karlsruhe in
1881, some regarded the centre of Wagner performances par excellence as shifting
with him, after Wagner's death, to this '*kleine* Bayreuth'.[33] Appointed in 1903 as
Hofkapellmeister in Munich and from 1904 Director of its Akademie der
Tonkunst, Mottl later assumed the directorship of music for the whole of Bavaria.
Only his failure in 1907 to secure release prevented his succeeding Mahler in
Vienna. He continued in Munich until he collapsed while conducting *Tristan und
Isolde* in 1911, dying a few weeks later.

Mottl's tastes were wide: his Mozart operas were thought outstanding (Berrsche
considered Beecham perhaps his nearest stylistic analogue (626)) and he championed French music, particularly Berlioz, copiously. But Wagner occupied centre
stage throughout Mottl's career and in his stylistic approach to the orchestral repertoire he adopted fully all that he had learned from the master – who by all accounts
was in practice even more extravagant in his freedom of tempo than his revolutionary advice to conductors suggested.[34] Mottl's practice in this respect was reinforced by his Bayreuth experiences when, from 1886 onwards, he submitted to
Cosima's demands for expanding hitherto hallowed tempos – with results in the
1888 presentation of *Parsifal* that caused Weingartner (who elsewhere claimed
friendship with Mottl) to impale it in 1897 as 'one of the greatest artistic crimes,
the greatest of all perhaps, that Bayreuth has ever perpetrated ... The new gospel
of the slow time was also preached in the concert hall and soon every fresh and
energetic tempo seemed to have disappeared ... [and] as one Berlin musician is
said to have expressed it, "he Mottlizes" ... Soon this dragging of the tempo à la
Bayreuth and these distortions à la Bülow, knowing the affinity of their natures,

---

[32] See Haas pp. 14–15 and Mittag pp. 23–7. (Felix) Otto Dessoff (1835–92) conducted the world
premiere of Brahms's First Symphony at Karlsruhe in 1876. The *New Grove Dictionary of Music and
Musicians* 2nd ed. vol. 17 pp. 232–3 gives Joseph Hellmesberger (Sr) as Mottl's conducting teacher.
Haas gives Dessoff as his conducting teacher, but Mottl played as timpanist in the Vienna Conservatoire
orchestra whose conductor was Hellmesberger; Mottl disliked him just as much as he did Dessoff: see
Haas p. 15.

[33] Haas p. 41.

[34] See Millington & Spencer, Clive Brown 'Performing Practice' p. 99 at pp. 117–18.

entered into the bonds of matrimony, and brought forth a strange child that was nothing else than the tempo rubato conducting which I have once before attacked.'[35]

Weingartner was not alone. On the occasion of Mottl's London concert debut in 1894, the critics, Bernard Shaw especially, welcomed his freedom of tempo in some powerful and convincing Wagner, but soon they were at play in objecting to his extravagant point-making and tempo distensions in a stream of masterpieces: Beethoven's Fifth and *Pastoral*, Tchaikovsky's *Pathétique*, Schubert's *Unfinished* – all, it seems, suffered from this unwonted strain of novelty. Although Mottl's *Eroica* finely brought out its 'constantly changing emotional phases', of Beethoven's Ninth in 1897 the *Musical Times* complained that, 'such a slow, lumbering *Adagio* we have never heard. The heavenly melodies appeared dragged out of all proportion.' In the following year even Wagner's then popular *Kaisermarsch* suffered from his 'tempo rubato reading', a *Musical Times* complaint which turned in the same notice with relief to the London debut of Felix Weingartner who, by contrast, was 'no tempo rubato faddist' but sane and direct, as well as undoubtedly great. Mottl's final London notices for his Covent Garden Wagner in 1900 were, as summarised in the opening pages of Chapter 1, no improvement.[36] By these persistent criticisms London writers pinpointed inescapable aspects of Mottl's style; furthermore, their notices contrasted sharply with the welcome for Steinbach's debut just two years after Mottl's last appearance, later expanding in a crescendo of approbation that established Steinbach in London eyes as one of the greatest conductors of his time – evidence, surely, of a telling difference of interpretative approach.

Weingartner's attacks and Mottl's reputation as a 'slow tempo' conductor barely touched his stature within the Austro-German world. Indeed, Berrsche's analysis of his way in, say, an expansive and songful Schubert Ninth (174) and the *Eroica*'s *Marcia funebre* were detailed and appreciative – he much preferred Mottl's Beethoven to Weingartner's 'hurried' and 'cool' approach (594). Further, Mottl's temperament, with his search for peace and harmony in music as in life, made him the ideal Viennese conductor in contrast to the uncompromising and fanatical Mahler.[37]

---

[35] Weingartner *Bayreuth 1876–1896* London: Weekes 1898, translated by Lily Antrobus, reprinted in Dyment 1976 pp. 97–110, this passage at p. 101. In a letter to Gaisberg dated 17 August 1938 Weingartner excused himself from the proposal that he record what he termed the Gluck-Mottl Ballet Suite (Mottl's 1896 suite of dances by Lully, Rameau, Grétry and Gluck) because 'Mottl was indeed a good friend of mine' but he had no sympathy for this suite (EMI).

[36] For Shaw's comments, see Shaw vol. 3 pp. 195–8. For the *Musical Times* notices, see 1894 vol. 35 June p. 391 (Beethoven's Fifth Symphony); 1895 vol. 36 July p. 455 (*Egmont* Overture), December p. 814 (Schubert's *Unfinished* Symphony); 1896 vol. 37 January p. 22 (*Eroica* Symphony), June p. 384 (*Pastoral* Symphony); 1897 vol. 38 May p. 313 (Beethoven's Ninth Symphony), December p. 817 (Tchaikovsky's Sixth Symphony); 1898 vol. 39 June p. 389 (Wagner's *Kaisermarsch*); 1900 vol. 41 July p. 477 (*Ring* cycle and *Tannhäuser*), August p. 537 (Mottl's *Meistersinger*, his final appearance in London, and Emil Paur's *Tannhäuser*, where items were 'for the first time this year ... [by contrast with Mottl] taken at the proper pace').

[37] See Haas pp. 350 and 352; Mittag p. 39.

Virtually all critics, however, conceded Mottl's failure in Brahms. His diaries record how, in his early years and particularly after he was enveloped by the atmosphere of Bayreuth, he found much that was boring and meaningless in the first two symphonies.[38] As Hofkapellmeister in Karlsruhe he conducted the Fourth Symphony in 1886, but this was an isolated effort and until the end of the century he ventured little into Brahmsian territory.[39] When in 1906 he essayed the Third Symphony in Vienna he was roundly condemned for his pains: 'In the first movement the correct shaping was missing, the woodwind phrases suffering from excessive haste. The graciousness of the *Allegretto* grew torpid with muddy heaviness and in the finale the conductor's temperament ... did not find the right transition to the radiant close.' The effort damaged his reputation.[40] Again, during his Munich years he could not avoid performing works by a composer whose stature was by then unchallengeable, but his diaries once more gave evidence of a continuing antipathy towards Brahms.[41] A later critic summed up Mottl's failings: 'the pupil of Wagner and interpreter of the pathetic and demonic, could make nothing of Brahms's scores; for a conductor who luxuriated in Wagnerian orgies of sound, the grey atmosphere of Brahms's orchestral palette was offensive.'[42]

In the absence of recordings, other than Welte-Mignon rolls including the *Tristan* prelude made in February 1907 and fragments in almost inaudible cylinders,[43] Mottl's star, like Steinbach's, has sunk below the horizon. Today he is remembered for his orchestrations, particularly of Wagner's *Wesendonk-lieder*, and as the influential Munich exemplar of Abendroth and also of Furtwängler, whose *Tristan*, according to Mottl's biographer, closely resembled his mentor's.[44]

Arturo Toscanini and Vittorio Gui

Turning to recording conductors, Toscanini's connection with and comments on Steinbach have been described in Chapters 11 and 12. Apart from the 1911 concert in Turin which he rehearsed for Steinbach, Toscanini witnessed him only at the 1909 Munich Festival; but included in that Festival, in which Steinbach conducted virtually everything, were (in addition to chamber music) the four symphonies, the *Haydn* Variations, the Violin Concerto, the *German Requiem*, the *Fest- und Gedenksprüche*, the *Triumphlied*, *Gesang der Parzen*, *Schicksalslied*, the Alto

[38] Haas pp. 27–8.
[39] Haas p. 172.
[40] Haas pp. 292–3.
[41] Haas p. 356.
[42] Dejmek pp. 152–3; translations from Dejmek courtesy Nicholas Chadwick.
[43] Haas pp. 354 and 425, Brown p. 722.
[44] Haas p. 355.

Rhapsody and the *Liebeslieder Walzer*. For Toscanini, once heard was to remember ever after. What is more remarkable was his lifelong consistency: he knew the work of nearly all the eminent Austro-German conductors senior to him in years – Levi, Richter, Schuch, Nikisch, Mottl, Fiedler, Muck, Weingartner – he heard them all and appraised them variously; but only for Steinbach did he always profess unqualified admiration to the end of his career. When, as already noted, Fritz Busch distanced himself from those seeking to denigrate Steinbach, he thought it sufficient answer to call in aid Toscanini's enthusiasm for Steinbach's Brahms performances, some of which, according to Fritz, the Italian conductor considered the most beautiful he had ever heard.

To whom else did Toscanini enthuse and did he ever explain in detail what struck him about Steinbach's interpretative approach – in addition, that is, to his virtuoso handling of the fifth *Haydn* Variation noted in Chapter 11? It is surely remarkable that the only Brahms conductor who in later years Alexander Berrsche praised unreservedly was an unexpected Italian. Berrsche did not witness Toscanini in Salzburg but, curiously, attended the Nazified 1938 Festival, when Vittorio Gui, not himself a fascist, nonetheless had little compunction in substituting for the missing Maestro. Berrsche reviewed two of his concerts, one with the Vienna Philharmonic in Salzburg including Brahms's *Tragic Overture*, the other in Augsburg containing the Fourth Symphony.[45] Gui had already conducted Brahms in Salzburg: Walter invited him in 1933[46] for a programme including the Second Symphony – perhaps the sprat to catch the Toscanini mackerel, which was duly hooked the following year when, alongside Gui's Brahms First Symphony, Salzburg audiences heard Toscanini's *Haydn* Variations and Third Symphony.[47] Now, in 1938, Berrsche was startled by Steinbach redivivus. He detailed at length the many elements in Gui's Fourth Symphony where 'all was as it was when Steinbach lived', such as the oboe solo at bar 17 in the first movement given with 'penetrating force, a sudden glowing accentuation', and in the Andante the 'sensitive espressivo' of the first violins' semiquavers, the 'scrupulous weighting' of the highly expressive accompanying cello cantilena (620) – two passages, as noted in Chapter 12, also unmistakably characteristic of Toscanini. As in the symphony, so it was in the overture, the like of which Berrsche had not heard since Steinbach (623).

Gui (1885–1975), wholly Italian trained, assisted Toscanini at La Scala for two

<hr/>

[45] Gui's 1938 Salzburg concert, 31 July 1938 in the Mozarteum, Kaut p. 446; 1938 Augsburg concert date unknown. Berrsche also praised Gui's Salzburg *Falstaff* (previously Toscanini's) as virtual musical perfection (618).

[46] Kaut p. 429.

[47] Toscanini's performances of all four Brahms symphonies with the Vienna Philharmonic 1933–37 were major successes with Vienna and Salzburg audiences: see Herbert Peyser in the *New York Times*, 14 November 1937. Gui's 1934 Brahms First Symphony at Salzburg was on 2 August, Toscanini's *Haydn* Variations on 23 August, his Third Symphony on 30 August.

Hans Richter   Colonne·   M-Fiedler

Chevillard   Mancinelli   Martucci

Serafin   Mascagni   Toscanini

Ricordo dei concerti dati dall'Orchestra Municipale di Torino al Teatro Vittorio Emanuele. Aprile e Maggio 1904.

Arturo Toscanini   Felix Weingartner

11 e 14 Maggio   21 Maggio

Cartolina Ricordo
Dei Maestri Direttori dei Concerti Orchestrali, dati dalla Società
di Concerti di Torino, al Teatro Vitt. Eman. nella Primavera 1905

Giuseppe Martucci   Oskar Nedbal

27 Maggio   31 Maggio

FIG. 59 –
'HE HEARD THEM
ALL': TURIN CONCERT
CONDUCTORS
1904–1905

years from 1923 and began his long association with Florence in 1928. He could hardly have avoided Toscanini's concert work with La Scala's orchestra, which often featured Brahms's Second Symphony, and he may also have heard his La Scala *Haydn* Variations in October 1925 and Fourth Symphony in October 1927; perhaps in addition he discussed the music with the Maestro. Certainly Gui went on to become the most important Italian Brahmsian of his generation, recording the Second and Third symphonies with his Florence orchestra in June 1946 and, again with that orchestra, choosing the Fourth Symphony for what turned out to be his last concert a few weeks before his death.[48]

To have reproduced Steinbach's characteristics without linkage of any kind would have been uncanny, but the putative Toscanini connection provides a possible solution to the mystery, to which Gui's recorded Brahms adds substance. His 1975 Fourth Symphony suggests a rather gentler, plainer facsimile of Toscanini in 1935 and in particular his passacaglia is indistinguishable in structure from Toscanini's. This performance is described further in the next section dealing with recorded evidence.

The Mottl acolytes: Hermann Abendroth and Wilhelm Furtwängler

Adhering to chronology, next are two recording conductors having an immediate connection with Felix Mottl. The Frankfurt-born Hermann Abendroth (1883–1956) received his musical education in Munich during 1901–05 where his teachers were Ludwig Thuille and Anna Hirzel-Langenhan.[49] Here without doubt Abendroth also witnessed and absorbed Mottl's 'authentic' Wagner presentations, among them *Die Meistersinger* and *Tannhäuser* in May 1904 and the *Ring* in August that year during the Summer Wagner Festival, held each year in the Prinzregenten-Theater.[50] As the reigning Hofkapellmeister at the summit of a great career, Mottl's approach to the

---

[48] Gui's Brahms recordings: Symphony No. 2: Parlophone/Cetra BB 25171–74, LP transfer Tempo MTT 2074; Symphony No. 3: BB 25163–66, LP transfer Tempo MTT 2040; Symphony No. 4: see p. 326 below. The Cetra recordings were made in June 1946, the Third on 12 June, the Second a few days later. The LP transfers were released in the USA in August 1951 (Symphony No. 3) and August 1952 (Symphony No. 2) but were neither advertised nor reviewed. Courtesy Michael H. Gray and Pennsylvania College, I have been able to confirm the clean, Classical character of Gui's recorded performance of the Third Symphony.

[49] Ludwig Thuille (1861–1907), German composer and teacher, professor of theory and composition at the Munich Akademie; Anna Hirzel-Langenhan (1874–1951), Swiss pianist and teacher, pupil of Leschetizky and resident in Munich from 1898.

[50] Abendroth's biographer suggests (Lucke-Kaminiarz p. 17) he also assisted Mottl at Munich and Bayreuth during his studies, but this is questionable: after five months as guest conductor in the United States, Mottl did not arrive as Munich Hofkapellmeister until May 1904 and took over as director of the Akademie der Tonkunst only in October that year. During Mottl's Munich years he conducted at Bayreuth in 1906 (*Tristan* – his last appearance there, on the eve of his break with Cosima Wagner and the Bayreuth musical establishment) and Abendroth is not listed among the Bayreuth musical assistants and répétiteurs for that year: Neupert pp. 64–5.

FIG. 60 HERMANN ABENDROTH IN 1909

repertoire in his Munich concert and opera presentations would necessarily have impacted deeply on the young conductor. Subsequently Abendroth was appointed Mottl's assistant conductor for the Wagner Festivals of 1907–10, when he helped him prepare the *Ring*, *Die Meistersinger* and *Tristan*.[51] At this time, too, Abendroth befriended Mottl's assistant Wilhelm Furtwängler; beyond doubt the two young conductors were thoroughly soaked in the Mottl style and method.

After early conducting experience in Munich before graduation, Abendroth was appointed Kapellmeister for concerts and opera in Lübeck, followed by his appointment in 1911 as Kapellmeister in Essen, a post he kept until May 1916. During these years he guest conducted in virtually all major German-speaking centres, including Berlin, Hamburg, Munich, Frankfurt and Vienna, and also in many others.

Did Abendroth find time in such a busy schedule to attend any of Steinbach's Brahms concerts in Cologne, just 70km distant from Essen? It is quite possible, but current scholarship about Abendroth's career provides no definite answer. In any event, his opportunities to hear Steinbach's Brahms would have been limited, because during the relevant period Steinbach gave, as was his custom, just one all-Brahms concert each year: on 15 March 1912, featuring the Third Symphony; on 28 March 1913, the First; and on 6 February 1914, the Fourth.[52] The recorded evidence is too thin to suggest Abendroth's attendance at any of these concerts save possibly the second; moreover, there was no Cologne/Steinbach Brahms Second Symphony during Abendroth's Essen period.

Less speculatively, in his Essen years Abendroth was already forging his own way with the repertoire, which necessarily bore the imprint of the wide and emphatic tempo changes typified by Mottl's practice. That way was observed by contemporary critics who enjoyed comparing the differing Brahms styles of Steinbach, Abendroth and his successor in Essen, the noted Brahms conductor Max Fiedler. Consistent with what we learn from Abendroth's recordings, he was singled out at this time as 'already ... a Brahms conductor of stature' who, by comparison with Fiedler, gave 'more emphasis to the architectural element' (in the sense of highlighting nodal points by major fluxes of tempo) and allowed 'the melodic aspect to sing out more profoundly'.[53]

As a forceful personality and, at thirty-two, already a greatly experienced

---

[51] The Festivals began in 1901; see Haas pp. 265, 309 and 328. Abendroth's appointment was noted in biographical details in EMI files, presumably compiled from material supplied by Abendroth or his agent. Other than details of his HMV recording sessions, nothing more about Abendroth survives in EMI's archive.

[52] See concert listing in Scharberth pp. 215–27. Steinbach's last Cologne performance of Brahms's Second Symphony was on 9 March 1909. Abendroth might have heard Steinbach's Brahms at one of the latter's geographically more distant Brahms festivals or on tour elsewhere, but evidence is wholly lacking.

[53] By Max Hehemann (1873–1933), the leading Essen critic for the Essen *Allgemeine Zeitung* quoted in Dejmek p. 149.

conductor, Abendroth was chosen unanimously from among some distinguished candidates as best qualified to succeed Steinbach in Cologne after the latter's flight.[54] On learning that Abendroth had accepted the post, Steinbach regretted that his favourite, Fritz Busch, had not gained it: from his Munich retreat he wrote to Adolf in January 1915, 'if they wanted a young man they could ... have taken Fritz'.[55] In fact, Fritz had been approached but felt that, just five years out of the Conservatoire, he could not tactfully step into his master's shoes and, shortly after, his call-up for war service ended that possibility.[56] Abendroth conducted in Cologne for twenty years, his first full season (1915/16) in tandem with the Essen concerts.

Although Brahms's First Symphony featured in one of Abendroth's earliest Cologne concerts, in March 1915, and eventually became one of his calling-cards as guest conductor in and outside Germany, in his Cologne repertoire Brahms was just one of many featured composers stretching from Bach to Schoenberg and Bartók, with Beethoven and Bruckner perennially and much to the fore.[57] Given that Abendroth was a master-conductor of his generation with already decided interpretative ideas almost certainly grounded in his experience of Mottl in particular, it cannot credibly be suggested that his Cologne players would have passed on any specific interpretative tradition in performing Brahms ('no, we do it this way'); and as mentioned above, he inherited score parts which gave few clues about his predecessor's approach.[58] There is no known evidence of a direct connection between Abendroth and Steinbach and, from the latter's correspondence quoted above, some suggestion to the contrary. If, therefore, Abendroth was aware of his predecessor's approach to Brahms, his knowledge would most probably have stemmed only from witnessing one or more of the three Gürzenich Brahms concerts noted above.

Abendroth introduced himself to London audiences with Beethoven's Ninth Symphony in 1927 and so impressed was the LSO that the orchestra urged HMV to place him under a major contract.[59] The company contented themselves with

[54] Lucke-Kaminiarz p. 36. Abendroth's rivals included Max Reger and Gustav Brecher (1879–1940), at the time first conductor of the Cologne Opera, who shared the 1914/15 season with Abendroth: Scharberth p. 227.

[55] Adolf Busch p. 115.

[56] Fritz Busch p. 99.

[57] Lucke-Kaminiarz pp. 44 and 51, and see concert listing in Scharberth pp. 227–45. The listing shows five Brahms First Symphonies (1915–33) and four each of the Second (1918–33), Third (1924–31) and Fourth (1916–33) plus five *German Requiems*; but Brahms is dwarfed by the sheer quantity of Beethoven.

[58] See p. 303 above. Steinbach's scores have, it seems, not survived, Musgrave & Sherman p. 276, but the parts used by Bülow, Brahms and Steinbach at Meiningen are preserved in the Meiningen Museum. Abendroth's scores disappeared in the 1970s and only his working parts for the First Symphony survived; these disclose nothing relevant to this essay. Information courtesy Irina Lucke-Kaminiarz, December 2009.

[59] Foss & Goodwin p. 120.

recording Brahms's Fourth Symphony on that first visit and the First in 1928 (there was also an unissued Bach Third Brandenburg recorded at the latter session). He again conducted the LSO in 1928/29 and in 1936/37. Because local politicians could not stomach his left-wing views, he had by then left Cologne; but in 1934, after Walter fled the Nazis in Leipzig, Abendroth nonetheless took over the Gewandhaus Orchestra. With this orchestra and the Berlin Philharmonic he recorded quite extensively, including further versions of Brahms's First and Fourth symphonies. Abendroth's post-war career in Soviet-occupied Europe, from which derive most of his broadcast recordings later issued on CD, is detailed elsewhere.[60]

The career of Abendroth's friend Wilhelm Furtwängler (1886–1954) is important in the present context only for the significance of his period as assistant to Mottl in Munich during 1907–09 when he absorbed the senior conductor's interpretative approach to, among others, Wagner, Strauss and Beethoven, as well as his skill as an opera-house administrator. As third conductor under Pfitzner[61] at Strasbourg from 1909, Furtwängler also fully absorbed that composer-conductor's views on the exalted place of the artist in society and the more misty concepts of German identity.[62] These diverse influences helped develop a style quite distinct from the Brahms-Steinbach line, with (like Mottl and Abendroth) structural signposts underlined by wide distensions of tempo and in later years (like Mottl but unlike Abendroth) a further admixture of inflated tempos often manipulated for expressive effect.

Comments on Furtwängler's Brahms performances in the 1920s make clear the distinction here proposed. His first performance of Brahms's Second Symphony as conductor of the Berlin Philharmonic on 22 October 1922 was criticised by one writer with a long memory for 'preciously stretched tempos' that 'Brahms himself never had taken.'[63] Berrsche's strong reservations about Furtwängler's Brahms Fourth Symphony in that year were rather different. He admired the clarity, the masterly logic of his structure (Berrsche would here be referring to the emphatic distensions of tempo which sought to clarify structure) but objected to his Beethovenish brio and dynamics which rode roughshod over the more sensitive inflections revealed in earlier times by Steinbach (609). The *Haydn* Variations in 1928 were better in

---

[60] Lucke-Kaminiarz pp. 107–51.

[61] Although he was a prolific recording conductor in the 1920s, Pfitzner's stature as a composer has since overshadowed that aspect of his career. As a Munich resident in the early 1900s, Pfitzner had substantial contact with Mottl, who programmed his music with some frequency, e.g. in his debut concert with the Vienna Philharmonic in November 1904 which included a work by Pfitzner preceding the *Eroica* Symphony: Haas pp. 274 and 302. Pfitzner's interpretative approach, e.g. his extreme changes of tempo in Beethoven (see Ch. 12 p. 243), may therefore have owed something to his experiences of Mottl. See p. 308 for suggestions as to Mottl's interpretation of the *Eroica* Symphony.

[62] For the influence on Furtwängler of Mottl and Pfitzner, see Shirakawa pp. 12–13.

[63] Leopold Schmidt in the *Berliner Tageblatt*, 24 October 1922, quoted in Shirakawa p. 49.

these respects, although the fourth variation was far too slow (and here again Berrsche pined for Steinbach's agogic inflections) while the crescendos in the seventh variation were exaggerated (611). In short, 'authentic' Brahms in the Meiningen way cannot be looked for in Furtwängler's interpretations.

Sir Adrian Boult

Hans Richter was the great conductor dominating the early years of Adrian Boult (1889–1983). Weingartner provided extra illumination and vitality in Beethoven while Fritz Steinbach came as a revelation in Brahms. Quite how many Steinbach concerts Boult attended is not clear; what is clear is his veneration for him and the benefit he received, noted above in his quoted descriptions of Steinbach's style and technique. Like Toscanini, he retained his memories of and respect for Steinbach throughout a remarkably long career.

Boult recorded the Brahms symphonies twice after the Second World War. His first cycle with the LPO in 1954 is the stronger and more firmly characterised; references below to his interpretative stance in Brahms draw principally on examples from that cycle.

Fritz Steinbach's pupils: the Busch brothers and Hans Knappertsbusch

Fritz Busch (1890–1951) entered the Cologne Conservatoire in 1906 and in October 1907 joined Steinbach's conducting class. More than any other recording conductor he had the chance to observe and absorb the Steinbach method and style and, as noted above, he was unsparing in his praise for this fearsome character, who nonetheless showed him 'remarkable sympathy ... on every sort of occasion'.[64] Ultimately Steinbach hailed him when he first conducted the Conservatoire orchestra as 'the conductor of the future!'[65] and, although they had their differences over stick technique, quickly forgotten, they remained in close contact after Fritz left Cologne. Steinbach wrote to him frequently in the following years and in 1914 became god-father on the birth of Fritz's first child, Hans Peter.[66]

Fritz always paid due tribute to Steinbach's Brahms and, as noted in Chapter 4, although he thought Toscanini's Oxford performance of Brahms's First Symphony in June 1937 was 'very lovely', he could not resist reminding his brother[67] that 'the

[64] Fritz Busch p. 56.
[65] Fritz Busch p. 62. Fritz records their quarrel over stick technique at p. 65.
[66] The Busch Brothers Foundation's archive contains sixteen letters from Steinbach to Fritz Busch (they include advice on the performance of Brahms) and five from Fritz in reply.
[67] See Ch. 4 p. 96; the emphasised passage from Adolf Busch vol. 2 p. 370.

Brahms I still have in my memory *even more warmly and convincingly as a whole by Steinbach*' [emphasis added]. By the late 1940s, however, when he came to compile his memoirs, he was content to cite Toscanini's approval of Steinbach's Brahms without comment of his own, noting only that Brahms was regarded as his teacher's speciality.[68] Perhaps by then he felt a greater independence of view; if so, Fritz's earlier recordings would be more likely to bear any surviving traces of the Steinbach imprint. Unfortunately, only one of his Brahms recordings dates from pre-war days. Fritz's post-war recordings of the Second and Fourth symphonies adhere closely to a pure Classical ideal, but the broadcast of the Second Symphony with his Dresden Staatskapelle from Berlin on 25 February 1931 shows him in a rather different light. Although the Classical line is here upheld, it is married to a free-flowing spirit which bends the tempo seemingly spontaneously and momentarily without interrupting the forward impetus. Midway between the two recordings of the Second Symphony lies the almost complete recording of the First Symphony drawn from Fritz's concert with the New York Philharmonic on 1 February 1942, which in many ways is as remarkable as the 1931 Second. This performance, his 1931 Second Symphony and his late recording of the Fourth Symphony are examined below for evidence of Steinbach's influence.[69]

Adolf Busch (1891–1952) entered the Cologne Conservatoire at the age of eleven and, in addition to his tuition in violin and piano, eventually joined Steinbach's composition class. His closeness to Steinbach cannot be over-emphasised: he was the chosen protégé of the Director who oversaw his progress in detail. Not long after graduation Steinbach enjoined him to 'Du' familiarity and to address him as 'Onkel.'[70] Their correspondence, before and after Steinbach's fall from grace (about which Adolf was the first to comfort his mentor), was copious. Nevertheless, Adolf left few observations about Steinbach's Brahms style – he was simply too close to and continuously familiar with it. In one letter he said to Steinbach 'no-one does [the Second Symphony] as beautifully as you do', but correspondence reveals little more. Significantly, however, after leaving the Conservatoire he played the Brahms concerto at least eight times under Steinbach and thereby, with his help, achieved supreme mastery in it; his robust, eloquent and unmannered recorded performances of it are living testament to the Steinbach legacy. Moreover, he had no hesitation in passing on to other conductors his knowledge of Brahms's wishes gained from this experience of playing the work under Steinbach.[71] Adolf's mentor also

---

[68] See letter, Fritz to Adolf Busch, 13 June 1949, Adolf Busch vol. 2 pp. 512–14.

[69] I am indebted to Peter Aistleitner for the opportunity to hear the recording of the First Symphony. Recording details of Fritz's post-war Brahms are in the text p. 326 and n. 88 below.

[70] Adolf Busch vol. 1 p. 39; the quoted remark about Brahms's Second Symphony, ibid. p. 87.

[71] For the occasions on which Adolf played the Brahms concerto under Steinbach, see Potter pp. 115, 118, 119, 120, 140 and 199; Adolf Busch vol. 1 pp. 32, 37 and 38–9. For an instance of Adolf passing on

conducted him in Brahms's Double Concerto and the Beethoven and Reger concertos. Clearly, he was as happy to play under Steinbach's direction as he was later under Toscanini's.

Adolf did leave illuminating, if brief, comments about other conductors. After playing the Mendelssohn concerto with Abendroth in Cologne in January 1915, he thought him a 'fine, serious musician, who is concerned about the work and not himself', but he 'did not have a *profound* impression' and he was 'not *yet* at the *top* though with his seriousness of working he has hope of *getting* there'. A few weeks later, after playing the Brahms concerto with Abendroth in Essen, Adolf remarked that 'it was very nice, and we understood each other very well'.[72] By contrast, a Gewandhaus Brahms concerto that month with Nikisch was less happy: 'the orchestra was a little loud ... and the tutti was somewhat arbitrary on Nikisch's part – but his performance of the D major symphony was wonderful and also his *Tragic Overture!*'[73] Of Toscanini's Zürich Brahms Second Symphony in 1924 which so incensed Furtwängler, he remarked 'Toscanini was wonderful – in the Brahms Second Symphony, thank God, there was even something *happening* for a change.'[74] Three years later Karl Muck was 'good but frightfully boring' as accompanist in two works.[75] The one conductor Adolf consistently slated was Furtwängler, whom in 1927 he accused of 'doing a lot of damage' with his 'hopelessly corrupt' manner of music-making and the two were never at ease with each other.[76] Furtwängler in his turn claimed that Adolf had no feeling for Brahms – more evidence, if it were needed, of the gulf between the Steinbach and Mottl lines. Clearly, for Adolf, Steinbach and Toscanini stood on the peak, Nikisch sometimes did, while Muck, Abendroth and Furtwängler took their places variously on the slopes.

Berrsche did not, it seems, hear Adolf in the Brahms concerto but referred to his performance by repute as placing him in the Joachim tradition. Moreover, he praised the Busch Quartet especially for its mastery of *adagio* movements, for its musical spirit and elasticity of tempo, from all of which he concluded that Adolf was the most interesting and musical of German violinists, as well as the most expressive and musically full-blooded (660–5).

---

his knowledge of Brahms's wishes (with Boult in March 1937), see Potter p. 646. Adolf's performance of this concerto is best heard in the recording of 18 July 1943 with the NYPSO conducted by William Steinberg, Music & Arts CD 1107; a 1951 performance with the Basel SO under Hans Münch is on Music & Arts CD 861. A 1949 performance of the Double Concerto with brother Hermann and the French National Radio Orchestra under Paul Kletzki is on Music & Arts CD 1083.

[72] Adolf Busch vol. 1 pp. 120–1.

[73] Adolf Busch vol. 1 p. 122.

[74] Adolf Busch vol. 1 p. 240.

[75] Adolf Busch vol. 1 p. 251.

[76] Adolf Busch vol. 1 pp. 253–4 and Potter p. 216. See also Potter p. 160 for Adolf Busch's relations with Furtwängler.

Hans Knappertsbusch (1888–1965) joined Steinbach's conducting class in 1908. Steinbach did not hesitate to tell him, as (with the exception of Fritz Busch) he did many another class student, that he had no talent for conducting.[77] Perhaps he resented Knappertsbusch's already well-developed Wagnerian sympathies, which were confirmed when his pupil left Cologne to assist Richter at Bayreuth. After succeeding Walter in Munich in 1922, Knappertsbusch frequently came under Berrsche's gaze. Apparently he never invoked Steinbach's name in connection with Knappertsbusch's Brahms performances, but he did praise his rendering of the Third Symphony in 1933 for carefully reconciling its formal and expressive problems, commending in particular the 'glowing and exuberant impetus' given to the transition back to the first movement's recapitulation (281–2). Unfortunately the mantle of *Parsifal* in most of Kna's post-war Brahms recordings, especially those derived from broadcasts in his old age, weighed him down in some bizarrely slow tempos – certainly no legacy of Steinbach.[78] Finally, another Steinbach pupil, Heinz Bongartz (1894–1978), conductor of the Dresden Philharmonic 1947–64, made dignified but not outstanding recordings of the two Brahms Serenades with that orchestra in 1962.[79]

Walter Blume

Walter Blume (1883–1933) was another pupil of Mottl in his Munich period but he achieved no great distinction as a conductor: his principal posts were at Coblenz, probably at the time of Steinbach's Cologne tenure, with the Konzertverein Orchestra in Munich during the First World War and with the Württemberg Tonkünstler from 1931. His claim to fame lies in his book, published from the manuscript typescript in 1933 by Ernst Surkamp (Stuttgart), entitled *Brahms in der Meininger Tradition: Seine Sinfonien und Haydn-Variationen in der Bezeichnung von Fritz Steinbach*. Jonathan R. Pasternack's complete English translation under the title 'Brahms in the Meiningen Tradition – His symphonies and Haydn Variations According to the Markings of Fritz Steinbach' also contains a valuable contextual introduction.[80] The brief extracts in English from Blume's book in the section below devoted to recorded evidence draw on Pasternack's translation, with possible alternatives and, where necessary, the German language original.

[77] Friedrich Herzfeld *Magie des Taktstocks* Berlin: Ullstein AG 1953 p. 107.
[78] E.g. Symphonies Nos 2 (27 November 1959) and 3 (4 November 1956) with the Dresden Staatskapelle, Tahra TAH 303–04: the outer movements of No. 2 are, respectively, 16 (without the repeat) and 11 minutes, those of No. 3 (without the first movement repeat) 11 minutes each; compare the timings in Table 1, below, p. 328.
[79] Berlin Classics CD 0013592BC.
[80] Doctoral dissertation for Washington University, 2004.

Like Berrsche, Blume was convinced that Steinbach's Brahms was uniquely authoritative and that, before all memory was lost, his interpretative approach, as Blume himself heard it, should be described in all possible detail. As the introduction to his book shows, it was a task he carried out with commitment and passion. Given that context, his book's dedication to [gewidmet] Fritz Busch assumes indisputable significance. It is not known whether the two conductors knew each other and it seems no correspondence between them survives; there is nothing in the Busch Brothers archive. It is, however, inconceivable that Blume would have dedicated his book to Fritz unless at the time of compilation he heard something of Steinbach's voice in the Brahms performances of his pupil; perhaps, indeed, he heard Fritz's 1931 broadcast of the Second Symphony noted above as he worked on his book. Fritz's exile in the year of publication, as well as Blume's racial origins and his death in that year, are sufficient explanation of the book's extreme rarity.

Blume wrote and compiled his work in the early 1930s principally from his notes made during and after Steinbach's Brahms performances. His main opportunity to witness Steinbach would almost certainly have been during his Coblenz years; the town is about 80km from Cologne. In his introduction, Blume says he obtained the score extracts with Steinbach's markings in Munich during 1914–15 when he came into personal contact with Steinbach and became his student, attending also his 'frequent' concerts there.

Blume's introductory observations, his detailed advice and his claims for the absolute authenticity of the reproduced score markings need critical assessment. There is no reason to doubt that Blume observed Steinbach's Cologne Brahms performances during his Coblenz years, but that period ended nearly twenty years before he made his compilation. As earlier noted, because of ill-health and other factors Steinbach apparently conducted very few concerts in Munich – certainly they were not 'frequent' as Blume maintains – and was incapacitated from early December 1915 until his death. If, as Steinbach often complained, he lacked paying engagements at that time, he may well have accepted the thirty-year-old Blume as a student; but, in the absence of live performances, what he could have imparted about nuancing and phrasing by words alone remains speculative, as is the extent to which Steinbach annotated his scores which Blume says he saw. As explained above, Steinbach's orchestral parts of the Brahms symphonies did not contain 'anything special' by way of annotation.

Whatever the source of Blume's advice, how helpful or reliable is it as an indicator of Steinbach's approach? As will be seen, a number of Blume's precepts reflect common currency among more sensitive later Brahms interpreters, with or without such further explication. And are Blume's written observations sufficiently precise to be more than a general indication? The tempo of the fifth *Haydn* variation, says Blume, should always be 'very lively'; hardly a helpful gloss on Brahms's *vivace* and conveying nothing of the virtuoso spirit with which, through Toscanini (and, as noted below, Henry Wood), we know that Steinbach addressed it. Where, by contrast, Blume is more explicit, his link with Mottl raises questions: Mottl's style, unsuited to Brahms, was quite distinct from Steinbach's, but it cannot be assumed that Blume himself remained wholly uninfluenced by its tendency to extremes. 'Make a strong crescendo' with the 'greatest possible tone', he says of the crescendo in the second part of the seventh *Haydn* variation; but as already noted, Berrsche – forever conscious of Steinbach's shadow – thought it a misplaced exaggeration when Furtwängler did just that. Was Blume here invoking Steinbach or Mottl (who performed the work in Vienna)?

If such advice is doubtful, so also on occasion are Blume's references to Brahms's scores, where he relies on a faulty memory rather than the scores themselves; for example, in Variation 17 of the Fourth's passacaglia he refers to the descending strings' fortissimo as a triple forte, a typical error of a kind footnoted in other instances by Pasternack. In a compilation concerned with the minutiae of expressive annotations, such lapses, minor though they are, must raise queries about the complete reliability of Blume's memory elsewhere.

Finally, it is unclear how far Blume's annotations reflect his own opinions as distinct from Steinbach's opinions and markings. That lack of clarity is underlined by his unexplained habit of, from time to time, 'quoting' some of his pithiest advice. Do such quotations signify Steinbach's very words, imparted personally to Blume? If so, with what degree of authority is the remaining advice, by far the greater part, to be treated? These unanswerable questions lead unavoidably to the conclusion that, as Pasternack puts it, 'in relationship to Brahms's work, Blume's text must be designated as a tertiary source'. Given Blume's evident commitment and sincerity, it is more likely than not that a substantial part of his annotations reflects Steinbach's practice, but his observations must be assessed critically and supplemented from other reliable sources whenever possible. For these reasons Blume is treated hereafter as an aid towards reconstructing the Meiningen way, rather than as an infallible guide.

Other conductors

Max Fiedler (1859–1939) gained an immense reputation as a Brahms conductor during the twenty years or so after returning from his stint with the Boston Symphony Orchestra in 1912, especially during his long tenure at Essen from 1916 to 1934. He was acquainted with Brahms during his early years in Leipzig and Hamburg but there is no evidence that Brahms heard him conduct his works. He left a small legacy of recordings including the Second (1931) and Fourth (1930) symphonies.

Although some German critics regarded Fiedler's Brahms as the best of its time, others were less enthusiastic. Boston and New York critics thought his renditions restless and formally unbalanced, while a Hamburg critic of a Brahms First Symphony which Fiedler conducted there early in 1915 found him striving after effects with excessive reliance on *luftpausen*, premature accelerandos and much stretching and forcing of tempos.[81] A few days later Fiedler repeated the work in Munich where, although some critics approved, Berrsche did not. Rather like his Hamburg colleague, he deplored a continuous excitability, which ignored the more sensitive and gracious side of the music; what a pity, as he thought, Fiedler chose to end his concert with this disappointing performance (599). It seems that, while Weingartner treated what he regarded as Bülow's excesses in his post-Meiningen Hamburg and Berlin years as a joke, Fiedler treated them as gospel.[82] Whatever may have been the virtues of his Brahms, described in detail elsewhere by the author, his approach to the composer was somewhat distant from Steinbach's.

All the more so was Felix Weingartner's, also detailed by the author elsewhere.[83] Although, as described above, Weingartner (1863–1942) gained Brahms's approval for his handling of the Second Symphony in 1895, he himself, as he admitted, had at that time 'obstinately hardened my heart against many of his works'.[84] So much was evident in the two early editions of his *The Symphony since Beethoven* published in the late 1890s; the fourth and final edition of 1926 wholly revised his attitude to Brahms the symphonist. Since he performed little else of Brahms during the composer's lifetime and, so far as is known, had no substantive contact with Steinbach at Meiningen, his recordings have no connection with the Meiningen tradition. That is not to say, however, that Weingartner's clean-limbed, uncluttered performances constitute a separate 'tradition' somehow in contrast to the Meiningen way: he did not properly appreciate or conduct the complete range of Brahms's orchestral works until well into middle age, by which time other eminent conductors with a variety of connections with the composer, direct or indirect, including Nikisch, Fiedler, Fritz Busch and Toscanini, were already performing Brahms with a variety of stylistic approaches.

Sir Henry Wood (1869–1944) was not quite in this league but he merits mention because he was a convinced devotee who annotated his Brahms scores in Steinbach's

---

[81] Hamburg concert on 4 January 1915, report in *Neue Hamburger Zeitung*, reproduced in Dejmek p. 85.

[82] See Weingartner *On Conducting*, Dover p. 19 and, as to Fiedler, Dejmek p. 30. For details of Fiedler's recorded Brahms, see Dyment, *CRC* Summer/Autumn 2002.

[83] See Dyment 1976 pp. 65 and 68; for the timings of his recordings, ibid. p. 83.

[84] Weingartner 1937 p. 221. For Weingartner's changing attitude towards Brahms the symphonist, see his *The Symphony since Beethoven* 2nd. ed. (English translation) London: William Reeves (undated) pp. 50–6 and final ed. Dover pp. 273–6.

way, after he heard him repeatedly in Cologne: 'I moulded my Brahms on Steinbach'; indeed, so closely moulded that he complained about London audiences' enthusiasm for Steinbach's Brahms as compared with the half-empty halls for his own purportedly identical readings.[85] Suggestively, his brisk 1935 recording of the *Haydn* Variations with a fifth variation outpacing even Toscanini's – presumably drawing on his Steinbach experience – was for a time mistaken by some as an unpublished Toscanini recording and transferred to CD as such.[86]

Bruno Walter (1876–1962) took over the directorship of the Munich opera in January 1913, in succession to Mottl and Franz Fischer. He may have heard Steinbach's few post-Cologne concerts there but there is no evidence that he did so. He is mentioned here because, together with selected recordings by Furtwängler, his pre-war recorded Brahms cycle (without the Second Symphony) is used below as an 'external' reference point in comparisons between various recorded performances where the Steinbach influence is more likely to be discernible.

This survey of documentary evidence has attempted to articulate and analyse the peculiar attributes of Steinbach's style, as observed by critics and subsequent generations of recording artists, and the ways in which that style differed from other conductors of his generation. Unsurprisingly, the conclusion must be that the subtleties of nuance and phrasing emphasised by Berrsche in Steinbach's highly flexible approach to Brahms would have been less likely to be observed by adherents of other traditions – those influenced, for example, by that complete Wagnerite, Felix Mottl, or the seeming extravagancies of Bülow in his later years. The next section examines the recorded legacies of those who observed Steinbach at work for any surviving evidence of his practice as described in the preceding pages.

RECORDED EVIDENCE: THE BRAHMS SYMPHONIES

The chosen recordings: an overview

The Brahms symphony recordings examined in the following pages are listed below. The choice of Abendroth, Boult, Fritz Busch and Toscanini is, given the documentary evidence, self-explanatory; so also is the inclusion of Gui's Fourth Symphony. Where there is a further choice between earlier and/or live performances as against later 'official' recordings, as is the case especially with Toscanini, the former are preferred because a live performance (as opposed to studio recording, mostly on 78rpm

---

[85] See Wood pp. 166–7; the index lists Steinbach under Emil, Fritz's brother. As to Wood's complaint about London audiences, see Pearton p. 32 fn.

[86] Decca K 763–64, transferred (identified mistakenly as conducted by Toscanini) Pearl GEMM CDS 9922.

discs) is more likely to reflect actual performance practice and, by its closer proximity to the Steinbach era, might expect to display his influence, if any, more explicitly. Abendroth's Brahms symphonies are preserved in several versions of each; choice was dictated by the foregoing criteria and also by ready availability. Walter and Furtwängler, esteemed by later generations as great Brahms conductors, are, given the documentary evidence, non-contenders in the Meiningen stream. They are included as 'outsiders' against whom to test the authenticist credentials of others. Walter's pre-war Brahms recordings are here preferred since they are free of the possible contentions of 'New World' influence or the undue relaxation of tension in old age sometimes raised against his American recordings. For these reasons, too, the Second Symphony, not recorded in the 1930s, is represented by his Paris performance of 1955.

In the following details all recordings are of concert or broadcast performances, save where the date appears *in italics*; selected commercial releases are identified (CD format unless otherwise stated).

HERMANN ABENDROTH

No. 1	London SO	*20 Mar 1928*	78: HMV D 1454–58
			Biddulph WHL 052
	Bavarian State Orchestra	16 Jan 1956	Tahra TAH 490
			Memories MR 2045/46
No. 2	Breslau RSO	15 Apr 1939	Music & Arts CD 1099
	Leipzig RSO	3 Mar 1952	Memories MR 2045/46
No. 3	Leipzig RSO	17 Mar 1952	Berlin Classics 0094332 BC
			Memories MR 2045/46
No. 4	London SO	*3 Mar 1927*	78: HMV D 1265–70
			Biddulph WHL 053
	Leipzig RSO	8 Dec 1954	Berlin Classics 0094332 BC
			Memories MR 2045/46

ADRIAN BOULT

No. 1	London PO	Nov 1954	Nixa NIXCD 1002
	London PO	*21/23 Oct 1959*	CRQ CD 022
No. 2	London PO	*Nov 1954*	Nixa NIXCD 1002
No. 3	London PO	*Nov 1954*	Nixa NIXCD 1002
No. 4	London PO	*Nov 1954*	Nixa NIXCD 1002

FRITZ BUSCH

No. 1	NYPSO	1 Feb 1942	
No. 2	Dresden Staatskapelle	25 Feb 1931	Profil Hänssler PH 07032
			Guild GHCD 2371
	Danish State RSO	*20/21 Oct 1947*	78: HMV C 4006–09
			EMI/IMG 724357510325
No. 4	Vienna SO	*Oct 1950*	Arlecchino ARL 77

WILHELM FURTWÄNGLER

No. 1	Berlin PO	10 Feb 1952	Virtuoso 2699072
No. 2	Vienna PO	28 Jan 1945	DG 4353242
	Berlin PO	7 May 1952	Virtuoso 2699072
No. 3	Berlin PO	18 Dec 1949	Virtuoso 2699072
No. 4	Berlin PO	24 Oct 1948	Virtuoso 2699072

VITTORIO GUI

No. 4	Orchestra del Maggio Musicale Fiorentino	5 Oct 1975	Warner Fonit 50467 12012

ARTURO TOSCANINI

No. 1	*NBC SO	25 Dec 1937	Pristine Audio PASC 275
	NBC SO	6 May 1940	Naxos 8.110806
	NBC SO	*10 Mar, 14 May, 11 Dec 1941*	78: HMV DB 6124–28
			78: RCA Victor M 875
			RCA GD 60277
			RCA 88697916312-26
No. 2	NYPSO	24 Feb 1935 (excerpts)	
	*NBC SO	12 Feb 1938	Pristine Audio PASC 283
	BBC SO	10 Jun 1938	Testament SBT 1015
No. 3	NYPSO	17 Mar 1935	
	NBC SO	15 Oct 1938	Guild GHCD 2211/12
	NBC SO	8 Feb 1941	Naxos 8.110827
	Philharmonia	1 Oct 1952	Testament SBT 3167
No. 4	NYPSO	7 Apr 1935 (excerpts)	
	*BBC SO	3/5 Jun 1935	EMI CDH 7697832
	NYPSO	15 Mar 1936 (excerpts)	
	NBC SO	27 Nov 1948	EMI/IMG 724356293922

* References in the analysis below are to this performance, except where otherwise stated

BRUNO WALTER

No. 1	Vienna PO	*3/4 May 1937*	78: HMV DB 3277–81
			Opus Kura OPK 2022
No. 2	French National RSO	5 May 1955	Tahra TAH 587–89
No. 3	Vienna PO	*18/19 May 1936*	78: HMV DB 2933–36
			Koch 3-7120-2
No. 4	BBC SO	*21 May 1934*	78: HMV DB 2253–57
			Koch 3-7120-2

A table of timings for each complete movement of the above recordings is at Table 1. Such timings have limited value here, since they give no hint of the extremely wide range of tempo variations within movements, while in the outer movements of the First Symphony the varying tempos taken for their introductions disguise the overall timings of the main Allegros. Table 1 therefore includes (bracketed) timings for these introductions while, from a selection of the recordings, Table 2 provides the metronome markings for the tempos taken at various equivalent points within specified movements. Other recordings mentioned in the following text are detailed in the footnotes.

Table 1: Timings of recordings

Symphony No. 1	I	II	III	IV	*Total*
Abendroth 1928	13:18 (2:54)	8:46	4:25	15:07 (4:47)	41:36
Abendroth 1956	12:58 (2:52)	9:00	4:19	15:04 (5:08)	41:21
Boult 1954	12:40 (2:26)	9:11	4:49	16:26 (4:44)	42:06
Busch	13:37 (2:39)	10:22	4:38	15:13 (5:00)	43:50*
Furtwängler	14:36 (3:15)	10:37	5:17	17:02 (5:10)	47:32
Toscanini 1937	12:20 (2:30)	8:40	4:19	16:36 (5:00)	41:55
Toscanini 1940	12:24 (2:30)	8:37	4:25	16:21 (4:39)	41:47
Walter	12:53 (3:01)	8:52	4:21	14:49 (4:12)	40:55

* The Busch off-air recording lacks bars 106–28 of the fourth movement, about 35 seconds of music at his tempo. Also, the end of the second movement, the third movement and the first six minutes of the finale (up to bar 106) are recorded at a slightly higher (incorrect) pitch. The timings here are adjusted to take account of these shortcomings.

Table 1: Timings of recordings continued

Symphony No. 2	I	II	III	IV	Total
Abendroth 1939	14:13	9:13	5:06	7:55	36:27
Abendroth 1952	13:58	9:02	4:58	8:12	36:10
Boult	15:01	9:24	5:05	9:40	39:10
Busch 1931	14:12	10:17	5:10	7:34	37:13
Busch 1947	13:24	8:41	4:44	7:53	34:42
Furtwängler 1945	14:07	10:05	5:44	8:21	38:17
Furtwängler 1952	15:28	10:37	5:51	8:56	40:52
Toscanini 1938/NBC	14:21	8:31	5:26	8:28	36:46
Toscanini 1938/BBC	14:08	8:15	5:20	8:22	36:05
Walter	14:26	9:42	4:55	8:14	37:17

Symphony No. 3	I	II	III	IV	Total
Abendroth	11:52*	8:25	5:56	7:34	33:47*
Boult	13:35	8:33	5:46	8:36	36:30
Furtwängler	13:09	9:36	6:17	9:09	38:11
Toscanini 1935	12:30	8:46	6:16	8:15	35:47
Toscanini 1938	12:04	8:02	6:03	8:11	34:20
Toscanini 1941	11:28	7:42	5:45	7:54	32:49
Toscanini 1952	12:29	8:32	6:18	8:35	35:54
Walter	11:22^	7:19	5:27	7:46	31:54^

* Repeat omitted; includes addition of a notional 2:56 (actual totals: 8:56 and 30:51)
^ Repeat omitted; includes addition of a notional 2:45 (actual totals: 8:37 and 29:09)

Symphony No. 4	I	II	III	IV	Total
Abendroth 1927	11:58	12:24	5:43	10:23	40:28
Abendroth 1954	11:33	12:30	5:48	10:04	39:52
Boult	12:33	9:45	6:28	10:30	39:16
Busch	10:57	10:50	5:50	9:49	37:26
Furtwängler	12:38	12:15	6:21	9:40	40:54
Gui	11:38	11:33	6:23	9:46	39:20
Toscanini 1935	11:35	11:33	6:04	9:18	38:30
Toscanini 1948	11:36	10:47	6:05	9:25	37:53

Table 2: Metronome marks

Symphony No. 1	I ($\downarrow$.=)			IV ($\downarrow$ =)		
bar	42	150	184	62	106	120
Abendroth 1928	100	69	120	104	160	160
Abendroth 1956	104	58	120	104	168	160
Boult 1954	100	84	104	112	132	126
Busch	92	72	100	126	144	152*
Toscanini 1937	96	72	112	104	132	138
Walter	100	84	108	112	132	144

* Exposition missing from the recording; tempo taken from the recapitulatory material at bar 301.

Symphony No. 2	I ($\downarrow$ =)				III ($\downarrow$ =)	
bar	1	50	136	212	1	120
Abendroth 1939	104	120	126	126	92	69
Boult	96	108	108	116	84	72
Busch 1931	104	116	120	132	92	76
Furtwängler 1945	108	130	126	136	88	66
Toscanini 1938/NBC	100	112	112	132	84	69

Symphony No. 3	I ($\downarrow$ =)		III ($\eighthnote$ =)	
bar	3	112	1	54
Abendroth	104	56	72	120
Boult	76	50	84	96
Toscanini 1935	92	42	84	88
Toscanini 1938	80	48	88	92
Toscanini 1941	92	56	96	100
Toscanini 1952	84	44	84	92
Walter	96	69	88	92

Table 2: Metronome marks continued

Symphony No. 4		I (♩ =)					IV (♩ =)		
bar	1	88	91	130	433	1	97	129	253
Abendroth 1927	112	160	132	160	176	84	72	108	168 (+accel.)
Abendroth 1954	116	184	132	168	184	104	72	132	168 (+accel.)
Boult	132	144	126	144	152	104	66	112	160
Busch	152	176	144	168	168	104	80	112	168
Toscanini 1935	108	152	126	160	170	96	88	96	168
Walter	126	152	120	160	176	104	69	120	184 (+accel.)

Although the tables have limited utility, some features stand out. First, Toscanini's pre-war performances include some of the slower examples among the great Brahms conductors; that conclusion would have been further emphasised if timings of Weingartner's late recordings of all four symphonies, dating from 1938–40, had been included in Table 1, since in many movements he outpaced Toscanini. Moreover, in the case of Toscanini's First Symphony, nothing before December 1937 has survived. An earlier performance would probably have disclosed still broader timings, a conclusion consistent with the timings of his earliest Brahms symphony performances tabled here.[87] Overall the timings also point to the post-war 'slow Brahms' phenomenon of which there is plentiful recorded and other evidence. Significantly, Steinbach pupil Fritz Busch was also unaffected by this tendency, although his slow movements were sometimes expansive.[88]

Secondly, Toscanini's range of tempos within those movements selected for comparison in Table 2, which include some of the structurally most complex and

---

[87] Toscanini's recordings of the *Tragic Overture*, not dissimilar in musical character to the first movement of the First Symphony, provide further evidence of his change of approach from 1935 onwards: the Philharmonic aircheck of 24 February 1935, the earliest Toscanini recording, lasts 13:55, the BBC SO recording of October 1937 12:42.

[88] See Musgrave & Sherman Ch. 4, Bernard D. Sherman 'Metronome markings, timings, and other period evidence regarding tempo in Brahms', pp. 115–19. An outstanding example among pre-war recordings which supports the post-war 'slow Brahms' thesis is the remarkable Stokowski/Philadelphia First Symphony recorded on 25–27 April 1927, HMV DB 2874–78, Biddulph CD WHL 017–18, in which the basic tempos are consistently faster than Toscanini's: I 12:21 (2:31); II 8:15; III 4:10; IV 15:00 (4:10), although these timings disguise some major fluctuations of tempo not present in any Toscanini performance. There is no evidence, either written (confirmation courtesy Edward Johnson) or deducible from this performance, that Stokowski might have experienced Steinbach's way during his European apprenticeship. As to Fritz Busch, further evidence of his general approach to Brahms tempos is provided by his live *Tragic Overture*, Danish State Radio SO, 7 September 1950, included with the 1947 Brahms Second Symphony in the EMI/IMG CD compilation noted at p. 326; this is similar in tempo to Toscanini's NYPSO performance referred to in n. 88.

expressively diverse, is wider than many; only in a minority of movements conducted by Abendroth and Furtwängler does Table 2 disclose a significantly greater emphasis on tempo fluctuation. This conclusion connects directly to the final observation: among those known to have witnessed Steinbach's performances (the 'Steinbach witnesses'), there are distinct similarities in structural and expressive emphases signified by modifications of tempo. The significance of these conclusions is considered in the context of each symphony below.

A final preliminary point pertains to textual fidelity. Toscanini first conducted the Second and Fourth symphonies in 1898 but delayed his first performances of the First until 1930, and of the Third until 1929. In the latter two he had problems in making the lead voices at certain moments sound as he wished and his recordings are evidence of his continued experiments to achieve what he heard in his mind's ear. The only disturbing element is his added timpani: in the coda of the First Symphony's finale, underlining the return of the chorale and (save in the Philharmonia performance) the rhythmic accompaniment preceding the final bars; and in the Third's finale, where his practice continually changed, only to be abandoned in favour of the score as written in his Philharmonia performance.[89] In the First Symphony's finale Busch adds timpani at the same points as Toscanini – whether by preference, or following Toscanini's Philharmonic parts, or because it accorded with his memory of Steinbach, cannot now be established. Again, Abendroth in 1956 added timpani rolls at bars 413–15 of the First's finale and Furtwängler freely added timpani in the Third's finale (bars 44–5 and 86 and in the recapitulation). Since, according to Blume, Steinbach himself was no purist in textual matters, further pursuit of these unorthodoxies is unprofitable.

In the following examination of recordings a number of passages are compared using Blume as a guide – but not, for reasons given, as an infallible observer. Other important elements in assessment include any observed consistency of approach among Steinbach witnesses, other possible influences on the chosen interpreters and the endistancing effect of the passage of time between the date of Steinbach's performances and the chosen recordings. Comment on all of Blume's observations relating to every movement would require a book-length thesis; this study is therefore limited to some obvious and vital elements, such as the tempo variation and phrasing for which Steinbach was peculiarly noted, in selected movements from each symphony, including those listed in Table 2.

---

[89] The timpani and other emendations are detailed in Harris Goldsmith's and Mortimer Frank's notes to the first RCA CD issues of the RCA recordings: Symphony No. 1, 6 November 1951, GD 60257; Symphony No. 1 (Toscanini 1941), GD60277; Symphony No. 3, 4 November 1952, GD 60259. See also the author's review of Symphony No. 3, Toscanini 1938, Guild GHCD 2011–12, *CRC* Autumn 2002, p. 81.

Symphony No. 1

In the first movement's introduction Blume is insistent on the *un poco* qualification of the *sostenuto*, beaten with fairly hard drumsticks in six but not slow, with a hint of a *luftpause* between forte and piano at bar 9 to avoid hall resonance covering the first pizzicato. These pizzicatos are to be 'stiff and rigid' and 'strictly in time', compared with the 'sighs' which follow, although whether that 'time' should be precisely the tempo primo Blume does not specify. Toscanini (references throughout are to the 1937 performance), Busch and Boult agree on the meaning of *un poco*, the tempo made plain by their evidently quite hard drumsticks; they leave minimal pauses between forte and piano, with Busch just audibly more flexible in this respect. All three keep the pizzicatos in tempo, although Toscanini slackens very slightly second time round (bars 13–14) in anticipation of the repeated 'sighs'. His achievement here, as elsewhere, is to meld continuity with expressivity. Abendroth starts more slowly but at a plausible tempo, the timpani indistinct in 1928 (probably the aged recording), with *luftpausen* far more obvious in 1956. In both, more so in 1928, he drops sharply in tempo for the pizzicatos, thereby breaking the musical line. By Blume's standards, Walter and more especially Furtwängler adopt implausibly slow opening tempos with much lingering later on. Toscanini, Boult and Busch are fully consonant with Blume, although the minimalist tendency of the first two in regard to *luftpausen* suggests a more modern approach. Abendroth, particularly in his (here very powerful) 1956 version, has a tendency to sectionalise and linger.

In the Allegro's main theme, bars 42–6, the non-slurred crotchets must be shortened and played *marcato*, says Blume. Toscanini, Boult and Busch (the last at a slightly broader tempo) agree entirely, other conductors less conspicuously so. Blume is further insistent on the accents on weak (last) beats in bars 51–7, a cross-accenting effect of which Brahms was very fond and frequently used. Toscanini reflects this advice in full with characteristic attack, abetted here by Busch and Boult but rather less forcibly by Abendroth and Furtwängler; Walter completely ignores it.

Moving to the lyrical passage commencing at bar 101 which includes the oboe's second subject from bar 131, Blume demands inter alia fleet playing of bars 101–2, broadening at 103–4, resuming as before at 105 until 114 where the tempo is to broaden again, resuming tempo primo at 121 and slowing at 130 in anticipation of the oboe's broadened second subject. Some of these expansions and contractions are obviously implied in the score and are sometimes adopted in performance today. In any event, Toscanini reflects them all and, in addition, in anticipation of the oboe's entrance, greatly expands the lyrical phrase commencing at 125, followed by an oboe second subject only modestly slower than tempo primo ($\bullet$.= 88 compared with 96). The expressive range of Boult and Busch compared with Toscanini is more reined in, although both recognise similar changes of mood and Busch slows his tempo for the oboe's entrance a little more. Abendroth in 1928 virtually ignores the expressive requirements until slowing at 128 in extended anticipation of a substantially broadened oboe theme; in 1956, like Toscanini, he is expansive from bar 125 onwards.

After the oboe second subject Blume advises the string chords from bars 145–6 be not 'connected together' and the dialogue between horn and winds be shaped with freedom until the tempo is 'revived' with the subsidiary theme at bar 157, implying a preceding broadening of tempo. Again Toscanini reflects these injunctions in full, Busch at his slightly broader tempo less generously but with clear emphasis on the final octave drop in the horns as Blume advises. Table 2 shows the degree to which the Steinbach witnesses manipulate the tempo here; it also shows how, by comparison, Abendroth slows extravagantly. His acceleration up to bar 185, where all conductors reach their maximum, is correspondingly greater. Blume merely asks for 'much more energy' for this passage with chords from 185 onwards very 'chopped' or 'incisive'. Once again Toscanini's incisiveness and rhythmic emphases on the weak beats as marked in the score stand out, as does his grappling at a broadened tempo with the entry into the development (from bar 190) which, for Blume, 'cannot be played too brilliantly or lushly'. His unusual term for this last word, 'vollsaftig', translates literally as 'extremely juicy'; perhaps 'tonally saturated', in which Toscanini excels, best conveys the sense.

In the fourth movement's introduction Blume asks for the first pizzicato passage not to increase in tempo significantly until two bars before it ends (bar 12). Toscanini reflects this and audibly retards the tempo at bar 8 (an effect he abandoned in later performances) before his marked *stringendo*. Boult is straightforward, the *stringendo* strongly marked in bar 10 onwards. Abendroth retards several times in bars 8 and 9, reflecting the hairpins (crescendos or diminuendos) also in his tempo, before a downplayed, very modest *stringendo* in bars 10–12. There appears to be no authority for this curiously contrived approach. Busch is here the prize: until bar 9 he replicates Toscanini but then accelerates ferociously in bars 10–12. So compelling is the result, one feels it must be Steinbach's own (and Brahms's) voice, a reaction reinforced as the movement progresses.

At the start of the main theme (bar 62) Blume dilates extensively on the length of the upbeat with which it commences, which requires full value and weight to be given to the crotchet, a 'slight broadening'. This much-discussed feature is played by Abendroth in 1928 as a full minim but in 1956 is distended to the equivalent of a full bar's length, self-consciously contrived and with disruptive effect. Toscanini's treatment is just short of minim length (that is, he extends it somewhat beyond the score's crotchet) but in later performances he conducts more or less in tempo, as do Busch and Boult. Abendroth in 1928 and Toscanini sound quite natural in effect while giving full value to the disputed note.

The theme itself should, says Blume, have internal variations of tempo, in both its first and second statement, the latter accelerating towards the *animato* at bar 94, where the theme must be 'felt either as alla breve or 4/4'. Busch alone at a faster tempo treats the theme with the fluxes of tempo suggested by Blume, with a barely contained rise of tension throughout the theme's statement and restatement. Neither Toscanini nor Abendroth makes any acceleration until the restatement at bar 78. From the first *animato*, however, Abendroth's treatment in 1928 and 1956 is unique: as Table 2 shows, he increases his basic tempo by an astonishing two-thirds. The observance of the *animato* by Toscanini, Busch and Boult is more modest, which has the virtue, in the case of Toscanini and Busch, of enabling them to set a faster tempo for the second *animato* at 120 as the music seems to require and where, as Blume now says unequivocally, there should be a genuine alla breve tempo.[90] (This *animato* theme lies within the missing section of Busch's finale – the foregoing comment relies on his handling of the same theme from bar 301 onwards). Illogically, Abendroth and Boult feel obliged to slow slightly for this second *animato*, impliedly contradicting Blume.

Abendroth's treatment of tempo in the rest of the movement continues to be uniquely extreme in pace. For several reasons, this singular approach probably does not reflect Steinbach's practice. First, Abendroth's orchestras find it impossible to play the notes at his forced tempos. In 1928 there are frequent scamped passages, such as those following bars 257 and 356; in 1956, when his approach was still more extreme, strings slither from 102 and 234 onwards, while from 352 the woodwind triplets go for nothing since they cannot be played audibly at such a furious pace, which at 356 reaches $\downarrow$ = 176. Even making full allowance for changing standards, styles and expectations of what was possible in terms of orchestral execution, if the LSO in 1928 and more especially the Bavarian orchestra in 1956 could not meet the score's demands at such tempos, it is scarcely credible that the Meiningen players – finely drilled by contemporary standards though they were – or Steinbach's Cologne and Munich players could have met them either. Secondly, Blume is insistent on the need throughout the movement to conduct with a mixture of alla breve and common time according to the character of the music, for example, from bar 168 onwards after appropriate expansion for the oboe theme at 132. Abendroth's wholesale rush makes such differentiation all but impossible, in contrast to the Steinbach witnesses who throughout vary the pace appropriately.

The strongest reason for rejecting any authenticist view of Abendroth's approach, however, lies in the contrast between his and Busch's finale. Table 1 shows their overall timing for the last movement to be very similar, indicating a radically faster

---

[90] As is shown by Toscanini's televised performance (3 November 1951, Testament SBDVD 1006, a performance very much in his 'late' style), he conducted this theme throughout in four, although the accelerated material later in the movement he takes in two (or one!) according to the pace and shaping required.

approach by these two conductors to the main body of this movement by comparison with most other recordings. But as shown by Table 2, Busch is exceptional in
his quick basic tempo for the finale's big C major theme; thereafter, while moving
consistently faster, structurally his shifts of tempo throughout reflect the integrated
approach of the other Steinbach witnesses. In the resulting combination of irre-
pressible impetus and structural coherence, the music surges forward with unrivalled conviction while permitting all details to be properly executed. Steinbach's
finale was by all accounts one of his great triumphs; for example the *Musical Times*
thought his performance with the LSO in October 1912 'the sensation of the evening
... a great interpretation, the playing of the final movement unforgettable'. Busch,
too, triumphs in recreating with supreme mastery what is surely his mentor's voice.

Two further passages in this movement merit examination. First, that leading
up to letter N, bar 285, extending to the lead back to the alla breve theme at bar 301.
Many conductors slow both before and after the cataclysmic chord at bar 285, so
losing the force of Brahms's *calando* at bar 297. Blume is insistent on the need to
conduct bars 279 onwards in two, bar 286 (alone) in four – that is, slower – then to
resume the previous tempo until relaxing at the *calando*. Toscanini, Busch and
Abendroth all preserve the scheme of things here, although with his faster initial
tempo at bar 279, $\downarrow$ = 160 as compared with Toscanini's 132, Abendroth's treatment
of the ten bars following 286 sounds the more radical. Toscanini's treatment is clar-
ified in 1941 where the various textual strands, including in particular the changing
tempo of the timpani from bar 289 onwards, are clearly audible. Busch, at $\downarrow$ = 152
from bar 279, maintains clarity and remarkable impetus while preserving absolute
structural coherence: his *animato* at bar 301 resumes again at the identical $\downarrow$ = 152.

Finally, the transition into the coda from the *stringendo* at bar 383 through the
ben marcato marking at 395: here Blume advises no *ritardando* before 390 but at
395, to reinforce the *ben marcato* character, the tempo is, in Pasternack's translation,
to be held back 'slightly'; Frisch's earlier translation has 'somewhat', a significant difference. Blume's term is 'etwas', which bears both meanings but, as will be seen from
his usage elsewhere, Pasternack's choice seems to be the more appropriate.
Toscanini's *stringendo* from 383 is modest, reaching $\downarrow$ = 96 at 390, a pace continued
through the transition without change. Busch once again heightens the drama with
an increase of pace to $\downarrow$ = 132 at 390, maintained steadily but very incisively until
the return of the chorale theme. Abendroth's *stringendo* is extreme, reaching in 1928
$\downarrow$ = 144, in 1956 $\downarrow$ = 152 at bar 390; but at 395 he pulls back in both recordings to
$\downarrow$ = 112, causing complete disjuncture from one note to the next.[91] He also stretches
the returning chorale theme in similarly unique fashion, in contrast to a modest

---

[91] This practice, with rather less disruption, has been taken up recently by Vladimir Jurowski in performances of the First Symphony: LPO 0043, 25 May 2008, and subsequently at a BBC Henry Wood
Promenade Concert in 2009.

expansion of tempo by Toscanini, Boult and Busch; Blume merely asks for the brass chords to be 'broad and strongly sustained'.

Blume's brief suggestions for the coda transition, and in particular for holding back slightly at the *ben marcato* marking, provide a number of valid interpretative options. First, this advice may simply warn the conductor not to give into the temptation to accelerate – a frequent course – but to hold back in tempo, an option most clearly audible in Toscanini (1941) where the remarkably incisive bowing gives full value to the *ben marcato* marking; Boult is very similar at this point. Although adopting a faster tempo throughout, Busch's approach is in structural terms the same, the articulation again very distinct. Secondly, the advice may suggest an emphasis combined with a slight modification of tempo, an option to be heard in Max Fiedler's handling of a somewhat analogous passage in Brahms's First Piano Concerto.[92] Blume's advice is, however, unlikely to signify an abrupt reduction in tempo by up to one-third as heard in Abendroth's recordings; this sudden change wholly disrupts the structure and musical line, a result inconsistent with all reports of Steinbach's general approach.

Abendroth's recordings of the First Symphony have been examined in detail elsewhere, with the proposal that they shine a unique light on the Steinbach tradition as described by Blume.[93] Hence the detail provided here which suggests an alternative view that takes into account the interpretative approach of the proven Steinbach witnesses. This examination makes clear that, in the typical passages chosen for comparison, Toscanini's and Boult's earliest recordings, together with Busch's nearly complete version, reflect far more closely the (then unknown) precepts of Blume than do Abendroth's. As a Steinbach witness in this work, Abendroth remains possible but far from proven or likely: the evidence of a few coincidences with Blume's advice is counterbalanced by many departures and also by fundamental differences between his approach and that of proven Steinbach witnesses.

Two further conclusions are, however, obvious. First, quite clearly the eye-witness conductors, proven or not, do not always accord with Blume. In approaching the First Symphony, they took only what they wanted from their memories of Steinbach, selecting what they needed to shape their own experience of the work. Sometimes, it seems, they either ignored seemingly vital points underlined by Blume or Blume must have misremembered Steinbach or read his own views into his description of the Steinbach way, which were not reflected in Steinbach's actual performances. For example, at the climactic point of the first movement (bars 470–5) Blume advises that the tempo be pushed ahead up to bar 473 but that the (slower) tempo primo be

---

[92] At bar 9 before B in the first movement; performance on 26 October 1936 by Alfred Hoehn, piano, and the Hamburg RSO: see Dyment *CRC* Autumn 2002 p. 47, CD ARBITER160.

[93] See n. 1 above.

resumed in the climactic bar 474 in preparation for the distinct 'jolt' (*Ruck* – a sudden start or shock) at bar 475. Of the conductors here examined, only Furtwängler, a Meiningen 'outsider', does anything approaching this: Abendroth and the eye-witnesses (save for a trace of Blume in Boult's 1959 recording) take bar 474 in their preceding accelerated tempo and wait for 475 and after to commence their deceleration. This short but crucial passage illustrates both the danger of treating Blume as gospel and the relevance of other aural and comparative evidence.

The foregoing analysis also affirms the importance of factors other than the Meiningen way in shaping the interpretative approaches of these recording conductors. For Boult, Richter's prolonged influence was probably as significant as his relatively few experiences of Steinbach. With his observant but balanced and phlegmatic outlook, it is therefore hardly surprising that Boult's interpretation in its high maturity, fiery though it is, contains its expressive effects within closer confines than those of other eye-witnesses.

Abendroth, developing his independent interpretative approach during his Essen years, could not escape his background in the ultra-Wagnerian practices of Mottl, to whom both he and Furtwängler were indebted; and the grand fluxing of tempo which features in their approach to wide swathes of the repertoire, including Brahms, is more likely to be linked to that source than to the subtleties of Steinbach. This background must also account for the exaggerated response in Abendroth's recordings of Brahms's First Symphony to certain elements which may possibly have had their origin in his memory of Steinbach in Cologne.

Fritz Busch is a unique source of information, not only in his direct relationship with Steinbach but more especially because we know that he treasured the memory of Steinbach's performance of this work, which, just five years before his own New York performance of it, he invoked as preferable to Toscanini's in its warmth and overall conviction. In his interpretation, certainly the introduction to the first movement and the whole of his electrifying finale for the most part ring true as remarkable recreations in the spirit of his teacher; so, too, do his broad, flexible but never inflated Andante second movement and his free-flowing but never pressurised Allegretto third movement (neither of them examined further here). But other long-term influences, such as Weingartner, who in his earlier years Busch greatly respected, may have contributed to the formation of his later conducting style; nor should one ignore the constant development of his independent interpretative viewpoint. Such factors may account for his less multi-faceted, more sober response to the expressive requirements of the first movement's Allegro than Toscanini and also for his divergence from Blume's lengthy plea for an extended upbeat commencing the finale's C major theme. Nevertheless, Busch's Brahms First Symphony must be counted among the prime documents available in the task of reconstructing the Meiningen way.

As for Toscanini, his capacious memory doubtless enabled him in the 1930s to recall in every detail what he heard in Munich in 1909. However, it seems clear that, while he deeply admired Steinbach, an admiration which helped ground his pre-war Brahms with a quite extraordinary expressive variety (in the 1937 First Symphony the metronome finds it difficult to pace more than any two bars in the same tempo), that admiration did not preclude him going his own way whenever he felt the letter of the score took precedence, even if, as Fritz Busch maintained, that sacrificed some of Steinbach's warmth. Notably in the finale, Toscanini's broad pacing probably differed in some degree from Steinbach; here Busch is a significant guide. But the dangers of the opposite extreme are only too vividly demonstrated in the scrambled incoherence of Abendroth's performances of this movement.[94]

Precisely how Steinbach himself interpreted the finale will never be known, but his approach did not meet with universal approbation. In contrast to the London critic quoted above, the foremost contemporary Essen critic who witnessed Stein-bach in a Cologne rendering of the work (probably the one in March 1913 noted above) thought that 'at the end of the last movement he needed to resort to purely dynamic effects which can certainly be read into the score but are hardly in accor-dance with its spirit. There occurred there a stretto with piling-up of the brass, which may have been Steinbach but was certainly not Brahms.'[95] The composer, as we know, took a different view, but that was two decades earlier. Who knows how Steinbach's way developed in the intervening years?

Symphony No. 2

In this symphony we know that Steinbach fully approved Toscanini's preparation of the work for him in 1911; Toscanini's approach (here principally his 1938 NBC Symphony performance) may therefore provide corroborative evidence of Stein-bach's practice. Noteworthy, too, is the structuring of the first movement suggested by Table 2, in which the Steinbach witnesses calibrate the fluctuations of tempo towards the point of maximum tension and resolution in the development, differing in this respect from the more varied treatment of the Mottl acolytes.

The exposition of the first movement has distinctive advice from Blume of which a selection follows. First, both the first theme from bar 2 and the second at bar 82 require, says Blume, slight 'separations' at the end of each of the short phrases.

---

[94] Günter Wand's interpretation of the finale has elements of Abendroth's approach, without the scramble, and in the film of his 1997 Kiel performance with the NDR SO he can be seen to conduct the *animato* themes freely sometimes in two, sometimes in four (24 August 1997, TDK DVWW-COWAND7). Wand studied in Cologne (though not conducting, in which he was largely self-taught) when Abendroth was still in post there and probably witnessed Abendroth conduct the work. However, nothing else in his interpretation bears signs of an Abendroth influence.

[95] Max Hehemann, quoted in Dejmek p. 150.

Toscanini reflects this advice and, indeed, in his February 1951 performance the degree of separation in the second theme's reprise is more marked than in any other: only his careful observance of the dynamics prevents an inappropriate swooning.[96] The other eye-witnesses are less consistent, while the Meiningen 'outsiders' opt for less inflected phrasing. Next, the much-discussed *quasi ritenente* (bar 118), where Brahms was unhelpful[97] in response to requests for elucidation, should be 'prepared', says Blume – that is, with a slight *ritenuto* beforehand, which many conductors insert – but should not be too broad: the emphasis should be on the 'quasi', meaning that it should remain 'internally proportional' (Blume's quotes) to the main tempo. Toscanini, Boult and especially Busch (1931) agree with a modest expansion, Abendroth in 1939 and 1952 is more emphatic and Furtwängler, especially in 1952, distends dramatically.

If the eye-witnesses in the last-mentioned passage are the most convincing, so also are they at two noteworthy points which follow. In the fortissimo climax at bar 134 Blume requires the trombones, which alone are marked forte, to commence *fp* with a crescendo to the fortissimo specified for the rest of the orchestra. Busch, Boult and Toscanini, so far as can be heard, ignore this here and in the recapitulation, following the score with a consistent forte/fortissimo through the two bars in question, complete with the marked emphases. The treatment by Abendroth in 1939 and Furtwängler in 1945 is, by contrast, curious: Abendroth imposes a crescendo by the whole orchestra at this point in both exposition and recapitulation, a practice he adjures in 1952 in favour of the score; Furtwängler in 1945 makes a sharp, full orchestra crescendo in the recapitulation (only) but follows the score in 1952. This crescendo has no authority either in the score or in Blume; it is not only Wagnerian in effect (compare the start of the Third Symphony below) but at these focal points in the structure virtually inverts the composer's own dynamic marking, with fatal effect.

Again, in the passage at bars 137–40 Blume prescribes a 'slight break' after each slur. Busch (1931) makes clean breaks, much less obvious in 1947 where his treatment parallels Toscanini who, while not ignoring the slur breaks, relies more on dynamic shading that favours greater continuity. Furtwängler gives no hint of breaks. The joker in the pack here is Abendroth who not only exaggerates the breaks (hardly 'slight') but in 1939 adds crescendos to each phrase, with self-consciously disruptive results; this effect is toned down in 1952. Who is closest here to the Meiningen way? The response depends on the degree of reliance placed on Blume but the differing extremes of Furtwängler and Abendroth at this point are both doubtful solutions.

---

[96] Performance of 10 February 1951, NBC SO, Carnegie Hall, Pristine Audio PASC 157.

[97] See Musgrave & Sherman Ch. 2, Styra Avins 'Performing Brahms's music: clues from his letters' p. 25; and Ch. 8 (Pascall & Weller) p. 228, quoting a letter of 28 October 1878 to Dessoff.

In the Adagio, says Blume, from bar 87 lead energetically back to the 4/4 at 97, relaxing the tempo before the double bar at that point. Toscanini relaxes slightly at 96, Busch (1931) a little more; by contrast Abendroth holds on to the last note of bar 96, extending the subsequent rests: two different ways of achieving the same aim, the first better maintaining continuity, the second bringing the music to a lingering halt. The one is Brahmsian in character, the other imports Wagnerian license, reflected also in Furtwängler's 1945 recording.

In the Allegretto Blume again advises characteristic separations in the phrasing of the first (oboe) theme, particularly distinctive in opening up the E–D intervals in bars 8–11. Further, he advises that the major–minor distinction in bars 25–26 be highlighted by urging forward and pulling back. Busch (1931) is the most forceful in articulating the oboe as per Blume and, indeed, his principal's distinctive tone sounds under strain from his demands here. Toscanini clearly articulates at least some of the separations and suggests, perhaps vestigially, the major-minor contrast. His BBC SO soloist a few months later does not follow his NBC colleague. Other conductors, including Abendroth, Furtwängler and Walter, largely bypass these sophistications, as they do also the separated downbeat crotchets advised by Blume at bars 114–17; but here again the three eye-witnesses accord with Blume. All conductors anticipate by several bars the *ritardando* at bar 124, commencing usually at 120; as is apparent from Table 2, the Steinbach witnesses do so to a modest extent, the Mottl acolytes to an extreme. Brahms wanted this movement to sound 'rather peaceful' and Toscanini is here the most relaxed in tempo; Furtwängler's longer timing is a consequence principally of the dying fall he imposes on the closing bars, a habit of his in so many of Brahms's quiet endings – perhaps one of the points occasioning the critical reception given to his first Berlin Philharmonic performance of the work in 1922.

In extreme contrast, Furtwängler's closing pages of the finale in 1945 are over-driven to the point of hysteria. His second subject *largamente* in the reprise, where Toscanini is the most generous of the eye-witnesses in broadening the tempo (only Max Fiedler is more pronounced), is minimally acknowledged in the rush while the Vienna brass in the final bars can barely articulate the notes. Such treatment contrasts sharply with Blume's advice that bar 387 be played 'heavily and holding back' (his quotes); that there be a gradual acceleration from 391 to 405; that at 408 and 412 a crescendo should lead to an abrupt cut-off at each rest; and that the closing horns and trumpets at 421–4 'above all' be clear and not rushed. Toscanini alone reflects all these demands and thereby demonstrates the accuracy of Blume's reportage here. The result in this 1938 performance is, as Steinbach's must also have been, both noble and transcendently thrilling, notwithstanding the deadening acoustic of Studio 8H.

As will be apparent, this Toscanini performance offers multiple insights into many of the Steinbach practices he heard thirty years before. The BBC SO performance only four months later disappoints expectations in this respect and others: the playing, save for some wind solos such as Aubrey Brain's horn, is unfocused by comparison with the NBC Symphony, for reasons given in Chapter 7. Yet the 1938 NBC performance itself marks a transition to a later, less inflected style: surviving parts of a New York Philharmonic aircheck from 24 February 1935, the third movement from bar 110 and a complete finale, are still more flexible, inflected and broader in tempo and, on these counts, afford even closer insights into the performance practices of Steinbach on which, in many respects, Toscanini sought to model his approach. The reprise of the finale's *largamente* second subject, for example, has unexampled breadth and intensity as well as Toscanini's usual lift and separation of phrasing reflected in Blume's advice.

Fritz Busch (1931) deserves the closest scrutiny, despite the remote and confusing sound. He conveys many notable Steinbachian insights in his spontaneity and freedom of approach within a Classical framework; the framework was retained in his 1947 recording but less of the freedom. Midway in time between the two, it is noteworthy that, of his Queen's Hall performance of this work with the LSO on 28 November 1938, the *Times* remarked the following day that, in its delineation of melody, it 'reminded us of Steinbach and what was said of Steinbach'.[98] By contrast, Boult's performances of Symphonies Nos 2 and 3, as may be inferred from Table 1, do not have the fire of his No. 1 although, in his observant but phlegmatic way, there is much insight in his Second in regard to matters of phrasing and significant detail.

It is unlikely that Abendroth heard Steinbach conduct this symphony. Steinbach did not perform it in Cologne during Abendroth's Essen tenure and the recorded evidence is still less persuasive than in the case of the First Symphony. In any event the scattering of eccentricities, Wagnerian idiosyncracies and exaggerations limit the value of Abendroth's 1939 performance as possible documentation of the Meiningen way; his later version also examined here has conspicuously less energy and rather less individuality.

Symphony No. 3

Documentation of Toscanini's approach to the Third Symphony dates back to the Philharmonic performance of 17 March 1935, his earliest extant complete recording of a Brahms symphony. In this work his repeated experiments, already noted in regard to textures, extended also to tempos and proportioning, from the lightness of his NBC broadcast of February 1941 to the listless heaviness of his RCA recording of November 1952. As mentioned in Chapter 11, his constant searching also signified his lifelong dissatisfaction in failing to recreate some of the characteristics he heard

[98] Quoted in Potter p. 1079.

in Steinbach's evidently persuasive way with the work in 1909. Both Tables indicate that in his last great performance of the work, with the Philharmonia in October 1952, he returned quite closely to the spirit of his 1935 reading.

As Toscanini knew too well, the opening Allegro is full of traps for even the most complete conductor. Blume advises that the two opening bars are simply distinct forte chords without crescendo. In the following theme, the pairs of crotchets, marked as phrased and staccato in bars 4, 6 and 8 must, he says, be played portamento, by which in this context he probably means distinct but joined (Pasternack suggests *portato*, on the same bowstroke); only in the unphrased pair in bar 10 should there be space between them. The theme's other notes, Blume continues, should be shaped sonorously rather than short and energetically. Every one of these precepts is exactly reflected in all of Toscanini's performances, sometimes at a quicker tempo, as in the 1935 New York Philharmonic and 1952 Philharmonia performances, at others in slightly more solid fashion, as in 1938. Boult at his slower tempo is similarly heedful. Abendroth, in extreme contrast, swells the second chord in an ear-splitting, distended crescendo straight out of Wagnerian *Trauermusik* (Furtwängler likewise). Each note of his opening theme, at headlong tempo, is articulated staccato without discrimination, heedless of Brahms's careful differentiation, with or without Blume's admonitions. Clearly, Abendroth never heard Steinbach in this work – or, if he did, ignored him completely.

The rest of the exposition is subject to Blume's micro-management, advice that Toscanini sometimes reflects, sometimes not. Two examples: of Blume's various suggested 'separation' marks in the 9/4 theme, in his early performances Toscanini clearly lifts the phrasing at the *pianissimo* in bar 38 but not elsewhere. Others are no more heedful. At bar 46 Blume suggests an accelerando to allow a longer rest at the end of the bar. Toscanini in 1935, like Abendroth in 1952, actually slows here but by 1938 takes it exactly in tempo, as he does in all later performances. The effect is startling enough.

In the much-analysed passage before the recapitulation, Blume advises a small *poco rit* before H (bar 112) with thereafter the conducting taken *alla breve*, thus not too slowly. As Table 2 shows, Toscanini interprets this as half-tempo in some performances and something rather quicker in others, especially in 1941. Abendroth also halves his tempo. Here only Boult and Walter adopt a moderate change of gear.

In the coda Blume wants a 'slight acceleration' at bar 183 continuing to the second beat of bar 194 with, after a distinct rest, an abrupt, downward, change of gear thereafter. No conductor precisely reflects this, the closest being Toscanini in 1935, although at 194 his change of gear is only slight. Boult rather placidly declines to do anything not indicated in the score. Abendroth markedly accelerates his already headlong tempo at 183, resulting in an incoherent scramble before 194, where he continues virtually without change.

The third movement Allegretto is also full of less acknowledged traps. For example, Blume suggests moving the first theme 'forward a bit' at bar 8, to relax again for the peaceful (*ruhig*) quintuplet at bar 11. In all the noted Toscanini performances this adjustment is finely judged with the quintuplet exquisitely realised. Boult is more straightforward. Abendroth, after a drowsy start, accelerates too much and fails to relax the tempo in time for the quintuplet, which is therefore (as recorded) indistinct.

Blume characterises the Trio as 'scherzando', at a tempo 'slightly [etwas] quicker'; the scherzando character is to be achieved in each bar by playing the second quaver rather short and emphasising the third, thereby suggesting that note values rather than increased tempo should contribute most to the musical effect. The following answering string phrase is to be 'slightly held back'. This distinction between the Allegretto and Trio is another instance in which Blume's description broadly reflects later practice, whether by Steinbach witnesses or not: it is quite usual to move the Trio forward at a faster pace.[99] The Steinbach witnesses adopt a distinctly modest change of pace, as Blume implies: Toscanini and Boult interpret the Trio as slightly quicker with modest distensions for the answering phrase. As Table 2 indicates, Toscanini varied his practice; the forward-pressing Trio is most explicit in his 1941 and 1952 performances. Other (non eye-witness) conductors are varied in approach. Walter's handling is similar to Toscanini, whereas Abendroth almost doubles his tempo for the start of the Trio, thereby making it impossible to characterise each note as Blume suggests; he then distends each answering phrase very markedly. Furtwängler alone does not change tempo for the Trio but distends both the answering phrase and the end of the movement in Wagnerian fashion.

Once again Toscanini's approach to this work sheds substantial light on Steinbach's practice but, if Blume is to be trusted (which is not always), the illumination is fitful. Boult's solid temperament displays its limitations most obviously in its dogged, if textually illuminating, adherence to the score: the architecture is immaculate, the Brahmsian fire stoked low, the evidence of the Steinbach legacy at best intermittent. Abendroth's overheated first movement and his alternately sluggish and exaggerated Allegretto suggest a kinship with Mottl's much criticised way with the work. In this symphony alone Blume advises the first movement repeat, presumably following Steinbach's practice and, implicitly, the composer's own preference. Toscanini made the repeat whenever he could, Abendroth seemingly did not, while Walter resolutely never made it, responses reflecting their relationship more generally with the Meiningen way.

---

[99] E.g. the distinct change of pace adopted by Stokowski with the Philadelphia Orchestra in their otherwise stylistically wayward recording of 25–26 September 1928, HMV D 1769–73, on Biddulph CD WHL 017–18, and Gui in his disciplined 1946 recording noted above at n. 48.

Symphony No. 4

All proven Steinbach witnesses left recordings of the Fourth Symphony, including Toscanini's 1935 BBC SO rendering that stimulated this essay. Brahms also left his own performance advice on the Fourth in the form of those later cancelled score notations earlier referred to[100] and it is necessary to consider how far his advice corresponds with Blume's and the practice of the eye-witnesses.

The opening of the first movement immediately presents a paradox in Blume's presentation of the opening theme with what he describes explicitly as Steinbach's markings – extended upbeats with a diminuendo on each downbeat; but that advice seems virtually to nullify the effect of Brahms's own diminuendos in bars 4 and 6. Most conductors, including Abendroth, Boult and Busch, simply play as written, although Abendroth starts with a lengthened first upbeat, exaggerated (as in the equivalent instance in the First's finale) in his later recording. Toscanini's solution in the BBC SO recording is a lengthened first upbeat, followed by even stresses with slightly lengthened upbeats until the two diminuendos, where the upbeat is distinctly stressed. Could Steinbach really have ignored the significance of the composer's own score markings here, as Blume implies, or was Toscanini's memory of him more accurate than Blume's? The latter seems more likely.

In the rest of the exposition none of the conductors reflects Blume's advice at all meticulously. In its moment-to-moment flexibility and full observance of the many hairpins, however, Toscanini's reading comes closest to the spirit of his advice and at some points certainly coincides with Blume's reproduction of Steinbach's score. For example, Toscanini observes fully the staccato separation of crotchets in bars 45 and 49 and the stress on the final upbeats in 131–3; but, like all the other conductors, he prefers a barely inflected singing line for the cello/violin theme from bar 57 rather than Blume's frequent separations. This eye-witness unanimity again throws doubt on the reliability of Blume's memory.

In the coda the composer's own cancelled markings conflict with Blume. At 393 Brahms marked *pesante* under the double bass line and directed 'no pressing forward right up to the end'.[101] Blume advises an increase in pace from 387, reining back emphatically in tempo at 393, with a gradually more flowing tempo from 398, kept at an 'unbroken' pace from 408 until broadening for the penultimate bar's timpani strokes. To accelerate or not? All conductors rein back in tempo at 393 with similar effect in every case – save only for Max Fiedler's giant *luftpause*, which surely exceeds by far what Brahms had in mind; further, contra Brahms, he then accelerates rapidly to the end. After bar 393 the rate and consistency of acceleration by the

---

[100] See p. 298 and n. 13.
[101] 'Nicht eilen bis zum Schluss!' (see Musgrave & Sherman p. 223).

examined conductors varies, as shown by Table 2, from Boult's sane intensification to Abendroth's 1954 race towards a doubling of pace. As ever, Toscanini adopts the *via media* with maximum tempos permitting clear articulation (still clearer, at a similar pace, in his incomplete 1936 Philharmonic performance).[102] In later performances, such as those of 1948 and 22 December 1951, Toscanini virtually eschewed an accelerando and thereby adhered all the more closely to Brahms's expressed wishes;[103] Gui's treatment was very similar. Table 2 again suggests structural similarities between the Steinbach witnesses and their marked differences from the others.

Those similarities are brought into sharp focus by the fourth movement passacaglia. As shown by Table 2, the eye-witnesses, together with Gui, agree on a similar pace for the 'exposition' variations, a moderate drop in tempo for the central variations (for example, in the flute solo – though here Boult reduces more markedly), resumption at or close to tempo primo as Brahms specifies at bar 129, with a proportionate increase in tempo for the coda at 253 which is maintained without acceleration to the end. By contrast, Abendroth, Walter and also Furtwängler (not included in Table 2) adopt a radical increase in pace at the tempo primo, bar 129, and accelerate markedly in the coda.

Among his other later withdrawn advice, Brahms himself wanted variation 8 (bar 57) slower and *pesante* with variation 9 back in tempo, variation 20 (bar 153) also *pesante* and variations 25–27 faster. Blume's advice differs from Brahms. Following through his annotations with Toscanini and the BBC SO reveals many striking similarities of which a few include: the *marcato* timpani at bar 24 (variation 4); the violins *marcato* and *largamente* from 33 (variation 5); the extreme precision of rhythm in variation 8 (which with Toscanini also has something of Brahms's desired *pesante*); and the slowing at the end of the flute variation (bars 103–4) where, as Table 2 indicates, Toscanini alone approximates to the specified equivalence of pace on which Blume insists.

At the tempo primo, bar 129 (variation 17), Blume, despite the obvious meaning of Brahms's marking, wants the music 'faster' than the opening. Boult and Busch disclose a barely perceptible increase while Toscanini waits until the following variation to step it up – logically so, since variation 17 largely replicates in outline the opening theme. Blume's advice here doubtfully reflects Steinbach, given that Boult marked his score with Steinbach's changes of tempo in this movement and that Brahms himself chose not to elaborate on his tempo primo marking. Toscanini continues with Blume's 'energetic accented staccato' at bar 153 (variation 20), hinting again at Brahms's desired *pesante*. Further, he accords with Blume's 'slightly [etwas]

---

[102] See Ch. 12 p. 248.
[103] The performance of 22 December 1951 on CD Hunt 706.

broader' tempo at variation 22 (bar 169), where the annotator's demands for 'resounding and well-sustained' trombones with 'short and energetic' chording could not better describe the effect Toscanini secures. Boult here broadens his tempo a little more, Busch a little less, whereas Abendroth presses on regardless at the increased basic tempo which he, like Walter and Furtwängler, adopts in the second half of the movement. The following variation 23 is, Blume exclaims, 'scherzando!' and, uniquely, Toscanini increases the tempo a little to achieve precisely that effect. The tempo in variation 27 (bar 209) should be 'flowing', says Blume, and here and in the following two unannotated variations, Toscanini moves the tempo gracefully forward. The coda from 281 onwards, says Blume, 'speaks for itself', implying no further change of tempo; and that is indeed the scheme to which all three eye-witnesses adhere.

There are a few differences between Toscanini's rendering of the passacaglia and Blume's advice, noted above. In general, however, the reflection of one in the other is remarkably close. Further, Toscanini's scheme of things, as well as much of the detailed handling of the variations, is corroborated by the other Steinbach witnesses. By contrast, in the outer movements of this symphony scrutinised above there is little evidence that Blume's advice is reflected in Abendroth's performances, which have more in common with those of Walter and Furtwängler. It seems unlikely that Abendroth heard Steinbach performing this work.

CONCLUSIONS

Each group of recordings of individual Brahms symphonies here examined shows, to a varying degree, the likelihood of some Steinbach influence in performances by the proven Steinbach witnesses. Given the broad conclusion reached above in regard to available documentary evidence, that can occasion no surprise: one corroborates the other in expected fashion, a conclusion considered in more detail hereafter.

The position of the possible but unproven eye-witness, Hermann Abendroth remains unresolved. There is, however, no disputing the merits of some of his Brahms recordings or some of Walter's and Furtwängler's: they have an urgency, musical pliability and overwhelming conviction lacking in so many more recent recordings of the canon. Although these performances may not point to the 'Meiningen way', with its particular characteristics which we know had Brahms's wholehearted approval, it does not follow that, in the absence of those characteristics, Brahms would have withheld approval from them. That conclusion is supported by Brahms's own cancelled markings in specified passages in the Fourth Symphony, which Blume's (perhaps not always reliable) annotations suggest that Steinbach performed in a quite different fashion. As has been remarked elsewhere, this contradiction is 'an index and valorisation of the tolerances of the readings endorsed and admired by Brahms',[104] an observation which leads inexorably to the conclusion adumbrated at the outset: that in performances of his orchestral music Brahms was willing to look favourably upon a wide range of deeply felt and cogent solutions to problems of form, shape and nuance.

If that broad conclusion is uncontroversial, what more specific conclusions may be drawn about the conundrum which motivated the present analysis of documentary and recorded evidence, the strange paradox of Steinbach's Classicist followers ranged against the sometimes extreme stylistic idiosyncracies of Abendroth, upheld elsewhere as an exemplar of the Steinbach tradition? The necessarily prolonged exposure of fresh evidence presented here suggests the chimerical character of that conundrum. Documentary evidence in the round leads ineluctably to examination of lines of authority and affinity – from Wagner onwards, from Brahms onwards – which in the field of orchestral performance indicate how the fundamental division between those two camps separated interpretative outlooks in the late nineteenth and early twentieth centuries almost as much as it did creative and critical endeavours. Wagner's advice on conducting, in particular his prescriptions for the frequency and extent of tempo modifications, had a near-universal influence; but the current temptation to conflate the approaches of all conductors of the time subject to that influence in one omni-German-Austro-Hungarian 'romantic' tradition has tended to obscure the significant distinctions between the principal actors such as Nikisch, Mottl, Steinbach, Fiedler, Muck and others. All had different approaches; but the differences were most acute among, on the one hand, those who followed Wagner's more extreme personal practices in his own performances, of which Mottl and Anton Seidl[105] were the prime exponents, and, on the other, those who specialised in the Classical repertoire. By the early twentieth century both streams practised their art in their various ways across the entire repertoire; but adherents of one or the other tradition continued to exhibit those marked differences of approach that have lived on in subsequent generations to cause continuing debate among aficionados and musical historians today.

As the documentary evidence shows, Abendroth and Furtwängler were in their distinct but related ways the descendants of ultra-Wagnerian practice through the

---

[104] Musgrave & Sherman Ch. 8 (Pascall & Weller) p. 237.

[105] (1850–98): see Ch. 1 p. 2. Seidl assisted Wagner from 1872, worked alongside Mottl at Bayreuth in 1876 and was responsible for the German opera (primarily Wagner) craze in New York from 1885. For Seidl's style, see Henry T. Finck (ed.) *Anton Seidl: A Memorial by his Friends* New York: Charles Scribner's Sons 1899 (Da Capo repr. 1983) pp. 67–8 (Finck), 116 (Huneker), 134–5 (Krehbiel, who notes Seidl's general lack of sympathy for Brahms, paralleling Mottl's similar attitude), 164–5 (Finck) and 258–9 (Jean and Edouard de Reszke). Unlike Mottl, Seidl left no followers who made any mark, which makes the task of reconstructing his approach in detail almost impossible; see Brown pp. 122–32, 737–8.

persuasive and powerful example of their mentor, Felix Mottl. The other recording conductors here examined were subject to many influences, including in substantial measure Fritz Steinbach who, save only to a significant extent in the performance of Brahms, was fundamentally a Classicist in the company of others such as Richter, Muck and Weingartner.

How best to assess Steinbach's undoubted freedom of approach in Brahms has been the primary purpose of the section dealing with recorded evidence. As earlier foreshadowed, the conclusion must be that, while no one recording conductor holds the key to Steinbach's practice and style, evidence of his approach is present to a varying degree in the chosen recordings of his eye-witness followers. Further research[106] may clarify uncertainties about the relationship between some of the major players in this analysis, such as Abendroth and Mottl, Abendroth and his Cologne players, Blume and Steinbach in Munich, Toscanini and Gui, as well other issues such as the frequency with which Boult attended Steinbach's concerts. The results are, however, unlikely to change significantly the conclusions presented in the following paragraphs.

Although evidence is entirely lacking, Abendroth may on occasion have observed Steinbach's Cologne performances of Brahms while he was in post at Essen; but whatever he heard or noted was subsumed in the experiences of an already well developed and dominant musical personality grounded in earlier and antithetical influences. As the examination of the First Symphony suggests, there may (just) be a few clues about some limited aspects of Steinbach's approach buried deep within Abendroth's recordings. But to rely on this fragmentary evidence as a key to Steinbach's approach would indeed be a chimerical pursuit, for, whether in lineage, artistic connections or virtually all recorded performances, there is nothing to link the two conductors.

The influences shaping Boult's approach to Brahms undoubtedly included Steinbach, whose performances were, he said, revelatory. But Boult witnessed him on only a relatively few occasions and it is by no means clear that he heard him conduct all the symphonies at a (musically) fully cognisant age. In any event, over a period of years before those occasions he also heard Richter across the whole repertoire and there is no doubt that the latter's monumental, sometimes unvaried approach remained a potent influence. Boult's finest Brahms recordings, made when he was in his mid-sixties, appear to retain only intermittent reminders of the Steinbach influence, although some are of substantial value in that connection, notably the outer movements of the First Symphony and the finale of the Fourth.

---

[106] Material about the performance of Brahms still awaiting assessment includes correspondence between Steinbach and both the Busch brothers and Max Reger held by the Busch Brothers Foundation at the Max Reger Institute (Karlsruhe); also the Brahms symphony score parts annotated by Brahms, Bülow and Steinbach held at the Meiningen Museum: see n. 58 above.

Fritz Busch's recorded Brahms legacy is relatively small but, given Steinbach's closeness to him as master and friend, immensely valuable. The greater part of his almost complete recording of the First Symphony is compelling evidence of the Meiningen way, particularly in the unique features of its finale. In his first recording of the Second Symphony from 1931, the spontaneous exuberance and the pliable, individual shaping of phrase are highly suggestive of Steinbach's practice, although in the outer movements Busch's tempos may outpace his master's. The controlled expansiveness of the slow movements in both the foregoing recordings (not here examined in detail) again strongly suggests Steinbach's unhurried approach. Busch's later recording of the Second Symphony has less fire and individuality but rather more polish. His recorded Fourth Symphony is certainly not lacking in fire and provides valuable corroborative evidence about Steinbach's approach to structure, particularly in the finale.

Corroborative because of that finale's similarities to Toscanini's approach. The focus here has for the greater part been on Toscanini's earliest Brahms recordings, some of them not widely available. That choice was occasioned not merely because of his earlier tendency towards greater breadth of tempo, a tendency that in this composer in particular cannot, as Table 1 demonstrates, be assumed. Indeed, there are so many exceptions in his recorded performances of Brahms as almost to nullify its validity as a generalisation: the late RCA versions of the Second and Third symphonies, for example, are his slowest complete recordings of the works. But what is remarkable about the Toscanini recordings here examined is the degree to which they retain a constant flexibility and multiple nuancing which became less apparent and less frequent in later years. Toscanini was already between sixty-eight and seventy-two years old at the time of these earliest recordings. He was just forty-two when he first heard Steinbach, probably little influenced until then by other interpretative approaches to Brahms. How he conducted Brahms in, say, the 1920s, when he invoked the shade of Steinbach in his exchange with Furtwängler, can only be guessed at between the lines of fragmentary reviews of limited value. But of the recordings that now remain the BBC SO Fourth Symphony from June 1935 retains the characteristics of Toscanini's early approach at their most eloquent. An 'explosive and generating force' recalling Nikisch, remarked Cardus of this performance of the passacaglia;[107] but as detailed in this essay, its direct and most obvious debt is to the Steinbach heritage. That recording of the finale locates with some precision where, with the assistance of Blume and all other supporting evidence – including in particular the (sadly incomplete) finale of Fritz Busch's recording of the First Symphony – the task of reconstructing the Meiningen tradition may best begin.

Affirming its central importance to our understanding of both Steinbach and

---

[107] See Ch. 2 p. 43.

Toscanini, this performance of the Fourth's passacaglia also underlines how vital for listeners today were the determined efforts of the HMV forces which saved this revelatory account for posterity, as recounted in Chapter 3 of the narrative. Gaisberg begged Toscanini in vain to let the public hear it. A wider public may henceforth appreciate its significance.

BIBLIOGRAPHY

ARCHIVES

The principal archival sources have the following abbreviations in footnotes:

ATC   The Toscanini Legacy collection in the New York Public Library for the Performing Arts, comprising sound recordings, documents and scores. Individual sound recordings and folders are identified in the relevant notes.

BBCA   BBC Written Archive, files R CONT 1/910; WACR 49/872/1; R30/2, 657-1; R30/2, 695-1.

EMI   EMI archive, Toscanini files 1902–.

GA   The Glyndebourne Archive – correspondence and other documents dated 1935–46.

MA   Mase archive memorabilia belonging to the Agrell family.

PUBLISHED WORKS

Books/articles are listed separately in the Bibliography and identified in the footnotes by the author's name and, in cases where more than one book by a particular author is listed, the year of publication. In a few instances, for brevity, a book is given a special abbreviation in footnotes, listed below in square brackets after the relevant entry; for example, '[ATL]' for Sachs *Letters of Arturo Toscanini* 2002. Where a footnoted citation is from a book published under different titles in the UK and USA as listed below, the citation refers to the UK publication. Concert review extracts in newspapers and journals are identified and dated in the text or in relevant footnotes.

Books on Toscanini

Antek, Samuel, and Hupka, Robert. *This was Toscanini*. New York: Vanguard, 1963.

Barblan, Guglielmo. *Toscanini e La Scala*. Milan: Edizioni della Scala, 1972.

Chotzinoff, Samuel. *Toscanini: An Intimate Portrait*. London: Hamish Hamilton, 1956.

Frank, Mortimer H. *Arturo Toscanini: The NBC Years*. Oregon: Amadeus, 2002.

Frassati, Luciana. *Il Maestro: Arturo Toscanini e il suo mondo*. Turin: Bottega D'Erasmo, 1967.

Haggin, B. H. *Conversations with Toscanini*. New York: Doubleday, 1959; revised and edited by Thomas Hathaway in *Arturo Toscanini: Contemporary Recollections of the Maestro*. New York: Da Capo, 1989.

Haggin, B. H. *The Toscanini Musicians Knew*. New York: Horizon, 1967; revised and edited by Thomas Hathaway in *Arturo Toscanini: Contemporary Recollections of the Maestro*. New York: Da Capo, 1989.

Hughes, (Patrick Cairns) Spike. *The Toscanini Legacy*. London: Putnam, 1959; revised ed. New York: Dover, 1969.

Marek, George R. *Toscanini*. New York: Atheneum, 1975.

Marsh, Robert Charles. *Toscanini and the Art of Orchestral Performance*. London: Allen and Unwin, 1956; revised and retitled *Toscanini and the Art of Conducting*. New York: Collier, 1962.

Matthews, Denis. *Arturo Toscanini*. UK: Midas, New York: Hippocrene, 1982.

Nicotra, Tobia. *Arturo Toscanini*. New York: Knopf, 1929 (Kessinger reprint, n.d.).

Sachs, Harvey. *Toscanini*. London: Weidenfeld and Nicolson, 1978.

Sachs, Harvey. *Arturo Toscanini from 1915 to 1946: Art in the Shadow of Politics*. Catalogue of travelling exhibition, Turin: EDT/Musica, 1987.

Sachs, Harvey. *Reflections on Toscanini*. New York: Grove Weidenfeld, 1991.

Sachs, Harvey (compiled, edited and translated). *The Letters of Arturo Toscanini*. London: Faber, New York: Knopf, 2002 [ATL].

Selden-Goth, Gisela (ed.). *Arturo Toscanini*. Vienna: Reichner Verlag, 1937.

Stefan, Paul (Introduction by Stefan Zweig). *Toscanini*. Vienna: Reichner Verlag, 1935; translated by E. and C. Paul, London: Heinemann, 1936.

Taubman, Howard. *Toscanini*. London: Odhams, 1951.

General

Avins, Styra. *Johannes Brahms: Life and Letters*. Oxford, New York: OUP, 1997.

Bailey, Cyril. *Hugh Percy Allen*. London: OUP, 1948.

Baillie, Dame Isobel. *Never sing louder than lovely*. London: Hutchinson, 1982.

Bennett, Keith. *Guido Cantelli: Eight Years of Fame*. Woodbridge: GC Publishers, 2009.

Berrsche, Alexander. *Trösterin Musika*. Munich: Hermann Rinn, 1949 (2nd ed.).

Bliss, Sir Arthur. *As I Remember*. London: Faber, 1970.

Blume, Walter. *Brahms in der Meininger Tradition: Seine Sinfonien und Haydn-Variationen in der Bezeichnung von Fritz Steinbach*. Stuttgart: Ernst Surkamp, 1933.

Boult, Sir Adrian. *My Own Trumpet*. London: Hamish Hamilton, 1973.

Boult, Sir Adrian. *Boult on Music*. UK: Toccata, 1983.

Brown, Jonathan. *Great Wagner Conductors: A listener's companion*. Canberra: Parrot Press, 2012.

Busch, Fritz. *Aus dem Leben eines Musikers*. Zürich: Rascher & Cie, 1949; translated as *Pages from a Musician's Life*. London: Hogarth, 1953.

Busch, Grete. *Fritz Busch, Dirigent*. Frankfurt: Fischer, 1970.

Busch-Serkin, Irene (compiled and translated by Russell Stockman). *Adolf Busch: Letters–Pictures–Memories* (vols. 1 and 2). New Hampshire: Arts and Letters, 1991 [Adolf Busch].

Camden, Archie. *Blow by Blow*. London: Thames Publishing, 1982.

Cardus, Neville. *Talking of Music*. London: Collins, 1957.

Cardus, Neville. *The Delights of Music*. London: Gollancz, 1966.

Carr, Jonathan. *The Wagner Clan*. London, Faber & Faber, 2008 (revised ed.).

Dejmek, Gaston. *Max Fiedler*. Essen: Vulcan, 1940.

Dyment, Christopher. *Felix Weingartner: Recollections and Recordings*. UK: Triad Press, 1976.

Ebert, Peter. *In this Theatre of Man's Life*. UK: The Book Guild, 1999.

Elkin, Robert. *Royal Philharmonic*. London: Rider, 1946.

Erskine, John. *The Philharmonic-Symphony Society of New York, Its First Hundred Years*. New York: Macmillan, 1943 (Da Capo reprint, 1979).

Evans, John, (ed.). *Journeying Boy: The Diaries of the young Benjamin Britten 1928–1938*. London: Faber & Faber, 2009 [Britten].

Fifield, Christopher. *True Artist and True Friend: A Biography of Hans Richter*. Oxford: OUP, 1993.

Fifield, Christopher. *Ibbs and Tillett: The Rise and Fall of a Musical Empire*. London: Ashgate, 2005.

Foss, Hubert and Goodwin, Noel. *London Symphony, Portrait of an Orchestra*. London: Naldrett, 1954.

Gaisberg, F. W. (Fred). (USA) *The Music goes Round*. New York: Macmillan, 1942; (UK) *Music on Record*. London: Robert Hale, 1947.

Goossens, (Sir) Eugene. *Overture and Beginners*. London: Methuen, 1951.

Gray, Cecil. *Musical Chairs*. London: Home and Van Thal, 1948; 2nd ed. London: Hogarth Press, 1985.

Grierson, Mary. *Donald Francis Tovey: a biography based on letters*. Oxford: OUP, 1952 (Greenwood Press reprint, 1970).

Haas, Frithjof. *Der Magier am Dirigentenpult: Felix Mottl*. Karlsruhe: Hoepfner-Bibliothek, 2006.

Haggin, B. H. *Music & Ballet 1973–1983*. New York: Horizon, 1984.

Henschel, Helen. *When Soft Voices Die*. London: Westhouse, 1944.

Heyworth, Peter. *Otto Klemperer, His Life and Times vol. 1 1885–1933*. Cambridge, 1983; vol. *2 1933–1973*. Cambridge, 1996.

Holmes, John L. *Conductors on Record*. Connecticut: Greenwood Press, 1982.

Hughes, Spike. *Second Movement*. London: Museum Press, 1951.

Hughes, Spike. *Glyndebourne, A History of the Festival Opera*. London: Methuen, 1965; 2nd ed. Newton Abbot: David and Charles, 1981.

Jackson, Gerald. *First Flute*. London: Dent, 1968.

Kaut, Josef. *Festspiele in Salzburg*. Salzburg: Residenz, 1969.

Kennedy, Michael. *Adrian Boult*. London: Hamish Hamilton, 1987; Papermac, 1989.

Kenyon, Nicholas. *The BBC Symphony Orchestra 1930–1980*. London: BBC, 1981.

Klemperer, Otto (ed. S. Stompor). *Über Musik und Theater*. Berlin (DDR): Henschelverlag, 1982.

Kolodin, Irving. *The Story of the Metropolitan Opera 1883–1950*. New York: Knopf, 1953.

Kutsch, K. J. and Riemens, Leo (translated by Harry Earl Jones). *A Concise Biographical Dictionary of Singers*. New York: Chilton, 1969.

Lehmann, Stephen and Faber, Marion. *Rudolf Serkin: A Life*. New York: OUP, 2003.

Lewis, Lawrence. *Guido Cantelli: Portrait of a Maestro*. London: Tantivy, 1981.

Lucas, John. *Thomas Beecham: An Obsession with Music*. Woodbridge: Boydell & Brewer, 2008.

Lucke-Kaminiarz, Irina. *Hermann Abendroth: Ein Musiker im Wechselspiel der Zeitgeschichte*. Weimar: WTV, 2007.

McKenna, Wayne. *W. J. Turner: Poet and Music Critic*. Kensington, NSW: New South Wales UP, 1990 (Gerrards Cross: Colin Smythe reprint).

Martland, Peter. *Since Records Began: EMI, The First 100 Years*. London: Batsford, 1997.

Matthews, Denis. *In Pursuit of Music*. London: Gollancz, 1966.

Meyer, Donald Carl. 'The NBC Symphony Orchestra' (University of California PhD thesis, 1994). Ann Arbor: UMI Dissertation Services, 1997.

Millington, Barry & Spencer, Stewart. *Wagner in Performance*. London: Yale UP, 1992.

Mittag, Erwin. *The Vienna Philharmonic*. Vienna: Gerlach & Wiedling, 1950.

Moore, Jerrold Northrop. *A Voice in Time, The Gramophone of Fred Gaisberg*. London: Hamish Hamilton, 1976.

Morreau, Annette. *Emanuel Feuermann*. London/New Haven: Yale UP, 2002.

Morrison, Richard. *Orchestra. The LSO: A Century of Triumph and Turbulence*. London: Faber & Faber, 2004.

Musgrave, Michael (ed.). *A Brahms Reader*. London/New Haven: Yale UP, 2000.

Musgrave, Michael and Sherman, Bernard D (eds.). *Performing Brahms: Early Evidence of Performance Style*. Cambridge/New York: CUP, 2003.

Neupert, Käte. *Die Besetzung der Bayreuther Festspiele 1876–1960*. Bayreuth: Ed. Musica, 1961.

Newman, Vera. *Ernest Newman, A Memoir*. London: Putnam, 1963.

O'Connell, Charles. *The Other Side of the Record*. New York: Knopf, 1947.

Osborne, Richard. *Conversations with Karajan*. Oxford: OUP, 1989; revised ed. 1991.

Osborne, Richard. *Herbert von Karajan: A Life in Music*. London: Chatto, 1998.

Pasternack, Jonathan R. 'Brahms in the Meiningen Tradition – His Symphonies and Haydn Variations According to the Markings of Fritz Steinbach, Edited by Walter Blume: A Complete Translation with Background and Commentary'. (Dissertation for the degree of Doctor of Musical Arts) University of Washington, 2004.

Pearton, Maurice. *The LSO at Seventy*. London: Gollancz, 1974.

Pettitt, Stephen J. *Dennis Brain, A biography*. London: Robert Hale, 1976, 2nd ed. 1989.

Pettitt, Stephen J. *Philharmonia Orchestra, A Record of Achievement 1945–1985*. London: Robert Hale, 1985.

Philip, Robert. *Early Recordings and Musical Style*. Cambridge: CUP, 1992.

Philip, Robert. *Performing Music in the Age of Recording*. London/New Haven: Yale UP, 2004.

Plaskin, Glenn. *Horowitz, A Biography*. London: Macdonald, New York: Morrow, 1983.

Potter, Tully. *Adolf Busch: The Life of an Honest Musician*. London: Toccata, 2010.

Reith, J. C. W. (Lord). *Into the Wind*. London: Hodder & Stoughton, 1949.

Rosenthal, Harold. *Two Centuries of Opera at Covent Garden*. London: Putnam, 1958.

Ryding, Erik & Pechefsky, Rebecca. *Bruno Walter: A World Elsewhere*. New Haven: Yale UP, 2001.

Sachs, Harvey. *Music in Fascist Italy*. London: Weidenfeld and Nicolson, 1987.

Sanders, Alan. *Sir Adrian Boult, a Discography*. London: Gramophone, 1980.

Sanders, Alan (ed.). *Walter Legge, Words and Music*. London/New York: Routledge, 1998 [Legge].

Scharberth, Irmgard. *Gürzenich Orchester Köln 1888–1988*. Cologne: Wienand Verlag, 1988.

Scholes, Percy A. *The Mirror of Music 1844–1944*. London: Novello/OUP, 1947.

Schwarzkopf, Elisabeth. *On and Off the Record, A Memoir of Walter Legge*. London: Faber & Faber, 1982.

Senior, Evan (ed.). *The Concert Goers Annual No. 1*. London: John Calder, 1957.

Shaw, Bernard. *Music in London*. London: Constable, 1932.

Shirakawa, Sam S. *The Devil's Music Master*. New York: Oxford University Press, 1992.

Shore, Bernard. *The Orchestra Speaks*. London: Longmans, 1938.

Shore, Bernard. *Sixteen Symphonies*. London: Longmans, 1949; London: Readers Union, 1950.

Southall, Brian, Peter Vince and Allan Rouse. *Abbey Road*. London: Omnibus Press, 2002 (2nd ed.).

Stansky, Peter. *Sassoon: The Worlds of Philip and Sybil*. London/New Haven: Yale UP, 2003.

Tanner, Michael (ed.). *Wilhelm Furtwängler: Notebooks 1924–1954*. London: Quartet Books, 1989.

Wagner, Friedelind. (USA) *Heritage of Fire*. New York: Harpers, 1945; (UK) *The Royal Family of Bayreuth*. London: Eyre and Spottiswoode, 1948.

Walker, Alan. *Hans von Bülow: A Life and Times*. New York/Oxford: OUP, 2010.

Walsh, Stephen. *Stravinsky, A Creative Spring*. London: Cape, 2000 (vol. 1); *Stravinsky, The Second Exile*. London: Cape, 2006 (vol. 2).

Weingartner, Felix. *Lebenserinnerungen*. Zürich: Orell Füssli, 1928 (vol. 1), 1929 (vol. 2).

Weingartner, Felix. *Buffets and Rewards*. London: Hutchinson, 1937.

Weingartner, Felix. *On Music & Conducting*. New York: Dover, 1969 – containing *On Conducting*, 3rd ed. 1905 translated by Ernest Newman with notes; *On the Performance of Beethoven's Symphonies*, 3rd ed. 1928 translated by Jessie Crosland; and *The Symphony since Beethoven*, 4th ed. 1928 translated by H. M. Schott [Dover].

Wood, Henry. *My Life of Music*. London: Gollancz, 1938.

Wright, Donald (ed.). *Cardus on Music*. London: Hamish Hamilton, 1988; Cardinal, 1990.

ARTICLES AND PAMPHLETS

Amis, John. 'Legge on Toscanini'. *Gramophone* vol. 68, June 1990, p. 9.

Armani, Franco. 'Toscanini/La Scala Orchestra – Postwar concerts'. *The Maestro* vol. 1 nos 3–4, July–December 1969, p. 17.

Blyth, Alan. 'David Bicknell'. *Gramophone* vol. 49, September 1971, p. 425.

Dyment, Christopher. 'Toscanini's European Inheritance'. *International Classic Record Collector*, Winter 1998, p. 22.

Dyment, Christopher. 'Max Fiedler Pt 1: Prophet of Brahms? Pt 2: Pauses for Thought'. *Classic Record Collector*, Summer 2002, p. 26, Autumn 2002, p. 44.

Dyment, Christopher. 'Adrian Boult, The Formative Years'. *Classic Record Collector*, Spring 2003, p. 38.

Dyment, Christopher. 'Franz Schalk: Greatness captured in time'. *Classic Record Collector*, Spring 2005, p. 10.

Dyment, Christopher. 'A whirlwind in London, Toscanini's HMV sessions'. *Classic Record Collector*, Winter 2006, p. 15.

Dyment, Christopher. 'Some "lost" Toscanini Recordings'. *Classic Recordings Quarterly*, Summer 2011, p. 39.

Fairclough, Pauline. 'The "Old Shostakovich": Reception in the British Press'. *Music and Letters* vol. 88 no. 2, May 2007, p. 266.

Fiske, Roger. 'Toscanini and Beethoven'. *Musical Times* vol. 75, August 1935, p. 703.

Foreman, Lewis. 'Saved from Oblivion'. *Classic Record Collector*, Summer 2007, p. 21.

Gaisberg, F. W. (Fred). 'Toscanini'. *Gramophone* vol. 21, June 1943, p. 6.

Gaisberg, F. W. (Fred). 'Battistini and others'. *Gramophone* vol. 21, February 1944, p. 131.

Gaisberg F. W. (Fred). 'All Roads Lead to the Scala'. *Gramophone* vol. 21, April 1944, p. 161.

Gerwer, Josef. 'Toscanini and the Lucerne Festival Concerts'. *The Maestro* vol. 2 January–December 1970, p. 62.

Gorlinsky, S. A. 'Toscanini in London – "Third Time Lucky"'. *Music and Musicians* vol. 5 no. 7, March 1957, p. 9.

Heinitz, Thomas. 'Toscanini, The Recorded Legacy'. *Records and Recordings*, March 1967, p. 22.

London Music Festival 1939: *The Festival Book*.

Mackenzie, Compton. 'Sir Louis Sterling'. *Gramophone* vol. 34, July 1958, p. 45.

Mase, Owen. 'The Other Dimension'. *Gramophone* vol. 32, June 1954, p. 6.

Mase, Owen. 'Memories of the Maestro'. *Music and Musicians* vol. 5 no. 7, March 1957, p. 13.

Matthews, Denis. 'Toscanini and Beethoven' (Pts 1 and 2). *Gramophone* vol. 34, March/May 1957, pp. 361, 441.

Matthews, Denis. 'Toscanini, A Centenary Tribute'. *Records and Recordings*, March 1967, p. 17.

Müller, Herta. 'Fritz Steinbach's Wirken in Meiningen und für Johannes Brahms von 1886–1903'. Meiningen: *Südthüringer Forschungen* 30, 1999, p. 87.

Parikian, Manoug. 'Playing Under the Maestro'. *Music and Musicians* vol. 5 no. 7, March 1957, p. 11.

Paterno, Anthony V. 'Arturo Toscanini, The Philharmonic Years'. *The Maestro* vol. 1 nos 1–2, January–June 1969, p. 12.

Paterno, Anthony V. 'Toscanini and the NBC Symphony'. *The Maestro* vol. 2, January–December 1970, p. 16.

Sanders, Alan. 'Arturo Toscanini'. Testament CD note, SBT 3167, 2000.

SOUND RECORDINGS

Camden, Archie. Interview with Christopher Dyment, 1972.

Goossens, Sidonie. Toscanini: BBC broadcast talk, 15 October 1972.

Hall, Ernest. Interview with Christopher Dyment, 1972.

Hamilton, David. 'Toscanini in Britain'. Lecture, New York Public Library of the Performing Arts, 4 December 2001.

Nifosi, Alex. Toscanini: BBC broadcast talk, 8 October 1972.

Toye, Francis. Toscanini: BBC broadcast talk, January 1957, repeated 15 October 1972.

INDEX

Abendroth, Hermann, 296, 312, 313, 319; influence of Mottl on, 314, 343; career of, 314, 315, 316, 348; performances of Brahms by, 314, 315, 324–5, 327–30, 331, 346–7 and see entries under each work
Agrell, Margery, (see Georgina Mase)
Aldrich, Richard, 10
Allen, Hugh, 93, 94, 95, 96
Amans, John, 19
American Ballet Theatre, 193
Anderson, W. R., 260
Arne, Thomas Augustine
    British National Anthem (*God Save The King/Queen*) 22, 23n, 24, 279, 283, 284
Asquith, Margot, 101, 121
Astor, John Jacob, 49
Astor, Violet, 49

Bach, Johann Sebastian, 101, 304, 305
    Brandenburg concertos, 130
    Brandenburg Concerto No. 2, 130, 285
    Brandenburg Concerto No. 3, 316
    Mass in B minor, 166
    (orch. Respighi) Passacaglia and Fugue in G minor, 27, 31, 280, 282
Backhaus, Wilhelm, 154
Baillie, Isobel, 112, 114, 117, 119, 283, 284, 288, 292
Baker, Bernard, 130n
Balfour, Margaret, 288
Bantock, Granville, 178n
Barbirolli, John, 47, 62, 101, 180
Barblan, Guglielmo, xiv
Bartlett, Ethel, 145, 286
Bartók, Béla, 315
Barzin, Leon, 127
Bavagnoli, Gaetano, 10
Bavarian State Orchestra, 325, 334
Bayreuth Festival, 2; 1888, 307; 1894, 5n;

1897, 5n; 1899, 5; 1902, 7; 1906, 312n; 1930, xxiii, 7, 55; 1931, xxiii; 1933, 49
BBC (British Broadcasting Corporation), xv, 34, 37, 50, 75, 79, 93, 122, 142, 152, 182, 186, 189, 214, 230; plans LMFs 1936–7, 66–7, 70–1, 77–8; plans LMF 1940, 172–3; plans Toscanini's wartime return, 178–81; plans Philharmonia Orchestra broadcasts, 215–6
BBC Chorus and Choral Society, 114, 150, 166, 167, 283, 284, 285, 288, 289
BBC Empire Orchestra, 173
BBC Symphony Orchestra (BBC SO), xiv, xvi, 26, 37, 38, 39, 45, 50, 110, 238; formation of, 34–5; personnel of, 34–5; first rehearsal and concert with Toscanini, xxiii, 40–2; critical views of playing by, 46–7, 80, 156; changes in personnel of, 82; parties for Toscanini given by, 170; opinion of Toscanini, 105, 169; characteristics of players' performances under Toscanini, 80–2, 84, 245, 248–9, 250–1, 252–3, 256–7; Toscanini's HMV recordings with, 262–70; concerts with Toscanini by, 280–9 and see entries under composers/works
BBC Theatre Orchestra, 173
Beard, Paul, 35n, 82, 83, 155, 167, 285, 290, 292
Beecham, Thomas, 12, 13, 24, 30, 34, 37, 48, 58, 126, 142n, 143, 152, 156, 206, 207, 307
Beethoven, Ludwig van, xxiii, 11, 14, 21, 24, 101, 150, 152, 169, 196, 230, 236, 304
    Fantasia for piano, chorus and orchestra, 205, 207, 293